CHARLES HARTSHORNE'S CONCEPT OF GOD

STUDIES IN PHILOSOPHY AND RELIGION

Volume 12

For a list of titles in this series see final page of the volume.

CHARLES HARTSHORNE'S CONCEPT OF GOD

Philosophical and Theological Responses

edited by

SANTIAGO SIA

Loyola Marymount University, Los Angeles, U.S.A.

KLUWER ACADEMIC PUBLISHERS

DORDRECHT / BOSTON / LONDON

Library of Congress Cataloging in Publication Data

```
Charles Hartshorne's concept of God : philosophical and theological
  responses / edited by Santiago Sia.
      p.   cm. -- (Studies in philosophy and religion ; 12)
  Includes index.
  ISBN 0-7923-0290-7
    1. Hartshorne, Charles, 1897-   --Contributions in concept of God.
  2. God--History of doctrines--20th century.  3. Process theology.
  I. Sia, Santiago.  II. Series: Studies in philosophy and religion
  (Martinus Nijhoff Publishers) ; v. 12.
  BT101.H37C42   1989
  211'.092--dc20                                              89-8154
```

ISBN 0-7923-0290-7

Published by Kluwer Academic Publishers,
P.O. Box 17, 3300 AA Dordrecht, The Netherlands

Kluwer Academic Publishers incorporates
the publishing programmes of
D. Reidel, Martinus Nijhoff, Dr W. Junk and MTP Press.

Sold and distributed in the U.S.A. and Canada
by Kluwer Academic Publishers,
101 Philip Drive, Norwell, MA 02061, U.S.A.

In all other countries, sold and distributed
by Kluwer Academic Publishers Group,
P.O. Box 322, 3300 AH Dordrecht, The Netherlands.

printed on acid free paper

Printed in the Netherlands

Table of Contents

Books by Charles Hartshorne

- *Anselm's Discovery.* La Salle: Open Court, 1967.
- *Aquinas to Whitehead: Seven Centuries of Metaphysics of Religion. The Aquinas Lecture, 1976.* Milwaukee: Marquette University Publications, 1976.
- *Beyond Humanism: Essays in the New Philosophy of Nature.* Chicago: Willett, Clark & Co., 1937. Bison Book Edition, with new Preface. Lincoln: The University of Nebraska Press, 1968.
- *Creative Synthesis and Philosophic Method.* London: SCM Press, Ltd., 1970. La Salle: Open Court, 1970.
- *Creativity in American Philosophy.* State University of New York Press, 1984.
- *The Divine Relativity: A Social Conception of God.* The Terry Lectures, 1947. New Haven: Yale University Press, 1948.
- *Insights and Oversights of Great Thinkers: an Evaluation of Western Philosophy.* State University of New York Press, 1983.
- *The Logic of Perfection and Other Essays in Neoclassical Metaphysics.* La Salle: Open Court, 1962.
- *Man's Vision of God and the Logic of Theism.* Chicago: Willett, Clark & Co., 1941. N.Y.: Harper and Brothers Publishers, 1948. Reprinted, 1964, by Archon Books, Hamden, Conn.
- *A Natural Theology for Our Time.* La Salle: Open Court, 1967.
- *Omnipotence and Other Theological Mistakes.* State University of New York Press, 1984.
- *Philosophers Speak of God* (With William L. Reese). Chicago: The University of Chicago Press, 1953. Reissued in 1976 in Midway Reprints.
- *The Philosophy and Psychology of Sensation.* Chicago: The University of Chicago Press, 1934. Reissued in 1968 by Kennikat Press.
- *Reality as Social Process: Studies in Metaphysics and Religion.* Glencoe: The Free Press and Boston: The Beacon Press, 1953. Reprinted by Hafner, 1971.
- *The Social Conception of the Universe* |3 chapters from RSP| edited by Keiji Matsunobu. Tokyo: Aoyama, and N.Y.: Macmillan, 1967.
- *Whitehead and the Modern World: Science, Metaphysics, and Civilization, Three Essays on the Thought of Alfred North Whitehead.* By Victor Lowe, Charles Hartshorne, and A. H. Johnson. "Whitehead's Metaphysics" by C. Hartshorne, 25—41. Boston: The Beacon Press, 1950. Reprinted by Books for Libraries Press, 1972.
- *Whitehead's Philosophy: Selected Essays, 1935—1970.* Lincoln: University of Nebraska Press, 1972.
- *Whitehead's View of Reality* (With Creighton Peden). N.Y.: The Pilgrim Press, 1981.
- *Wisdom as Moderation: a Philosophy of the Middle Way.* Albany: SUNY, 1987.
- *Collected Papers of Charles Sanders Peirce, Vols I—VI.* Edited by Charles Hartshorne and Paul Weiss. Cambridge: Harvard University Press, 1931—1935.

CHARLES HARTSHORNE
1897—

Preface

Charles Hartshorne's considerable writings have been influential in contemporary religious and philosophical thought.[1] Not only is he regarded as the leading living representative of process thought as well as a much respected interpreter of Whitehead, but he has also established himself as an original and creative thinker in his own right.[2] The literature on his philosophy has been rapidly increasing. His thought and influence have also been the subject of a number of conferences and gatherings of scholars.[3]

One of Hartshorne's most notable contributions to contemporary philosophy and theology is his concept of God.[4] In his writings he has set out "to formulate the idea of deity so as to preserve, perhaps increase, its religious value, while yet avoiding the contradictions which seem inseparable from the idea as customarily defined."[5] The result of his efforts has been the development of the concept of a "dipolar God" (insofar as contrasting metaphysical predicates, e.g. relative/absolute, contingent/necessary, finite/infinite and so on, are affirmed as applicable to God although always in an eminent way). Inasmuch as he has elaborated this concept in close dialogue with classical theism, he also refers to it as "neo-classical". Because of the emphasis he places on the reality of change and becoming in his metaphysics (which regards God as the chief exemplification of metaphysical principles), the term "process" has likewise been used to describe his notion of God.[6]

Since Hartshorne aims to formulate a concept of God with a "religious value", by which he means "the power to express and enhance reverence or worship on a high ethical and cultural level", and one which "an enlightened person would find to be free of logical absurdity and which he could associate with the God he worships",[7] it seemed worthwhile to invite a number of philosophers and theologians from diverse backgrounds to evaluate Hartshorne's concept of God from a particular perspective. This collection, therefore, contains essays from the perspectives of feminist theology (Sheila Greeve Davaney), black theology (Theodore Walker), Indian thought (Arabinda Basu), Thomism (W. Norris Clarke), Buddhism (John Ishihara) and Judaism (William E. Kaufman). Other essays compare and contrast Hartshorne's theism with Latin American liberation theology (Peter C. Phan), with phenomenology and Buddhism (Hiroshi Endo), with European philosophy (André Cloots and Jan Van der Veken). One essay (by Randall Morris) focuses on Hartshorne's political thought, another (by Piotr Gutowski) on his conception of theology, and a third essay (by David A. Pailin) on his contributions to philosophy of religion and philosophical theology. One article (by Martin McNamara) examines some of the biblical evidence for process thought while another (by Joseph Bracken) deals with Hartshorne's interpretation of the God-world relationship and assesses that interpretation with particular reference to the doctrine of the Trinity. Charles Hartshorne was invited to respond to these essays, and he has written a lengthy piece at the end of this collection. The actual arrangements of the essays as they appear in published form follows the suggestion of Charles Hartshorne, who explains his reason in his response. Although an attempt was made to include as many and as differing perspectives as was possible, certain limitations, including my own, prevented this ideal from becoming a reality. It is hoped, however, that the present collection gives a good idea of the extent of the interest in Hartshorne's achievements.

A collective undertaking such as this would not be possible without the full co-operation of all the contributors. I would like to record my sincere thanks to each of them for their active participation in this work. Charles Hartshorne deserves my special gratitude not only for accepting graciously, despite a busy schedule, the invitation to respond to the essays but also for his continued support for and encouragement of this project and of many others. I am also indebted to John Cobb for suggesting possible contributors to the collection. A number of individuals who had reluctantly to decline the invitation due to other commitments expressed considerable interest in this project. Their positive comments made the work more worthwhile and are much appreciated. The publishers and the staff of Kluwer Academic Publishers are likewise to be thanked for transforming what was a proposal into the present work.

EDITOR

NOTES

1. Charles Hartshorne, regarded as one of the most creative contemporary American philosophers, was born in Pennsylvania in 1897. He studied at Haverford College in Pennsylvania and Harvard University and did postdoctoral studies at the Universities of Marburg and Freiburg. He was an Instructor and Research Fellow at Harvard University from 1925 to 1928, during which time he was an Assistant to A. N. Whitehead, who exercised considerable influence on his philosophy. However, Hartshorne was already developing his own ideas before his contact with Whitehead. He moved to the University of Chicago in 1928 and remained there until 1955. Subsequently he held Professorships of Philosophy at Emory University (1955—62), and at the University of Texas at Austin (Ashbel Smith Professor 1962—76 and Professor Emeritus since 1976). His illustrious

career includes a number of Visiting Professorships in various universities throughout the world and several awards. For his biography and intellectual development, see among others, his "The Development of my Philosophy," in *Contemporary American Philosophy* 2nd series, ed. by John E. Smith (London: Allen & Unwin, 1970), pp. 211—228, and Eugene H. Peters, *Hartshorne and Neo-classical Metaphysics: an Interpretation* (Lincoln: Univ. of Nebraska Press, 1970).

Hartshorne is a prolific writer. His wife, Dorothy, has compiled bibliographies, arranged chronologically, of his writings and of secondary sources. The list of Hartshorne's writings (until 1976) appeared in *Process Studies*, VI, 1 (Spring, 1976), pp. 73—93. An updated list of his work (up to 1980) was published in *Process Studies*, XI, 2 (Summer, 1981), pp. 108—112. The bibliography of secondary sources can be found in *Process Studies*, III, 3 (Fall, 1973), pp. 179—227 and XI, 2 (Spring, 1981), pp. 112—120. For a selected bibliography (main focus on his concept of God) of primary and secondary sources until 1985, see S. Sia, *God in Process Thought: a Study in Charles Hartshorne's Concept of God* (Martinus Nijhoff, 1985), pp. 125—147.

2. Charles Hartshorne is featured in a forthcoming volume of *The Library of Living Philosophers* series. There is also a growing number of dissertations and theses on Hartshorne's philosophy. An early listing was published by Dean R. Fowler in *Process Studies*, III, 4 (Winter, 1973), pp. 304—307. Addenda to that list, compiled by Philip Ricards, appeared in the same journal, XI, 2 (Summer, 1981), pp. 151—152. This journal regularly publishes abstracts of dissertations and articles on process thought, including Hartshorne's neo-classical theism.
3. Among the meetings and conferences devoted to Hartshorne's thought were those which took place in Leuven, Belgium; Chicago and Austin, USA.
4. Hartshorne develops his concept of God in various writings. For a systematic summary, see S. Sia, *op. cit.*
5. Hartshorne, *Divine Relativity: a Social Conception of God* (New Haven: Yale University Press, 1948), p. 1.
6. The term "process" has been used to refer to the school of thought influenced by Whitehead and Hartshorne. However, some of its followers prefer the phrase "process-relational" since it affirms not only the basic category of becoming but also of relation.
7. Hartshorne, *DR*, p. 1.

List of Contributors

Arabinda Basu, Sri Aurobindo Ashram, Pondicherry 605002, India.

Joseph Bracken, Dept. of Theology, Xavier University, 3800 Victory Parkway, Cincinnati, Ohio 45207-1096, USA.

W. Norris Clarke, Dept. of Philosophy, Fordham University, Bronx, N.Y. 10458-5163, USA.

Sheila Davaney, Iliff School of Theology, 2201 South University, Denver, Colorado 80210, USA.

Hiroshi Endo, Dept. of Philosophy, Waseda University, 1-24-1, Toyama-cho, Shinjuku-ku, 160 Japan.

Piotr Gutowski, Dept. of Philosophy, Catholic University of Lublin, Al. Rackawickie 14, 20-950 Lublin, Poland.

Charles Hartshorne, 724 Sparks Avenue, Austin, Texas 78705, USA.

John Ishihara, Chikushi Jogakuen College, 2-12-1 Ishizaka, Dazaifu-shi Fukuoka-ken, 818-01 Japan.

William E. Kaufman, Temple Beth E., 385 High St., Fall River, Mass. 02720, USA.

Martin McNamara, Sacred Heart Missionaries, Moyne Park, Coolarne, Athenry, Co. Galway, Ireland.

Randall Morris, Dept. of Religion Studies, Texas Christian University, Fort Worth, Texas 76129, USA.

David A. Pailin, Dept. of Philosophy of Religion, Faculty of Theology, University of Manchester, Oxford Road, Manchester M13 9PL, England.

Peter Phan, School of Religious Studies, Dept. of Theology, The Catholic University of America, Washington, D.C. 20064, USA.

Santiago Sia, Dept. of Philosophy, Loyola Marymount University, Loyola Blvd. at West 80th St., Los Angeles, CA 90045, USA.

Jan Van der Veken and *André Cloots*, Hoger Instituut voor Wijsbegeerte, Katholieke Universiteit Leuven, Kardinaal Mercierplein 2, 3000 Leuven, Belgium.

1. Hartshorne's Neoclassical Theism and Black Theology

THEODORE WALKER, Jr.

In this essay I shall offer some critical reflection upon Charles Hartshorne's neoclassical conception of God from the perspective of black theology.

I. BLACK THEOLOGY AND CLASSICAL THEISM

The term "black theology" is here used to refer primarily to those contemporary African-American and native African systematic theologies which understand that the Christian witness to the modern world is more than less in accord with the liberation agenda of "black power."[1] Accordingly, black theology understands that a liberating answer to questions pertaining to the circumstance of oppression and the struggle for freedom is essential to the Christian witness.

This understanding of Christian witness yields a particular vision of God which has been summarily formulated by James Cone and others under the conception of God as "God of the oppressed."[2] When black theologians speak of God as God of the oppressed, we do not mean merely that God is present with, related to, worshipped by, or somehow involved with those who are oppressed. This would be to understate the matter. From the perspective of black theology, to speak of God as God of the oppressed is to affirm that God actually experiences the suffering of those who are oppressed. Moreover, black theology knows, from the data of human experience, that the experience of suffering from oppression entails a desire to be liberated from such suffering. Hence, it follows that the God who experiences the suffering of the oppressed also desires their liberation.

Black theology has its deepest rootage in the experience of enslaved and oppressed Africans, and in their appropriation of the witness of scripture; but *not* in the philosophical and theological traditions of the Western academy and in its medieval and Greek forebears. The essentially non-Western rootage of black theology is often concealed by the fact that most African-American communities of worship wear the labels of Euro-American Protestant denominations. It must be remembered however that African-

S. Sia (ed.), Charles Hartshorne's Concept of God, 1–22.

American denominations are not "protestant" in the sense of having been born in protest to alleged Catholic abuses; instead, African-American denominations are protestant in the very different sense of having been born in protest against oppression by Euro-American protestant denominations. For example: the African Methodist Episcopal Zion Church is called "Methodist Episcopal" largely on account of the fact that white members of the John Street Methodist Episcopal Church of New York city were so oppressive of their black members that in 1796 about thirty African-Americans, under the leadership of James Varick, separated themselves from that white congregation and formed an independent denomination.[3] Most other African-American denominations and racially separated churches were born of similar protest, and typically, African-Americans retained the name of whichever Euro-American denomination or church they happened to have stood in protest against. As such, when African-American congregations are referred to by Euro-American denominational titles, one must understand that, ironically, such titles signify differences more so than similarities. Black theology's rootage in the tradition of that other great protest, schism, and reformation which produced the racially separate African-American congregations determines that it is not at all committed to that predominantly white-Western theological tradition which Hartshorne calls "classical theism."

To be sure, black theology is defined in considerable measure by its protest against the prevailing Western theological tradition. History has taught us that classical Western theism is quite capable of abiding peaceably with, and even of being very supportive of, such oppressive activities as the enslavement of Africans and the genocide of native Americans. It is characteristic of black theology to be unforgivingly critical of any theology which fails to affirm that God favors the struggle for liberation. If God is conceived so as not to favor our struggle for liberation, then God is thereby conceived so as not to experience fully our pain and suffering. Such a conception of God is contrary to the Christian witness to God's suffering as indicated by the cross, and it is contrary to the vision of God as that utterly unsurpassable Friend whose love is perfect and all-inclusive. The logic of black theology is this:

(first)   The most basic existential datum of black theology is that the experience of suffering from oppression entails or produces a desire, and inevitably a struggle, for liberation.

(second) The most basic religious datum of black theology is that human experience becomes divine experience, that our suffering becomes divine suffering, in that God actually experiences our experience of humiliation, pain, and suffering.

(third)   Therefore, the most basic theological affirmation of black theology is that God desires and strives to achieve the liberation of those who are oppressed.

To experience suffering from oppression is to desire, and inevitably to struggle for, liberation. Because we know that God actually experiences our oppression, we know that God favors our struggle for liberation. This is as far as can be removed from such classical attributes of God as immutable, totally impassible, wholly other, and unmoved mover. From the perspective of black theology, the prevailing classical Western (white) theism is logically, existentially, and religiously anathema. Insofar as classical theology aids and abets the structures of oppression, James Cone would describe it as the theology of the Antichrist.

We may then begin this critical reflection upon Hartshorne's "neoclassical theism" or "process theology" with the observation that both black and neoclassical theologies are defined in large part by their opposition to or protest against certain features of classical Western theism. This is an important observation, but one that is somewhat deficient in providing positive information about the status of the two theologies with respect to each other. To say x is contrary to y, and that z is also contrary to y, is to say little about the status of x with regard to z. The opposition between black theology and classical theism, on the one hand, and the opposition between neoclassical theism and classical theism, on the other, tell us little about the status of black theology in respect to neoclassical theism. Thus, it is appropriate that we further the relatively new conversation between black theology and neoclassical theism.[4]

The purpose of this essay is to advance the dialogue between black and neoclassical theologies by offering several systematic indicators of important similarities and differences. I believe that these indicators will support my general thesis, which is that the African-American conception of God as God of the oppressed is far more in accord with Hartshorne's vision of God than with those classical Western theologies which are affiliated with denominations and traditions from which African-American congregations have sought to liberate themselves.

II. THE CHALLENGE THAT BLACK THEOLOGY PRESENTS TO NEOCLASSICAL THEISM

At a November 1985 conference on process theology and the black experience at the University of Chicago (and in partnership with the Center for Process Studies and Meadville-Lombard Theological School) William R. Jones presented a paper in which he observed that process theology emphasizes the unconditional, indiscriminate, and universal character of God's love in a way that typically fails to indicate that God favors the struggle of the oppressed for liberation from economic, social, and political oppression.[5] Rather than indicating that God sides with the oppressed in their struggle for liberation, process theology seems to place God on everyone's side; and if God sides with everyone, says Jones, then God effectively sides with no one. Thus, from Professor Jones's perspective, black theology cannot find process theology acceptable until process theology is able to indicate that God is the

God of the oppressed rather than merely that God's love is unconditional and universal. If neoclassical theism, like classical theism, is unable to present its vision of God in a way which indicates that God favors the struggle of the oppressed, then the neoclassical alternative will be unacceptable to black theology. Furthermore, Jones stipulates that the "litmus test" for compatibility is process theology's ability to "accommodate counter-violence."[6]

In challenging process theology to state explicitly that God sides with the oppressed, and to do so in a way that does not rule out the possibility of righteous counter-violence, I understand Jones to be challenging process theology to explicate the social-ethical consequences of accepting certain metaphysical truths in order that black theology might measure its ethical content against the needs of the struggle for liberation. Broadly conceived, black theology asks not only about the metaphysical status of process theology, but also, and more importantly, Can process theology illuminate social-political ethics in a way that contributes favorably to the liberation struggle?

In the fourth chapter of *Man's Vision of God* — "God and Righteousness" — Hartshorne teaches us how neoclassical theology illuminates ethics in a way that is socially critical and intellectually honest, that is, in a way that is adequate to both ethical and metaphysical criteria. Hartshorne holds that, "In general, the possibility of a theology depends upon the possibility of making our basic conceptions adequate to a supreme instance."[7] Hence, theology can illuminate ethics when ethics stands in critical relationship to an adequate understanding of the supreme instance and "maximal degree" of divine goodness — "perfect love."

In this chapter Hartshorne refutes the view that there can be no such thing as perfect love, and hence, by implication, that theology cannot illuminate ethics, but rather, "far from being able to illuminate ethics, theology pre-supposes and merely applies an ethic."[8] According to this mistaken view, love is thought to be necessarily imperfect because all motivation can be reduced, finally, to self-interest. Hartshorne finds this view to be erroneous in that it neglects the requisite temporal distinctions between a present self and other future selves (including one's own future self). Hartshorne holds that "the present self never acts merely for itself, but always for some other self."[9] What unites a present self to other selves is "the sympathetic character of imaginative realization" according to which "self and other self are scrambled together in motivation."[10] Thus, for every conceivable self, "the ultimate motive is love, which has two equally fundamental aspects, self-love and love for others."[11] Where a given individual displays foolish altruism or egoism, it is because self-love and love for others are not given a proper balance; but it cannot be the case that one or the other of these two fundamental aspects is altogether absent. Given, then, the requisite temporal distinctions, and given the social nature of the self, we can see that all motivation is not reducible to sheer self-interest; and therefore, the view that all motivation reduces to self-interest, being false, cannot be used to deny the possibility of perfect love. Hence, the argument against the possibility that theology can illuminate ethics fails.

Furthermore, attending to temporal distinctions and to the social character of reality, Hartshorne discovers that ethics needs a divine memory. Hartshorne reasons that if the past is not in some sense eternally and perfectly preserved, that is, if the past is not immortal, then it follows that in the more or less distant future, it will be the same as if we had never chosen one action as opposed to any other; indeed, it would be the same as if we had never existed at all. Thus, ultimately, the essential ethical view that some choices are better than others requires an eternal reality; otherwise, in the long run, no choice is better or worse than any other.

While ethics needs divine memory, there is, says Hartshorne, no ethical need for divine providence or timeless perfection. In fact, Hartshorne shows that to conceive that God has certain foreknowledge of absolutely every detail, and that God's perfection is such as to be capable of no increase whatever, is to deny the metaphysically and ethically necessary possibility of temporary values "and with it choice, activity, or purpose, in any intelligible senses."[12]

Hartshorne finds, then, that ethics is related to theology in that the very possibility of meaningful ethics requires a divine reality which includes the immortality of the past. Moreover, the possibility of meaningful ethics excludes theological affirmations of absolute divine providence and timeless perfection.

After having taught us something about how ethics informs theology, Hartshorne proceeds to teach us how theology informs ethics. In developing a theism which conceives of the supreme instance of goodness in terms of perfect love, Hartshorne argues that this "religious ideal of love" is "not a mere emotional glow toward others," but rather, love is "action from social awareness."[13] Hartshorne says, "The divine love is social awareness and action from social awareness."[14] According to the Hartshornian understanding of perfect love, we might interpret the scriptural command — "Be ye perfect" — to mean that we are commanded to act from a social awareness that is perfectly responsive to the interests of all others, and for the purpose of promoting the greatest liberty for all. Insofar as we fail to fully sympathize with the interests of others and to act accordingly, our love is imperfect, and we are not fully ethical. Hartshorne says that if ethical means "being motivated by concern for the interests of others, then God alone is absolutely ethical."[15] Thus, on Hartshorne's view, ethical status is measured by love, that is, by action from social awareness which takes account of the interests of others. While God alone is absolutely ethical (perfectly loving), we are commanded to be as nearly ethical, that is, as nearly perfect in action from social awareness, as we can. Here, then, Hartshorne's theological understanding of the supreme instance of goodness gives us the ideal towards which human ethical behavior must aspire.

From the perspective of black theology, it is important to observe that

6

Hartshorne's account of theological ethics displays a sensitivity which is characteristic of liberation theologies in general. Hartshorne notes that an important ethical objection to classical theism is that it tends toward a faith which disarms criticism of and struggle against predominant social arrangements. Hartshorne describes the propagation of such sentimental faith as "smoothing the path of the oppressor."[16] In contrast to a view of divine love which does not admit that God sides with the oppressed, Hartshorne holds that God favors the creaturely exercise of freedom up to the point where it becomes excessive and is a threat to the freedom of others to pursue their interests. Hartshorne emphasizes "the energy of his [God's] resistance to the excesses of creaturely will at the point where these excesses threaten the destruction of creaturely vitality."[17] Thus, the logic of Hartshorne's conception of divine love is such as to place God decisively on the side of the oppressed in their struggle for liberation.

In the same chapter, Hartshorne rejects dogmatic pacifism by arguing that the religious ideal of love as action from social awareness "seems clearly to include the refusal to provide the unsocial with a monopoly upon the use of coercion."[18]

> Coercion to prevent the use of coercion to destroy freedom generally is in no way action without social awareness but one of its crucial expressions. Freedom must not be free to destroy freedom.[19]

The kind of action from social awareness that is demanded by perfect love is such as must admit the tragic reality that there are people who are genuinely intent upon using their freedom to destroy the freedom of others, and that, under certain circumstances, love itself may dictate that "It is better that many should die prematurely than that nearly all men should live in a permanent state of hostility or slavery."[20] Difficult though it is for humans with imperfect love, the demands of perfect love may, nonetheless, require that we kill an oppressor with whom we have sympathy. Hartshorne says,

> To decide to shorten a man's life (we all die) is not ipso facto to lack sympathy with his life as it really is, that is, to lack love for him.[21]

> To veto a desire is not necessarily to fail literally to sympathize with it; for sympathy only makes the desire in a manner one's own, and even one's own desire one may veto, because of other more valuable desires.[22]

Violent coercion and sympathy are not mutually exclusive. Thus, Hartshorne concludes that "The logic of love is not the logic of pacifism or of the unheroic life."[23]

Hartshorne's theological ethics is consistent with such expressions of black theology which, drawing upon the philosophy of black power, maintain that, under certain circumstances, the oppressed may be compelled to engage in violent struggle against an oppressor. We see, then, that Hartshorne's theology can be acceptable to black theology insofar as it does not smooth the path of the oppressor by disarming the oppressed, and also in that Hartshorne's vision of God supports the basic affirmation of all black and liberation theologies — that God sides with the oppressed in their struggle for liberation.

An Alternative Formulation of the Challenge: The God of the Oppressed is Greater than the Universal God of All

The challenge that black theology presents to the neoclassical alternative is sometimes formulated in this way: How is it possible to reconcile the so-called "particular" vision of God as the God of the oppressed (G-of-O) with the so-called "universal" vision of God as the God of all-embracing love (G-of-A)? In more Hartshornian language, the question is this: How does one reconcile the apparently restrictive theological assertion that God favors the struggle of the oppressed with apparently unrestrictive neoclassical assertions — for example, that God is "the subject of all change?"[24] (It is commonly said that the conceptions of God which stress the universality of divine love are incompatible with the conception of God as God of the oppressed, because the latter conception is insufficiently comprehensive. I do not know that Hartshorne, or any other neoclassical/process theologian, has given explicit attention to this matter.)

I trust dialogue between black and neoclassical theology will be helped somewhat if I were to offer an African-American perception of the way in which it is possible to conceive without contradiction or confusion that God is both the subject of all change (G-of-A), and the God of the oppressed (G-of-O). That I should care to reconcile G-of-A with G-of-O is typically African-American. Throughout history, from the secret beginnings of the "invisible institution," through the second great schism and reformation up to the present, African-American religion has affirmed simultaneously both conceptions of God.

Frederick Douglass is an illuminating example. Douglass (1817—1895) was an African Methodist Episcopal Zion (AME Zion) clergyman who was born into slavery and who escaped from slavery and joined the abolitionists' struggle as an internationally known orator, fund raiser, newspaper publisher, and editor. Douglass wrote a letter to the man who had once been his slave master in which he said that God is the God of all, the God of master and slave alike, that God is "our common Father and Creator."[25] In the same letter Douglass wrote that God is — in Douglass's own words — "the Most High, who is ever the God of the oppressed."[26] Here, and in other writings Douglass expresses a traditional African-American commitment to both G-of-A and G-of-O.

The question of how to reconcile indiscriminate and all-embracing love with siding with the oppressed is one that Douglass gave attention to in his May 12, 1846 speech at Finsbury Chapel in Moorfield, England. On this occasion, Douglass was asking "the people of Britain" to join the struggle against American slavery. In order for his appeal to be successful Douglass knew he would have to reconcile a certain pious regard for the well-being of slave owners with supporting the slaves' struggle for liberation. The audience at Finsbury Chapel would want to know how it was possible to side with the oppressed without being against the oppressor. Douglass argued that they should support the abolition of slavery not only because slavery was not in the best interest of African slaves, but also because slavery was not really in the best interest of slave owners and Americans in general.

In his life as a slave who was passed from one owner to another in the manner of chattel property, Douglass saw first-hand how becoming a slaveholder could alter one's existence. Here are two examples that Douglass offers on this point:

Mrs. Auld ... a most kind and tender-hearted woman ... on entering upon the career of a slaveholding mistress ... When I went into their family, it was the abode of happiness and contentment ... Slavery soon proved its ability to divest her of these excellent qualities, and her home of its early happiness. Conscience cannot stand much violence.[27]

A change had taken place, both in Master Hugh, and in his pious and affectionate wife. The influence of brandy and bad company on him, and the influence of slavery and social isolation upon her, had wrought disastrously upon the characters of both.[28]

Douglass summarized the influence of slavery upon the slaveholders by saying that "slavery can change a saint into a sinner, and an angel into a demon."[29] Douglass maintained that slavery had a corrosive influence upon the "character" and general well-being of the slave owner and of the whole slaveholding community, and that therefore the British could be appealed to "as strongly by their regard for the slaveholder as for the slave, to labor in this cause."[30] There is here an implicit distinction between the apparent self-interest of the slaveholder and the real self-interest of the slaveholder which allowed Douglass to maintain that it was genuinely in the best interest of the slaveholder that slavery be abolished.

We might add also that another corrosive influence upon the character of the oppressor is the kind of self-deception which an oppressor is driven to engage in in order to maintain his/her self-image. One has only to examine statements by slaveholders to the effect that their activity was for the purpose of Christianizing Africans who would otherwise spend eternity in hell to see the tortuous self-deceptions to which slaveholders were subject. I hold a similar regard for statements by white South Africans who seeks to convince us that apartheid is in the best interest of colored and black peoples, as well as for statements by American entrepreneurs who argue that they have invested in South Africa for the purpose of enhancing the standard of living for black workers. Douglass is correct. Insofar as the oppressor is driven to such colossal acts of self-deception, oppression does indeed corrode the character of the oppressor.

A similar testimony is provided by another African-American abolitionist — William Wells Brown (1814—1884). Brown's life parallels that of Douglass in that he too was born into slavery and escaped to become an abolitionist, writer, and orator, who gave nearly a thousand lectures favoring the abolitionist cause in England, Ireland, Scotland, Wales, and France. Like Douglass, during his career as a slave, Brown was the chattel property of several families, and he also recorded that slavery had a corrosive influence upon the character and well-being of the slaveholders and their families. In particular Brown noted the damaging influence of slavery upon the children of slave-owners. To this end, Brown quoted from a 1788 letter by Thomas Jefferson in which Jefferson said,

The parent storms, the child looks on, catches the lineaments of wrath, puts on the same airs in the circle of smaller slaves, gives loose to his worst passions; and, thus nursed, educated and daily exercised in tyranny, cannot but be stamped by it with odious peculiarities.[31]

William Wells Brown, Frederick Douglass, Thomas Jefferson, and many others have observed that slavery was contrary to the genuine self-interest of slaveholders, their families, and the surrounding community. Thus, the abolitionists maintained that siding with the oppressed in their struggle for liberation is also a being for, rather than against, the genuine well-being of the oppressors and the community of oppression.

That siding with the oppressed can be a being for the oppressor has obvious theological implications. The God who is "the God of the oppressed" can also be "our common Father and Creator" (G-of-A) in that siding with the oppressed in their struggle for liberation is genuinely in the best interest of all.

We can represent these theological reflections in the form of two deductions which show that, given the reality of oppression, the G-of-A must be the G-of-O.

first deduction:
(1) God experiences all experience.   (G-of-A)
(2) African-Americans have suffered from oppression.
(3) To suffer from oppression entails a desire to be liberated from such suffering.
(4) God experiences the suffering of the oppressed.
(5) Therefore, God desires the liberation of the oppressed.   (G-of-O)

second deduction:
(1) God experiences all experience.   (G-of-A)
(2) Anglo-Americans have been oppressors.
(3) Being an oppressor entails a corrosion of one's character and well being as well as that of one's community.
(4) God experiences the corrosion of the oppressor's well-being.
(5) Therefore, God desires that the oppressor cease being an oppressor. (G-of-O)

There are instances when it might seem that God does not desire the liberation of the oppressed. For example, according to the book of Exodus, God might choose to "harden Pharaoh's heart" so as to make conditions more oppressive. But, again, according to the Exodus account, this is done for the sake of contributing, in the long run, to the struggle for liberation. Sometimes it is better in the long-run that certain short-run interests be sacrificed. This is somewhat akin to the New Testament analogy according to which an eye might be sacrificed for the sake of liberating the whole body. Hartshorne's theism, also, allows for the possibility that God might choose to sacrifice some particular interests for the sake of other more inclusive interests, and that such sacrifice does not imply that God fails to sympathize with the interests which are sacrificed.[32] According to Hartshornian and to biblical theism, then, what may appear to be God's failure to sympathize with the interests of the oppressed is never that; and furthermore, when God sacrifices some interests in favor of other interests, it is always for the sake of promoting the greatest liberty for all. Thus, while our perception may, on account of its limited scope, indicate otherwise; nonetheless, the truth is that God never fails to promote the greatest liberty for all. In the words of Douglass, God is "the Most High, who is ever the God of the oppressed."

It is only by inserting a contingent statement — given the reality of oppression — that an unrestrictive theological statement — say, for example, that God is the subject of all change — can come to entail what I wish to call a "restrictive yet necessary statement" — that God is the God of the oppressed. Strictly speaking, that God is the God of the oppressed is not "necessary" in the sense in which metaphysical necessity is opposed to contingency; however, given the reality of oppression, that God be G-of-O is not a factual contingency in the sense that God could fail to be the G-of-O. In that God is the subject of all change, if oppression is among the changes to which God is subject, then God cannot fail to desire the liberation of the oppressed. But, of course, oppression is a contingent reality. Thus, while strictly speaking, the conjunction of a contingent statement — that oppression is real — with a metaphysically necessary statement — that God is G-of-A — yields what is technically another contingent statement — that God is G-of-O; there is a certain undeniable ineluctability about the truth that if oppression is real, then God cannot fail to be G-of-O, which compels me to indicate its ineluctable character by saying that it is "restrictive yet necessary" (and here necessary does not mean metaphysical necessity). This is somewhat analogous to Hartshorne's language of "hypothetical necessity." In any event, without the insertion of a contingent statement affirming the reality of oppression, it would seem impossible to bridge the gap between an unrestrictive theological assertion and the characteristic and partially restrictive assertion of black theology — that God favors the struggle of the oppressed for liberation.

The status of a strictly metaphysical assertion, taken alone, or only in combination with other strictly metaphysical assertions, is a matter about which black theology and most other theologies of liberation have shown little interest, and this is so for the best of reasons. The obvious reason is that strictly metaphysical assertions are, with regard to ethics, singularly uninteresting. If, according to neoclassical metaphysics, a properly metaphysical assertion is one that is affirmed by every actual and every conceivable fact;[33] then it would follow that nothing actual or conceivably actual is contradicted by a metaphysical assertion so that, in the words of Ivan Karamazov, "all things are lawful." But if, on the other hand, the metaphysical assertion that God is the subject of all change is conjoined with an assertion of the reality of oppression, then we can deduce that God favors the struggle against oppression, and that there are theological reasons for holding that some things are lawful and some not lawful. It is at this point that neoclassical metaphysics becomes relevant to ethics generally, and to the liberation agenda of black and liberation theologies in particular.

The principles of method outlined by Charles Hartshorne in *Creative Synthesis and Philosophic Method* are entirely consistent with our liberation agenda. For example, Hartshorne says, "Philosophy has two primary responsibilities: to clarify the non-empirical principles and to use them, together with relevant empirical facts, to illuminate value problems of personal and social life."[34] Thus, the central challenge posed by black theology is that neoclassical metaphysics consider the realities of oppression as among the most important, if not *the most important* of the relevant empirical facts to be used together with non-empirical principles for the illumination of value problems of personal and social life. The varied circumstances of oppression have been too seldom among the relevant empirical facts considered by neoclassical theism. From the perspective of most of the world's people, the reality of suffering from oppression is not one fact among a great many others; rather, it is *the fact* of social existence to which so many others are subordinate. The challenge is, then, not a contrary view, but rather, a stimulus to follow through with the neoclassical logic in ways that further illuminate the problems faced by the world's oppressed majority.

Perhaps the most important theological point in this essay, is that neoclassical theism, according to its own principles of method, must — given the reality of oppression — join black theology in affirming a certain priority for the conception of God as God of the oppressed. While, on the one hand, many critics of black theology regard the vision of God as God of the oppressed as an insufficiently comprehensive vision of God; Hartshorne's theism, on the other hand, must insist that the partially restrictive and partly contingent vision of God as God of the oppressed is *more inclusive* than any abstract vision of God as merely the universal God of all. In Chapter V — "Some Principles of Method" — of *Creative Synthesis and Philosophic Method*, Hartshorne argues that, in accordance with the principles of formal logic, "the necessary cannot include the contingent, and that the total truth, assuming there are both contingent and necessary truths, must be contingent."[35] In the same way that "Becoming includes Being, as the contingent includes the necessary,"[36] black theology maintains that its vision of God as G-of-O includes the abstract vision of God as the G-of-A, while the converse cannot be true. Therefore, the vision of God as G-of-O is greater than and altogether inclusive of the vision of God as the G-of-A. Insofar as the logic of Hartshorne's neoclassical theism requires us to affirm the priority of G-of-O over any wholly abstract vision of God, neoclassical theism is to this considerable extent more in accord with black theology than are most Western orthodox and neo-orthodox theologies.

III. THE CHALLENGE THAT NEOCLASSICAL THEISM PRESENTS FROM THE PERSPECTIVE OF BLACK THEOLOGY

In one of his more recent books — *Omnipotence and Other Theological Mistakes* — Hartshorne summarizes the neoclassical challenge to traditional or classical theism. Here, Hartshorne identifies "six common mistakes about God" which taken together describe what he calls "classical theism." Hartshorne understands classical theism to be characterized by mistaken conceptions of (1) divine perfection, (2) divine omnipotence, (3) divine omniscience, (4) divine sympathy, (5) immortality, and (6) revelation. (1) The classical conception of divine perfection is faulty in that it concludes wrongly that in order for God to be perfect, God must therefore be conceived as unchangeable/immutable in every respect. (2) The classical conception of divine omnipotence is found to be faulty in that it concludes that in order for God to be omnipotent that whatever happens must be divinely caused to happen. (3) The classical conception of divine omniscience is wrongly conceived in that it holds that whatever happens must have been eternally known in every respect by God. (4) Divine goodness is misconceived in that God is thought to be good, yet unsympathetic. The classical misconception holds that God's unsympathetic goodness is such that God's goodness is "like the sun's way of doing good, which benefits the myriad forms of life on earth but receives no benefits from the good it produces."[37] (5) Classical theism errs in conceiving of "immortality as a career after death."[38] (6) And finally, classical theism is marked by an erroneous conception of infallible revelation according to which, "The idea of revelation is the idea of special knowledge of God, or of religious truth, possessed by some people and transmitted by them to others."[39]

The first four of the mistakes are of the same class in that each violates "the principle of dual transcendence" by failing to conceive that God is not only transcendent and unsurpassable as an "agent" with power to be the cause of events, but also that God is transcendent and unsurpassable as "patient" in having a uniquely excellent capacity to be an effect. According to Hartshorne's principle of dual transcendence, God is unsurpassable as both agent and as patient. Hartshorne conceives that God is not only eternal, but eternal *and* temporal; not only spiritual, but spiritual *and* physical; not only infinite, but infinite *and* finite; not only abstract, but abstract *and* concrete; not only active, but active *and* passive; not only independent, but independent *and* dependent; not only simple, but simple *and* complex. This is a "dipolar" conception of God. Classical theism, on the other hand, accepts that only one of any pair of such metaphysical contraries applies to God, and it thereby, in violation of the principle of dual transcendence, produces a monopolar conception of God. Hartshorne attributes this consistent violation of the principle of dual transcendence to the fact that classical theism has placed too much faith in Greek philosophy, and to a Western prejudice according to which absolute independence along with the power to be the cause of events is regarded as a superior attribute while relativity and the capacity to be an effect is mistakenly regarded as an inferior attribute."[40]

It is clear that black theology does not share the classical Western prejudice against relativity (After all, nothing can be more supremely relative — "surrelative" — than the view that God experiences all experience.), and we have also seen that black theology is not much indebted to Greek philosophy. (1) Unlike classical theism, black theology has never conceived of divine perfection in such a way as to entail that God is wholly immutable. (2) Unlike classical theism, black theology has never conceived divine omnipotence in a way that entails that whatever happens is entirely deter-mined by God. On the contrary, black theology has consistently and explicitly rejected such a conception of divine omnipotence. (3) Unlike classical theism, black theology has never conceived divine omniscience in a way that denies that the future is at least partly open. (4) And finally, black theology has steadfastly opposed the view that divine goodness is unsympathetic with its view that God is maximally sympathetic. Thus, as regards the four theological mistakes which Hartshorne describes as various violations of the principle of dual transcendence owing to a faulty Greek inheritance and a Western prejudice which favors absolute independence over relativity and partial dependence, the Hartshornian foil touches black theology hardly at all. We may then pass over the whole group of four in order to consider the remaining two — (5) immortality and (6) revelation — from the perspective of black theology.

Mistake # 5

Hartshorne characterizes the classical conception of after-death as that which recognizes only two possibilities: either death reduces us to a mere corpse with no enduring meaning or value, or, we survive death to experience a new career of heavenly or hellish existence "in which our individual consciousness will have new experiences not enjoyed or suffered while on earth."[41] Classical theism opts for the second alternative in the form of conventional views of personal immortality. Neoclassical theism offers a third possibility according to which we do not survive death in the form of having an after-death career of new experiences, but according to which this lack of an after-death career does not reduce us to nothing because there is, in Whiteheadean terminology, an "objective immortality of the past." While this third alternative denies personal immortality in the conventional sense, there is, nonetheless, an objective immortality of the past insofar as every past event is a permanent item in the subsequent present. Our existence is, then, permanently and perfectly preserved in ultimate reality.

It might seem that the Hartshornian denial of personal immortality would be a direct challenge to African-American religion and thus to black theology, but, upon careful reflection, we shall see that this is not altogether the case.

We may begin with the observation that African-American religion is not characterized by a univocal commitment to the conventional vision of personal immortality, especially as formulated in the classical Greek conception of immortal souls. One has only to attend to funeral services among African Baptist and African Methodist congregations to see that this is so. For example, it is very common to find three clearly distinct and somewhat incompatible views of after-death affirmed at a single funeral in an African-American church. Very commonly one will find that a minister will, in the course of a single funeral ceremony, affirm each of the following: (1) that death is the inevitable way of all the earth, that we must all return to the earth — "dust to dust, ashes to ashes" — that, in short, when you're dead, you're dead; (2) that the deceased is now at home with God, that her/his soul has gone to its eternal home — hopefully heaven, but perhaps hell; and (3) that the deceased will rest here, asleep, in the grave until that great day of judgment when Gabriel will blow a trumpet whereupon the dead will be resurrected in the body to face the last judgment. The first view is akin to ancient Hebrew visions according to which there is no personal immortality. The second view is akin to the classical Greek vision of an immortal soul being liberated from imprisonment in the physical body. And the third view is akin to an early Christian (Pauline) vision of the general resurrection or resuscitation of previously deceased bodies based upon the model of the bodily resurrection of Jesus. Typically, all three visions of after-death are affirmed by African-American Christians.

Obviously, African-American Christianity has given no systematic attention to this matter, otherwise it could not conceivably affirm three incompatible visions of after-death. Moreover, to my knowledge, black theology has given no systematic attention to this matter either. What is unambiguously clear, however, is that African-American funeral rites reflect an unshakable religious conviction that ultimate meaning and value rests "in God's hands," and that while we do not know the programmatic details, we remain certain that the value of our past life can be entrusted to God's care. This much is clearly affirmed, while the conventional notions of personal immortality, especially as rendered in the classical Greek vision of immortal souls, represent programmatic details which are not univocally affirmed; for indeed, such unknowable details are not essential to the fundamental religious conviction that we can entrust our deceased to God's tender loving and eternal care. This last fundamental religious conviction is, to my knowledge, as much as black theology in North America has ever affirmed, and there is nothing essential in this which is overturned by preferring objective immortality to personal immortality and immortal souls.

Traditional and ancient African religions are resources which are essential to black theology, and since existence after death is a topic about which African religions have much to say, we shall now consider their contribution. At this point black theology may rightly criticize Hartshorne's treatment of existence after death. Hartshorne's analysis in *Omnipotence and Other Theological Mistakes* is defective insofar as it recognizes only three possibilities — the two identified by classical theism and the third which is Whitehead's doctrine of the objective immortality of the past. These are not the only possible or actual views of existence after death, and we are licensed to criticize Hartshorne for speaking as if they were by Hartshorne's own criteria of evaluation. In *Creative Synthesis and Philosophic Method*, Hartshorne provides us with a list of seven criteria by which a metaphysician can be evaluated, and the fifth of these refers to "an ability to grasp diverse possible or historical perspectives on problems (why should we trust his choice of a view if he does not know what views have been or can be held?)"[42] Thus, we turn now to consider a historical perspective on the problem of existence after death which Hartshorne has not considered — the traditional black African vision.

In *African Religions and Philosophy*, John S. Mbiti addresses the question of what remains after one's physical life by drawing upon a traditional African distinction between (1) the living, (2) the "living dead," and (3) the "completely dead," or as some others prefer to say, the "dead dead." While there are significant philosophical inconsistencies inherent in Mbiti's description, he still succeeds in making the essential point that among traditional Africans a deceased individual, while physically dead, is not thought to be reduced to a mere corpse. Such a one is appreciated for the difference that s/he made and for the difference that this continues to make to the surviving community. For so long as the surviving community is conscious of the fact that its existence is, and will be, different on account of its having creatively synthesized the contributions of the deceased and for so long as the surviving community can remember the deceased by name, that person, though physically dead, continues to live in that his/her previous existence continues to make a difference to and is remembered by the community; and thus, such a one is classified as "living dead." One of the conceptual flaws in Mbiti's description is that he describes this as a "state of personal immortality."[43] It is clear that Mbiti does not really mean "immortality" because he goes on to tell us that the "living dead" do eventually die insofar as sooner or later, perhaps generations later, the surviving community will forget the contributions and even the name of the deceased person at which time s/he becomes "completely dead"/dead-dead. Thus, there is, according to traditional African thought, existence after death — that of the living dead, but not such as can be properly described as "personal immortality."

Mbiti describes the traditional African conception of time by using two Swahili words — "Sasa" and "Zamani." Traditional Africans conceive that events move backward in time from the Sasa period of time into the Zamani

16

period. The Sasa period of time is the period of conscious living. The living participate in Sasa self-consciously while the living-dead participate insofar as the surviving community remembers their names and the differences made by their having lived. When the living-dead die, that is, when they become dead-dead, they disappear from human consciousness as they move backward into a realm of eternal reality called "Zamani." Mbiti describes the process in this way:

> Death becomes, then, a gradual process which is not completed until some years after the actual physical death. At the moment of physical death the person becomes a living-dead: he is neither alive physically, nor dead relative to the corporate group. His own Sasa period is over, he enters fully into the Zamani period; but as far as the living who knew him are concerned, he is kept "back" in the Sasa period, from which he can disappear only gradually. Those who have nobody to keep them in the Sasa period in reality "die" immediately, which is a great tragedy that must be avoided at all costs.[44]

It is important to note that while Zamani is a realm beyond the reach of human remembering, it is not a realm of unreality. Thus, not even the dead dead who have moved back into the Zamani period are reduced to utter nonreality. While it is unfortunate that the living-dead die, it is nonetheless true that the fact that they were once among the living makes an ineluctable difference, albeit an invisible difference, to the existence of those who are presently living and to all subsequent reality. In this sense, Mbiti rightly refers to the Zamani as a realm of "collective immortality" when he says that, "the living-dead do not vanish out of existence: they now enter into the state of collective immortality."[45] Death is, then, another instance of the more general way in which all history and all events move backward in time "from the Sasa period to the Zamani, from the moment of intense experience to the period beyond which nothing can go."[46]

Traditional African philosophy, then, offers us a conception of existence after death which does not partake of a mistaken vision of personal immortality. Thus, Hartshorne is quite wrong in saying that, "Only the ancient Jews and some of the ancient Greeks were nearly free from this flight from what, for all we really know, is the human condition."[47] Given that both the living and the living-dead die, strictly speaking, there is no notion of an immortal career involved with the traditional African conception of existence after death. Moreover, the traditional African perception that events move backward in time from Sasa to Zamani reminds me of Whitehead's doctrine of perpetual perishing; and also, the perception that all events are preserved in the eternal reality of the Zamani — "the state of collective immortality" — reminds me of Whitehead's doctrine of the objective immortality of the past.

Mistake #6

The last of the six common theological mistakes identified by Hartshorne is a view of infallible revelation which tends to obliterate any distinction between an infallible God and fallible humans. Christian fundamentalism is taken to be the most extreme form of the erroneous claim to possession of an exclusive and infallible revelation. Hartshorne wishes to correct this kind of extreme claim by offering a more moderate view which grants that there are some religious guides which may be regarded as more reliable than most; but given that all such revelations are mediated by fallible humans, no one revelation can be taken as utterly absolute to the exclusion of all others.

Black theology has never been fundamentalist, but there are some theologians who have argued that at least some black theologians tend to be overly Barthian in their exclusive focus upon the "special revelation" of Christ to the neglect of other "general revelations" about God. Deotis Roberts, for example, says that "the 'exclusive' Christocentrism of Cone is inadequate."[48] (In fairness to James Cone we must observe that in recent years he has developed a progressively more inclusive approach to theology which has included dialogue with Third World, feminist, Asian, traditional African, and other Christian and non-Christian perspectives.) Roberts recognizes that black theology is now being done in a post-colonial, post-Barthian, multicultural and interethnic context which requires new dialogical encounters with traditional African, Third World, and other theological perspectives. Accordingly, in *Roots of a Black Future: Family and Church*,[49] Roberts draws heavily upon traditional African resources to develop his vision of the black church as an extended family, and in *Black Theology in Dialogue* he dialogues with South Korean Minjung theology and with Jewish liberation theology. Charles Long, a black historian of religion, has long sought to widen the scope of black theology so as to include serious dialogue with African, Islamic, and other non-Western and traditional religions. And more recently, Jacquelyn Grant, Henry Young, Archie Smith, Thandeka and other African-Americans have sought to increase dialogue between black theologians and process theologians. Here and in numerous other instances it is clear that black theology is willing to engage and employ traditional African and other non-Christian resources in ways which indicate that, on the whole, black theology does not believe that it has possession of an exclusive and wholly infallible revelation of God.

Black theology's tendency to avoid extreme exclusivist conceptions of the "special revelations" of Christianity is partly determined by its appropriation of the traditional African vision of "general revelation." Gwinyai Muzorewa quotes with approval a fellow African — E. B. Idowu — as saying, "There is no place, age, or generation which did not receive at some point in its history some form of revelation."[50] Additionally, it has been well documented that a monotheistic conception of ultimate reality is indigenous to almost all of traditional African culture, and that it is highly probable that traditional African theism, like Judeo, Christian and Islamic theism, has its historical genesis in the monotheism of a black pharaoh of ancient Egypt — Iknaton — who was the first person known to have popularized the religious conviction that there is one, and only one, god. It is also among the black Africans of ancient Egypt that one finds the earliest conviction that God can be manifest and revealed in human incarnations. And perhaps, therefore, it is no mere coincidence that according to ancient Hindu religions, God became incarnate in the form of a black man — Krishna (the very name Krishna means "the black one"). Therefore, ancient African and traditional African resources have determined that black theology would appropriate Christian revelations in ways that do not entail extreme fundamentalist claims to exclusivist particularity.

Another Mistake

Another of the classical Western notions that is challenged by Hartshorne is what I call the Western conception of the atomic individual. In *Creative Synthesis and Philosophic Method* Hartshorne says, "Our whole Western tradition is warped and confused by the concept of individual taken as ultimate."[51] Hartshorne understands the philosophical conception of the individual taken as ultimate to be an unfortunate consequence of an erroneous "substance theory." According to neoclassical metaphysics, there are, strictly speaking, no enduring substances. Rather than speaking of individuals, things, and substances, metaphysical exactness demands that we speak of "event-sequences or Whiteheadean 'societies.'"[52] Hartshorne's philosophy of "event pluralism" allows that "highly-ordered sequences of events" which normal discourse abstractly calls a self or individual to be properly recognized as a society of events participating in a larger society of events. Thus, Hartshorne opposes the classical Western conception of the atomic individual as ultimate with a social conception of the self, and indeed, with a social conception of all reality.

Black theology, insofar as it draws upon traditional African resources, must side with Hartshorne against the classical Western conception of the atomic individual. This is so because the traditional African conception of human existence is primarily social rather than individual. Again, John Mbiti is our teacher. He says:

> In traditional life, the individual does not and cannot exist alone except corporately. He owes his existence to other people, including those of past generations and his contemporaries. He is simply part of the whole. The community must therefore make, create or produce the individual; for the individual depends on the corporate group. . . . Only in terms of other people does the individual become conscious of his own being, his own duties, his privilege and responsibilities toward himself and towards other people. When he suffers, he does not suffer alone but with the corporate group; when he rejoices, he rejoices not alone but with his kinsmen. . . . Whatever happens to the individual happens to the whole group, and whatever happens to the whole group happens to the individual. The individual can only say: "I am, because we are: and since we are, therefore I am."[53]

Mbiti describes this as "a cardinal point in the understanding of the African view of man."[54] Mbiti's point is buttressed by another native African theologian, Gwinyai H. Muzorewa, who says, "Most African scholars agree that in traditional religion humanity is to be conceived as 'being in relation.' "[55]

Black theology agrees with Hartshorne against classical Western thought also insofar as black theology appropriates a traditional African view of the cross-generational character of ethical responsibility. The cross-generational character of African ethical thought is a consequence of its social conception of human existence. John S. Pobee teaches us in the "African World View" that the basic unit of African society is the family, and that the family "consists of the living, the dead, and the yet-to-be-born."[56] Thus, according to the traditional African vision, a person is not defined as an atomic individual, but as a member of an extended social community that stretches across generations — past, present, and future. The ethical implication is that moral responsibility is not confined to consequences which obtain for only our contemporaries in the present generation. A member of African society has a moral responsibility to past generations to venerate the ancestors; a moral responsibility in regards to the present generation to consider the well-being of his/her contemporaries throughout the community; and a moral responsibility in regards to future generations to create conditions which serve the well-being of those who are called "the beautiful ones" by Ayi Kwei Armah in his classic novel — The Beautyful Ones Are Not Yet Born.[57]

From the perspective of those who see ethics in such cross-generational terms as never to neglect the well-being of the not-yet-born, nothing is more strikingly characteristic of Western systematic ethics than its failure to concern itself with the beautiful ones. Typically, Western ethics, on account of its atomic individualism, is governed by considerations which extend not much beyond the immediate difficulties of a single generation. This is, in fact, one of the reasons why Western ethics has been so unable to deal adequately with long-term ecological difficulties. In contrast to the classical Western neglect of the beautiful ones, there is the Hartshornian theory of "contributionism" which, like traditional African thought, maintains that, given a social conception of human existence, "the rational aim of the individual must in principle transcend any mere good of that individual."[58] Hartshornian contributionism emphasizes the need to contribute to future life, that is, to the well-being of the beautiful ones.

IV. BLACK POWER AND NEOCLASSICAL THOUGHT

It is a historical fact that the philosophy of black power is one of the resources which has shaped black theology.[59] Insofar as black theology remains consistent with the philosophy of black power, it cannot but welcome a metaphysics which conceives that freedom has a metaphysically necessary aspect. Hartshornian metaphysics conceives that freedom is inherent in all existence. For Hartshorne, to be actual at all is to be an instance

of creative synthesis, and this means to have power to be partially deter-
minative of self and others, as well as to have the capacity to be partly
determined by other selves. Thus, insofar as Hartshorne conceives that
freedom, power, and creativity are necessary aspects of all existence, neoclassical thought can be received as a metaphysical foundation for the
philosophy of black power.

The philosophy of black power insists that, given the reality of oppression,
there will be struggle against oppression. One of the founders of the contemporary philosophy of black power is Kwame Ture (Stokely Carmichael).
Ture says that no matter how overwhelming the might of the oppressor is, it
is in the very nature of the people that they will struggle and struggle and
struggle for as long as they are oppressed until at last they achieve their
liberation.[60] Vincent Harding's history — There is a River — emphasizes the
inevitability of the African-American struggle for liberation.[61] From Harding
we learn that while the meaning of liberation and the character of the
struggle are variable, the fact that there will be struggle against oppression is
a constant. Thus, for the African newly-chained to the deck of a ship
anchored at a West African harbor, the meaning of liberation and the
character of the struggle are very different from that of the African-American
who, three generations later, like Frederick Douglass and William Wells
Brown, must consider how best to conduct an abolitionist campaign. We
might add that the meaning of liberation and the character of the struggle
were yet and again different for young Huey Newton (founder of the Black
Panther Party) as he lay hand-cuffed and under armed guard even while in
surgery as the result of being shot by two policemen in 1967. Thus, Vincent
Harding, Kwame Ture, Winnie Mandela, and many others have spoken in
accordance with the philosophy of black power in maintaining that where
there is oppression, there will also be some form of protest and struggle for
liberation.

The late Howard Thurman once described the necessary aspect of the
struggle for liberation by using an analogy form nature.[62] Thurman recalled
that on one occasion during his childhood in Daytona Beach, he happened
upon a tiny green snake crawling along a dirt path. In the mischievous way
that is typical of a boy child, he pressed his bare foot on top of the little
snake. Immediately, the little snake began to struggle to free itself. Young
Thurman felt the tremor of the snake's struggle as it vibrated up his leg and
through his body. Thurman reasoned that it is divinely given to the nature of
all creatures, even to little green snakes, to struggle and protest against
oppression.

The necessity of struggle against oppression can also be described through
the use of neoclassical resources.[63] According to such resources, it is inevitable that the oppressed will struggle for liberation. Moreover, it is characteristic of black power philosophy to insist, with Hartshorne, that, under
certain conditions, those who support the struggle may rightfully engage in
armed resistance to oppression.

Black power philosophy, and therefore black theology, can find neoclassical metaphysics acceptable, also, insofar as each perceives that powerlessness is contrary to the just demands of any people for fully human existence. The agreement between black power and neoclassical philosophies can, therefore, be symbolized by transforming the black power slogan — "Power to the People" — into a more neoclassical formulation — Creative Synthesis to the People; and reciprocally, the neoclassical philosophy of creative synthesis can be understood as a metaphysical way of saying "Power to the People."

NOTES

1. James H. Cone, *Black Theology and Black Power* (New York: The Seabury Press, 1969).
2. James H. Cone, *God of the Oppressed* (New York: The Seabury Press, 1975).
3. Bishop William J. Walls, *The African Methodist Episcopal Zion Church: Reality of the Black Church* (Charlotte, NC.: A. M. E. Zion Publishing House, 1974).
4. Note J. Deotis Roberts's call for black theology to increase its dialogical activity in *Black Theology in Dialogue* (Philadelphia: Westminster Press, 1987).
5. William R. Jones, "Process Theology: Guardian of the Oppressor or Goad to the Oppressed? Insights from Liberation Theology." A paper presented at a conference on process theology and the black experience at the University of Chicago (and in partnership with the Center for Process Studies and Meadville/Lombard Theological School), November 9, 1985.
6. *Ibid.*, p. 17.
7. *MV*, p. 144.
8. *Ibid.*, p. 143.
9. *Ibid.*, p. 148.
10. *Ibid.*, pp. 148–150.
11. *Ibid.*, p. 151.
12. *Ibid.*, p. 159.
13. *Ibid.*, p. 166.
14. *Ibid.*, p. 173.
15. *Ibid.*, p. 162.
16. *Ibid.*, p. 165.
17. *Ibid.*, p. 173.
18. *Ibid.*
19. *Ibid.*
20. *Ibid.*
21. *Ibid.*, p. 168.
22. *Ibid.*, p. 167.
23. *Ibid.*, p. 173.
24. See chapter eight — "The Subject of All Change (Cosmological Argument)" — in *Man's Vision of God*.
25. Frederick Douglass, *My Bondage and My Freedom* (New York: Arno Press and the New York Times, 1969) p. 427.
26. *Ibid.*, p. 422.
27. *Ibid.*, pp. 152–153.
28. *Ibid.*, p. 183.
29. *Ibid.*, p. 142.
30. *Ibid.*, p. 417.
31. From Lucille Schulberg Warner's *From Slave to Abolitionist: The Life of William Wells Brown* (New York: Dial Press, 1976).

22

32. *MV*, p. 166.
33. *LP*. "Metaphysical truths may be described as such that no experience can contradict them, but also that any experience must illustrate them" (p. 296).
34. *CSPM*, p. xiv.
35. *Ibid.*, p. 84.
36. *Ibid.*, p. 84.
37. *OOTM*, p. 4.
38. *Ibid.*, p. 4.
39. *Ibid.*, p. 5.
40. The Western prejudice against relativity is discussed in Hartshorne's book — *The Divine Relativity: A Social Conception of God*. Here, Hartshorne shows that the relative includes within itself, and exceeds in value, the nonrelative or absolute "as the concrete includes and exceeds the abstract" (p. ix).
41. *OOTM*, p. 4.
42. *CSPM*, p. 41.
43. John S. Mbiti, *African Religions and Philosophy* (New York: Anchor Books, 1979) p. 32.
44. *Ibid.*, p. 208.
45. *Ibid.*, p. 33.
46. *Ibid.*, p. 29.
47. *OOTM*, p. 32.
48. J. Deotis Roberts, *Black Theology in Dialogue* (Philadelphia: Westminster Press, 1987) p. 41.
49. J. Deotis Roberts, *Roots of a Black Future: Family and Church* (Philadelphia: Westminster Press, 1980).
50. Gwinyai Muzorewa. *The Origins and Development of African Theology* (Maryknoll, NY: Orbis Books, 1985) p. 9.
51. *CSPM*, p. 190.
52. *CSPM*, p. 204.
53. Mbiti, *op. cit.*, p. 141.
54. *Ibid.*, p. 141.
55. Muzorewa, *op. cit.*, p. 17.
56. John S. Pobee, *Toward an African Theology* (Nashville: Abingdon, 1979) p. 49.
57. Ayi Kwei Armah, *The Beautyful Ones Are Not Yet Born* (New York: Collier Books, 1969). Also, see Ngugi wa Thiong'o's *Petals of Blood* (New York: E. P. Dutton, 1978).
58. John B. Cobb and Franklin I. Gamwell (eds.), *Existence and Actuality: Conversations with Charles Hartshorne* (Chicago: University of Chicago Press, 1984) p. 188.
59. See James Cone's *Black Theology and Black Power* (New York: The Seabury Press, 1969).
60. Here I am paraphrasing from Kwame Ture's speech at Southern Methodist University in Dallas, Texas of 23 October, 1986.
61. Vincent Harding, *There is a River: The Black Struggle for Freedom in America* (New York: Harcourt Brace, and Jovanovich, 1981).
62. Howard Thurman narrated this story from his youth when I had a personal conversation with him on the occasion to his visit to Livingstone College in Salisbury, North Carolina, during the spring of 1978.
63. Again, this is not strict metaphysical necessity; rather, it is what cannot fail to be the case given the reality of oppression.

2. The Dipolar God and Latin American Liberation Theology

Anyone reasonably familiar with the contemporary theological scene of the North and South Americas will readily recognize that process and liberation theologies are the two predominant currents of thought, the former in the northern hemisphere and the latter in the southern. Chronologically process thought is the elder sibling; and though it originated in modern times with Alfred North Whitehead[1] primarily as a cosmology and metaphysics, its basic insights have been appropriated by a number of theologians to revitalize classical Christian theology which, in their judgment, had suffered atrophy on account of the static substance metaphysics it employed.[2] On the other hand, liberation theologians, also disillusioned with classical Christian theology, the primary purpose of which they perceive as the achievement of contemplative wisdom and rational knowledge, propose instead as the proper task of theology a critical reflection on political, economic, and social praxis in favor of the integral liberation for the poor and the oppressed.[3]

In this paper I shall limit my considerations of process thought to the system proposed by Charles Hartshorne[4] and of liberation theology to the writings of Latin American theologians.[5] The choice of Hartshorne, besides being dictated by the purpose of the volume, is, I trust, abundantly justified since there is little doubt that he is acknowledged as the ablest and most prolific exponent of Whitehead and an influential and original thinker in his own rights. The restriction to Latin American theologians is equally warranted since *de facto* liberation theology was first given expression in Latin America. The paper is an exercise in *Auseinandersetzung* of the doctrine of God of these two schools of thought with a view to identifying areas in which they can enrich each other.

There have been, of course, attempts to compare and contrast process thought and liberation theology with the purpose of correcting and complementing each by the insights of the other. So far, however, the effort has been carried out almost exclusively by process theologians, such as Schubert Ogden, Delwin Brown, and John B. Cobb, Jr.[6] Liberation theologians, either because of their educational background or because of their alleged distrust of academic pursuits, have exhibited little interest in constructing an appro-

S. Sia (ed.), Charles Hartshorne's Concept of God, 23–39.
© 1990 *Kluwer Academic Publishers. Printed in the Netherlands.*

priate metaphysics to undergird their theological position.[7] Schubert Ogden correctly sees the challenge of liberation theologies for philosophical theologians in that "they typically focus on the existential meaning of God for us without dealing at all adequately with the metaphysical being of God in himself."[8] On the other hand, as John B. Cobb, Jr. acknowledges, while justice is the central concern of liberation theology, "process theology has failed to deal extensively with the issue of justice, at least under that rubric."[9] Hence, a mutual confrontation between process thought and liberation theology will no doubt be beneficial to both.

In what follows I will first of all discuss the methodological divergencies between Hartshorne and Latin American liberation theologians, and secondly I will elaborate their respective concepts of God, focusing on how the dipolar God of Hartshorne and God the Liberator of liberation theology are two mutually complementary concepts.

I. STARTING POINT, METHODOLOGY, AND TASKS: CONVERGENCES AND DIVERGENCES

The differences in starting point, methodology, and tasks between process thought and liberation theology are brought forth indirectly by Jon Sobrino's illuminating comments on the divergencies between European theology and Latin American theology.[10] Sobrino identifies three areas in which these divergencies occur. First of all, liberation theology fosters the "liberating" character of theological understanding. Whereas European theology attempts to overcome the crisis produced by the first phase of the Enlightenment (Kant) by liberating theology from dogmatic authoritarianism, historical error, and myth, and by *explaining* the existential meaning of religious truth, Latin American theology takes up the challenge of the second phase of the Enlightenment (Marx) by seeking to liberate the wretched state of the real world marked by exploitation, slavery, oppression, and poverty and to *transform* that sinful condition. Theological understanding is thus inseparable from the practical and the ethical and cannot be reduced to the attempt to reconcile faith with the meaninglessness experienced by the subject. Because European theology is interested in restoring the meaning to religious truths, it naturally has recourse to philosophy as the model for universal understanding and the tool for the expression of meaning. On the other hand, since the concern of liberation theology is the transformation of the social condition, it turns spontaneously to the social sciences as suitable mediation for theological understanding.

Secondly, whereas for European theology the starting point is a deposit of truths that must be transmitted, explained, interpreted, and made meaningful, and hence orthodoxy is its primary concern, for liberation theology the starting point is experiential praxis of liberation, however inchoative, rather than past theological tradition, and hence its primary interest is orthopraxis.

The method of liberation theology is then not critical reflection on the way travelled to reach theological understanding but is identified with the travelling itself. In other words, understanding is obtained not by means of the history of ideas but by means of correct practice.

Thirdly, liberation theology insists that there is a "break" in theological epistemology. Whereas in the epistemology of European theology analogy functions as a way of going *beyond* natural knowledge but not *against* it (that is, analogical knowledge presupposes that like is known by like), in Latin America, where beauty, love, peace, and justice are in short supply and the plight of the masses catastrophic, theological discourse is much more dialectical than analogical, more practical than analytical. Besides the analogical understanding of reality, liberation theology proposes a *dialectical* understanding of it; that is, it takes the wretched conditions and the situation of sin and oppression as the point of departure and a stimulus for theological thinking about the means to eliminate them. Consequently, liberation theology is not interested in constructing a natural theology in which the God-question begins with what is positive in the world; rather its task is to answer the question of theodicy the starting point of which is what is negative in the world: How is the existence of God to be reconciled with the real wretchedness and evil in the world? As Sobrino puts it sharply: "The 'problem of God' is not tackled as extensively and directly in Latin American theology as it is in European theology. The reason for this is not that God has ceased to be a problem or a question . . . , but rather that the theme is approached indirectly. The epistemological break in theodicy does not consist fundamentally in explaining, at the level of thought, the true nature of God, but in experiencing the reality of God in the effort to build his kingdom. The reality of God is proved in the effort to reconcile him with the real world."[11] That is why the "death of God," which ever since Hegel and Nietzsche has exercised theism in First World theology, is not for liberation theology an issue to be debated in natural theology but an anthropological question. That is to say, the "death of God" is seen through the death of the human being, especially the death of the poor and the oppressed, which reveals itself as the triumph of injustice and sin.[12]

These observations on the starting point, method, and tasks of European theology and Latin American theology help us understand the similarities and divergencies between process thought and liberation theology. Both schools of thought are critical of classical theism, which is said to be founded on a static concept of being and substance, but for basically different reasons. Hartshorne rejected what he terms classical theism on logical, metaphysical, moral and religious grounds. The classical concept of God may be described as supernaturalistic, dependent on the Greek notion of deity as timeless, and based upon a hierarchical ordering of reality.[13] Hartshorne's neoclassical view of God was developed as a response to the crisis of *meaning* in this classical theism. He radically reinterpreted the three fundamental concepts of classical metaphysics — substance, causality, and deity — because he thought that they were logically incoherent, metaphysically inadequate, and morally and religiously barren.[14] Of course Hartshorne did elaborate the ethical and religious implications of classical theism as well as his own version of neoclassical theism, both on the individual and social levels. Indeed, it may be argued, as Santiago Sia has done,[15] that the starting point and frame of reference for Hartshorne's understanding of deity is religion. Religious experience provides the intuitive insight into deity which philosophy seeks to express with appropriate conceptuality. Hartshorne contends that his process philosophy expresses more adequately than classical theism the nature of religion as "devoted love for a being regarded as superlatively worth of love"[16] and the nature of God as the worshipful one, who is all-inclusive, one and unsurpassable in his goodness, power and knowledge, and whose happiness is affected by others.[17] Hartshorne has also pointed out the nefarious ethical consequences of classical theism, namely, otherworldliness, power worship, asceticism, moralism, optimism, obscurantism, and the confusion between deity and humanity.[18] What Hartshorne meant by these aberrations and how they can be eschewed by adopting his neoclassical theism or the doctrine of "surrelativism," we will determine shortly.

Despite these religious and ethical strands in Hartshorne's dipolar doctrine of God, it remains true that his philosophical project was primarily animated by the concern to overcome the challenge of the first phase of the Enlightenment. Indeed it is significant that not infrequently Hartshorne polemicized against Hume and Kant, especially in his attempt at establishing the possibility of natural theology.[19] This concern for the meaning of reality naturally led Hartshorne to defend the legitimacy of metaphysics as the science that "deals with what is common and *necessary* to all possible states of affairs and all possible truth."[20] Consequently his philosophical method, though based on language and experience, makes abundant use of formal logic and mathematics on the one hand to achieve coherence, necessity, and universality of metaphysical truths (hence, the importance of making an exhaustive survey of possible standpoints) and enlists the help of natural science on the other hand to ensure their adequacy.[21]

Another important methodological presupposition of Hartshorne's doctrine of God is the legitimacy of our God-talk. He distinguishes three different ways of speaking of God: symbolic (or material), literal (or formal), and analogical. Symbolic predication occurs when God is compared to a concrete species of reality, e.g. rock, king, shepherd, parent. In literal predication God is described in terms of purely abstract and general philosophical categories such as space, time, becoming, necessity, infinity. Literal predication can be either negative or positive. Negative God-talk uses literal language but denies that it is applicable to God. Hartshorne is critical of negative theology because he believes that some formal predicates of deity are not exclusively negative and that some positive properties can be ascribed to deity literally (non-symbolically, even though differently when ascribed to creatures). Thus one can speak of God not only literally but also positively.[22] Finally, our predication of God is analogical when it describes God in terms of the psychological properties common to deity and creatures, e.g. knowledge, love, and will (panpsychism).[23] In sum, as far as our predication of God is concerned, Hartshorne says that "God is symbolically ruler, but analogically conscious and loving, and literally both absolute (necessary) in existence and relative (contingent) in actuality — that is, in the concrete modes of his existence."[24]

These considerations of Hartshorne's conception of the starting point, method, and tasks of metaphysics clearly show the differences between his view and that of liberation theologians. As pointed out above, Latin American liberation theology takes up the challenge of the second phase of the Enlightenment by seeking to liberate and transform the wretched condition of the real world. Of course, liberation theologians are aware, as Hartshorne is, of the deficiency of the classical doctrine of God, in particular its inability to foster and sustain a liberative praxis in favor of the poor and the oppressed and its tendency to preserving the status quo. Sobrino puts it quite starkly: "The Greek metaphysical conception of God's being and perfection renders any theology of the cross impossible. A truly historical theology of liberation must view suffering as a mode of being belonging to God."[25] This incapacity of Greek metaphysics to formulate a truly adequate conception of the Christian God is the consequence of its view of divine perfection. In terms remarkably reminiscent of Hartshorne, Sobrino writes: "In this respect liberation theology must get beyond Greek thought. It must ask itself in what sense suffering and death can be a mode of being for God. Bound up with this difficulty in Greek thought is its conception of perfection. That conception . . . associates perfection with immutability. Something that is perfect is also eternal and ahistorical. Those traits must therefore be of the very essence of the deity. Suffering implies some form of passivity and mutability, hence it must be alien to God. Greek thought cannot picture suffering as a divine mode of being because that would imply a contradiction."[26]

But instead of systematically re-evaluating classical theism from the standpoint of natural theology and our language about God, liberation theology chooses to formulate a theodicy and a doctrine of God from the experience and perspective of the poor. The poor here include not only the economically poor but also those who, as Matthew L. Lamb has accurately described,[27] are victims of classism, sexism, racism, technocentrism, and militarism. The point of departure of liberation theology is not a body of metaphysical principles but a liberative praxis, a living commitment to and a struggle with and for the poor. Theology is critical reflection on praxis; it is the second act following the first act, historical praxis, the true *locus theologicus*. From and out of this praxis, liberation theology is articulated in three steps: socio-analytic mediation, hermeneutic mediation, and practical mediation.[28]

Because it is interested in transforming the socio-economic and political situation of the poor, liberation theology appeals not to logic, mathematics, and the natural sciences, as Hartshorne did, but to the social sciences, in particular sociology and politics, with a view to explaining the phenomenon of poverty. Poverty as a social phenomenon is seen neither as the result of vice (the empirical explanation) nor as backwardness (the functional explanation) but as oppression (the dialectical explanation). The last explanation, also known as the 'historico-structural' approach, sees poverty as a collective and conflictive phenomenon which can be overcome only by replacing it with an alternative economic-social system through revolution. In performing this socio-analytic mediation liberation theology makes use of Marxist social analysis, particularly its emphasis on the importance of economic factors, class struggle, and the mystifying power of iedologies.[29]

In the hermeneutic mediation, which is the formally theological stage, liberation theology attempts to reread the Bible and the Christian tradition from the viewpoint of the oppressed, and insofar as the doctrine of deity is concerned, it sees God mainly as the liberator of the poor from every kind of oppression. It is a liberative hermeneutics: it seeks application rather than explanation; it looks for the textual meaning but as a function of the practical meaning; it attempts to discover and activate the transforming energy of biblical texts; and lastly, it stresses the social context of the message.

Finally, in the practical mediation, liberation theology seeks to foster pastoral practices of transformation, that is, action for justice, work for love, conversion, renewal of the church, and transformation of society. For liberation theology, faith is not only "also" political, but above all else political. Of course such practical mediation is extremely complex; wisdom and prudence will dictate what course of action is feasible, morally permissible, and historically viable.[30]

Liberation theology's emphasis on its social context of oppression and poverty leads it away from the use of analogy in its theo-logy. Analogy presupposes continuity and harmony, central features of Hartshorne's metaphysics and God-talk. On the contrary, liberation theology gives priority to dialectics, which underlines contrast and distance, in its theology of God. Sobrino makes the point clearly: "Greek epistemology, which was based on analogy and wonder, makes it impossible for us to recognize God in the cross of Jesus. Liberation theology must add further principles here. To the principle of analogy it must add the principle of dialectics; to the principle of wonder it must add the notion of suffering as a font of knowledge leading us to the concrete practice of transforming love."[31] God, then, is known not only through what is positive in his creatures, e.g. their beauty, order, intelligence, wisdom, and so on, but also, and primarily, through what is negative in reality. God appears on the cross *sub specie contrarii*. Further, analogy presupposes that some correlation exists between the object to be known and the knowing subject. And, according to Aristotle, it is intellectual wonder that enables us to grasp this correlation. Liberation theology suggests that this sense of wonder takes on a special form, namely, sorrow. Sorrow wells up in the face of the evil embodied in oppression and injustice. It is the cognitive attitude that serves as an analogy between the believers and the cross of Jesus and it enables them to grasp by means of a sympathy and a con-natural knowledge the presence of God on the cross of Jesus and in the sufferings of their fellow human beings. Sorrow, however, must be active, and so analogical knowledge through active sorrow is transformed in socio-political action.

The foregoing comparison and contrast between liberation theology and Hartshorne's process thought are not intended simply to highlight their divergencies, important though they are, but also to show how they can be mutually complementary and enriching. As John Cobb, Jr. has clearly shown,[32] process theology has just begun and should continue to reflect on its social context and the effects of that context on its work. Further, there is nothing inherent in process thought that would prevent it from moving from the first phase to the second phase of the Enlightenment.[33] After all, as has been mentioned above, Hartshorne was fully aware of the ethical and social implications of what he considered a mistaken notion of deity of classical theism. Whether or not these pernicious effects flow from monopolar theism is a moot point; nevertheless, there is no doubt that the errors that Hartshorne decries are also heartily rejected by liberation theologians. Both Hartshorne and liberation theologians strongly object to the flight from the task of promoting human welfare to that of saving souls (otherworldliness), the divorce of the notion of power from that of sensitivity in the concepts both of deity and of church and state authority (power worship), the failure to genuinely synthesize 'physical' and 'spiritual' values (asceticism), the notion that courageous creative action in art, science, and statesmanship is religiously neutral or secondary (moralism), the idea that all violence is wrong (optimism), the theory that we can best praise God by indulging in contradiction and semantical nonsense (obscurantism).[34]

Hartshorne contends that such moral and social ills can be eschewed by adopting his dipolar doctrine of God. On the other hand, liberation theologians attempt to construct a concept of God as liberator "from the underside of history" (Gustavo Gutiérrez), that is, history from the perspective of the poor. Are the Dipolar God and God the Liberator mutually complementary concepts of deity? Schubert Ogden has argued that liberation theologies "typically are not so much theology as witness."[35] Leaving aside the question of whether Latin American liberation theology is only "witness," that is, whether it fails critically to inquire into the meaning and truth of its faith assertions, it is of interest to examine whether Hartshorne's neoclassical metaphysics can serve as a coherent and adequate conceptuality for liberation theology's doctrine of God.

II. GOD THE LIBERATOR AND THE DIPOLAR GOD:
THEOLOGY AND METAPHYSICS

Liberation theology's concept of God is succinctly summarized by the two Boff brothers:

a. Liberation theology recovers the image of God *as creator of life*, a God whose glory is the "human being alive." Among a people for whom death is not a simple figure of speech but a daily reality thrust upon their attention in infant mortality, violent conflict, kidnappings, and torture, a theology of God as creator and sustainer of life acquires a piercing relevancy.

b. To an oppressed people, God also appears as *Yahweh the Liberator,* who wills that his people go *free* from all slavery. Here the Exodus is no longer a "typological luxury, serving as counterpoint for a moral-and-spiritual salvation" (José M. González Ruiz), but is the model, in the full sense of the term, of any and every liberation process that has ever been or ever will be — without ceasing to be a "type" of the Paschal Mystery, from the viewpoint of salvation-in-its-transcendency.[36]

It seems that these two concepts of God, God the creator of life and Yahweh the Liberator, closely parallel Schubert Ogden's notion of God as the *Redeemer* and *Emancipator,* which he bases on the two key process principles, namely, "nothing whatever, not even God, can wholly determine the being of something else" and "whatever is, even God, is in part determined by the being of other things."[37]

On the basis of the theology of the cross of Jesus, Sobrino develops a doctrine of God emphatically in terms of process. The best way to show how Sobrino's theology of God closely resembles that of process thought is to reproduce some of the key texts:

On the cross of Jesus God himself is crucified. The Father suffers the death of the Son and takes upon himself all the pain and suffering of history. In this ultimate solidarity with humanity he reveals himself as the God of love, who opens up a hope and a future through the most negative side of history. Thus Christian existence is nothing else but a *process* of participation in this same *process* whereby God loves the world and hence in the very life of God.[38]

God himself must be part of the whole *process* of protest rather than remaining aloof of it. So the question is: Do we find any theological experience where God himself is against God? The answer is yes: the cross. On the cross we find a *process within God himself.* The Father surrenders the Son, abandoning him to the power of sin.[39]

The Christian belief in God as a Trinity takes on a new and dynamic meaning in the light of the cross. God is a *trinitarian "process"* on the way to its ultimate fulfillment (1 Cor. 15:28), but it takes all history into itself. *In this process God participates in,* and *lets himself (be) affected by,* history through the Son; and *history is taken into God in the Spirit.*[40]

Alongside the notion of God as a *"process",* then, we have Christian existence as a "way" based on the following of Jesus. When we view Christian existence as the following of Jesus, we are not simply viewing it in ethical terms that flow from a prior faith. Strictly speaking, we are viewing it as a participation in the very life of God himself. ... We are made children of God *by participating in the very process* of God.[41]

The cross suggests that the reality of God may be viewed as a *process* that is open to the world. Through the Son, God actively incorporates himself into the historical *process*; through the Spirit, human beings and history are *incorporated into God himself.*[42]

Apart from terminological coincidences, these five passages express a doctrine of God that possesses startling similarities with that of process thought. God the Liberator clearly is not the *Actus Purus* who is absolute, immutable, impassible, eternal, independent, all-powerful. Rather, he reveals himself as the God of love, as suffering love; the God who is crucified, who internalizes all the pain, sorrow, and horrors of history, who takes the side of the poor against their oppressors, who participates in the changing process of history, who "lets himself (be) affected by" human history; the God who is the liberator, the vindicator (*Go'el*), the God of life "who vanquishes death and re-creates life." In short, the God who is process. Victorio Araya sums up the theo-logy of Latin American liberation theology: "*The liberator God is the God of the kingdom.* The God who continues to be manifest in history on the calvary of the world, on the side of the poor — hidden in them, in loving, suffering solidarity with them — as salvific praxis (liberation, justice, and life), is revealed in a process: the process of the kingdom."[43]

Is the liberation theology God then a dipolar God? It must be pointed out here that while many Latin American theologians have voiced sharp criticisms of classical theism as seriously inadequate to the task of expressing the Christian understanding of God, they have failed to elaborate what Ogden calls "the metaphysics of faith and justice" appropriate to the biblical witness to God's activities in and relation to the world and credible in terms of contemporary experience.[44] Nevertheless, consideration must be given to Sobrino's attempt at constructing a "dipolar" *theology* (not metaphysics) of God from the experience of the Church of the poor: God reveals himself both as the "Greater God" (*Dios Mayor*) and the "Lesser God" (*Dios Menor*), or more precisely, the "Greater God" reveals himself *as* and *in* the "Lesser God." In other words, one cannot know the "Greater God" in himself except through the experience of the "Lesser God."

By the "Greater God" Sobrino means God as mystery who is beyond control, the totally other: God in absolute otherness, the Holy, the Inconceivable, the Transcendent, the *mysterium tremendum.* This aspect of God may be experienced in various ways, but especially in the process of conversion, which includes two components: (1) the turning away from and changing of the direction of one's life, and hence rupture; and (2) the turning away from the idols toward the true God. The experience of conversion is an experience of God as the "Siempre Mayor" (the Ever Greater) because he differs radically from every other beings.[45]

But this *Dios Mayor*, though omnipresent, is not equally present in all things and cannot be reached directly. The "Greater God" is a partisan God; he lets himself be reached in and through the poor and the oppressed. Consequently, says Sobrino, "out of this situation emerges the expression 'the lesser God', an expression metaphorically correct, but no less metaphorical than that of 'the greater God'. This expression means that one cannot approach God in the same way from all experiences, but rather that such an approach must take place from adequate experiences and, more specifically, from those experiences which prima facie would seem to have absolutely nothing to do with God."[46] Thus, access to the transcendent *Dios Mayor* comes through contact with the *Dios Menor*, the *mysterium fascinans* hidden in the poor, crucified on the cross of Jesus and on the countless crosses of the oppressed of our day.

It is extremely tempting to see a parallel, if not a correspondence, between the *Dios Mayor/Dios Menor* on the one hand and the absolute/relative, abstract/concrete, necessary/contingent, single/multiple, eternal/temporal, active/passive aspects of the dipolar God on the other. Of course the "Greater God" and the "Lesser God" are not two different Gods; rather the latter is the modality in which the former manifests himself historically to us. Consequently, in the order of knowledge at least, the "Lesser God" is the primary reality in contrast to which, *dialectically*, we come to know the "Greater God." Similarly, for Hartshorne, it is the second members of the pairs of metaphysical contraries (i.e. relative, concrete, contingent, multiple, temporal, passive) that are both epistemologically and ontologically primary to which the first members of the pairs are subordinate.[47]

Since liberation theologians explicitly affirm that God "lets himself (be) affected by history through the Son," that "history is taken into God in the Spirit," that "God actively incorporates himself into the historical process," and that "through the Spirit, human beings and history are incorporated into God himself," they should have no serious objection to Hartshorne's concept of God as all-inclusive, God as supreme, yet indebted to all, and God as absolute, yet related to all. It will be recalled that for Hartshorne God is "unsurpassable by others," not only by beings actually in existence but by any conceivable reality. The *Dios Mayor*, insofar as he is the wholly Other, the Holy, the Transcendent, can be said to be "unsurpassable by others." But the dipolar God is also "self-surpassable" in some respects, insofar as he can be affected by what others do. Similarly, the *Dios Menor*, insofar as he lets himself be affected by history and incorporates human beings and history into himself, can be said to be "self-surpassable." Thus, to use Hartshorne's language, God is neither "perfect in no way" nor "perfect in all ways" but "perfect in some ways";[48] in other words, God is "absolute perfection in *some* respects, relative perfection in all others."[49]

Consequently, the doctrine of *Dios Mayor* and *Dios Menor* can be said to exemplify the "Law of Polarity," enunciated by Morris Cohen and appropriated by Hartshorne, which affirms that "ultimate contraries are correlatives, mutually interdependent, so that nothing real can be described by the wholly one-sided assertion of simplicity, being, actuality, and the like, each in a 'pure' form, devoid and independent of complexity, becoming, potentiality, and related contraries."[50]

Liberation theologians would also in principle be sympathetic to Hartshorne's view of divine creativity and supreme power. He categorically
rejects the notion of divine omnipotence as "being able to do whatever is
intrinsically possible or self-consistent" since, in his view, such power would
suppress the creativity and freedom of the creatures. Rather he suggests that
God's power should be designated as "unsurpassable power over all things"
or "adequate cosmic power," that is, "power to set conditions which are
maximally favorable to desirable decisions on the part of local agents."[51]
Such power, which God alone possesses, makes him uniquely able to
guarantee the survival of human society. But God's power does not do for
the cosmos things that could only be done by non-universal agents. Furthermore, God's power is exercised not over the powerless but over real powers.
It enables the powerless to act powerfully. Each being is self-creative and is
endowed with a degree of power. Supreme creativity permits and demands a
division of creative power and, to use Hartshorne's favorite phrase, "creative
synthesis."

Liberation theologians, too, strongly emphasize the obligation of all
human beings, especially Christians, to collaborate with God's kingdom.
Araya, speaking from his Protestant tradition with its self-styled anti-Pelagian
anthropology, warns that theological slogans such as "history is failure,"
"God, not the human being, will have the last word," may promote historical
escapism and preserve the status quo of injustice. On the contrary, says he:
"The 'logic' of the biblical bipolarity is very different. It is true that human
beings are not God, but they are called to be the deputies, the vicars, of God.
The true God does not replace human beings in the task of re-creating and
transforming the world. God created the world and a humankind associated
in the preservation and ongoing transformation of the world. . . . That is,
there is a space in which God has invited men and women *to act on their
own*. God will never invade this space as a rival."[52] Again, Sobrino says
forcefully: "Conformity to the reign of God involves not only hope that the
kingdom *is coming* but also a practice whereby it actually *becomes a reality*.
. . . It is secondary here whether this practice is required *because* the
kingdom is coming or *in order that* it may come. The important thing is that
God's will is *that* the kingdom should come, *that* human beings should act in
a particular way, and *that* their action should have an objective content in
conformity with the reign of God."[53]

Furthermore, since for liberation theologians God lets himself be affected
by history, they would not be adverse to Hartshorne's notion of God's power
as also the ability to be affected by the other agents or creators. They would
very likely take offence at Hartshornian language of God as "creative, effect,
derivation, and passive," even though in an eminent and supreme way.[54]
However, there is no doubt that for them humans contribute to the emergence of the kingdom of God through their struggle for justice and freedom.

God's ability to let himself be affected by others is supremely manifested
in his love. Hartshorne understands perfect or divine love as "absolute

adequacy to the object,"[55] that is to say, because God's *concrete* knowledge includes all actual entities with adequacy, his love embraces all without exclusion. Hence he is able to posit the optimal conditions for the maximal creative synthesis of the creatures. And because God is love, he suffers with and for the creatures. Indeed, God's concrete knowledge is so adequate that he is united with the sufferings of others much more fully than we can ever sympathize with them. Not only does he know that we suffer but he also feels our pain and misery and suffers them with us. Furthermore, this love is not pacifist; at times it may require the use of violence against the oppressors to prevent them from monopolizing coercion to destroy the freedom of others: "The divine love is social awareness and action from social awareness. Such action seems clearly to include the refusal to provide the unsocial with a monopoly upon the use of coercion. Coercion to prevent the use of coercion to destroy freedom generally is in no way action without social awareness but one of its crucial expressions. Freedom must not be free to destroy freedom. The logic of love is not the logic of pacifism or of the unheroic life."[56]

No doubt liberation theologians would heartily agree with much of Hartshorne's reflections on God as love and on the legitimacy of the use of violence as the last resource. They emphatically affirm that it is through the cross of Jesus that the definition of God as love receives its ultimate concretion: "The cross is the contradiction of humanity, but it is grounded on an ultimate solidarity with it. In the Son's passion, the Father suffers the pain of abandonment. In the Son's death, death affects God himself — not because God dies but because he suffers the death of the Son. Yet God suffers so that we might live, and that is the most complete expression of love."[57] Such love demands that we in turn concretize our love for the poor and the oppressed by hearing, accepting, and serving them, by being the voice of the voiceless, by accompanying them in their efforts for liberation, by imbuing them with the Christian spirit, by keeping the active hope of the poor alive in their difficult moments, and by celebrating life in the depth given it by faith.[58] At times, this may require, as the last resource, doing violence to the oppressors so that they may be liberated from their own self-oppression.

The primary intention of this paper has been to trace the points of contact between Hartshorne's process philosophy and liberation theology, especially in their doctrines of God. Readers familiar with both schools of thought will have noticed that I have interpreted them *in optimam partem*, with the view to identifying parallels and even correspondences between them. My objective was to inquire whether Hartshorne's neoclassical theism with its dipolar conception of God can serve as the appropriate metaphysics for liberation theology's concept of God as the Liberator of the poor and the oppressed and whether liberation theology's response to the challenge of the second phase of the Enlightenment can expand and enrich the starting point, method, and tasks of process thought. No attempt has been made to take a critical stance toward either school of thought, nor have I implied to assert that Hartshorne's dipolar deity is the metaphysical equivalence of liberation theology's God the Liberator. But there seem to be sufficient commonalities between them to suggest that dipolar deity might not be the procrustean bed to which God the Liberator is chained. Further, the crisis of meaning in natural theology provoked by the critique of the first phase of the Enlightenment need not be resolved exclusively by devising a more coherent theism; ultimately it may be the case that the meaning and meaningfulness of the God-question is restored only by a praxis in favor of justice and freedom.

NOTES

1. For a popular but highly informative exposition of Process theology, see John B. Cobb, Jr. and David Ray Griffin, *Process Theology: An Introductory Exposition* (Philadelphia: The Westminster Press, 1976).
2. For an overview of the development of Process theology, see *ibid.*, pp. 176—85.
3. For a liberation theology critique of classical theology, see Gustavo Gutiérrez, *A Theology of Liberation* (Maryknoll, New York: Orbis Books, 1973), pp. 3—15 and Jon Sobrino, *The True Church and the Poor* (Maryknoll, New York: Orbis Books, 1984), pp. 7—38.
4. For a brief biography of Hartshorne, see Eugene H. Peters, *Hartshorne and Neoclassical Metaphysics* (Lincoln: University of Nebraska Press, 1970), pp. 1—14. For monographic studies on Hartshorne's concept of God, see Ralph E. James, *The Concrete God: A New Beginning for Theology — The Thought of Charles Hartshorne* (New York: The Bobbs-Merrill Co., Inc., 1976) and Santiago Sia, *God in Process Thought: A Study in Charles Hartshorne's Concept of God* (Dordrecht/Boston/Lancaster: Martinus Nijhoff Publishers, 1985). The latter book contains a selected bibliography of Hartshorne, pp. 125—138. Another monographic study of Hartshorne's concept of God in contrast to that of Karl Barth's deserves notice, Colin E. Gunton, *Becoming and Being: The Doctrine of God in Charles Hartshorne and Karl Barth* (Oxford: Oxford University Press, 1978).
5. It is well known that liberation theology, though originating in Latin America, has spawned other theological movements in diverse parts of the world, e.g. Asian and African, Black, Hispanic and feminist liberation theologies. My focus here is only on Latin American liberation theology. For a classic exposition of Latin American liberation theology, see Gustavo Gutiérrez, *A Theology of Liberation* (Maryknoll, New York: Orbis Books, 1973). Other good introductions are: Leonardo Boff and Clodovis Boff, *Introducing Liberation Theology* (Maryknoll, New York: Orbis Books, 1987); *Salvation and Liberation: In Search of a Balance Between Faith and Politics* (Maryknoll, New York: Orbis Books, 1984); *Liberation Theology: From Confrontation to Dialogue* (San Francisco: Harper & Row, Publishers, 1986); Phillip Berryman, *Liberation Theology: Essential Facts about the Revolutionary Movement in Latin America and Beyond* (Philadelphia: Temple University Press, 1987). For critiques of liberation theology by the Roman Catholic Congregation for the Doctrine of the Faith, see *Instruction on Certain Aspects of the "Theology of Liberation"* (August 6, 1984) and *Instruction on Christian Freedom and Liberation* (March 22, 1986), English translations by the United States Catholic Conference. For scholarly critiques of liberation theology, see James V. Schall, *Liberation Theology in Latin America* (San Francisco: Ignatius Press, 1982); Ronald H. Nash (ed.), *On Liberation Theology* (Milford, Michigan: Mott Media, Inc., 1984); Andrew J. Kirk, *Liberation Theology: An Evangelical View from the Third World* (Atlanta: John Knox, 1980). For our considerations of liberation theology's method and doctrine of God, the following works are essential: Juan Luis Segundo, *The Liberation of Theology* (Maryknoll, New York: Orbis Books, 1976); Clodovis Boff, *Theology and Praxis:*

36

Epistemological Foundations (Maryknoll, New York: Orbis Books, 1987); Juan Segundo, *Our Idea of God* (Maryknoll, New York: Orbis Books, 1974); Victorio Araya, *God of the Poor: The Mystery of God in Latin American Liberation Theology* (Maryknoll, New York: Orbis Books, 1987). For a good reader of Latin American liberation theology, see Rosino Gibellini (ed.), *Frontiers of Theology in Latin America* (Maryknoll, New York: Orbis Books, 1979) which features articles by Gustavo Gutiérrez, Raúl Vidales, Joseph Comblin, Luis G. del Valle, Leonardo Boff, Hugo Assmann, Ronaldo Muñoz, Segundo Galilea, Enrique Dussel, Juan Carlos Scannone, Juan Luis Segundo, José Míguez Bonino, Rubem Alves. To this list one should perhaps add Jon Sobrino, Clodovis Boff, Ignacio Ellacuría, and many other younger theologians.

6. See Schubert M. Ogden, *Faith and Freedom: Toward a Theology of Liberation* (Nashville: Abingdon, 1979); Delwin Brown, *To Set at Liberty: Christian Faith and Human Freedom* (Maryknoll, New York: Orbis Books, 1981); John B. Cobb, Jr., *Process Theology as Political Theology* (Philadelphia: The Westminster Press, 1982). See also the special issue of *Process Studies* devoted to liberation theology, Volume 14/Number 2 (Summer/1985) with articles by Joseph A. Bracken, Marjorie Suchocki, Schubert M. Ogden, Matthew L. Lamb, and John B. Cobb, Jr.

7. Most Roman Catholic Latin liberation theologians completed their graduate studies in Europe at the time when process thought was largely unknown, e.g. Gutiérrez, Assmann, the two Boff brothers, Dussel, Muñoz, Scannone, and Segundo. As regards liberation theology's suspicion of academic pursuits, some of its practitioners seem to reject all intellectual work as fundamentally self-alienating.

8. *Faith and Freedom*, p. 34.

9. "Points of Contacts between Process Theology and Liberation Theology in Matters of Faith and Justice," *Process Studies*, Vol. 14/No. 2 (Summer/1985), p. 130.

10. See *The True Church and the Poor* (Maryknoll, New York: Orbis Books, 1984), chapter 1 "Theological Understanding in European and Latin American Theology," pp. 7—38.

11. *Ibid.*, p. 30. Gustavo Gutiérrez expresses the same view succinctly: "A goodly part of contemporary theology seems to take its start from the challenge posed by the *nonbeliever*. The nonbeliever calls into question our *religious world*, demanding its thoroughgoing purification and revitalization. . . . In a continent like Latin America, however, the main challenge does not come from the nonbeliever but from the *nonhuman* — i.e., the human being who is not recognized as such by the prevailing social order. . . . These nonhumans do not call into question our religious world so much as they call into question our *economic, social, political, and cultural world* . . . " quoted in Rosino Gibellini (ed.), *Frontiers of Theology in Latin America* (Maryknoll, New York: Orbis Books, 1979), p. x.

12. Despite these differences, it must be acknowledged that Latin America theologians derive many of their concepts from European political theology enunciated by Johannes B. Metz and Jürgen Moltmann. For liberation theology's critique of political theology, see Hugo Assmann, *Theology for a Nomad Church* (Maryknoll, New York: Orbis Books, 1976), pp. 29—40. For the similarities between the two theologies, see Arthur F. McGovern, *Marxism: An American Christian Perspective* (Maryknoll, New York: Orbis Books, 1980), p. 176. The book also contains an excellent account of liberation theology, especially in relationship to Marxism. See pp. 172—209.

13. For a brief exposition of this classical concept of God and the factors causing its decline, see Colin Gunton, *Becoming and Being: The Doctrine of God in Charles Hartshorne and Karl Barth* (Oxford: Oxford University Press, 1978), pp. 1—7.

14. For an explanation of Hartshorne's critique of classical metaphysics, see Colin Gunton, *Becoming and Being*, pp. 11—23.

15. See his *God in Process Thought*, pp. 9—18.

16. Charles Hartshorne, *Man's Vision of God and the Logic of Theism* (Chicago: Willett, Clark & Company, 1941), p. 3. Henceforth, *MVG*.

17. See Charles Hartshorne, *A Natural Theology for Our Time* (La Salle, Illinois: Open Court, 1967), pp. 1—28. Henceforth, *NTOT*.
18. See Charles Hartshorne, *The Divine Relativity: A Social Conception of God* (New Haven and London: Yale University Press, 1948), pp. 148—149. Henceforth, *DR*.
19. See, for instance, *NTOT*, pp. x—xi: "The possibility of natural theology, or a theory of divinity appealing to 'natural reason' . . . is often said to have been thoroughly discredited by Hume and Kant. I do not share this trust in the ability of these men whose climate of opinion was not ours — to settle for us, or for all time, the relations of theoretical reason to religion." See also his *The Logic of Perfection* (LaSalle, Illinois: Open Court, 1962), pp. 116—117. Henceforth, *LP*.
20. *DR*, p. xv. See also *Creative Synthesis & Philosophic Method* (La Salle, Illinois: Open Court, 1970), pp. 19—42; 159—172. Henceforth, *CSPM*. In terms of propositions, metaphysics formulates non-restrictive, necessary, existential, and unfalsifiable propositions. Metaphysical statements do not describe factual and contingent things, rather they say something common to, or true of, every actual or conceivable reality.
21. For a full discussion of Hartshorne's metaphysical method, see *CSPM*, pp. 69—130; Santiago Sia, *God in Process Thought*, pp. 19—31; and Eugene H. Peters, *Hartshorne and Neoclassical Metaphysics*, pp. 15—28.
22. See *LP*, pp. 133—147 and *DR*, pp. 30—40.
23. For Hartshorne's doctrine of panpsychism, see *LP*, pp. 216—233; Eugene H. Peters, *Hartshorne and Neoclassical Metaphysics*, pp. 39—42.
24. *LP*, p. 140.
25. *Christology at the Crossroads* (Maryknoll, New York: Orbis Books, 1978), p. 195. See also pp. 373—374.
26. *Ibid.*, pp. 196—197. Compare Sobrino's statement with Charles Hartshorne and William L. Reese, *Philosophers Speak of God* (Chicago: The University of Chicago, 1953), p. 15: "Evil in the sense of suffering, however, is indeed, we believe, a category. And, if so, the dipolar view must hold not only that God contains suffering but that he suffers and that it is in his character to suffer, in accordance with the suffering in the world. Here the Christian idea of a suffering deity — symbolized by the Cross, together with the doctrine of Incarnation — achieves technical metaphysical expression." Henceforth, *PSG*.
27. See "Liberation Theology and Social Justice," *Process Studies*, Vol. 14/No. 2 (Summer/ 1985), pp. 102—104. For the concept of the poor, see also Leonardo Boff and Clodovis Boff, *Introducing Liberation Theology*, pp. 28—32; 46—49.
28. The most sophisticated and sustained treatment of the method of liberation theology is Clodovis Boff, *Theology and Praxis: Epistemological Foundations* (Maryknoll, New York: Orbis Books, 1981). For shorter discussions, see especially Gustavo Gutiérrez, "Liberation Praxis and Christian Faith," in *Frontiers of Theology in Latin America*, ed. Rosino Gibellini (Maryknoll, New York: Orbis Books, 1979), pp. 1—33; Raúl Vidales, "Methodological Issues in Liberation Theology," *ibid.*, pp. 34—57; Leonardo Boff and Clodovis Boff, *Introducing Liberation Theology*, pp. 22—42; Leonardo Boff and Clodovis Boff, *Salvation and Liberation*, pp. 4—12; 48—56.
29. For the relationship between Marxism and liberation theology, see Leonardo Boff and Clodovis Boff, *Liberation Theology: From Confrontation to Dialogue* (Maryknoll, New York: Orbis Books, 1986), pp. 22—23, 65—72; José Miranda, *Marx and the Bible: A Critique of the Philosophy of Oppression* (Maryknoll, New York: Orbis Books, 1974); Fernando Belo, *A Materialist Reading of the Gospel of Mark* (Maryknoll, New York: Orbis Books, 1974); Michel Clévenot, *Materialist Approaches to the Bible* (Maryknoll, New York: Orbis Books, 1985); Arthur F. McGovern characterizes liberation theology's relationship to Marxism as follows: "Liberation theology is not grounded in Marxism. It is grounded in the experiences of the peoples of Latin America and in faith reflection. The pervasiveness of Marxist thinking in Latin America does affect liberation theology. It uses Marxism 'heuristically', that is, it takes certain insights from Marxism and uses these to

38

gain insight both into situations in Latin America and into the faith. It draws especially upon Marxist insights into the relation of theory to praxis, the political — economic causes of underdevelopment, and the relation between ideology and social structures." See *Marxism: An American Christian Perspective* (Maryknoll, New York: Orbis Books, 1980), p. 203.

30. In this context it must be pointed out that liberation theologians in principle favor non-violent means to violent ones.

31. *Christology at the Crossroads*, p. 198.

32. See "Points of Contact Between Process Theology and Liberation Theology in Matters of Faith and Justice," *Process Studies*, Vol. 14/No. 2 (Summer/1985), pp. 124—133. Cobb mentions three areas in which liberation theology can and should learn from liberation theology: reflection on social location, theological methodology and the concern for justice. In pp. 133—140, he suggests two areas which are quite different but potentially mutually enriching, namely, 'interest' and 'perspective' viewpoints and ecology.

33. Hartshorne has said a propos of the transforming power of his theory of surrelativism: "The doctrine of divine relativity is not entirely unconnected with the great drive toward a synthesis of freedom and order which . . . is our political goal. . . . In this vision of a deity who is not a supreme autocrat, but a universal agent of 'persuasion', whose 'power is in the worship he inspires' (Whitehead), that is, flows from the intrinsic appeal of his infinitely sensitive and tolerant relativity, by which all things are kept moving in orderly togetherness, we may find help in facing our task of today, the task of contributing to the democratic self-ordering of a world whose members not even the supreme orderer reduces to mere subjects with the sole function of obedience" (*DR*, p. xvii).

34. See *DR*, pp. 148—149.

35. *Faith and Freedom*, p. 33.

36. *Liberation Theology: From Confrontation to Dialogue*, pp. 25—26.

37. *Faith and Freedom*, pp. 76, 79, 82—95.

38. *Christology at the Crossroads*, p. 224. Emphasis added.

39. *Ibid.*, p. 225. Emphasis added.

40. *Ibid.*, p. 226. Emphasis added.

41. *Ibid.*, pp. 226—227. Emphasis added.

42. *Ibid.*, p. 234. Emphasis added. In his process view of God Sobrino is heavily influenced by Jürgen Moltmann's book *The Crucified God* (New York: Harper and Row, 1974).

43. *God of the Poor*, p. 75.

44. See Schubert Ogden, "The Metaphysics of Faith and Justice," *Process Studies*, Vol. 14/No. 2 (Summer/1985), pp. 87—101. Ogden contends that the revisionary metaphysics developed by Alfred Whitehead and Charles Hartshorne is indispensable to theology if the strictly metaphysical implications of faith and justice are to be explicated and validated both appropriately and credibly. See in particular pp. 92—99.

45. See *The True Church and the Poor*, pp. 144—148.

46. *Ibid.*, p. 149. See also, Victorio Araya, *God of the Poor*, pp. 34—39; 50—58.

47. For an itemized list of metaphysical contraries, see *CSPM*, pp. 100—101.

48. See *Reality as Social Process: Studies in Metaphysics and Religion* (Glencoe: The Free Press, 1953), pp. 155—157 and 182—183. Henceforth, *RSP*. In this connection see also Hartshorne's analysis of the notion "unsurpassability" in *MVG*, pp. 6—9.

49. *MVG*, p. 8. For a clear analysis of Hartshorne's doctrine of God's perfection, relativity, and absoluteness, see Santiago Sia, *God in Process Thought*, pp. 35—45.

50. *PSG*, p. 2. This law of polarity as applied to God Hartshorne terms "the principle of dual transcendence"; as applied to creatures "the principle of dual immanence." The infinite superiority of God over creatures Hartshorne calls "categorical supremacy."

51. *DL*, p. 135. For Hartshorne's discussion of divine omnipotence, see *ibid.*, pp. 134—142 and *Omnipotence and Other Theological Mistakes* (New York: State University of New York Press, 1984).

52. *God of the Poor*, p. 150.
53. *The True Church and the Poor*, pp. 43—44.
54. *CSPM*, p. 237. For a discussion of God's supreme power and creativity, see Santiago Sia, *God in Process Thought*, pp. 73—85.
55. *MVG*, p. 145. For Hartshorne's earliest treatment of love, see *ibid.*, pp. 142—173.
56. *Ibid.*, p. 173.
57. Jon Sobrino, *Christology at the Crossroads*, pp. 225—226.
58. See Victorio Araya, *God of the Poor*, pp. 142—143.

3. Competition and the Common Good: The Liberal Politics of Charles Hartshorne

RANDALL MORRIS

In the Preface to *Science and the Modern World* Whitehead says that the "mentality of an epoch springs from the view of the world which is, in fact, dominant in the educated sections of the communities in question."[1] He goes on to assert that the cosmology which has been in the ascendancy in the western world for the past three centuries is that derived from science. The repercussions of this 'scientific cosmology,' heavily influenced as it was by the metaphysical theory of atomism and dominated by the fundamental assumption of matter with the property of 'simple location', reverberated throughout the European intellectual world. One important consequence of this new way of understanding nature was that it opened up novel ways of understanding human nature and society as well (e.g. the mechanistic materialism of Thomas Hobbes).

The scientific cosmology which has been preeminent in western societies has, of course, been challenged and it is well known that Charles Hartshorne is among those who have done so. In place of the atomistic theory of reality in which discrete bits of matter are merely externally related one to another Hartshorne advances a social theory of reality and adheres to a theory of asymmetrical internal relations. The question which this leads me to ask is whether process theology, like scientific materialism before it, opens up new ways of understanding man and society? Also, is it possible to see a link between Hartshorne's metaphysics and his social and political views? Such questions cannot be answered in the space of a single essay; however, I do hope to begin to address this issue by discussing one feature of Hartshorne's political thought, namely, the use of coercive force by the State.

I have selected the issue of power for investigation for two reasons. First, process theology has made a significant contribution to the analysis of the concept of power generally, and of God's power in particular. Moreover, power is an important political concept. Therefore, this might be one area in which we can detect a linkage between Hartshorne's political views and his metaphysics. The second reason for selecting the issue of power as the focus for this essay is that it proved to be such a contentious and divisive one among liberal political theorists around the turn of the century. The move

S. Sia (ed.), Charles Hartshorne's Concept of God, 41–55.
© 1990 *Kluwer Academic Publishers. Printed in the Netherlands.*

away from an abstract individualism and a mechanistic theory of society towards an organic conception of man and society was not peculiar to Whitehead and Hartshorne. Quite the contrary. Recent historians of liberal thought have emphasized the monumental developments within that tradition from the time of J. S. Mill until the First World War.[2] Far from being a static dogma the liberal tradition was a dynamic theory which developed over several centuries. Thus while classical liberals such as Locke generally viewed man as "essentially independent, private and competitive beings who see civil association mainly as a framework for the pursuit of their own interests," modern liberals such as J. S. Mill and L. T. Hobhouse are "more apt to stress mutual dependence over independence, co-operation over competition, and mutual appreciation over private enjoyment."[3] The importance of this development in liberal political ideology has been largely overlooked by theologians seeking to ascertain the contribution which process theology might make to political theory.[4] As a consequence some scholars have, in my opinion, exaggerated the uniqueness of this contribution.[5] In what follows I hope to provide evidence that Hartshorne stands in what by his time was a well-established political tradition and that several main tenets of his process metaphysics reflect his own commitment to a liberal ideology.

I. INTERVENTION AND THE OPTIMIZATION OF FREEDOM

For process metaphysics there is always a mixture of self-determination and determination by others in human relationships. Not only is absolute freedom an impossibility, but from a process perspective, were such a state conceivable, it would hardly be an ideal condition. This is because our relationships with other individuals not only determine the area of real possibility open to us for self-determination, and thus restrict our freedom in a negative sense, but they simultaneously provide us with the necessary data for a rich experience, and thus enhance our freedom in a positive sense. In Hartshorne's words, "The social limitation upon freedom is what gives it positive content and value."[6] The problem of social freedom is an aesthetic one and reflects the metaphysical fact that the creative process is a "creative synthesis." It is creative in that the past does not fully determine what values will be realized in the present occasion; but it is also a synthesis which means that the occasion depends upon the data it prehends in order to achieve intense experiences.

Although coercion is an unavoidable element of social interaction, we should remember that what limits our freedom is other freedom: "[F]reedom is causality in the making, causality is crystalized freedom, the influence of past acts of self-determination by countless creatures upon this act now taking place."[7] Hartshorne explains the tragic aspects of existence by reference to his theory of freedom. An individual is self-active, and since "what is many must act as many," the harmonious activity of the many cannot be guaranteed.[8] There are multiple centers of individuality and freedom, and therefore a multiplicity of decisions and relationships irreducible to a single decision. Some of these relationships will be characterized by social harmony, and others by discord; but the character of any particular relationship is partly a matter of chance. No absolute co-ordination of creaturely decisions is possible. To guarantee harmony "the cosmos must completely coerce the lesser individuals, that is, must deprive them of all individuality. Existence is essentially social, plural, free, and exposed to risk. . . ."[9] Thus for the details of our existence we depend upon the choices which others make. Every individual is fate for other individuals, divine providence being a "superfate" for us all.[10] Hence, because of the social nature of existence, tragedy is in principle, although not in particular, an unavoidable fact of human social life.

In general, tragedy is the unavoidable consequence of a world in which there are multiple centers of creative freedom. In this instance, tragedy is unfortunate but accidental, a product of chance. However, not all tragedy is accidental. In Hartshorne's opinion, the cross of Jesus symbolizes the supreme tragedy in the world. The world is tragic "not only because conflict is inevitable between free and ignorant beings, but because there is an inner conflict in men between their will to serve a common good and their desire to promote a private or tribal goal."[11] This is the meaning of sin. Tragedy is not only a matter of chance; it can also be a matter of choice. As such it is not the unforeseen consequence of the decisions made by many free beings, but the result of a conflict of interests within a single individual.

Although tragedy is in principle unavoidable, this does not mean that the scope for tragedy is beyond control. We recall that, according to Hartshorne, divine providence means not that God determines what will happen in its full definiteness, but that God places limitations on the operation of chance. Without God's ordering, without his providential activity, "individuals could not form even a disorderly world, but only a meaningless, unthinkable chaos in which there would be neither any definite good nor any definite evil. This is the same as no world. With God there is an order, a world in which good and evil can occur."[12] Creatures have freedom because of, and not in spite of, the limitations which God imposes upon the creative order. The successive states of God's concrete nature limit the possibilities available for realization by finite agents. God "controls, checks, encourages, redirects" the impulses which are produced by finite individuals.[13] God's concrete states are his reactions to the finite actions by which he "absorbs and transmutes all influences into a counterinfluence, integrative and harmonizing in tendency, discouraging excessive factors and encouraging insufficient ones."[14] By this activity God establishes a situation which provides for a maximal surplus of opportunities over risks. If God were to allow more freedom then the increase in risks would exceed that of opportunities gained. Similarly, additional restrictions would result in a larger decrease in opportunities than in risks. Thus God's universal activity establishes at each moment conditions which express the optimal risk-opportunity ratio.

Hartshorne believes that what the divine monarch does for the universe, so also political and social institutions should do for human society.[15] The perfection of the divine activity consists in God's exerting an "optimum of control" and thereby "maximizing the promise of freedom."[16] "Hartshorne gives priority to creativity," writes Santiago Sia, "and interprets divine power in terms of the existence of this value. Power that would violate such a value is judged wrong."[17] God establishes a "golden mean" between risk and opportunity; similarly, the function of government is to establish an environment which optimizes the opportunities of its citizens. Like the divine ruler, human government, then, is *not* characterized by insensitivity to the needs of its citizens, that is, it is not necessarily the case that the less government intervention in the affairs of the people the better. Society must arrange and continue to rearrange itself so as to optimize the opportunities for development for all its members.[18] The best government is the one which is sensitive and responsive to its citizens' needs. The proper adjustment of chance and love "requires that destructive conflict arising from incompatibility of values should be mitigated without paying too high a price in loss of individuality, from which spontaneity, chance, and danger cannot be eliminated."[19] One criterion of good government, then, is that in response to decisions of its constituents it supplies sufficient coercive force to ensure the maintenance of an ordered environment without unduly restricting the options of the citizens for self-development.

It is questionable as to how far Hartshorne intended to push the analogy between the divine governance of the universe and good state government. For example, we recall that God does not intervene in particular situations to send us particular evils; rather, he "establishes an order in which creatures can send each other particular goods and evils."[20] The question is whether, for Hartshorne, good government is similarly characterized by 'universal' action. In other words, should a government intervene in affairs of particular citizens, or should its legislation be applicable to the whole body politic? If this analogy is acceptable then it would secure legislative impartiality as a virtue of good government. That Hartshorne did have such an analogy in mind is supported by a passage in *The Logic of Perfection*:

> To rule is to sway all by a *common* influence; but something must, in each individual case, be freely added to constitute the response to the influence.
> Ruling or governing is always the imparting of certain *common* characters or limits to the self-determining of the ruled or governed.[21]

The principles of good government are special instances of the metaphysical principles of freedom and causality. According to Hartshorne, causality is the restriction of logical possibility. Within the range of real possibility determined by the cause there will be factors *common to the entire set*. These features are "conditional necessities," that is, features which invariably will be realized by the event. However the event is not fully determined by its antecedent causes. There remains an element of "chance," an element of uncertainty which follows from the self-creativity of the event. Similarly government should ensure that certain "common characters or limits," e.g. rights, are shared by the citizens thus retaining a level of social order within which those citizens are free to act. At the same time, however, government must avoid an excessive restriction upon the freedom of its citizens: "[P]eople need first of all to be themselves, and this self-hood no tyrant, human or superhuman, however benevolent, can impose upon them."[22] It is clear that Hartshorne agrees in principle with Hobhouse's claim that law is essential to liberty. "Law, of course," writes Hobhouse, "restrains the individual; it is therefore opposed to his liberty at a given moment and in a given direction. But, equally, law restrains others from doing with him as they will. It liberates him from the fear of arbitrary aggression or coercion, and this is the only way, indeed, the only sense, in which liberty *for an entire community* is attainable."[23]

What Hartshorne is advocating is a *balance* between corporate and individual responsibility. This was a common emphasis among Idealists and new liberals alike although the different theorists did not always strike the same balance. Idealists such as Green, Arnold Toynbee, and Bernard Bosanquet had a fundamental concern for the character of the individual.[24] Hence while the government had a responsibility for providing citizens with the minimal requirements necessary for self-development, it must not "interfere with the growth of self-reliance ... with the moral autonomy which is the condition of the highest goodness."[25] In an extended passage reminiscent of Hartshorne[26] Green writes:

> It is one thing to say that the state in promoting these conditions must take care not to defeat its true end by narrowing the region within which the spontaneity and disinterestedness of true morality can have play; another thing to say that it has no moral end to serve at all, and that it goes beyond its province when it seeks to do more than secure the individual from violent interference by other individuals. The true ground of objection to 'paternal government' is not that it violates the 'laissez faire' principle ... but that it rests on a misconception of morality. The real function of government being to *maintain conditions of life* in which morality shall be possible, and morality consisting in the disinterested performance of self-imposed duties, 'paternal government' does its best to make it impossible *by narrowing the room for the self-imposition of duties* and for the play of disinterested motives.[27]

Among the new liberals Hobhouse presents us with a similar position. Where there is a harmony in social relationships individuals co-operate freely together and this results in a "heightening and fulfilling [of] their natural capacities."[28] However, to some degree constraint as well as co-operation is involved in every society. "High organisation may be achieved on these lines," writes Hobhouse, "but at a cost to social vitality proportioned to the degree of constraint exerted, and in the extreme case ruinous."[29] Since repression leads to a diminution of the vitality within society which is located within individuals, the state should limit its action to securing those *common ends* in which uniformity or concerted action is necessary and which cannot be secured without compulsion.[30] Over-legislation and too much corporate responsibility was thus regarded as dangerous as under-legislation and too little responsibility.

II. INTERVENTION AND PERSONAL DEVELOPMENT

Hartshorne acknowledged the necessity of governmental coercion in order to maintain an acceptable social order in which individuals may prosper. Without adequate protection, the liberty of the strong results in the oppression of the weaker members of society. Yet perhaps it might be argued that the strong must also be free to develop their capacities and that governmental intervention places an undue restriction upon them which runs counter to the general aims of society. Hartshorne's belief that tragedy is inevitable, that individual goods are mutually exclusive, and that competition may be necessary to induce individuals to exert themselves[31] provides grounds for suspecting that he would sympathize to a point with such an argument. It is a metaphysical principle that "every good excludes some possible good" and consequently "[s]omething must always be renounced that would not be valueless if realized." This principle has according to Hartshorne "political applications."[32] These political applications, although not specified by Hartshorne, are clear. While the state is responsible for establishing the optimum risk-opportunity ratio within its area of jurisdiction, the members are left free to compete among themselves in their efforts to realize their opportunities for self-creativity. The social nature of existence, together with the incompatibility of finite values, means that in such a competitive world A's success means B's failure.

Hartshorne's thought tends to lean at times towards a classical liberal position. The idea of personal development as competitive, an idea based on his belief that tragedy is inevitable, seems to be one of those points. However, he also makes statements which show a divergence from classical liberalism. Although some tragedy is unavoidable, there is also a form of tragedy which stems from "an inner conflict in men between their will to serve a common good and their desire to promote a private or tribal goal. Some conflicts are chosen where a less destructive, more fruitful form of interaction is known."[33] Hartshorne is suggesting that the supreme tragedy (sin) is a failure to realize those forms of interaction which produce a wider harmony, pursuing instead a path which is known to involve the sacrifice of the common good to a private goal.[34] Presented thus, Hartshorne's position is indistinguishable from that of Cobb who believes we should adopt a relational/communal model of human relations according to which "the growth of our good is a function not primarily of competitive advantage but of communal well-being."[35] Such a shift will not "do away with all of the oppositions which lead to trade-off thinking" for in some instances sacrifices are unavoidable. "But we will look primarily for ways in which both desirable variables can be increased in mutually supportive fashion rather than quickly settling for the trade-off."[36]

What are we to make of these two different attitudes? It appears that Hartshorne falls between classical and modern liberalism. The individualism of the classical liberals is evident in his emphasis on the inevitability of conflict between partially free beings. Conflict is unavoidable owing to the social nature of reality and the incompatibility of individual goods. What practical consequences follow from this? "To try so to act that no conflict results is to adjust oneself to fairyland, not any real world. . . . What we have to do is to prefer the less deadly, the more constructive or fruitful, forms of conflict."[37] A stress on the tragic element in the world leads Hartshorne to propound a policy of semi-acquiescence to human conflict. Our aim and the function of the state should be to limit the scope for conflict among individuals as they compete for the realization of their own goods. The idea of a harmonious realization of individual aims is consigned to "fairyland." Conflicts, and hence trade-offs, are the stuff of reality. Thus he concludes that "[e]very legislative act excludes things which for some are genuine values. *Always* someone loses or suffers. This is an element of tragedy in process itself."[38]

Although Hartshorne lays considerable stress upon the tragic nature of process, his acceptance of competitive individualism is tempered by his concept of God. Hartshorne sees that we are not just dealing with society and competition, but also with God. When God is brought into consideration this alters one's perspective. Pure self-interest is ruled out because we are all part of the one divine life. Competition must be balanced by an ideal of harmony. We are enjoined to pursue the general welfare of humanity because that welfare, as a whole, is "effectively enjoyed by a single subject in a single satisfying experience."[39] Our ultimate purpose is to serve God which we do by promoting the creative process, by contributing to the general welfare or common good."[40] Within the common good each person's own future happiness is included so far as compatible with that of others.

While tempering competitive individualism, the introduction of God into the equation does not make the common good noncompetitive. The pursuit of our own self-development can in theory conflict with a similar pursuit by other members of society. Part of what it means to contribute to the common good is to respect the freedom of others to actualize their private preferences.

> No one individual can decide unilaterally that there shall be harmony; for an individual cannot give up all personal preference and conform purely passively to the preferences of others. To be an individual is to have and act upon some distinctive preference or other.[41]

Hartshorne leans towards a preferential theory of the good according to which "the nature of one's self-interest is solely a matter of preference, so that one's happiness is defined in whatever way one pleases."[42] This is a characteristic feature of classical liberalism. "[T]he goals of liberalism can be succinctly stated. In general, they are that as many individuals as possible realize as many of their private preferences as possible."[43] God's aim "seems to be zestful creaturely activity, the creation of intense and predominantly harmonious experiences, in order that these may be appreciatively appropriated by the divine love, of which our own love is a faint image."[44] To love another person is to respect their freedom and to accept their decisions as objects of appreciative awareness.[45] Therefore we love God when we respect the freedom of our neighbour to act upon his or her preferences. Owing to the incompatibility of individual preferences, conflict is unavoidable. Free beings must "harmonize themselves together as best they can."[46]

A modern liberal would object that Hartshorne's emphasis upon conflict stems from an inadequate grasp of the organic nature of society and of the common good. What Hartshorne has done is to emphasize the metaphysical principle that freedom *limits* freedom at the expense of the equally important principle that our environment *provides* us with our real potentialities. The past both limits and supplies.[47] An emphasis on this latter aspect opens the way for entertaining the ideal of a common good which is noncompetitive.

In contrast to Hartshorne's claim that the exclusion of possibility from actualization is necessarily tragic Hobhouse argues that not every development of the individual is socially desirable, but only those which are in accordance with the conditions of social harmony. "For after all," he writes, "it is not every development of every faculty that can reasonably be desired for the sake of progress. There are mischievous as well as benevolent talents capable of cultivation, and if we are asked for a test to distinguish the two, we can give none more simple than that of the capacity of harmonious working in an ordered society."[48] The development of the aristocracy, for example, or of the bourgeoisie, is not an adequate form of development because it involves the suppression of others. Such developments are, according to Hobhouse, only partial:

> [W]hat there is of social progress in them does involve a development of individuals, while, on the other hand, in so far as the life of any member of society is cramped and mutilated by them, there is social stagnation and decay. Any such development is not fully harmonious. Gain on one side is set off by loss on another. The problem of true social progress is to find the lines on which development on one side does not retard development on another, but assists it.[49]

Similarly Green argues that while it is possible for an individual to realize himself in ways that make the world wonder, yet the social effect of such individual realizations may be the hindrance rather than the development of the human spirit. This is not to deny that such a person "is living for ends of which the divine principle that forms his self alone renders him capable, but these ends, because in their attainment one is exalted by the depression of others, are not in the direction in which that principle can really fulfil the promise and potency which it contains."[50]

The notion of a common good which is noncompetitive dominates the minds of modern liberals such as Hobhouse and Green. The good of the individual could not be considered in abstraction from the good for everyone else. The salvation of each was dependent upon the salvation of all. Hence Green writes that "the idea of a perfection, of a state in which he shall be satisfied, for himself will involve the idea of a perfection of all other beings, so far as he finds the thought of their being perfect necessary to his own satisfaction."[51] Far from accepting the inevitability of trade-offs whereby A's success means B's failure, modern liberals hold that true development is cooperative rather than competitive. Individual development made possible through the suppression of other members of society is an inadequate form of development. Social progress involves the development of a form of order which promotes this common good.

Only those individual developments which promote the development of other members of the society are good. The lopsided development of a portion of society must be avoided, either by self-restraint or governmental coercion. Mill expresses this well in a lengthy passage from *On Liberty*:

> In proportion to the development of his individuality, each person becomes more valuable to himself, and is therefore capable of being more valuable to others. There is a greater fullness of life about his own existence, and when there is more life in the units there is more in the mass which is composed of them. As much compression as is necessary to prevent the stronger specimens of human nature from encroaching on the rights of others, cannot be dispensed with; but for this there is ample compensation even in the point of view of human development. The means of development which the individual loses by being prevented from gratifying his inclinations to the injury of others, are chiefly obtained at the expense of the development of other people. And even to himself there is a full equivalent in the better development of the social part of his nature, rendered possible by the restraint put upon the selfish part.[52]

The aim of society is the development of the capacities of its members. Because of the organic nature of society, each person's development is, in Mill's words, "valuable" to others. We are partially dependent upon each other for the development of our own capacities.

I believe that the metaphysical principles of process theology render it sympathetic with this 'mutual stimulation' argument although it is more evident in Whitehead's writings than in Hartshorne's.[53] For example, Whitehead holds that types of order are to be rated "according to their success in magnifying the individual actualities. . . ."[54] An individual, on the other hand, is rated on a double basis, "partly on the intrinsic strength of its own experience, and partly on its influence in the promotion of a high-grade type of order. These two grounds in part coalesce. For a weak individual exerts a weak influence."[55] An individual is rated, not only on the basis of the strength of his or her *individual* experience, but also on that individual's contribution to the development of *society as a whole*. If, therefore, there is a danger that an individual will develop his or her own capacities without regard for the rights of others to develop their potentialities, the state is justified in coercing that individual for the sake of the common good. Lopsided development gained at the expense of others is as undesirable as its consequential by-product, viz. underdevelopment. Yet if the restraints are just *and* are recognized by the individual as such, then they need not have pathological consequences.[56] This would be an example of what Whitehead terms control by "reasonable persuasion." In this instance legal restraints are not perceived as coercive because the individual acknowledges their propriety. Indeed, as we see, the individual gains in the development of the social part of his nature. The agent's loss of 'minor intensities' which he would have enjoyed by pursuing his own development at the expense of others, is compensated for by a 'finer composition' of feeling which results from the harmonious development of the whole.[57]

III. CONCLUSION

The positive contribution which coercion can make to social progress stems from the social nature of reality in general, and of human persons in particular. When people were considered to be atomic individuals each of whom possessed a fully formed nature it was easy to attribute personal or moral failures wholly to the individual. Character development could be brought about simply by exercising one's will autonomously. Social progress was then seen to be dependent upon each person's improvement of his or her own character. But with the advent of a social conception of human nature the importance of the environment for the development of character became a prominent theme of social reformers. "[T]he misleading juxtaposition of character versus environment made way for the improvement of environment *and* will power as means to character."[58] The ideological struggle now was over "the priority and relative weight of environmental factors in individual and social life. . . ."[59] The Charity Organisation Society, for instance, stressed the individual responsibility whereas liberals like Hobhouse and D. Ritchie emphasized the social conditions.

Process theology reflects the same tension between environmental factors and individual will. No doubt Hartshorne, like liberals generally, stresses the importance of self-reliance and individual character. Society can provide us with a good environment but in the end we are free to decide what we will be within the limits imposed upon us. A civilized society cannot be built upon coercion alone. This is because the good of the individual is not simply development, but *self*-development. Every individual is in part self-created or *causa sui*. An excess of coercion will suppress individuality which is an essential element in an intense and harmonious experience. Hence the value of persuasion as a means of social control.

However, there is a danger of over-emphasizing process theology's stress on persuasion. While Hartshorne views persuasion as the preferable means of social intercourse because it is consistent with the meaning of good as self-activity, he recognizes that the use of coercive power is an unavoidable feature of social life. Every occasion of experience emerges from its actual world and bears in its own essence the scars of its birth. Here Hartshorne would, I believe, be in agreement with Whitehead who wrote: "[A] species of subject requires a species of data as its preliminary phase of concrescence. But such data are nothing but the social environment under the abstraction effected by objectification."[60] Like actual occasions, "man is a social animal."[61] Therefore if we desire to see a particular type of person emerge within human history this will require the provision of an environment appropriate for such development. This is the metaphysical justification of the social reformer. It is also an apologetic for the reformer's use of coercive power. Coercion is necessary in order to prevent individuals from using their freedom in a way which impedes the (positive) freedom of others. "Coercion to prevent the use of coercion to destroy freedom"[62] is a 'crucial expression' of the divine love. Because we are influenced by our environment it is appropriate that we structure that environment so that it furthers our ideals. Coercion is therefore justified by the increased opportunity it brings to individuals for the full and free realization of their capacities. The sole legitimate aim of state intervention is finally the optimization of the promise of freedom. In doing this we are, at least on Hartshorne's analysis, only doing on the local level what God does in his governance of the cosmos.

Having said this, we must be careful not to overlook a tension within Hartshorne's thought concerning the use of coercive force by government and self-development. Because he does not regard human societies as being fully organic structures in the modern liberal sense Hartshorne tends to emphasize the tragic element in life. These features of his metaphysics correspond to the commitment which he appears to make to certain key elements of classical liberalism. These include his stress upon the competitive nature of personal development, his belief that individual goods are mutually exclusive, and his support for a preferential theory of the good.[63] However, Hartshorne's concept of God tempers his acceptance of competitive individualism. Unlike human societies, God is a fully organic society inclusive of all reality; therefore, competition must be balanced by an ideal of aesthetic harmony. We are enjoined to promote the general welfare of others because it contributes to the welfare of God. Only a supremely relative deity can, in Hartshorne's opinion, provide human beings with a good which is truly common to all. This is because there are no fully organic wholes inclusive of human persons apart from God. Consequently competition and tragedy are unavoidable at the level of human social interaction. Thus we find ourselves in the uncomfortable position of being encouraged by one aspect of his thought towards a policy of competitive individualism and by another feature to pursue the general well-being of others. To the extent that the quasi-organic nature of human societies is stressed Hartshorne leans towards a classical liberal position; however, when he emphasizes the fully organic nature of the cosmic society, i.e. God, he defends values more clearly identified with modern liberalism. Either way, it is clear that Hartshorne himself finds the metaphysical principles of process theology conducive to his personal commitment to *some* form of liberal ideology. What still needs to be assessed, however, is whether these principles have enabled Hartshorne to point a way forward towards a harmony of the ideals of classical and modern liberalism, or whether this tension reveals a latent contradiction in his position and represents merely a step backwards from a more progressive modern liberal position towards the conservative 'classical' position which, ironically, coincides with the cosmology he seeks to replace.[64]

NOTES

1. A. N. Whitehead, *Science and the Modern World* (Cambridge: Cambridge University Press, 1926), p. ix.
2. See Michael Freeden, *The New Liberalism: An Ideology of Social Reform* (Oxford: Clarendon Press, 1978); Gerald F. Gaus, *The Modern Liberal Theory of Man* (New York: St. Martin's Press, 1983); Andrew Vincent and Raymond Plant, *Philosophy, Politics and Citizenship: The Life and Thought of the British Idealists* (Oxford: Basil Blackwell, 1984).
3. Gaus, *Modern Liberal Theory*, p. 7.
4. An exception to this is Douglas Sturm who has noted that a similarity exists between Whitehead's philosophy and the organic political theories of Hobhouse and T. H. Green. See Douglas Sturm, "Process Thought and Political Theory: Implications of a Principle of Internal Relations," in *Process Philosophy and Social Thought*, John B. Cobb, Jr. and W. Widick Schroeder (eds.) (Chicago: Center for the Scientific Study of Religion, 1981), p. 98.
5. For example, see John Cobb's essay, "The Political Implications of Whitehead's Philosophy," in *Process Philosophy and Social Thought*, pp. 11—28.
6. Hartshorne, "Politics and the Metaphysics of Freedom," *Enquête sur la liberté, Fédération internationals des sociétés de philosophie*, Publié avec le concours de l'u.n.e.s.c.o., (Paris: Hermann and Cie., Editeurs, 1953), p. 80.
7. Charles Hartshorne, *The Logic of Perfection* (La Salle, Illinois: Open Court Publishing Company, 1962), pp. 307—8.
8. Hartshorne, "Organic and Inorganic Wholes," *Philosophy and Phenomenological Research* 3/2 (December, 1942), p. 133.
9. *Ibid.* In a similar vein Hobhouse declared that "[n]othing short of omniscience could establish a perfect harmony in all social relations at once" *Social Development: Its Nature and Conditions* (London: George Allen and Unwin, 1966), p. 69. Hartshorne, of course, denies that even divine omniscience is sufficient to establish a perfect harmony since within the world there are numerous centers of free creativity. See Hartshorne, "A Philosopher's Assessment of Christianity," in *Religion and Culture: Essays in Honor of Paul Tillich*, Walter Leibrecht (ed.) (New York: Harper and Brothers, 1959), p. 170.
10. Hartshorne, *The Logic of Perfection*, p. 314.
11. Charles Hartshorne, *Reality as Social Process* (Glencoe, Illinois: The Free Press, 1953), p. 149.
12. Charles Hartshorne, "A New Look at the Problem of Evil," in *Current Philosophical Issues: Essays in Honor of Curt John Ducasse*, F. C. Dommeyer (ed.) (Springfield: C. C. Thomas, 1966), p. 206.
13. Hartshorne, *The Logic of Perfection*, p. 203.

14. Charles Hartshorne, *The Divine Relativity: A Social Conception of God* (New Haven: Yale University Press, 1953), p. 50.
15. Hartshorne, *Reality as Social Process*, p. 41. "The question confronting God's love is this: Within what limits can the creatures be allowed to be their own and each other's destinies? It is these limits of freedom which provide for the cosmos the predictability which legal forms aim to achieve for human society" Hartshorne, "A Philosopher's Assessment of Christianity," p. 177.
16. Hartshorne, *The Logic of Perfection*, p. 204. It should be noted that God does not act so as to maximize freedom *per se*, but to maximize the *promise* of freedom. God's interest in maximizing the opportunities for self-realization in the universe, to be fulfilled, requires both freedom and restraint.
17. Santiago Sia, *God in Process Thought: A Study in Charles Hartshorne's Concept of God* (Dordrecht: Martinus Nijhoff, 1985), p. 80.
18. Hartshorne specifically states that "while the search for a risk-free utopia seems vain," he would "heartily support the search for a better system of risk-opportunity, more appropriate to our technology than we have now." As an example he says that the major dangers of pollution, nuclear war, and unjust extremes of rich and poor can only be effectively counterbalanced by restricting the freedom of each national group to be judge in its own cause. See Hartshorne, "Beyond Enlightened Self-Interest: A Metaphysics of Ethics," *Ethics* 84 (1973—74), pp. 211—12.
19. Hartshorne, *Reality as Social Process*, p. 108.
20 Charles Hartshorne, *A Natural Theology for Our Time* (La Salle, Illinois: Open Court Publishing Company, 1967), p. 120.
21. Hartshorne, *The Logic of Perfection*, p. 231. Emphasis added.
22. *Ibid.*, p. 204.
23. L. T. Hobhouse, *Liberalism* (Oxford: Oxford University Press, 1944), pp. 23—24. See also pp. 153—54.
24. Vincent and Plant, *Philosophy, Politics and Citizenship*, p. 73. Green, for example, describes the end of human activity as "a character not a good fortune, as a fulfilment of human capabilities from within not an accession of good things from without, as a function not a possession." The true good is "the perfection of human character" which is achieved through the activity of the individual as he fulfills his capabilities "according to the divine idea or plan of them." T. H. Green, *Prolegomena to Ethics*, A. C. Bradley (ed.) (Oxford: The Clarendon Press, 1890), p. 267.
25. T. H. Green, "Lectures on the Principles of Political Obligation," *Works*, Vol 2, R. L. Nettleship (ed.) (London: Longman, Green, and Co., 1891), p. 345. Green specifically mentions the Poor-law which, in his estimation, "takes away the occasion for the exercise of parental forethought, filial reverence, and neighbourly kindness." *Ibid.*
26. See Hartshorne, *The Logic of Perfection*, p. 204.
27. Green, "Principles of Political Obligation," pp. 345—46. Emphasis added. Cf. Hartshorne's similar strictures against paternalism in "Individual Differences and the Ideal of Equality," *New South* 18 (February 1963), p. 6.
28. Hobhouse, *Social Development*, p. 76.
29. *Ibid.*
30. L. T. Hobhouse, *Social Evolution and Political Theory* (Port Washington, N.Y.: Kennikat Press, 1968), pp. 195—96.
31. See Charles Hartshorne, *Creative Synthesis and Philosophic Method* (London: SCM Press, 1970), p. 313f.
32. Charles Hartshorne, *Insights and Oversights of Great Thinkers: An Evaluation of Western Philosophy* (Albany: State University of New York Press, 1983), pp. 224, 225.
33. Hartshorne, *Reality as Social Process*, p. 149.
34. The use of the word 'private' is misleading insofar as it suggests an ultimate bifurcation between individual experience and public utility. Process social theory holds that "every action is at once a private experience and public utility." A. N. Whitehead, *Adventures of*

Ideas, (Cambridge: Cambridge University Press, 1933), p. 39. 'Narrow' or 'restricted' would be a more accurate phrase. 'Sin' is the result of intentionally disregarding the relevance of our actions for our social environment beyond an excessively narrow area. It thus leads to forms of self-development which, while beautiful in themselves, introduce unnecessary disharmony within the wider social context: "With a larger view and a deeper analysis, some instance of the perfection of art may diminish the good otherwise inherent in some specific situation as it passes into its objective actuality for the future. Unseasonable art is analogous to an unseasonable joke, namely, good in its place, but out of place a positive evil" (*Ibid.*, p. 345).

35. John B. Cobb, Jr., *Process Theology as Political Theology*, (Manchester: Manchester University Press, 1982), p. 98.
36. *Ibid.*, p. 99.
37. Hartshorne, *Reality as Social Process*, pp. 148—49.
38. *Ibid.*, p. 99. Emphasis added.
39. Hartshorne, *The Divine Relativity*, p. 133.
40. *Ibid.*
41. Hartshorne, "A Philosopher's Assessment of Christianity," p. 170.
42. Franklin I. Gamwell, "Happiness and the Public World: Beyond Political Liberalism," *Process Studies* 8 (Spring 1978), p. 22. It is this preferential view of the good which underlies Hartshorne's claim that "every legislative act excludes things which for some are genuine values. Always someone loses or suffers. This is an element of tragedy in process itself" Hartshorne, *Reality as Social Process*, p. 99.
43. Kenneth M. Dolbeare and Patricia Dolbeare, *American Ideologies*, p. 6. Found in Gamwell, "Happiness and the Public World," p. 22. See Hartshorne, *Insights*, p. 226: "No one else feels and knows the needs and desires of an individual as intimately and constantly as that individual does. Hence each person should be permitted to design his or her lifestyle so far as this is compatible with others doing the same."
44. Hartshorne, "A Philosopher's Assessment of Christianity," p. 176.
45. *Ibid.*, p. 168.
46. *Ibid.*, p. 170.
47. These two aspects of human interrelationships are also acknowledged by Hobhouse when he says: "In living together, consciously and unconsciously we exert pressure and constraint upon one another, and consciously and unconsciously we co-operate and draw out from each other capacities which would otherwise lie dormant." *Social Development*, p. 70. The perfect organic harmony in which each person's development serves society and society sustains the development of each individual's capacities, is an ideal. But at the same time it is the criterion for determining what sort of individual development is to be considered good.
48. Hobhouse, *Democracy*, p. 227.
49. Hobhouse, *Social Evolution*, p. 87 n. 1.
50. Green, *Prolegomena*, p. 183. See also pp. 202, 257.
51. *Ibid.*, p. 414.
52. J. S. Mill, *On Liberty*, *Works* 18: 266.
53. This phrase is borrowed from Gaus, *Modern Liberal Theory*, p. 64.
54. Whitehead, *Adventures of Ideas*, pp. 376—77.
55. According to Whitehead civilization is a work of art. The details of its composition "make their own claim to individuality, and yet contribute to the whole." *Adventures of Ideas*, p. 364. Its aim is at "fineness of feeling" and therefore civilization should "so arrange its social relations, and the relations of its members to their natural environment, as to evoke into the experiences of its members Appearances dominated by the harmonies of forceful enduring things. In other words, Art should aim at the production of individuality in the component details of its compositions" (*Ibid.*, p. 363).
56. See Mill, *On Liberty*, *Works* 18: 266.

57. A. N. Whitehead, *Process and Reality*, Corrected Edition, David R. Griffin and Donald Sherburne (eds.) (New York: Free Press, 1978), p. 15(23).
58. Freeden, *New Liberalism*, p. 172.
59. *Ibid.*
60. Whitehead, *Process and Reality*, p. 203(309—10).
61. *Ibid.*, p. 204(311).
62. Charles Hartshorne, *Man's Vision of God and the Logic of Theism* (Hamden, Conn: Archon Books, 1964), p. 173.
63. It is also evident in his defence of the classical liberal ideals of liberty and equality as expounded by Milton and Rose Friedman. See Hartshorne, *Insights*, p. 229.
64. For a more detailed examination of Hartshorne's political thought see my forthcoming book *Process Philosophy and Political Ideology* (State University of New York Press).

4. God, Power and the Struggle for Liberation: A Feminist Contribution

SHEILA GREEVE DAVANEY

I. INTRODUCTION

While revolutions have ever been a part of human history, the modern era has been particularly marked by the rise of the dispossessed of the world. The poor, persons of color, and women of all races and classes have each, in turn, challenged centuries-old patterns of domination and structures of oppression.[1] And as these groups have developed their analyses of gender, class and race, they have as well, asserted that the realities of oppression are not separated from religious and theological beliefs and ideas, but that there exists a profound interconnection between these visions of reality and the systems that deny so many their humanity. In particular, proponents of liberation theology, black and feminist thought have focused their examination on the central symbols of the Western Christian tradition and most importantly the idea of God, in order to clarify the implications of this symbol system for political and social reality.[2] This critical analysis is not an interesting but irrelevant sidelight for the powerless of the world. Rather, it is an imperative dimension of movements for liberation for, according to these thinkers, such analysis reveals how religious visions of reality function to sanction and provide support for oppressive political and societal structures and institutions; this critical exploration makes clear, in the words of liberation theologian, Juan Luis Segundo, that "our unjust society and our perverted idea of God are in close and terrible alliance."[3]

Feminists, in particular, have undertaken this critical task. In the nineteenth century, during the first wave of feminism in the United States, suffragette Elizabeth Cady Stanton argued that religion and oppression were deeply intertwined and that women's subjugation would not be overcome until a radical transformation of religious visions took place. Feminist theology on the current scene has echoed Stanton's insights, insisting that Western religious traditions have been primary contributors to the oppression of women and that the liberation of women will, by necessity, entail the rejection or transformation of much of the religious frameworks we have inherited.

S. Sia (ed.), Charles Hartshorne's Concept of God, 57–75.
© 1990 *Kluwer Academic Publishers. Printed in the Netherlands.*

Moreover, women have argued that a, perhaps the, major locus of change must be the idea of God. There are a number of reasons for focusing on the idea of the divine. First, it is the central symbol of Western theisms, expressing their basic convictions about the nature of reality and embodying the primary values and commitments of these traditions. In so far as this symbol incorporates ideas, values and attitudes negative towards women, the worldviews it anchors will continue to be powerful reflections and sustainers of misogynist societies and cultures. The most obvious example of this has been the perennial identification in Christianity in particular, and Western theisms in general, of maleness and God. While these traditions have always asserted that God was not literally a male, the preponderance of male images for the divine and the lack of and, indeed, seeming horror of female images for God have resulted in the *de facto* divinization of maleness both in theological reflection and popular imagination.[4] Although the levels of sophistication and subtlety have varied in this process of apotheosis, the results have been singular — the alliance of the traditional idea of God and the oppression of women. For as Mary Daly succinctly put it in 1973, "when God is male, the male is God."[5]

It is, however, not merely the fact the male images have been used most frequently in relation to the divine. If this were the case, then the utilization of non-gender specific images or a greater variety of metaphors would substantially correct the situation. While such diversification of religious language has often proved helpful it has also served to obscure the truly critical questions about Western theism. The danger is that we will alter our images and metaphors for the divine without significantly challenging the visions and values embedded in the idea of God as it has developed in the West; that is, the names for the divine will change, but the God will remain the same.[6] What is, therefore, called for is the exploration, critique and reconstruction of the fundamental convictions that find expression in and through the idea of God. Without the radical transformation of these, the change of metaphors and images will be, at best, a half-way measure that makes us feel better while insidiously perpetuating oppressive interpretations of reality on other, less obvious, though perhaps more fundamental levels.[7]

It is important to note that the idea of God in Western Christianity has not developed in a singular or uniform fashion. A wide variety of competing claims about the divine has emerged in Western history, each vying for philosophical and theological justification and popular acceptance. However, despite this diversity and at the risk of offering a caricature, it is possible to delineate the central characteristics of what has come to be termed the classical idea of God. In this classical interpretation, God is viewed as other, as that which is infinitely distinct from the finite world. This God, despite the assertion by many theologians that Jesus provides the central clue to the meaning of divinity, is not understood as identified in a primary manner with any dimension of creaturely existence. Although this God entered into relationship with the world, this has been theologically given a subordinate position and God in Godself has been understood to have existence and value in Godself and apart from any relation with humanity or the world. This God is characterized by the attributes of sovereignty, self-sufficiency, unsurpassibility, and omnipotent control. The divine, conceived in this manner, has been understood to be absolute creator and ruler of creaturely existence. And while God's creativity and lordship have been interpreted as expressions of divine benevolence and love, such notions have been controlled by and subordinated to the ideas of absolute power, autonomy and independent existence that suffuse the classical understanding of God. Although God is graciously related to the human sphere, this connection is finally secondary and unnecessary, for the classical God is self-completed, needing nothing outside of Godself. Indeed this God of classical theism represents, in the words of Thomas Altizer, "the primary embodiment of a solitary and isolated selfhood."[8]

Challenging this traditional idea of God has not been only the province of women and other proponents of liberation movements. Much of modern philosophy and theology, literature and art can be interpreted as a struggle against the repressive elements of classical theism. It would, however, be a profound mistake to interpret feminist, black and liberation theologies as merely variations of this modern rebellion against this classical worldview. For a curious thing has happened in the modern rejection of this omnipotent, self-completed deity. The attributes deemed so problematic in relation to God have been neither thoroughly rejected nor transformed but rather they have been relocated in humanity. The autonomous, self-completed God has been replaced by the autonomous, independent, modern self. Even the radical cry that God is dead has not resulted in the loss of these values, but in their inversion; now humanity, not God, bodies forth "solitary and isolated selfhood." In the words of Mark C. Taylor, "the humanistic atheist denies God in the name of self by transferring the attributes of the divine creator to the human creature."[9]

This inversion of values is not to be found only in humanistic atheism. Rather, it permeates much of modern thought, including liberal, "progressive" theology; here, too, autonomous, free selfhood is the norm. It is precisely this failure to subvert, but only to invert, that causes proponents of liberation, black and feminist perspectives to distance themselves from much of modern theology. There has been a variety of ways of expressing this differentiation. Latin American theologian, Gustavo Gutierrez, argues that liberal progressive theology with its focus on the problematic of the "modern human being," i.e. the autonomous self, is, in fact, the product of the emergence of the bourgeois middle class in Europe and the United States. And, Gutierrez contends, ". . . the oppressed and marginalized are oppressed and marginalized precisely by the interlocutor of 'progressive' theology — by the bourgeois class."[10] Thus, far from being another expression of the modern spirit, liberation theology is in "historical contradiction" and "dialectical opposition to bourgeois ideology," including its theological forms.[11]

Black thinker, Cornel West, has argued along similar lines, suggesting that the Western worldview, with its "normative gaze," is inherently racist and must be replaced, not merely revised. It is no unfortunate historical accident that racism, imperialism and colonialism have characterized much of Western experience. Rather, these are the inevitable expression of the Western world-view.[12] And, finally, feminist theologians have vigorously insisted that both the classical idea of God and its mirror image, the autonomous, substantial self, are expressions of male experience, values and power. As such, they not only exclude women but function to sanction our ongoing oppression. Seen in this light, modern thought, including its theological critique of the classical idea of God, does not fully embody the ideals of emancipation for all, but is a form of "patricide" in which the Father God is killed, so that the sons might now receive their inheritance.[13] Not only has patriarchy not been trans-formed in modernity, but there is a real sense in which it has extended itself in the absence of the restraining presence of the transcendent God.[14]

While there are many ways in which the proponents of liberation, feminist and black perspectives are "modern," increasingly these thinkers share a common conviction that not only must the classical idea of God be challenged, but insofar as modernity represents a subtle, often hidden, relocation of the values embodied in that idea of the divine to the modern self, then this latter notion and all it entails must, also, be critically re-assessed. Put succinctly, more and more thinkers emerging from and representing oppressed groups are calling not for the reform of the Western worldview but for its dis-mantlement.

It is with this call for radical transformation of our basic convictions about reality, God and the human self that there opens up the possibility for dialogue between thinkers committed to liberation agendas and proponents of perspectives critical of much that has been associated with the Western worldview. Chief among these latter thinkers on the current scene who have rejected central tenets of the Western conception of reality have been the articulators of process philosophy and theology. And premier among such thinkers has been philosopher, Charles Hartshorne.[15] Hartshorne has devoted a philosophical lifetime to the critique of the classical idea of God and this notion of the autonomous individual self, and to the construction of an alternative interpretation that might not only be more coherent but also provide a basis for a more humane existence. In the remainder of this essay, I would like to examine several of Hartshorne's central claims in order to see how they might resonate with and contribute to liberation efforts, in general, and feminist ones, in particular, to construct more liberating understandings of reality. Such a conversation is fraught with difficulties for Hartshorne, as do the vast majority of process thinkers, represents precisely that group — white, Euro-American males — that oppressed peoples are struggling against. But if this is so, it is also the case that we live in dangerous times wherein the fate not only of oppressed groups is at stake but also the survival of the world. It is imperative, therefore, that all people of good will engage in such dialogue, recognizing our differences, but building upon our shared conviction of the necessity for radical change.

In particular, I want to focus my examination upon Hartshorne's understanding of power both in its divine and non-divine forms. The interpretation of power is of special importance in the present context for it has played not only a central role in defining God and the human self, but also because it is precisely on this point that feminists have been most critical of the classical concept of deity and of the humans that have mirrored such a God. At this juncture, I want to turn first to Hartshorne's creationist metaphysics, and to his ideas of God and divine power and then, in the following sections, to the repercussions of these notions for a range of issues including suffering, responsibility and the hope for change.

II. HARTSHORNE AND CREATIONIST METAPHYSICS

Charles Hartshorne represents, in many ways, a continuation of the expectations of the Enlightenment and modernity. While he has rejected a good many of the tenets of this period, he has nonetheless continued to espouse an unquestioning confidence in reason's capacity to know reality or at least its general structure.[16] Moreover, Hartshorne's trust in human cognitive capacities finds expression in his conviction that there is, or can be, a basic congruence between reality and human ideas about it. While Hartshorne acknowledges that the congruence is much closer on the preconscious and prelinguistic levels of experience, and that consciousness, with its increased complexification, often results in distortion, he also argues that truth, understood as correspondence to reality, remains a possibility.[17] If Hartshorne embodies these central convictions of modernity, he also has asserted that the modern project has failed. However, he believes it has done so not because of a naive faith in reason or the correspondence theory of truth, but because it continued, sometimes unconsciously, to operate out of a classical metaphysics that was, at heart, incoherent, inconsistent and morally problematic. Hartshorne proposes that rather than eschewing modernity's appeal to reason as the foundation for and arbitrator of claims to truth, we should re-think the basic convictions about the nature of reality that have rendered the Western worldview and especially the traditional ideas of God and the human self so questionable in our era. That is to say, Hartshorne concurs that there is indeed a crisis concerning God-talk, but insists this crisis is really about the traditional or classical understanding of deity outlined above and the metaphysical vision in which it is grounded. And while he has argued strenuously for the rejection of *this* idea of the divine and its metaphysical foundations, he has also asserted, in contrast to many modern thinkers, that such rejection need not entail leaving behind all conceptions of God.

Hartshorne locates his alternative understanding of God in the context of what he terms a creationist metaphysics. In order to understand Hartshorne's conception of the divine it is important to keep in mind the basic tenets of this metaphysical vision. First and foremost, Hartshorne argues, the fundamental form of reality is, from the perspective of a creationist metaphysics, concrete actuality.[18] The primary focus of the metaphysician must be on concrete realities, not ideal forms or universals. These latter are abstractions, which do not exist apart from the concrete moments of experience.

Further, Hartshorne contends, when concrete actuality is carefully considered it can be seen to be *social, creative, sentient and temporal.* Since these four characteristics play a foundational role in Hartshorne's interpretation not only of finite creaturely reality but also of God, it is necessary to consider each in turn. First, to be a concrete actuality is to be an experiencing subject internally related to other experiencing subjects. No concrete reality exists in utter isolation from its world or environment, but rather co-exists in a web of interdependence with other equally social entities. There is no "wholly other," neither God nor the substantial self, in a creationist metaphysics.[19]

Moreover, within creationist metaphysics, these socially defined concrete entities are understood to be distinct momentary units of experience.[20] Such momentary units are not self-enclosed egos or free-floating bits of lifeless matter, but are understood as dynamic processes which are, in fact, the product of their social relatedness. For Hartshorne, each moment of experience is literally the integration and creative synthesis of the data of the social world into new reality. Central to this argument is Hartshorne's insistence that to exist at all means to be internally related to the world, that is, to be determined by and dependent upon the other momentary units of experience that comprise reality. Thus, social relativity entails dependency upon the other.

Hartshorne further delineates the nature of this social relatedness by arguing that its structure is a thoroughly temporal one.[21] To say this means, according to Hartshorne, that there are fundamental distinctions between past, present, and future. In this schema, the past is settled, finished. It has reached completion and is available as data, raw material for future events to appropriate. The present is the province, so to speak, of experiencing subjects. Each moment of experience comes into existence as it takes account of, integrates and synthesizes its past. This is another way of stating that the present is constituted by and dependent upon its social environment understood as both the immediate and the more distant past; the past is therefore, the *cause* and the present, the *effect*.[22] As temporal beings we are, by necessity, products of our personal and communal histories.

If the past is settled and determined actuality, and the present is coming to be actuality, then the future, in Hartshorne's framework, is not actual at all. The future is the realm of the not-yet, the open arena of possibility. Although the past and present, as it reaches completion and thereby becomes past, will shape the future, its exact content and contour are yet to be determined. In this schema the historical process is open-ended; an end of history is ruled out.

If the past contributes to, indeed, constitutes and so determines much of the present it does not do so in a complete or absolute manner. For freedom and creativity are also characteristic of each moment of experience. Hartshorne argues that each experiencing subject must take account of its past, its social world, but how such data is synthesized and integrated is a matter of self-determination.[23] While the amount of creativity will vary according to the level of experience, ranging from little potential for creativeness on the subatomic level to enormous possibility for novelty and the emergence of the new on the cosmic level, no experiencing subject is without the capacity to receive creatively the influence of others and transform it in that very reception. Thus, all experience is a form of creative self-determination. Moreover, how a subject constitutes itself as it appropriates the past determines what it will offer to the future. To be a subject is thus to be open to the influence of the past and, in turn, to offer oneself to the future. Such movement from past to present to future, with its characteristics of both determination and creativity, constitutes the ongoing process which is, for Hartshorne, reality itself.

And, finally, underlying the above assumptions of the social, temporal and creative character of subjectivity is Hartshorne's adamant insistence that such subjectivity is a universal affair. That is, Hartshorne argues, every actual entity is or once was an experiencing subject. While collections of concrete actualities, such as stones or doors are not subjects, every individual reality that has internal unity and coherence, including the microcosmic ones that make up stones and doors, must be understood as not entirely devoid of experience. This claim is important for Hartshorne not only because it extends the notion of subjectivity to the subhuman level where it has so often been denied, but because it also suggests that subjectivity is as characteristic of the macrocosmic level of reality as well. That is, Hartshorne argues that the universe, understood as an integrated entity, is also an experiencing subject.[24] This idea of cosmic subjectivity will presently be seen to be central to Hartshorne's interpretation of God as the universe unified or the cosmic whole.

In sum, according to Hartshorne's creationist metaphysics, reality is composed of experiencing subjects which can best be characterized as social, temporal, sentient, and creative or self-determining. The all-important question must be how and to what extent such features can be said to characterize God. It is to this issue that we now turn.

III. HARTSHORNE'S CONCEPTION OF GOD

Charles Hartshorne has insisted, along with other process thinkers, that the notion of God as wholly other sharing no features in common with the world, is finally incomprehensible. Rather than this utterly transcendent deity, distinguished by total difference, Hartshorne has argued for an understanding of God as the cosmic subject who shares the characteristics of social relatedness, temporality, creativity and capacity for experience articulated

64

above, but who embodies these in a radically superior manner.[25] As a means of unpacking Hartshorne's notion of divine subjectivity, I want to focus on his interpretation of divine power. For it is here that Hartshorne and feminists alike have most clearly challenged the classical conception of God.

Traditionally, divine power has been conceived as the capacity to constitute first Godself and subsequently all creaturely reality in an all-determining manner. In this view, power is understood primarily in agential terms as the capacity to act, to influence, to determine. Thus, God is always active agent, creating the world, determining history and eventually bringing history to its conclusion in the eschaton. Perhaps the premier example of such omnipotent agency, in which all real power is concentrated, is the notion of the Creator God bringing the universe into existence *ex nihilo*.

Hartshorne thoroughly rejects what he terms this "monopoly notion of power."[26] His first reason for such a rejection is that if one begins with a creationist metaphysics and therefore with a social universe, then the idea of the concentration of all real power in one individual agent is contradictory and nonsensical. Moreover, Hartshorne argues that this notion is morally and existentially reprehensible. It, in fact, represents the ideal of domination in which difference and otherness must be controlled and repressed. It is the ideal of a despot, a tyrant and as such is to be resisted, not worshipped.[27]

Out of the canons of his creationist metaphysics, Hartshorne calls for the re-interpretation of this idea of divine power. He suggests that power is not a simple notion to be conceived only in agential terms. Rather, in an interdependent universe, power too must be seen as social in character entailing both the capacity to influence and the ability to receive the influence of others. That is, power has not only an agential dimension but also a receptive, responsive, patient form. Further, Hartshorne contends, this latter capacity to be open to the influence of others, to be shaped by them, is not a lesser form of power but is equal to its agential counterpart.[28] Moreover, it is precisely the ability to receive the world into oneself that is the foundation for creative and sensitive subsequent influence upon other social realities. Without such prior openness, the power to determine others is blind and dangerous.

Thus, Hartshorne argues that in a social universe, power — including divine power — entails the capacity both to receive influence and, in turn, to contribute to the determination of others. In this view, God, therefore, is not only cause but also effect. It is important to explore this divine receptivity for it has been almost completely absent from the classical interpretation of God.

Hartshorne details his understanding of divine receptivity most clearly in his analysis of God's knowledge. For Hartshorne, knowledge is the term that refers to the appropriating, integrating and creative synthesizing process whereby an entity takes account of its world and by so doing constitutes itself. Such knowledge is therefore responsive, entailing the determination of the knower by the known. Moreover, God in the Hartshornian schema is the perfect knower, the cosmic subject that receives all of reality into Godself.

Thus, in stark and radical contrast to the classical vision of deity in which God created the world by virtue of God's knowledge, the world influences, shapes and in a very real way determines God as God knows and thereby, receives the universe into Godself.

My own way of speaking of this perfect receptivity is to state that in Hartshorne's vision God's knowledge is conformal, inclusive and preservative.[29] Conformal here means that God knows things just as they are.[30] That is, divine knowledge is temporal; God knows things when they have taken place, not before. Moreover, counter to much of the Christian tradition, God's knowledge does not create creaturely reality nor cause it to take place in a certain way. Thus, both foreknowledge and predestination are ruled out. Further, divine knowledge, in this view is never complete. As creaturely reality changes, so does God's knowledge of it. Therefore, Hartshorne's God can never be understood as self-completed or fulfilled but only as ever-growing, increasing in richness and value.

Another way of viewing divine receptivity understood as knowledge is to state that it is inclusive. This is perhaps the most controversial aspect of Hartshorne's notion of God. For, he argues, God literally, as perfect knower, includes all of reality within God's life. Such radical inclusion leads Hartshorne to define God as the Inclusive or Cosmic Whole. That is, God is the integration and synthesis of all worldly experience into one unified divine reality.[31] Such interpretation of God follows from Hartshorne's argument that individual units of experience are the synthesizers of the multiplicity of past experiences into present reality. God, as the perfect knower, is this process on a cosmic scale.

This vision of God as the cosmos unified and thus understood as a sentient, experiencing, knowing individual, is not, Hartshorne contends, another form of simple pantheism. Rather God, like every individual, is never merely the sum of its constitutive parts, but is rather the creative unity whereby the world is not only known but also evaluated and harmonized.[32] Thus, God is not only determined, but is in that reception of the world creatively self-determining. God's freedom, therefore, lies not in freedom from influence but in the capacity to receive influence in a creative and trans-forming manner.

A third way to analyze divine receptivity in the Hartshornian framework is to say that it is preservative. That is, God not only knows the world but also remembers all creaturely experience forever. This conception of divine power as the capacity to remember and thereby continue to be influenced by creaturely reality is existentially all-important for Hartshorne. For, Hart-shorne contends, creaturely reality, as finite, is faced with the inevitable end of experience. Eschewing all claims for individual immortality, Hartshorne argues that what is important is not whether we as creatures live forever, but whether our experience has meaning. Such meaning is insured, according to Hartshorne, only by a divine knower who preserves our experience forever within the divine life. Thus, for Hartshorne, our only immortality and the only kind of immortality that matters, lies in our contribution to God's life and the divine ability to continue to be shaped by such offerings.[33]

And finally, I would suggest that Hartshorne understands God's knowledge to be perfect in each of these forms because it is a form of love.[34] In much of the tradition, God's love has been conceived, as has God's power, as only agential in nature. It was always outgoing, never passive. But Hartshorne argues that love, too, has a receptive form whereby it is the power to make the experience of others one's own. God's love is hence sympathetic awareness issuing forth in perfect conformity to reality, and the radical inclusion and ongoing preservation of the experiences of the world.

The Hartshornian vision of God's power interpreted as perfect receptivity has, I believe, a certain priority in Hartshorne's schema. For it is literally the way God continually comes into ever new being. Moreover, this form of divine power has been almost totally neglected in the Western tradition. But if Hartshorne has focused on the notion of power as the ability to be open to the world, he has developed, to a lesser degree, the idea of God's agential power, as well. This more agential power can be discerned in several ways.

First, Hartshorne insists, as was mentioned above, that God's receptive power is always creative and evaluative. The process whereby God constitutes Godself through the synthesis and integration of worldly reality not only conforms to that reality but also transforms it. Hence, receptivity is always, for God, a form of creativity. Second, God not only is shaped and influenced by the world, God in turn influences and contributes to creaturely reality. But God does so not by the means articulated by much of the Christian theological tradition; God influences not by divine absolute control, as predestination or foreknowledge. Rather, God shapes the world by offering Godself to God's creatures. That is, God influences the world — just as we contribute to God's life — by being an object to be appropriated. We are influenced by God through the gift of Godself and the possibilities and limitations inherent in that gift.

It is clear that in this schema, Hartshorne argues for an understanding of God's power that is far from the tradition's notion of divine omnipotence. In this vision, absolute control is impossible. God seeks, through the gift of Godself, to persuade the world but cannot finally force compliance. For Hartshorne, "the mode of influence is the dialogue — I speak, you listen, and then you speak and I listen."[35]

The claims concerning the mode of God's influence upon the world further emphasize Hartshorne's assertion that not only *does* God not control all that occurs, but God *cannot* exercise such all-encompassing control. What actually takes place depends upon the possibilities God offers the world and upon the world's response. That is, it depends in part upon worldly creativity and freedom. And freedom, interpreted as choice among alternatives, brings with it the possibility of wrong or mistaken choices, of evil and tragedy. There is no way in the Hartshornian schema to escape the *possibility* of evil. Moreover, the greater the range of possibilities and the greater the creative potential, the greater the risk of tragedy. For Hartshorne, freedom, creativity and the potentiality for evil as well as the opportunities for good decrease or increase together. In his words, "The risks of freedom are inseparable from freedom and the price of its opportunities."[36]

Thus, in this vision, the possibility of evil is inherent in freedom and therefore God cannot eliminate evil or at least the potential for such evil. In the universe interpreted according to the canons of creationist metaphysics, all power, including that of the cosmic subject, is social and entails the existence of an infinite number of creaturely subjects capable of their own decisions which shape and determine, in their own small way, the development of reality. As long as life is creative process, there can be no final victory that eradicates the potentiality for evil or eliminates the tragic repercussions of freedom.

In sum, Charles Hartshorne has developed a radical alternative to the metaphysics of being that emphasized a transcendent, self-completed, omnipotent deity and an isolated, independent, autonomous self who has in modern thought increasingly sounded like a caricature of this traditional God who has become so problematic. Thus, he has insisted that not only must the God of classical theism be rejected but he has also refused the move so characteristic of the modern era to relocate the attributes of deity in a divinized form of the human self. Succinctly put, Hartshorne has contributed to the dismantling of Western culture's worldview. And in its place he, with other process thinkers, has proposed an interpretation of reality as fundamentally interrelated, composed of social individuals who have both the capacity to receive influence from other social entities and who, in turn, through their self-constitution, contribute to the shaping of the world. God, in this schema, is not, as God finally was in the classical tradition, the epitome of self-satisfied, completed Being who exercised absolute, if gracious, control over creaturely reality. Rather, God is the cosmic instantiation of social relatedness whose power is always social and hence never absolute. In the Hartshornian vision, such absolute power with both its implications of domination and its promise of victory over evil is irrevocably lost.

IV. SUGGESTIONS FOR CONVERSATION

Charles Hartshorne's vision of an interdependent universe and a social God is, I believe, suggestive for those who, like him, have found the Western conceptions of God and self increasingly problematic. In particular, I believe Hartshorne's position, as does process thought in general, opens up a place for conversation with feminists. In this section, I would like to focus upon several areas in which fruitful dialogue might take place.

The first area centers on Hartshorne's articulation of power as receptive. Within Western culture, the ideal of the self, both on the divine and human levels, has been defined in terms of autonomy and independence. Further, such autonomous selfhood has been secured through the exclusion and domination of the other. In an essentially non-social universe, encounter with the other is always a threat. Hence, both the transcendent God and the autonomous human self have sought to be free from the influence of others, to be if you will, impermeable. But on a human level, this ideal of the impenetrable and unpierceable self has not been envisioned as the goal of *all* humans; it has, in fact, been understood to be the province of men, indeed many would suggest white males of the upper and middle classes. Women of all races and classes and men of color have been interpreted precisely as those others who must be excluded and controlled. Moreover, women, in particular, have been seen as the other for we have been defined precisely as that which is permeable, open to others, literally constituted by and through our relations. In a worldview in which relationship understood as mutual conditioning, is devalued both on a divine and human level, those who embody such relationality will inevitably be feared and understood negatively. It is, therefore, no accident that the Western ideas of God and self have been so closely associated with patriarchy and the oppression of women.

As contemporary women have rejected patriarchy, we have struggled to redefine both God and the human self. In particular, feminist theologians have sought to avoid simply extending the ideals of autonomy and independence, i.e. the ideals of the male self, to women. Instead, we have attempted to reconceive divine and human selfhood precisely along the lines that Western theology and philosophy have so often repudiated. That is, we have begun to articulate a worldview in which relationality is the guiding motif rather than autonomy. It is to this effort that I believe Charles Hartshorne's work lends strong support.

Hartshorne's vision, as detailed in the previous section, suggests that the ideal of the separate self — whether divine or human — exercising power as domination, is not only morally reprehensible but also descriptively inaccurate. Independent selfhood is not a reality and its ceaseless pursuit is bound inevitably to fail. (Perhaps this is why it is sought so violently.) Power in this alternative schema is not first the ability to control and dominate, to separate and exclude. Rather, power in its primary mode, is the power of inclusion, the capacity to receive and to be constituted by one's world. God, as was argued above, is not the premier example of independent selfhood, but the prime exemplification of radical inclusion.

Such claims resonate well with the insights of many feminist thinkers. Women long identified with relationality and then devalued for this, are insisting that connection, not separation, lies at the heart of reality. In particular, women are reclaiming and re-interpreting our bodily experience as the foundation for claims of the centrality of constitutive relationality.[37] Perhaps the most obvious examples of such mutual dependency are the experiences of conception, pregnancy, childbirth and lactation; at the emergence of life itself there is no isolated, self-sufficient autonomous individuality. Rather, life literally depends for its survival on the mutual well-being of mother and child. Without such mutual enhancement, both are put at risk.

This recognition of the importance of connectedness has found expression as well in how women interpret our moral relations with others. The research of Carol Gilligan on women's moral development suggests that many women live out of what she terms an ethic of care which presupposes the priority of connectedness.[38] In contrast, many males, and especially white males, assuming the normativity of the separate self, interpret moral decision in terms of rights. For the latter, the moral question centers on how to adjudicate among competing, often incompatible, rights, while for the former the concern is how to meet the needs of all. Such a commitment to the needs of all represents the attempt to see connection as fundamental and with it the importance of nurturing the web of interrelationship and thereby undermining the norm of autonomous selfhood and with it its "economy of domination." In Gilligan's words, ". . . in the different voice of women lies the truth of an ethic of care, the tie between relationship and responsibility, and the origins of aggression in the failure of connection."[39]

This ethic of connection has perhaps found its most significant embodiment in the feminist vision of women's community. Historically, women have not only been devalued by males but have been taught to devalue one another. We have lived intimately with our oppressors and in isolation one from the other. As feminist poet, Robin Morgan, states there has been

> No colonized people so isolated one from the other
> for so long as women.[40] . . .

In contrast to a world of self-enclosed selves, characterized by confrontation and competition, feminists are articulating a vision of community in which the possibilities of individual selves are based on the richness of the experience of others. As with mother and child so, too, with women together, we depend upon each other for the sustenance of life.

This ideal of community, grounded in a social worldview and embodied in a relational ethic, is shared by many women. Nonetheless, it has been an ambiguous ideal for at times it has served to mask the radical differences among women and the ways in which we have participated in one another's oppression. In particular, women of color have raised the question of the compliance of white women in racism.[41] This ideal of community does not, therefore, point to an achieved reality but rather to that towards which we struggle and whose intimations in our lives ground our hope.

If the claims of community and solidarity have sometimes seemed premature especially to women of color, the vision of a social self, literally constituted by its relations has raised for others the specter of the loss of all integrity and uniqueness. Have women, in articulating an interpretation of reality as radically relational, foregone the self we never had? The creationist metaphysics I have been outlining is suggestive on this concern as well. For, in the Hartshornian schema, literal inclusion does not result in the loss of individuality; for every moment of existence is constituted by the *creative* reception of the world whereby each entity is not only influenced by its environment but determines itself as well. The work of feminist theologian,

Catherine Keller, is particularly fruitful on this point. In her book, *From a Broken Web*, Keller, utilizing the insights of process thought, argues that radical relationality does not necessarily lead to the "soluble self" that has been so oppressive to women.[42] Instead she contends, differentiation and individuality depend upon the capacity to receive creatively the world into oneself and to make it one's own. Indeed, for Keller, uniqueness is predicated on the complexity of relations of which the individual self is capable. The more one can include, synthesize and integrate, the greater the richness of the individual experience. And in this process view, if this link between individuality and the capacity for inclusion is true on a human level, it is especially true for God whose richness of life literally depends upon the quality of creaturely experience.

It was argued in the previous section that when Hartshorne unpacked his ideas of fundamental relationality and radical inclusion, he concluded that God was the Cosmic Whole, the integration of reality on a cosmic scale. Within feminist theology there is much debate about the utility of God-talk versus Goddess-language and about the status of such notions of the divine. Despite the lack of consensus about these issues there is emerging, I believe, the outlines of an understanding of the divine that resonates with the process vision. The work of Rosemary Radford Ruether is suggestive at this point. She argues that God/ess is the matrix of reality, the cosmic process out of which life emerges and returns. Steadfastly repudiating the transcendent, disembodied, isolated deity of much of the Christian tradition, Ruether argues for an "earthy," naturalistic interpretation of the divine in which the dualism of body and spirit, nature and transcendence, female and male are overcome.[43] In her words, "The God/ess who is the foundation of our being — new being does not lead us back to a stifled, dependent self or uproot us in a spirit-trip outside the earth. Rather it leads us to the converted center, the harmonization of self and body, self and other, self and world."[44] In this vision of God/ess, the ideas of the separate, isolate self and the "soluble" non-self are rejected as the only options and replaced by the relational interpretation of God and world.

The recent work of theologian, Sallie McFague, also moves in this direction. While insistent upon the metaphorical nature of God-talk, she nonetheless argues for the greater appropriateness of certain metaphors for our nuclear era. In particular, she argues for images that find persistent echoes in the work of Charles Hartshorne — the world as God's body; God as lover, mother, friend.[45] In each instance, her metaphors point to the relational quality of life and embody values of inclusiveness, non-dualism, mutuality, reciprocity and responsibility. Moreover, she argues that not only are these metaphors more adequate, albeit metaphorical, expressions of our contemporary experience, they are also more conducive to our survival in this nuclear age. She contends that the notions of a transcendent, omnipotent deity and a substantialist, independent self have not only issued forth in the oppression of women but in fact have brought us to the brink of the nuclear abyss.

With this assertion that the transcendent God of the tradition and its mirror-image, the autonomous self, have contributed to the threat of nuclear annihilation, McFague and other critics of classical theism are making an interesting claim. It is that the omnipotent God, in whose name was promised final victory, cannot save us from ourselves and that indeed, it has been the idealization and worship of non-relational power that have brought us to this time and place; that which promised salvation instead has brought death.

If the idea of a relational and radically inclusive God, articulated by feminist and process thinkers, does not issue forth in the same oppression and dangers to life as the traditional notion of God, neither can it offer its own version of the traditional promise of victory over evil. For such a promise was predicated upon the existence of the omnipotent Being who created, sustained and fulfilled creaturely existence according to an irresist-able divine plan. With the departure of the omnipotent God goes the assurance that the triumph over evil will ever be complete. What does the loss of the traditional promise of the effectiveness of God's will suggest for peoples who struggle for liberation? Related to this concern is the issue of the purpose of God's relation with the world; can God be said to be on the side of the oppressed, and if so what does such partisanship mean for the quest for a just and equalitarian community? These questions are especially important in assessing the viability of the process idea of God. For process thinkers, including Hartshorne, have focused upon aesthetic categories, rather than moral ones, for interpreting how God relates to the world; God's principal aim in receiving the world into Godself is the intensification of aesthetic enjoyment. How does such a divine pursuit of aesthetic value fit with the partisan search for a just order?

Hartshorne's work suggests several responses to such concerns. First, he insists that while aesthetic categories are more inclusive and hence more cosmically applicable, he does not see them in opposition to moral ones. According to the canons of Hartshorne's creationist metaphysics the primary aim of the process of synthesis and integration whereby reality comes into being is the actualization of beauty, the realization of the intensity and harmony in experience. But in a social universe where the richness of the experience of each depends upon others, the aim of *moral* action does not deny this aim toward the aesthetic good but seeks the realization of such value on increasingly wider scales. Hence, for Hartshorne, "*to be ethical is to seek aesthetic optimization for the community.*"[46] On a divine level this means that God, as the cosmic subject, seeks the optimization of experience for all creaturely reality whose richness of life in turn contributes to the depth of divine actuality.

Such divine purpose can be interpreted on several levels as a form of God's commitment to the pursuit of liberation. First, as was argued earlier, God's reception of the world into Godself is never mere repetition or retention. It is a creative — indeed evaluative process. God can thus be said not only to receive the world into Godself, but in such reception to judge the world as well. That is to say, the mode of God's self-constitution, as it seeks the greatest possible value, is a form of judgment on creaturely reality. Moreover, how God constitutes Godself determines how God will in turn, influence the world. Hence, it can be argued that in the gift of Godself to the world, God seeks universal value and opposes all that diminishes the richness of experience. On a human level, oppression must be understood as chief among those evils which inhibit the growth of value and, therefore, as that which God seeks to transform. Hence, although Hartshorne has not explicitly concentrated on the interconnection between God's pursuit of aesthetic value and a divine commitment to the transformation of oppression, I do think his construal of aesthetic value in social terms, his interpretation of God's receptive power as both creative and evaluative, and, finally, his understanding of God's self-constitution as the form of God's influence upon the world, interpreted as weighted in the direction of the universal increase of value, are all supportive of a view of a God who is not indifferent or unaffected by the realities of oppression and suffering in the creaturely order.

Indeed, in this Hartshornian vision, not only is God not indifferent to the world, but the richness of God's concrete life depends upon the realities of the creaturely realm. The content and quality of the divine experience depend upon the world as God's social partners. Hence, oppression and other forms of evil affect not only creatures but resound in God's life as well; oppression is not merely a form of rebellion against God's purposes, but the direct diminishing of God's very life. In Hartshorne's words, "Thus God has a destiny, things happen to him — not indeed from without but from within. He is tortured, not by himself, but by the creatures who, in injuring each other, in some degree or manner crucify deity itself."[47] Thus, it makes sense for Hartshorne to concur with his fellow process philosopher, Alfred North Whitehead that God is "the fellow sufferer who understands."

But if it is possible to argue that within the Hartshornian schema God can be interpreted as an opponent of oppression who suffers with creaturely reality and seeks to transform the world in a manner which enhances value for all, it is not possible to claim that this God can now or at a future time insure a complete triumph over oppression. A social universe, composed of multiple powers, is always at risk. Hartshorne's God is thus a companion in our suffering, and fellow struggler against evil who can nourish the possibilities of freedom and mitigate its negative consequences but who can never eliminate its risks. For, as Hartshorne states, "freedom is our opportunity and our tragic destiny."[48]

Hartshorne's message is a somber one, especially for oppressed persons. It suggests that change is always possible but success is never guaranteed. Such a position may not satisfy many who struggle against oppression. However, I, as one feminist, am absolutely convinced that if we reject the notion of an omnipotent deity we must as well forego the comfort of the *promise* of victory. There are, indeed, reasons for hope but it is a hope grounded in the fallibilities of a social universe, and finally shorn of the triumphalist confidence of classical theism.

V. CONCLUDING REMARKS

I believe it can be seen from the foregoing analysis that there are significant areas of agreement or at least resonance between Hartshorne's creationist metaphysics and certain elements emerging in feminist thought. Both share the rejection of the whole apparatus of Western thought and the common project of articulating an alternative worldview. In particular, Hartshorne's work and the general consensus among feminists points to the recognition that we cannot simply transfer the attributes of an oppressive deity to a now divinized humanity. Instead, thorough-going reconstructions of not only God, but of the self and history are required as well.

This essay has suggested possible directions for such reconstruction along the lines of a social interpretation of reality. There is, I believe, much promise in the work already accomplished. But much remains for future consideration. In particular, I believe that the proponents of a process vision must articulate more explicitly their understanding of God's relation to the political struggle of oppressed peoples. And I believe feminists and other liberationists must come to terms in a more adequate fashion with the recognition that in a social universe with a social God there is no promise that we will indeed overcome the realities of oppression. There is only the promise of the struggle. It is to these issues that I hope future conversation will turn.

NOTES

1. For the purposes of this essay, I have made reference to several common claims heard in liberation, black and feminist theology. While such general reference is justified, it is imperative to keep in mind that great differences exist among these groups and within them as well. Any easy assumption of commonality is inaccurate and inadequate to their distinctive concerns.
2. In this essay, I am concentrating upon the Christian theological schema. Moreover, while other frameworks have developed in the West, this article presupposes the dominance of Christianity in defining the "Western worldview" and hence identifies Western and Christian for the purposes of this essay.
3. Juan Luis Segundo, *Our Idea of God* (Maryknoll, NY: Orbis Books, 1974) p. 8.
4. Sallie McFague, in *Models of God* (Philadelphia: Fortress Press, 1987) p. 97, stresses that it is not just the presence of male metaphors but the *absence* of female images for the divine that is so problematic.
5. Mary Daly, *Beyond God the Father* (Boston: Beacon Press, 1973) p. 19.
6. This concern about obscuring the convictions embedded within our images for God is behind the dis-ease by many women at the attempt to translate male language about God, found in traditional sources such as the Bible, into gender neutral or more inclusive terminology. Such translation does not resolve the questions of the male character of the classical God but often hides what is really at stake.
7. While I agree with Sallie McFague concerning the strategic importance of developing new metaphors, I think that it is imperative that the presuppositions "behind" these images be made clear and fully developed.
8. Thomas J. J. Altizer, *The Descent into Hell* (New York: Seabury Press, 1979) p. 183.
9. Mark C. Taylor, *Erring* (Chicago: The University of Chicago Press, 1987) p. 13.

74

10. Gustavo Gutierrez, *The Power of the Poor in History* (Maryknoll, NY: Orbis Press, 1983) p. 92.
11. *Ibid.*, p. 93.
12. Cornel West, *Prophesy Deliverance* (Philadelphia: Westminster Press, 1982).
13. Mark Taylor, in *Erring*, portrays the modern era, with the death of God and the elevation of the human-male-self, as a drama of patricide.
14. The current nuclear threat gives credence to the claim that the death of the transcendent God without a complimentary "deconstruction" of the autonomous self has led us to the brink of disaster.
15. There is considerable question about how far process thinkers have engaged the post-modern critique of foundationalism and the correspondence theory of truth. Many process thinkers, and especially Charles Hartshorne, appear to assume a good deal about reason and nature of knowledge that has long been under attack elsewhere. Thus, while the alternative process views of God and self seem ready places for dialogue with other opponents of classical theism, the status of such views is matter of an as yet unsettled debate.
16. Charles Hartshorne, *Reality as Social Process* (New York: Hafner Publishing Company, 1971), p. 164, hereafter cited as *RSP*. Much of this section follows closely my book on Karl Barth and Charles Hartshorne, *Divine Power* (Philadelphia: Fortress Press, 1986).
17. As was stated in note 15, such claims have long been criticized. See Nancy Frankenberry, *Religion and Radical Empiricism* (Albany, NY: State University of New York Press, 1987) for a process philosophy that seeks to avoid both foundationalism and the correspondence theory of truth.
18. Hartshorne, *Creative Synthesis and Philosophic Method* (LaSalle, Ill.: Open Court, 1970) pp. 22, 27. Hereafter cited as *CSPM*.
19. Hartshorne, "Philosophy of Creative Synthesis," *The Journal of Philosophy* 55 (22) (October, 1958) p. 948.
20. Hartshorne, *CSPM*, pp. 128—129.
21. Hartshorne, *The Logic of Perfection and Other Essays in Neoclassical Metaphysics* (LaSalle, Ill.: Open Court, 1962) p. 149. Hereafter cited as *LP*.
22. Hartshorne, *Whitehead's Philosophy: Selected Essays, 1935—1970* (Lincoln, Nebraska: University of Nebraska Press, 1972) p. 175. Hereafter cited as *WP*.
23. *Ibid.*, p. 132; *CSPM*, pp. 1—3.
24. Hartshorne, *RSP*, p. 70; *CSPM*, pp. 141—2.
25. Hartshorne, "Process and the Nature of God," *Traces of God in a Secular Culture*, George F. McLean (ed.) (Staten Island, NY: Alba House, 1973) p. 134.
26. Hartshorne, *A Natural Theology for Our Time* (LaSalle, Ill.: Open Court, 1965) p. 120. Hereafter cited as *NTOT*.
27. Hartshorne, *WP*, p. 184.
28. Hartshorne, *Man's Vision of God and the Logic of Theism* (Hampden, Connecticut: Archon Books, 1964) pp. 105, 273.
29. See Davaney, *Divine Power*, pp. 151—164.
30. Hartshorne, *WP*, p. 74.
31. Charles Hartshorne and W. L. Reese (ed.), *Philosophers Speak of God* (Chicago: University of Chicago Press, 1953) pp. 18—19. Hereafter cited as *PSG*.
32. Hartshorne, "Interrogation of Charles Hartshorne," in *Philosophical Interrogations*, Sydney and Beatrice Rome (eds.) (New York: Holt, Rinehart and Winston, 1964) p. 331.
33. Hartshorne, *RSP*, pp. 143—44; *WP*, p. 110.
34. Hartshorne, *NTOT*, p. 13; *CSPM*, pp. 262—63.
35. Hartshorne, "Divine Absoluteness and Divine Relativity," in *Transcendence*, Herbert W. Richardson and Donald R. Cutler (eds.) (Boston: Beacon Press, 1969) p. 166.
36. Hartshorne, "A New Look at the Problem of Evil," in *Current Philosophical Issues: Essays in Honor of Curt John Ducasses*, Frederick C. Dommeyer (eds.) (Springfield, Ill.: Charles Thomas, Publisher, 1966) p. 208.

37. See Davaney, "Feminism, Process Thought and the Wesleyan Tradition," in *Wesleyan Theology Today*, Theodore Runyon (ed.) (Nashville, Tenn: Kingswood Books, 1985), for a discussion of these debates.
38. Carol Gilligan, *In a Different Voice* (Boston: Beacon Press, 1982).
39. *Ibid.*, p. 173.
40. Robin Morgan, "Monster," *Monster* (New York: Vintage Books, 1972) p. 85.
41. Bell Hooks, *Feminist Theory* (Boston: South End Press, 1984).
42. Catherine Keller, *From a Broken Web* (Boston: Beacon Press, 1986), esp. Ch. 4.
43. Rosemary Radford Ruether, *Sexism and God-Talk* (Boston: Beacon Press, 1983) pp. 68—71.
44. *Ibid.*, pp. 70—71.
45. McFague, *Models of God*, esp. Chs. 3, 4, 5, 6.
46. Hartshorne, "Beyond Enlightened Self-Interest," in *Religious Experience and Process Theology*, Harry James Cargas and Bernard Lee (eds.) (New York: Paulist Press, 1976) p. 318.
47. Hartshorne, *PSG*, p. 210.
48. Hartshorne, *LP*, p. 14.

5. Religion, God and Indian Thought

I am grateful to the editor of this volume being published to honor Professor Charles Hartshorne for inviting me to contribute to it. It is my privilege to join this chorus of tributes to a thinker and writer who is justly considered a leading luminary in the world of philosophy of religion. Anyone who is acquainted with Professor Hartshorne's writings does not have to be convinced of his earnestness in thinking out ways and means of stating philosophically the nature of God, in relation to man and the world. He is a seeker of the truth and even if he is not a mystic, it is certain his intelligence has that clarity which is capable of reflecting the truth in his mind.

Professor Hartshorne is a humble man whose humility is genuine in that though he is full of confidence in his philosophical ability, he is never dogmatic. I know from personal experience that he very patiently hears out other people's comments on his ideas and arguments even when these are attempts to demolish them. This, to my mind, is a great quality in a philosopher.

This article will be a brief exposition of Professor Hartshorne's concepts of religion and God. It is well known that religion does not mean the same thing to everybody. Professor Hartshorne has a distinct idea of the nature of religion. Whether that idea is comprehensive enough to include the great religions of the world will be critically examined. I will also briefly look at Professor Hartshorne's concepts of God and review it in the light of a few strands of Indian thought on the ultimate reality. If I may anticipate a little, it will be found that his concept of God is not absent in some Indian philosophies of religion. It must however be pointed out that the Indians' ideas do not completely agree with those of Professor Hartshorne's. The difference is not so much one of substance as one of emphasis. It will be seen that except for one extreme philosophy of the supreme reality in India, most other doctrines will be found to agree with Professor Hartshorne's stress on the presence of God in the world though Indian thought emphasizes the transcendence of the Deity.

Professor Hartshorne himself has said that his fundamental ideas on religion have been shaped by his upbringing in a family in his younger days

S. Sia (ed.), Charles Hartshorne's Concept of God, 77–87.
© 1990 Kluwer Academic Publishers. Printed in the Netherlands.

which was deeply Christian. In his philosophy of religion, as it is well known, he has rejected what he considers as limitations of the concept of God in classical theism. It will not be wrong to say that his idea of religion is rooted in the Judeo-Christian tradition, but that his philosophy of religion has been nurtured by his deep and life-long study of the great systems of the doctrine of God current in the Western world. He is primarily a philosopher and despite his many references to God and other topics in certain Indian philosophies of religion, he is not a comparative religionist. Nevertheless, his concept of God cannot be dissociated from his idea of the essence of religion. Indeed it is true to say that what he thinks is the nature of religion has influenced his concept of God. A comparative review of his thought on some Indian doctrines of religion and of God as indicated above will show that his own thinking on the subject is not unknown to Indian philosophers of religion and theologists.

This is not to deny his originality but is an attempt to show that serious and earnest philosophical thinking runs on parallel lines in different countries and climes and ages. Philosophy is one fundamentally though extremely varied even as God is One with many aspects. On this idea that God though One has many aspects we shall say little more later.

Professor Hartshorne has said that in order to find out the religious idea of God we must go to religion itself. Whatever philosophical formulation is made of the concept of God, religion is the primary source for discovering that idea. Religion is experiential and intuitive. There are such things as religious experience and religious intuition. Experience and intuition of a religious kind are pre-philosophical. Professor Hartshorne believes that religion and philosophy have influenced each other, a fact which is recognised but not yet admitted. It is difficult to disentangle the pre-philosophical elements of religion. Indeed Professor Hartshorne holds that religion becomes mature after the development of philosophy. Nevertheless, he states that religion still has to be the source of our knowledge of the idea of God.

What does maturity of religion mean? Is it that religion becomes intellectually mature or that religious experience and intuition become deeper and more capable of knowing more of the mystery of the Divine Being? Religious experience is a developing process and with the progressive practice of psychological disciplines, a religious seeker can have a deeper, clearer and more comprehensive experience of the truth of the Spirit and its relation with the world and man. It can also give us a wider and maturer knowledge of morals, both individual and collective and of the destiny of man. A religious aspirant *qua* religious aspirant does not need to formulate his experiences and intuitions logically. This raises the difficult question of the nature of religious experience, whether or not it has any truth-claim. Professor Hartshorne says that religious experience does not *prove* (emphasis mine) the existence of God. To prove is an intellectual exercise. Religious experience, according to those who have them, carries its own evidence. In fact, it may be said that all experience does so. I do not have to prove to myself logically that I am seeing the desk in front of me. The seeing of it is sufficient proof for me of the existence of the desk that I am in direct contact with through my eyes. It is only when a second experience shows the previously experienced object to be something else that it raises a doubt in my mind. I have then to think out what it was that my previous experience showed me and how it is that I am now seeing the same thing as a different object. There is no suggestion that all experiences are valid. Nevertheless, when an experience occurs, it carries its self-evidence and it is only when a subsequent experience contradicts it that the question of a logical consideration of the two experiences arises.

The same idea of self-evidence can be applied to religious experience. Of course it must be made clear what is meant by religious experience. Many people see visions and hear voices. But there are visions and visions, voices and voices. Some of them may be authentic, revealing some truth of the nature of the world or of the Deity. Many, if not most of them, are not genuine and many be, often are, suggestions thrown up by a person's own subconscience. But there are other religious experiences, of peace, power, delight which are revelatory of the nature of the spiritual reality. Of course, these experiences also can be deepened, widened and heightened. And some of these experiences reveal different aspects of the same spiritual reality. It is not that a particular religious seeker will have all these experiences. He may have an undisturbed calm and peace but may not have the experience of uncaused spiritual delight. He may see God as a sheer transcendent reality having no relation with the world, — a possibility that Professor Hartshorne not only does not approve of but also will not admit as a plausible experience. Nevertheless, countless religious seekers coming from different cultural backgrounds and religious traditions have had this experience and others still have it. At the same time God can be directly felt as immanent in the world, not only as a Presence but also as a Power sustaining its existence. These are some of the experiences which ar the stuff of religion. And a religious seeker who is interested in attaining his spiritual goal does not care for philosophical formulation or logical proof of *what he knows* by direct intuition and experience of the ultimate, or even, in some experiences, of the only reality. He may wish to describe his experience, he may even want to formulate it philosophically. But then he is not only a religious person but a philosopher as well.

Professor Hartshorne is absolutely right in saying that there is a need of philosophical formulation of religious experience. As I understand it, man's consciousness is extremely complex. And in his religious quest it is the same consciousness which is applied to the development of religious intuition and experience. Not only the followers of the primitive religions but also those of the great civilized religions are not free from the mixed character of human consciousness. And man is also preeminently a mental being, a thinker in his external organized nature. Even if he is primarily interested in his religious evolution, he cannot entirely avoid pondering over the significance and value of his intuitions and experiences. But this only helps the clarity of his mind and the ability to interpret his intuitions and experiences, which in its turn assists his growth in consciousness. However, it cannot be gainsaid that a certain religious experience can be broadened and deepened by another religious experience and not by any philosophical consideration and examination. What he knows by non-intellectual means can be given intellectual form by philosophy. Religion enormously gains by clarity of thought, yet its ultimate appeal is to experience.

Professor Hartshorne considers worship to be the essence of religion. God is supremely worshipful and man's approach to him is by means of worship. Professor Hartshorne believes that the centrality of worship can be shown by a study of Judaism, Christianity, some phases of Hinduism and Buddhism, and Zoroastrianism. He also finds evidence of it in the inscriptions of Ikhnaton. The phases of Hinduism and Buddhism are not identified by him. It is true of Hinduism but certainly not of original Buddhism. Buddha did not believe in God, and did not consider himself a divine being. Early Buddhism required austere self-help. The aspirant of Nirvana was not to depend on anyone, not even on Buddha for progress in his religious life. The story is well known that at the time of his demise his disciples were shedding bitter tears at the prospect of the impending separation from their Master. Buddha is reported to have advised them not to give way to weakness and delusion, asked them whether they had forgotten all his teachings about the transitory nature of all things, and then told them to be lamps unto themselves and their own refuge. Mahayana Buddhism may be said to have brought into Buddhism an element of devotion and worship. It is certainly true that as Buddhism travelled outside India, the Buddha was deified and worshipped. Professor Hartshorne may not wish to call early Buddhism a religion because of the absence of worship in it. But then some other designation should be invented for it.

I think it can be said that all phases of Hinduism include worship as an important element. The Vedanta of Shankara may seem to be an exception to this. But whatever his metaphysics may be, as far as religious life is concerned, Shankara emphasized worship of the Saguna Brahman who is full of auspicious qualities. In fact, his Vedanta even says that without the grace of Ishwara, personal Lord or the qualified Brahman, liberation is not possible. True that liberation is freedom from the wrong sense of the separation of Jiva, individual soul, from Brahman, and is the *anubhava*, direct experience, of their identity. Let students of non-dualistic Vedanta of Shankara consider whether giving a place to worship and devotion in the religious life of the seeker is logically consistent with his metaphysics. After all, the qualified Brahman is a reflection in Maya of the unqualified Brahman which is the sole reality. In other words, the qualified Brahman is not really real. Nevertheless, it is the considered judgment of non-dualistic Vedanta that the seeker has to concentrate exclusively on the Lord, the Saguna or qualified Brahman because it helps him to take his attention away from the unreal world of many and facilitates concentration on the idea 'I am Brahman' the maturity of which leads to liberation. This exclusive concentration helps him to reject his identification with body, life, senses, mind, intelligence, the separative ego-sense which is indispensable to preliminary deep meditation on the identity of the individual self and the absolute Self or Brahman and the concentration on Ishwara includes the sentiment of devotion and the practice of worship. Professor Hartshorne perhaps will not consider worship in non-dualistic Vedanta as genuine. However, practical religious psychology shows that even the imagined mercifulness and grace of the Lord helps the seeker to attain the state of mind which enables him to prepare for liberation.

All other systems of Indian spiritual philosophy and religion give a high place to worship. It may be interesting to note here that the monistic philosophies based on the Tantric tradition have a very special idea of worship. The individual self and the world are real. But both are results of self-limitation by Shiva, the absolute Self. In so far as the individual self is concerned, it is the Absolute under limitation by self-contraction or self-concealment but in essence it is that Reality. In its religious discipline, worship plays a very important part. But the worship is given — and this may appear not only paradoxical but also blasphemous to a Christian-oriented temperament — by the individual self to its own absolute unlimited essence and not to another reality. In this system the destiny of the individual self is recognition of itself as the Absolute. It blends devotion and knowledge, religion and metaphysics in a fine harmony.

In appears that Professor Hartshorne's idea of religion is exclusive in that it leaves out some of the great religions from its scope. I suggest that religion may be defined as pursuit of a supreme value, something that is considered to be the highest and the best thing to be realized. As the Bhagavad-Gita puts it, the supreme value is that "attaining which nothing else is adjudged more and better than it, and established in which one is not perturbed by the fiercest assault of grief." Admittedly different people have different ideas about the supreme value. It may be identity with the Absolute, union with God, separation of the spiritual self, Purusha, from the unconscious Nature, Prakriti, dwelling in the Supreme Impersonal-Personal God with utter devotion, love and adoration for him and working as an instrument of him in this world for the maintenance of the world and its progress. This last notion, union with the Supreme in all ways — works, knowledge and love — is the *summum bonum* according to the Bhagavad-Gita. But what is common to all of these religious ideals is the sense of the seeker on the different paths, that they are pilgrims in quest of the supreme value, supreme according to their respective ideas of the reality.

Professor Hartshorne is a process philosopher. One of the most important doctrines of process philosophy is this, that God is not only outside the world, detached and aloof from it, but also is immanent in it and in intimate connection with the world-process. Indeed he is himself in the process of fulfillment here. That the world is a process need not be pointed out. It is a movement and nothing in it is unmoving. Professor Hartshorne argues that

God is most worthy of worship, for if he were not so, worship would not be offered to him. We have seen that according to him worship is the essence of religion. And God is unsurpassable in worshipfulness. But he is not, says Professor Hartshorne, impassible. He is very much in relation with his creatures, caring, loving, even suffering with them. If he were impassible he could not have this characteristic. God is not impervious to change. If a devotee is suffering, that makes God sympathise with him, excites in him emotion, causes him to console and succour the helpless and hapless. Thus, it is maintained by Professor Hartshorne that God is subject to change.

Indian thought is in complete agreement with Western process philosophy that the world is process. The Sanskrit word for world is *jagat*, which is derived from the root *gam*, 'to go'. The Isha Upanishad described all this, the whole phenomenal world as the world of individual motion in the world of universal motion. All things are 'going', *jagat* is the term employed, in *jagati*, universal going or moving. Where the Upanishad differs from process philosophy is that it says all this phenomenal movement and all things in it are for the habitation by the Lord who is not a phenomenon in the universal motion but its unmoving source in his essence. This does not mean that he is not change either. The same Upanishad also says that he really knows who knows That, the Self, the Lord, as both becoming and not-becoming, *sambhūti* and *asambhūti* respectively. Sambhuti is from the root *bhu* which always has the sense of 'becoming'. The *a* in the second term is privative or negative. So the Lord is non-becoming, Being, who is also Becoming. Aristotle's God is the unmoved Mover. The God of the Veda, the Upanishads and the Bhagavad-Gita is at the same time unmoved Mover and self-moving. It is said over and over again in these scriptures that God became, *abhavat*, all things. Process philosophy holds that there is no substance underlying the world process. If substance in this context means permanent, then this is simply not true. Whitehead holds the view that in one aspect God is unchanging and also that there is nothing permanent or substantial underlying the world. This would imply that the unchanging God is not in the world. But change has no meaning except its reference to something unchanging. At least according to Upanishadic Vedanta the Eternal Reality is at the core of everything transitory and ephemeral. The idea that God is immanent in the world movement and is himself that movement is as old as the Vedas as well as the idea that he is transcendent of all movement and process.

Western scholars have branded Vedic and Upanishadic thought as pantheism. This idea is only partially correct. For God is also transcendent of the world. It is true that God is all that has become and all that will become, but he also remained and always remains beyond the universe in his essential being. As the Veda puts it, God transcended the world by 'ten fingers.' This phrase is admittedly figurative. But the idea that of which it is a figure is quite plain. While 'all this is Brahman' according to the Upanishad, he is also 'not this, not this'. The doctrine of God in the Vedas, the Upanishads and the Bhagavad-Gita subtly harmonizes both classical and non-classical theism, pantheism and transcendentalism. The Bhagavad-Gita speaks of One — but triple — Purusha. One is the mutable spirit and is in the flux of the world, the second the immutable spirit, inactive but supporting the world process by its very presence but not involved in it, and the third and the supreme Spirit synthesizes in his being both status and dynamism, and is seated in the heart of all creatures.

The monistic systems of philosophy belonging to the Tantric tradition also are at one with the Vedic doctrine that God is both transcendent of and immanent in the world. Indeed, God is not immanent in the world, he is the world. It is his Shakti, conscious creative Power — Shakti is derived from the root *sak* meaning ability, capacity, force, energy — that has become the world whose material is God. Indeed God has an innate sense of 'I', a sense of identity with everything that he has become. This 'I' is not the separative ego-sense but the transcendent-immanent self-sense of God as identical with all and precisely because of the identity with everything, not confined cribbed and cabined in anything. If God is *sat*, Being, he is also *sakti*, force of Becoming. Everything is a concentration of Force manifesting the Master of Force.

Thus we see that process thought is not unknown to the Vedas, the Upanishads, the Bhagavad-Gita and the Tantric philosophies. But what is not known to Western process thought is that the ultimate Reality is not only Becoming but also Being in the heart of Becoming and unlike Whitehead's God, he is not a creature subject to Creativity but the Creator, the Lord of Creativity.

In our own day Sri Aurobindo (1872—1950), a Vedantin and not a Tantric, has developed an evolutionary philosophy of God. The supreme Absolute is unknowable by discursive intellectual thought but is self-aware and self-knowing, manifests itself to awakened human consciousness as Being-Consciousness — Consciousness-Force — Delight which may in relation to the world be described as God. God is self-luminous. Consciousness here does not stand for mental intelligence which is only one level of consciousness. Indeterminable, God has the inherent power of self-determination, self-limitation and self-absorption. Creation is both a self-concealing and a self-manifestation of God. It is the result of progressive descent of Consciousness till it reaches the state of the Inconscient which is a hood and mask of consciousness but not showing any sign of it. Evolution is the progressive manifestation of consciousness and is described as its ascent. Evolution has manifested Matter, Life and Mind, in the world. Mind, the crown of creation now, however, is not the summit of evolution. It is only an instrument for seeking knowledge which it does not possess. It has been said before that God is self-aware and self-knowing; Self-awareness of God is pure Consciousness and uncreative. God's self-knowledge is a result of a movement of Consciousness. The self-knowledge of God is creative and is called the supermind by Sri Aurobindo. It is the integral Knowledge-Will of the Divine by which he knows himself and also the world which is his self-expression and the effect of his conscious Will. Mind is not the perfect instrument of God's unveiled manifestation in the world. To that overt revelation of Divine consciousness in the world the creation is moving and evolution is manifesting the perfect instrument of it which is the Supermind, the integral and infallible Knowledge-Will of creative God. Man can co-operate with this process of the Divine's progressive revelation in the world. In him evolution has become a conscious process. But it is not fully conscious because Mind is not the highest power of Consciousness. Therefore Sri Aurobindo says that the supermind must be manifested, must evolve here in the world as the instrument of realizing God's purpose in the world.

In Sri Aurobindo's philosophy God has three statuses: transcendental, universal and individual. Despite his self-manifestation effected by God for the sheer delight of becoming, he always remains immutably self-existent beyond the manifestation. He is at the same time All and yet more than All. The individual is in manifestation a distinct center of God's action but is one in the essence of its being with the Deity. According to Sri Aurobindo, individuality is the result of a movement of the Divine Being and Consciousness. He describes it as the Divine as the individual, and also as the individual Divine. In the universe it is the pivot of evolution through which the universe grows progressively conscious. To fulfill God in life is man's manhood, which is also God's self-fulfillment in Nature. "In the conscious individual," writes Sri Aurobindo, "Prakriti (Nature) turns back to perceive Purusha (conscious Soul), World seeks after Self; God having entirely become Nature, Nature seeks to become progressively God."[1]

From another point of view, Brahman the Absolute has three aspects — Atman or Self, Purusha or Conscious Being and Soul, and Ishwara, God the Lord and Master of creation. Self is passive and silent and its Power is the conceptive conscious Maya and it supports creation by its presence, Soul sanctions creation and its power is the conscious executive Prakriti whose creation it enjoys, Ishwara is the freely active controller of the creative process and his Power is the conscious Shakti who is at the same time conceptive, executive and creative. Ishwara is the harmony of Self and Purusha. Though creative, he is free from creation, free to create and free in creation. Thus it can be seen that God is the Stable Master of Process — Sri Aurobindo speaks of the procession of God — and Process itself. Nevertheless, he is in his essential being beyond all process which proceeds from him and in which he is immanent and the inner truth of everything, progressively revealing himself while remaining always that which is transcendent of Being and Becoming. The idea that God is free from creation and free in creation also may perhaps be compared to Professor Hartshorne's concept of the double transcendence of God.

Sri Aurobindo emphatically rejects the idea of what he designates as extra-cosmic God by which he means a Deity who has created the world outside of his being and exists apart from it. He expounds the concept of a supra-cosmic God who is transcendent of the world which nevertheless exists in him and in which he exists and moves. The idea of an extra-cosmic God, says Sri Aurobindo, raises insurmountable difficulties for the problem of evil. A God who creates a world and creatures in it, and also suffering and pain and evil to which they are helplessly subject is morally deficient and impotent. The supra-cosmic God not only suffers with his creatures, as Whitehead says, but also suffers in them.

But why pain and suffering and evil at all? Sri Aurobindo says that it must be recognized that evil is not a universal feature. Evil does not exist in the sub-human living world and certainly not in the inanimate world or what is apparently so. It belongs only to human existence and sensibility. Sri Aurobindo's solution of the problem of pain and suffering is briefly this. First, they are results of the loss of the sense of essential unity of all existence. It is based on a sense of duality and separation. Man feels that the forces of stimulation come from an other which he cannot receive in the right manner with the sense that they ultimately originate in God. Second, as one's consciousness, so one's power — for consciousness is power — and if man can raise the conscious power in him, he can lessen the feeling of physical pain and emotional suffering. This is certainly psychologically true. Space prevents us from discussing the problem of moral evil in the light of Sri Aurobindo's philosophy. Suffice it to say now that it is there because man lives in a divisive consciousness and not in the spiritual soul which has an innate sense of the good. The soul in man when fully evolved is supra-moral and supra-ethical, evil is a thing foreign to it.

While I am discussing some strands of Indian thought and pantheism, I may mention that even Shankara's philosophy has been mentioned as an example of pantheism in the book *Philosophers Speak of God*[2] by Charles Hartshorne and William A. Reese. This is not a correct description of the philosophy of the great Vedantin. There is not and there cannot be any doubt that he considered the world to be *mithyā*, false. Brahman without quality, features, attributes, space, time, causality and creative Power is the *sole* reality, and the world is a magical apparition which never *is* but always appears. The two statements that Brahman is one with the world and that the world is utterly unreal contradict each other. The two authors of the book mentioned above have taken the Saguna, or qualified Brahman of Shankara's philosophy as the real Brahman. They say that Brahman has knowledge which is not Shankara's idea of Brahman. The reality is *cit* (chit), Pure Consciousness which is not knowledge. Shankara does not admit any kind of dynamism in Brahman. There is no movement of consciousness and therefore there is no self-knowledge in Brahman which is also devoid of will. The Saguna or qualified Brahman is endowed with knowledge, will, features and creative Power which is Maya. But Maya is unconscious and mechanical Power and thus is absent in Brahman which is Pure self-luminous Consciousness. In his commentary on Brahma-sutra II.1.14, Shankara clearly says that omniscience, omnipotence etc. are attributed to Brahman only when it is considered as being in association with Maya. In itself Brahman is not omniscient or omnipotent. Shankara takes recourse to Saguna Brahman to explain the apparent order, system, rationality if you like, in the world. He found the Indian systems current in his time — Materialism, Nyaya, Sankhya, Yoga etc. — could not explain the evidence of the work of intelligence in the world and fell back upon the qualified Brahman as the fundamental principle of the process that the universe is. So far so good. But Shankara then examined the concept of qualified and creative Brahman and found it wanting as a logical account of true Reality and rejected it as real. The lower and empirically real but transcendentally unreal Brahman is only the reflection of the real Brahman, qualityless and passive, in Maya, the magical power "capable of accomplishing the unaccomplishable," *aghatana-ghatana-patiyasi*, that is to say, of perpetually making the world appear though it is never real. Brahman is the only reality. Thus Shankara is not a pantheist. Shankara himself says that space, time, causality, qualities, power are non-existent in Brahman and that as such Brahman might seem to be Shunya, Void. But he adds that Brahman is not Void but *sat*, mere Existence.

I must touch upon another point because Professor Hartshorne has discussed it and because it is very important. In his article "God of Philosophy And God of Religion"[3] he says that according to some religions human beings are immortal. Is there any religion which holds this doctrine? At least Hinduism does not do so. There is something in man which is immortal but that is not the natural man but the spiritual, self, *atman* in him. Man in the world is a combination of *atman* and non-*atman*, the latter comprising the physical body, vitality, the senses, sense-mind which co-ordinates the function of the senses, the intelligence and the separative ego-sense which persuades man that his true being is not the self but that he is a complex of body etc. The natural constituents of man's worldly existence are ephemeral and subject to decay, disintegration and dissolution. Death is the lot of the natural human personality. But the self which may be termed the real Man is unborn, immortal and free from the defects of the natural elements of man's worldly being. Christian anthropology came to believe in the immortality of the soul only after its contact with Greek philosophy. Even then the soul is not deemed indestructible in principle but is said to be kept in existence by God because he created it and saw that it was good. There is in Christianity no concept corresponding to atman in Hindu religious thought. *Psuché* in St. Paul's writings is only the animating principle of the body which corresponds to *prána* or vitality of Hindu thought. He says that *pneuma*, spirit, is another aspect of man's personality. However, he points out that it is not the same as the Spirit of God. There is nothing in man which is of the same essence and nature of God. The individual atman according to the Upanishads and the Bhagavad-Gita is of the same nature as that of God, the same in essence as God, the Supreme Self, that is to say, the individual self is also unborn, undying and perfect. But it is not true that Hinduism holds the doctrine that human beings are immortal.

Professor Hartshorne says that God includes everything which is one of the ideas of God held by Ramanuja on whose philosophy he has written an excellent book entitled *The Divine Relativity*.[4] God creates the world in his own being and this includes the creation in it. This is one of the ideas of God found in the Upanishads, the Gita and other realistic monistic schools of Vedanta and also the monistic and realistic systems of thought arising from the Tantras as has been shown above. But it is not the only relation conceived of God and the world in Vedanta and Tantra. The relation between God and the world cannot be described in terms of a single pattern, the Divine being indeterminable though capable of self-determination. Sri Aurobindo calls his philosophy integral spiritual idealism. In his comprehensive knowledge of the ultimate Reality "God or Para Purusha (the supreme Person) is Parabrahman (the supreme Absolute) unmanifest and inexpressible and turned towards a certain kind of manifestation or expression of which the two eternal terms are Atman and Jagati, Self and the Universe. Atman becomes in self-symbol all existences in the universe; so also the universe when known, resolves all its symbols into Atman. God being Parabrahman is Himself Absolute, neither Atman nor Maya nor un-Atman, neither Being nor not-being, (*sat, asat*), neither Becoming nor non-Becoming (*sambhúti, asambhúti*), neither Quality nor non-Quality (*saguna, nirguna*), neither Consciousness nor non-Consciousness (*caitanya, jaḍa*); neither Soul nor Nature (*puruṣa, prakṛti*), neither Bliss nor non-Bliss; neither man nor God nor animal; He is beyond all these things. He maintains and contains all these things in himself as world; He is and becomes all these things."[5]

NOTES

1. *The Life Divine*, Sri Aurobindo Birth Centenary Library, Vol. XVIII, p. 45.
2. (University of Chicago, 1976), p. xiii and pp. 169—177.
3. *Talk of God: Royal Institute of Philosophy Lectures*. Vol. II, 1967—68 (Macmillan, 1969), pp. 152—167.
4. (Yale University Press, 1948).
5. "The Hour of God," *SABCL*, XVII, p. 68.

6. The World: Body of God or Field of Cosmic Activity?

JOSEPH BRACKEN

Certainly one of the more widely quoted and therefore influential articles written by Charles Hartshorne in the course of his illustrious career has been "The Compound Individual," originally composed for a Festschrift in honor of Alfred North Whitehead in 1936.[1] Therein Hartshorne reviewed the history of Western metaphysics on the key issue of substance or individuality and concluded that Whitehead alone had found a way to explain how organisms can be composed of much smaller entities (e.g., cells or, smaller yet, atoms) and still exist as functioning individuals in their own right. Organisms are colonies or societies of actual occasions "interlocked with other such individuals into societies of societies" so as to constitute the macroscopic realities of common sense experience.[2] Some of these structured societies, to be sure, do not possess a dominant subsociety which coordinates the activities of all the other subsocieties. But all higher-order animal species with central nervous system and brain clearly do give evidence of the presence and activity of a dominant subsociety of actual occasions to unify and coordinate bodily functions. Moreover, says Hartshorne at the end of the article, the God-world relationship may be explained in similar fashion. That is, God and the world are a compound individual, with God acting as the mind or soul of the world, and the world as the body of God. Thus, just as cells within the human body are substantial entities in their own right and yet under the direction of the soul make up a single macroscopic individual, so human beings and all other finite entities under God's unifying activity make up a single cosmic organism at any given moment.

Hartshorne expanded upon this organismic model for the God-world relationship some years later in *Man's Vision of God*.[3] While freely admitting that no analogy drawn from human experience will ever perfectly satisfy the requirements for such an intangible and all-comprehensive relationship, he still maintained that, just as the human mind is on a feeling-level in touch with the various organs of its body and exercises some measure of control over their proper functioning, so in a much more eminent way God may be said to know, control and suffer with the finite entities making up the world at any given moment.[4] Moreover, just as individual organs (still less, cells)

90

within the human body do not normally resist the unifying and directive activity of the mind, so, too, human beings and other finite entities within the universe should not resent the presence and activity of the divine mind in their midst. Even more than the human mind with respect to its bodily organs, God suffers with all creatures in bringing their otherwise disconnected activities into the unity of a cosmos, an integrated whole.

Many distinguished Whiteheadians have followed Hartshorne in accepting this organismic understanding of the God-world relationship. Schubert Ogden, for example, in his influential essay "The Reality of God" notes that God "is related to the universe of other beings somewhat as the human self is related to its body."[5] He immediately adds, however, that while the human self "interacts with little more than its own brain cells, and so is always a localized self, limited by an encompassing external environment," God as the pre-eminent Self interacts immediately and directly with every finite entity, hence, "can never be localized in any particular space and time but is omnipresent."[6] John Cobb in *A Christian Natural Theology* calls attention to the fact that this way of interpreting the God-world relationship (and, even more so, the relationship between body and soul within human beings and other higher-order animals) is not directly Whiteheadian but derivative from Hartshorne; at the same time, he believes that it provides a coherence and consistency lacking in Whitehead's own somewhat ambiguous remarks on these important topics.[7]

It seems safe to say, then, that the organismic understanding of the God-world relationship is the preferential way to deal with that all-important topic within process-relational metaphysics. Yet the burden of this essay will be to challenge that "received" interpretation and to offer another in its place for two reasons. First of all, it is difficult to accommodate traditional Christian belief in God as triune to the organismic model of the God-world relationship; God, in other words, appears to be necessarily unipersonal rather than triune if God is to relate to the world as the soul to the human body. Admittedly, this first reason is not in itself probative since there are many ways to understand the triune reality of God, some of which merely emphasize the tridimensionality or threefold functioning of a basically unipersonal God.[8] But, if one chooses to regard "Father," "Son" and "Holy Spirit" of traditional Christian theology as somehow distinct personalities within the unity of one God, then the body-soul analogy for the God-world relationship clearly does not work. Secondly, and much more importantly, however, I am challenging this model of the God-world relationship because it both reflects and to some extent reinforces what I regard as a partly erroneous conception of the nature and function of Whiteheadian societies. Furthermore, given what I consider to be the more accurate understanding of this key notion of society, a much more explicit trinitarian understanding of God within process-relational metaphysics immediately becomes possible.

The principal purpose of these reflections, then, is to defend a trinitarian understanding of God in process-relational terms. For, while one does not have to justify the central position of the doctrine of the Trinity within Christian belief, one is obliged continually to reinterpret it, render it intelligible, within the larger body of Christian doctrine and, indeed, within one's overall world view (in this case, process-relational metaphysics). At the same time, I also have in mind to set forth a new interpretation of Whitehead's doctrine of societies which will allow for a genuinely trinitarian understanding of God within the latter's philosophical scheme. In brief, I will be suggesting that Whiteheadian societies should be understood as structured environments or unified fields of activity for the emergence of successive generations of actual entities. While not themselves subjects of experience like their constituent actual entities, they are not simply aggregates in the classical sense but objective ontological unities of a higher order than their constituent occasions (even though they subsist only in and through the interrelated activity of those same occasions from moment to moment). With respect to the God-world relationship, this new understanding of Whiteheadian societies implies that the world is a cosmic field of activity brought into being and sustained in existence by constantly new generations of actual entities. The world itself, however, is contained within the even more comprehensive field of activity created by the dynamic interrelationship of the three divine persons to one another from all eternity.

Perhaps one final preparatory remark should be made before undertaking an analysis of Whitehead's doctrine of society. In *Man's Vision of God*, Hartshorne reminds his readers that the world is much more complex than sense perception would suggest: "the seeming solidarity of the body is an exaggeration of sense perception, due to the fact that perception is . . . on the macroscopic scale, while the real individuals in the body are microscopic." [9] What I am proposing here requires an even further leap of the imagination. For not only is the body to be understood as made up of individual entities smaller than itself; but these smaller individual entities (e.g., cells, molecules, even atoms) are themselves to be understood as hierarchically structured fields of activity for the energy-events (actual occasions) continuously taking place within them. Hence, the human body as a whole is a very complex field of activity within which the soul at any given moment is a single energy-event, albeit the key one since it contributes much more to the overall pattern for the field (the human body as a whole) than any of its contemporaries. Details of this scheme will be given below. Here it is only important to note how the common sense image of the body-soul relationship has disappeared in favor of a picture of energy-events being shaped by and in turn helping to shape an enormous number of interrelated and overlapping fields that alone perdure as the energy-events themselves come and go. Such a picture of reality may very well be what Whitehead intuitively grasped but only imperfectly expressed in words.

At this point we may profitably examine some of Whitehead's own comments on the nature and function of societies. In *Process and Reality* within the chapter entitled "The Order of Nature," he gives perhaps his most detailed analysis of the nature of a society. Noting that a society is "self-sustaining," he continues:

Thus a society is more than a set of entities to which the same class-name applies: that is to say, it involves more than a merely mathematical conception of 'order.' To constitute a society, the class-name has got to apply to each member, by reason of genetic derivation from other members of that same society. The members of the society are alike because, by reason of their common character, they impose on other members of the society the conditions which lead to that likeness.[10]

Specifying further what is meant by this "likeness," Whitehead states that "a certain element of form" is a "contributory component" to the satisfaction of each individual occasion within the society and that, when these occasions are objectified for prehension by their successors in the same society, that common element of form tends to be carried over into the satisfactions of these other members also. Thus the society provides its own "environment" for the perpetuation of its defining characteristic among successive generations of actual occasions.

Continuing this discussion of a society as "an environment with some element of order in it," Whitehead comments:

Every society must be considered with its background of a wider environment of actual entities, which also contribute their objectifications to which the members of the society must conform. . . . But this means that the environment, together with the society in question, must form a larger society in respect to some more general characters than those defining the society from which we started. Thus we arrive at the principle that every society requires a social background, of which it is a part.[11]

Societies, accordingly, should be seen as constituting "layers of social order" for their constituent actual entities. The broader, more elementary societies (e.g., the society of electromagnetic occasions) contain a minimum of order because they include virtually all actual occasions in existence at any given moment. The more restricted societies have a progressively more elaborate pattern of organization because they account for the conjunction of occasions to form, first, atoms, then molecules, cells, organs, entire organisms, communities and/or environments, etc.

Hence, even though actual entities "are the final real things of which the world is made up,"[12] societies as the progressive "layers of order" into which they are organized are clearly of equal importance for the self-constitution of the universe from moment to moment. For, without these structured environments for the emergence of subsequent generations of actual occasions, there would be no effective guarantee that the present and future would be continuous with the past. Change, to be sure, does take place as new generations of occasions subtly modify the structure or pattern of organization which they have inherited from their predecessors in the same society (societies). But such evolution of structure must be, especially at the inanimate level, very gradual if the cosmos is not to degenerate into chaos. Whitehead summarizes the reciprocal interaction of the society or "social environment" on the constituent occasions and vice-versa in the following manner:

> The causal laws which dominate a social environment are the product of the defining characteristic of that society. But the society is only efficient through its individual members. Thus, in a society, the members can only exist by reason of the laws which dominate the society, and the laws only come into being by reason of the analogous characters of the members of the society.[13]

In the above quotation, Whitehead states that a society is only efficient through its individual members. This very wording raises the question whether through the interrelated agencies of its individual members a society equivalently exercises a type of collective agency, at least the agency necessary to preserve the pattern of interaction for its constituent occasions from moment to moment and thus to assure its ongoing identity in space and time. This, of course, is a key point of difference between myself, on the one hand, and Hartshorne and Cobb, on the other. For they insist that, wherever individuality is present, it is due to the self-constituting activity of an actual occasion. Hence, if a nexus of actual occasions behaves as a unitary reality, then, a higher-order occasion must be present to exercise that measure of agency for its contemporaries within the nexus. As Cobb readily admits in "Overcoming Reductionism," this is not what Whitehead himself proposed in *Process and Reality*.[14] But it is consistent with Whitehead's statement elsewhere in *Process and Reality* that "agency belongs exclusively to actual occasions"[15] and it does circumvent the charge of reductionism (atomism) which Ivor Leclerc and others have leveled against Whitehead in the past.[16]

My own solution to this dilemma would be, on the contrary, to affirm with Whitehead that agency in the strict sense belongs exclusively to actual occasions, but also to claim that the effect of the interrelated agencies of the occasions within a society is to produce a collective agency necessary for the society to preserve its pattern of order or ongoing self-identity from moment to moment. By this I do not mean to say, however, that a society thus becomes a subject of experience capable of self-constitution through its own immanent "decision." Only actual entities are subjects of experience capable of such decisions. Where a given society appears to be a subject of experience (e.g., a human being or other higher-order animal), it is so only through its soul or dominant subsociety. A society composed of inanimate actual occasions, therefore, is not a subject of experience; but, in and through the interrelated agencies of its constituent occasions, it does exercise the collective agency necessary to preserve its own self-identity as an atom or molecule of a peculiar shape or consistency. It is not, in other words, a mere aggregate whose constituent occasions alone possess individuality and/or substantiality, as Hartshorne seems to claim.[17] It is rather a patterned environment or unified field of activity for the emergence of successive generations of actual occasions. As such, it is "self-sustaining; in other words, ... it is its own reason."[18]

Somewhat later in the same chapter on "The Order of Nature" in *Process and Reality*, Whitehead introduces the notion of a "structured" society, i.e., a society composed, not of actual occasions as such, but of subordinate societies and subordinate nexūs of occasions.[19] Subordinate societies are those which basically retain their distinctive self-identity within the larger structured society (like molecules within a cell); hence, they can survive the dissolution of the higher-order society. Subordinate nexūs, on the other hand, are groups of occasions whose character is derived exclusively from the role which they play in the structured society; hence, when and if that "level of social order" dissolves, they, too, go out of existence. This distinction between subordinate societies and subordinate nexūs of occasions within structured societies is extremely important for Whitehead's discussion of "living" societies a few pages later. For, according to Whitehead, a structured society is considered living if it contains a sufficient number of "living" actual occasions organized into spontaneous nexūs which are "regnant" over a much larger number of stable subsocieties of inanimate occasions.

The key point here, at least for our purposes, is that the structured society as a whole is alive because of the interrelated individual agencies of its constituent occasions. As Whitehead comments, "[a] complex inorganic system of interaction is built up for the protection of 'entirely living' nexūs, and the originative actions of the living elements are protective of the whole system. On the other hand, the reactions of the whole system provide the intimate environment required by the 'entirely living' nexūs."[20] In effect, then, the structured society in question (e.g., a cell) is alive in virtue of a collective agency derivative from the interrelated individual agencies of its constituent occasions. Some of these occasions are living; the great majority, however, are inanimate. But, in any case, there is no need to postulate the presence of a personally ordered subsociety of occasions (the equivalent of a primitive soul) to account for the life of the cell.

Commenting on this same passage in *Process and Reality*, John Cobb remarks: "Whitehead at that point was forced to explain the order in the cell in terms of its molecular structure, to which spontaneity was denied, and to explain the life of the cell in terms of the events in its empty space, which he depicted as radically unordered. It is hard to think that this combination can account for the type of order and the type of spontaneity actually exemplified in a cell."[21] On the contrary, given the presumption of a collective agency for the cell as a whole, it makes excellent sense to account for the stability of the cellular structure in terms of societies of inanimate actual occasions with their ongoing transmission of fixed patterns and for the vitality of the cell in terms of the nexūs of entirely living occasions with their higher degree of novelty and originality. The confluence of these two types of individual agencies produces the collective agency of the living cell as a whole. Cobb's difficulty with the passage, accordingly, is to be traced to his unquestioning acceptance of Hartshorne's earlier assumption that individuality and/or substantiality within societies of actual occasions can be accounted for only in terms of the agency of an individual dominant occasion, not the collective agency of the society as a whole.

In the final section of "The Order of Nature," Whitehead sets forth his analysis of structured societies with a regnant subsociety of personally ordered occasions (e.g., mind or soul in human beings and other higher-order animal organisms). For the purposes of this paper, it is especially important to note carefully what Whitehead says here since this special type of structured society implicitly serves as the paradigm for Hartshorne and Cobb in their understanding of all other kinds of structured societies. Whitehead begins thus:

> An 'entirely living' nexus [i.e., nexus of 'living' occasions] is, in respect to its life, not social. . . . But a living nexus, though non-social in virtue of its 'life,' may support a thread of personal order along some historical route of its members. Such an enduring entity is a 'living person.' It is not of the essence of life to be a living person. Indeed a living person requires that its immediate environment be a living, non-social nexus.[22]

Just as nexūs of living actual occasions, therefore, are reciprocally interrelated with a massive infrastructure of subsocieties of inanimate occasions, so a "living person," i.e., a personally ordered society of such living occasions, is reciprocally interrelated with an infrastructure of living occasions organized into one or more nexūs. Life in the form of living occasions, accordingly, must be present in abundance before the "thread of personal order" spoken of by Whitehead can initially arise and then survive. Still more importantly, however, the agency proper to the living person would likewise seem to be dependent upon the smooth functioning of the societies of inanimate occasions which provide the infrastructure for the living occasions. Even in this specialized case, then, it is the collective agency of the entire structured society which is at work here to support a "thread of personal order" among the living occasions. Put in other terms, the human being or higher-order animal organism is an ongoing subject of experience in and through its dominant subsociety of occasions; but the coordination therewith required to sustain the flow of consciousness can only be achieved through the collaboration of literally every occasion within the organism.

Whitehead himself seems to make the same point when he states a few paragraphs later:

> The living body is a coordination of high-grade actual occasions. . . . In a living body of a high type there are grades of occasions so coordinated by their paths of inheritance through the body, that a peculiar richness of inheritance is enjoyed by various occasions in some parts of the body. Finally, the brain is coordinated so that a peculiar richness of inheritance is enjoyed now by this and now by that part; and thus there is produced the presiding personality at that moment in the body.[23]

The fact that the constituent occasions of the living person or personally ordered subsociety do not have to be spatially contiguous with one another in some localized part of the brain is implicit indication that in Whitehead's view the structured society or organism as a whole is the ultimate agent here. The presiding occasion, to be sure, adds its unique agency to the "common element of form" or specialized pattern of behavior for the structured society at any given moment. But it is the society itself as a unified field of activity which survives to provide the necessary environment for the emergence of the next generation of actual occasions, including the next presiding occasion. Equivalently, then, that successor presiding occasion prehends the mentality of its predecessor(s) in the dominant subsociety, not directly through spatial contiguity, but through the patterns in the overall field of activity which is the organism or structured society as a whole. Otherwise stated, the organism or structured society as a unified field of activity exercises collective agency in faithfully transmitting to new generations of actual occasions the structural patterns necessary both for ongoing self-identity and for creative adaptation to the external environment. All this is done, of course, through the interrelated agencies of its constituent occasions (including the presiding occasion). But it is the organism or structured society as a whole which thereby continues to exist and undergo various changes.[24]

At this point, we may profitably turn to a consideration of the God-world relationship in the light of the new understanding of the nature and function of Whiteheadian societies developed above. What is immediately apparent, of course, is that the body-soul analogy is no longer really suitable. If the presiding occasion is successively located in different parts of the brain, as noted above, then, analogously God would have to be located now in this part, now in that part, of the universe. Furthermore, one would have to say that God is no more than a contributor, albeit the chief one, to the ongoing existence of a cosmic field of activity which God shares with all creatures. For, within this scheme, fields, not the individual energy-events taking place within them, are what ultimately survive.

On the other hand, a trinitarian understanding of the God-world relationship in terms of hierarchically ordered fields of activity seems quite possible. If the three divine persons, for example, are interpreted as three personally ordered societies of actual occasions which by their dynamic interrelation from moment to moment sustain a democratically organized structured society, then, their joint field of activity could be said to envelop and support the field of activity brought into existence at every moment by the interrelated activity of all finite actual entities. In the remainder of this essay, accordingly, I will offer such a field-oriented explanation of the God-world relationship. Since Whitehead himself was not very precise about the details of the God-world relationship, I will equivalently be doing what Hartshorne did fifty years ago: namely, on the basis of certain other features of Whitehead's philosophy, to construct a model of the God-world relationship which is basically Whiteheadian in inspiration.

My starting-point will be with the notion of the three divine persons as co-constituting from moment to moment a field of activity which is their reality as one God. As I see it, they are one God in three persons, rather than three gods in close collaboration, because they share without remainder this common field of activity. Human beings are separate individuals even though they co-exist within the same family or community because their fields of activity do not perfectly coincide. They do things either alone or with "outsiders" which help to shape their personal history (field of activity) as something distinct from the history (field of activity) of the family or community. With the divine persons, on the other hand, personal history and corporate history are one and the same. They have no personal identity apart from the roles which they play within the divine community (field of activity).

In earlier publications, I have outlined these roles in some detail.[25] Here I offer only a summary. Within the divine community, the "Father"[26] as the first person is identified with the primordial nature of God. That is, although all three are aware of the panoply of possibilities thereby presented to them, it is the role of the Father to select at each moment one such possibility for their communal existence and present it to the "Son" as the second person within the Godhead for actualization. The "Son" is thus identified with the divine consequent nature since it is by the "Son's" decision that all three become what they are for that moment. Finally, the "Spirit" as the third person within the Godhead may be identified with what Whitehead calls the superjective nature of God,[27] since the "Spirit" is responsible for the continuity of the dialogical relationship between the "Father" and the "Son" from moment to moment. That is, as the "living memory" of their communitarian life, the "Spirit" prompts the "Father" to offer and the "Son" to respond over and over again but always with a sense of purpose and direction so as to maximize the perfection of their life together.

As already noted, the three divine persons are incapable of existence apart from their life together as a community. Hence, the decision whereby the "Father" as an individual actual entity is constituted from moment to moment is identical with a choice of a possibility for all three of them to exist at that moment. Likewise, the self-constituting decision of the "Son" at that same moment is simultaneously the decision whereby all three of them achieve actuality as the divine community for that instant. Finally, the decision whereby the "Spirit" is "Spirit" for that moment is at the same time the decision to prompt the "Father" to offer and the "Son" to respond and thus to sustain the divine communitarian life for that interval. Since what results is a single unified field of activity with three foci or interrelated centers of activity, they are one God, not three gods in close collaboration. The divine reality, moreover, is intrinsically social since what ultimately exists is a unified field of activity for three individual existents whose personal identity is totally identified with their communal existence.

Within this same field-oriented model for the God-world relationship, the world is to be understood as a unified field of activity sustained from moment to moment by the decisions of successive generations of finite

98

occasions. Naturally, this cosmic field of activity is itself built up of hierarchically ordered subordinate fields of activity: from the very minute (e.g., atoms and molecules) to the extremely large (solar systems and entire galaxies). The entire field, however, is positioned within the field of activity proper to the divine persons. Just as the "Father," in other words, continuously offers to the "Son" a possibility for their communal existence as one God, so, too, the "Father" offers an initial aim, i.e., a range of possibilities, to every occasion coming into existence within the world of creation. By accepting that initial aim and responding to it in some measure, the finite entity implicitly aligns its "decision" with the response of the "Son" to the "Father" for that same moment. The order of the universe from moment to moment is thus the combined result of the decision of the divine "Son" plus all the decisions of finite occasions at that same moment. Put in other terms, the actuality of creation is part of the actuality of the triune God at every moment. Finally, just as within the immanent Trinity, the "Spirit" is active to prompt the "Father" to offer and the "Son" to respond, so, too, within the God-world relationship, the "Spirit" inspires the "Father" to keep offering initial aims to all finite occasions and inspires these same entities to respond as fully as possible to the "Father's" proposal and thus to align themselves with the response of the "Son" for that same moment.

The three divine persons, accordingly, do not occupy fixed spatial positions within the field of activity proper to the world. One might say, to be sure, that creation is centered on the "Son" since all finite entities join themselves to the reality of the "Son" in the latter's response to the "Father" at every moment. But, from another perspective, the "Son" is present to every finite occasion in its place within the extensive continuum since through the divine initial aim union with the "Son" is the implicit goal of its process of internal self-constitution. In thus being simultaneously everywhere within the world of creation, the "Son" is, strictly speaking, nowhere. The same could be said, of course, of the presence and activity of the "Father" and the "Spirit" within the world of creation. The "Father" is present to every occasion in and through the offer of an initial aim, and the "Spirit" is present to facilitate the occasion's response. They, too, then, are everywhere and nowhere within creation at every moment.[28]

Much more space would be needed to indicate how the eternal "Son" became incarnate in the man Jesus of Nazareth without violation of the latter's human consciousness and freedom of decision from moment to moment. Likewise, a complete account of this trinitarian God-world relationship should take into account how evil comes into the world through the disordered decisions of finite occasions which then become perpetuated as societal patterns within their respective fields of activity. Finally, attention should be given to the way in which the Christian Church as the extension in space and time of the person of Jesus and the other world religions as the corporate expression of the charism of their founders provide focus and direction for the efforts of human beings everywhere to combat the effects of sin, the "collective power of evil," in the world. But all these details are contained in my book *The Triune Symbol*.[29] Hence, it seems best to conclude by drawing attention to what I have attempted to accomplish in this article. My purpose was not simply to use insights from process-relational meta-physics to vindicate a more or less traditional understanding of the Trinity.[30] Nor was it, on the other hand, to use trinitarian language to describe the different "natures" or dimensions of the Whiteheadian God.[31] Rather, I had in mind creatively to synthesize the two lines of thought, the one philosophi-cal, the other theological, so as to resolve problems which are endemic to both systems taken separately.

Within trinitarian theology, for example, the overriding problem has been how to reconcile genuine threeness of persons with antecedent belief in one God. At least in the West, the clear tendency has been to move in the direction of functional modalism: i.e., to think of God primarily as "Father," but also to profess belief in Jesus as God Incarnate and in the Spirit as the "soul" or animating principle of the Church. The underlying fear of tritheism, belief in three gods rather than one God, has thus paralyzed efforts to think creatively about this issue: e.g., to question the basic philosophical assumption that in the end only individual entities exist, hence, that if one affirms three distinct persons within God, one ends up with three gods. Whiteheadian metaphysics, on the other hand, although obviously representing a break with the focus on individual substance in Aristotelian metaphysics, nevertheless, as I see it, has not yet explored the full implications of its own event-oriented ontology. Whitehead himself was ambivalent on this point. For, as I have pointed out above, his discussion of the nature of societies in *Process and Reality* seems to indicate that structured environments or patterned fields of activity are what survive the passage of time. But in Part Five of that same work, he describes God as the one actual entity which never achieves satisfaction and thus which alone survives as an entitative or substantive reality in a world of interlocking fields of activity.

The significance of the notion of field as developed in this article is that it both solves the problem of threeness in oneness for Trinitarian theology and renders Whiteheadian process-relational metaphysics internally more consistent. That is, it solves the Trinitarian problem because the divine community or divine field of activity exists only in virtue of the dynamic interrelatedness of the divine persons to one another; and the persons continue to relate to one another in the same way because of the structural patterns already resident within the field. Just as within classical Trinitarian metaphysics, the divine nature is not really (but only rationally) distinct from the divine persons, so within this scheme there is no real distinction between the divine field of activity and its constituent actual occasions, namely, the successive moments in the lives of the divine persons. Furthermore, this field-oriented understanding of the triune God likewise renders Whiteheadian metaphysics internally more consistent because now, even with respect to God, it remains true that only fields survive the becoming and perishing of actual occasions. Stated more precisely, "God" is thus understood to be the Judaeo-Christian-Islamic name for Ultimate Reality, i.e., the all-comprehensive field of activity in which energy-events in enormous profusion continually take place. The key energy-events, of course, are the successive moments in the lives of the three divine persons as they continue to relate to one another and to all their creatures. But the successive generations of finite occasions likewise play their role in filling out the extensive continuum and thus constituting what I call the cosmic society.[32]

Other essays in this volume will critique Charles Hartshorne's concept of God from a Buddhist or feminist perspective. Hence, I refrain from commenting further here on the way in which a revised notion of "God" as a cosmic field of activity might contribute either to the Buddhist-Christian dialogue or to a more feminist understanding of reality. The major hurdle to such a new understanding of the nature of God remains, of course, the effort required to set aside accepted ways of thinking about divinity (and, indeed, about reality as a whole) and to conceive the hitherto inconceivable. In that respect, Charles Hartshorne's achievement in "The Compound Individual" fifty years ago still stands as a reminder to his disciples and admirers today that truly creative thinking will usually require an imaginative leap, a radical change of metaphor to open up new possibilities for thought and action.

NOTES

1. Charles Hartshorne, "The Compound Individual," *Philosophical Essays for Alfred North Whitehead* (New York: Russell & Russell, 1936).
2. *Ibid.*, p. 211.
3. Charles Hartshorne, *Man's Vision of God and the Logic of Theism*, 2nd ed. (Hamden, CN: Archon Books, 1964), pp. 174—211. Still another extended exposition of this idea is to be found in *The Logic of Perfection and Other Essays in Neoclassical Metaphysics* (La Salle, IL: Open Court Publ. House, 1962), pp. 191—215.
4. *Man's Vision of God*, p. 200.
5. Schubert M. Ogden, *The Reality of God and Other Essays* (New York: Harper & Row, 1963), p. 59.
6. *Ibid.*, p. 6.
7. John B. Cobb, Jr., *A Christian Natural Theology* (Philadelphia: Westminster Press, 1965), pp. 82—91, 192—96. Cf. also a more recent article by Cobb in which he espouses Hartshorne's rethinking of Whitehead on these points: "Overcoming Reductionism," *Existence and Actuality. Conversations with Charles Hartshorne*, John Cobb and Franklin Gamwell (eds.) (Chicago: University of Chicago Press, 1984), esp. pp. 158—62.
8. Hartshorne himself seems to endorse such a modalist conception of the Trinity in the Epilogue to *Man's Vision of God*, pp. 351—52.
9. *Ibid.*, p. 176.
10. Alfred North Whitehead, *Process and Reality*, David Griffin & Donald Sherburne (eds.) (New York: The Free Press, 1978), p. 89 (137). N.B.: The number in parentheses corresponds to the pagination of the original edition of *Process and Reality* published in 1927, also by Macmillan.
11. *Ibid.*, p. 90 (138).
12. *Ibid.*, p. 18 (27).

13. *Ibid.*, pp. 90—91 (139).
14. Cobb, *art. cit.*, pp. 155—58.
15. Whitehead, *op. cit.*, p. 31 (46).
16. Cf., e.g., Ivor Leclerc, *The Nature of Physical Existence* (New York: Humanities Press Inc., 1972), pp. 289—91; also by the same author, *The Philosophy of Nature* (Washington, D. C.: The Catholic University of America Press, 1986), pp. 118—22.
17. Hartshorne, *art. cit.*, p. 215: "The dualism of common sense is due to thinking of composites as more unified and individual than their parts, whereas the reverse is true. A stone is better interpreted as a colony of swirls of atoms (crystals) than are its atoms interpretable as servants or organs of the stone. The atoms and crystals are the substances, the stone-properties, the accidents."
18. Whitehead, *op. cit.*, p. 89 (137). Cf. also on this point Dorothy M. Emmet, *Whitehead's Philosophy of Organism* (London: Macmillan & Co., 1932), pp. 174—219. Emmet speaks of the "interaction between the character of individual actual entities and the character of the society in which they find themselves" (*ibid.*, p. 212) in such a way that for her, too, the society is a functioning totality.
19. Whitehead, *op. cit.*, pp. 99—100 (151—53).
20. *Ibid.*, p. 103 (157).
21. Cobb, *art. cit.*, p. 156.
22. Whitehead, *op. cit.*, p. 107 (163).
23. *Ibid.*, pp. 108—09 (166). Cf. also on this point Whitehead's later works: *Adventures of Ideas* (New York: Free Press Paperback, 1967), pp. 207—08; *Modes of Thought* (New York: Free Press Paperback, 1968), pp. 163—64.
24. The fact that Whitehead allows for the possibility of several "living persons" within the animal body either successively or even simultaneously (cf. *Process and Reality*, p. 107 [164]) is still further evidence that for him the organism as a whole is the ultimate ontological agent.
25. Cf. *The Triune Symbol: Persons, Process and Community* (Lanham, MD: University Press of America, 1985), esp. pp. 36—47. Cf. also "Process Philosophy and Trinitarian Theology — I & II," *Process Studies* 8 (1978), 217—30, and 11 (1981), 83—96.
26. The traditional divine names are set in quotation marks to indicate their purely metaphorical, non-sexist use in this article.
27. Whitehead, *op. cit.*, p. 88 (135): "The 'superjective nature' of God is the character of the pragmatic value of his specific satisfaction qualifying the transcendent creativity in the various temporal instances."
28. It would be beyond the scope of the present article to indicate in detail how this field-oriented approach to the God-world relationship might be compatible with the reflections of Bernard Meland and Bernard Loomer on the reality of God in a process-relational world. Both of them are reluctant to ascribe personality to God, but instead think of God as somehow identified with the totality of the world process (cf., e.g., Bernard E. Meland, *Fallible Forms and Symbols: Discourses on Method in a Theology of Culture* [Philadelphia: Fortress Press, 1976], pp. 150—152; Bernard M. Loomer, "The Size of God," in *The Size of God: The Theology of Bernard Loomer in Context*, William Dean and Larry E. Axel (eds.) [Macon, GA: Mercer Univ. Press, 1987], pp. 41—42.) Presumably they are objecting (at least, in part) to the notion of an unipersonal God who, as Hartshorne suggests, is the soul of the world; for, the world is then incomplete without God as its transcendent unifying principle. Within the trinitarian model of the God-world relationship, however, finite actual entities constitute from moment to moment a field of activity proper to themselves. Moreover, while this field of activity is indeed situated within the field of activity proper to the divine persons, the influence of those same divine persons on their creatures, being all pervasive, is not readily detected except through the eyes of faith. Phenomenologically, therefore, one should not expect to experience the presence and activity of the divine persons as more than "Creative Passage" or "the ultimate mystery inherent within existence itself."

29. Cf. above, n. 25.
30. Cf., e.g., Illtyd Trethowan, *Process Theology and the Christian Tradition: An Essay in Post Vatican II Thinking* (Stillriver, MA: St. Bede's Publications, 1985). Trethowan illustrates quite well the tendency among many Roman Catholics familiar with process-relational metaphysics to use process-oriented language in describing the God of Aristotelian-Thomistic metaphysics. In my judgment, this will not work any better than the opposite tendency of Whiteheadians to use trinitarian language in describing the different functions of the Whiteheadian God. One has to synthesize both traditions through the creation of a third position which represents something genuinely new both for Trinitarian theology and for process-relational metaphysics. Aquinas seems to have done something similar in the thirteenth century when he synthesized a basically Platonic understanding of Christian doctrine with Aristotelian metaphysics. The result was something new, namely, Thomism, which was inevitably looked upon as heretical by more "orthodox" theologians of his own day. At the same time, it is not pure Aristotelianism since Aristotle did not employ the category of existence nor suggest that the ultimate instantiation of potency and act is the relation of essence to existence. This insight for Thomas presumably came out of his reflection on the Christian tradition, in particular, the received interpretation of Exodus 3/14.
31. Cf., e.g., Lewis S. Ford, *The Lure of God: A Biblical Background for Process Theism* (Philadelphia: Fortress Press, 1978), pp. 99—111. By his own admission, Ford seems to have moved away in recent years from the metaphysical position taken in this chapter.
32. Cf. Chapter VIII of a new book, *Spirit and Society*, now in preparation, in which I show how the three divine persons and all their creatures co-constitute an ever-expanding cosmic society.

7. Charles Hartshorne's Philosophy of God: A Thomistic Critique

W. NORRIS CLARKE

Let me begin by saying quite sincerely that I find Hartshorne's philosophical theology a truly "noble" one. It articulates a rich religious sensitivity and presents us with a God that is a totally admirable person, worthy of deep religious reverence and love. It is not surprising to me that some of the authors who have written on it declare that this is the only brand of theism they could accept.

He also reveals himself as a genuine metaphysician of a high order. His remarks on what metaphysical "proofs," or "arguments" (as he now prefers to call them) can be expected to deliver today, his notion of cumulative arguments for the existence of God, his critique of negative theology and defense of meaningful positive language about God, and many other observations, all show a highly developed philosophical as well as humane wisdom. Some of his arguments, too, for the existence of God, especially from cosmic order, I find quite good, or at the least very helpful in refining my own.

In what follows I shall not focus on his arguments for the existence of God. That would be too long and technical a job to be carried out adequately here. I wish to concentrate on the conception of God which results from his analyses, to investigate whether or not it satisfies adequately the exigencies of a reasonable metaphysical explanation of our world and experience — which is what he too admits is the goal of a philosophy of God. My point of view will be basically inspired by the metaphysics and natural theology of St. Thomas, but with a certain independence of traditional expositions of Thomism, as will appear, an independence in fact inspired by my own sympathetic study of process philosophy. I believe St. Thomas's metaphysics can go much further in solving the key problems of natural theology — truly difficult for any philosophical system — than Hartshorne is willing to admit, though too often Thomas does not proceed far enough in articulating the resources of his own system. In fact I do find that Hartshorne systematically misunderstands — to my mind — some of the key metaphysical issues which St. Thomas is trying to come to grips with in his conclusions and so inevitably misinterprets St. Thomas himself in these cases. I shall focus on a few key points.

S. Sia (ed.), Charles Hartshorne's Concept of God, 103–123.
© 1990 *Kluwer Academic Publishers. Printed in the Netherlands.*

I. IS GOD THE CAUSE OF THE BEING OF CREATURES?

The religious intuition which nourishes Hartshorne's metaphysical explications is very rich, and so is what I might call without pejorative connotations his literary and rhetorical expression of what he understands to be the religious implications of his metaphysical analyses. Thus in particular he speaks movingly of God as the ever-present collaborating — though not totally determining — cause of all creatures and their activities. But my difficulty arises when I press the metaphysics hard to see if it adequately supports the descriptive statements. Here I must say that I find less than meets the eye. Hartshorne's God does not seem to be the genuine cause or source of the very *being and power* — creativity — of creatures. He does indeed provide their initial subjective aim, set the general limit laws of the cosmos for their activity, and influence them by allowing them to prehend his intentions, etc. But all this is *influencing* them only. It presupposes they are somehow *there* for Him to influence, at least with some initial inchoate being handed on from their predecessors. But He is not the radical ultimate source of their very being itself, or of their power to act with a certain creative spontaneity. Hartshorne is so afraid of making God the "tyrant" determiner of all activity — which I agree with him is certainly an intolerable view — that he is reluctant even to let God be the source of the *power* of His creatures to be creative.

He would answer by rejecting creation *ex nihilo* as implying an absolute beginning of the cosmos, which he finds opaque in intelligibility. Thus there are always previous entities which as they perish are partial causes, with God, of the new actual entity. But even if one concedes the intelligible possibility of an infinite series of entities or events in a universe without beginning or end, as he does — which, by the way, I am now coming to think more and more, contrary to St. Thomas, does not make sense — one is still left with the situation that nowhere can one find any *sufficient reason* for the actual existence and real power of any of God's creatures, all of which are contingent creatures. An infinite eternal series of all contingent beings never can add up to an adequate sufficient reason for the being of any of them.

Let me put it this way. God is not the ultimate radical source for the very being and power of contingent beings. He influences them profoundly, but always presupposes their initial being as handed on by their predecessors. So the predecessors are in fact more the cause of the actual power-filled being of their successors than God is. But the trouble is that none of these prior contingent beings is the adequate sufficient reason for its own being and power, since that depends on the gift of a prior, and the latter in turn depends on a prior, and so on to infinity. Thus we are endlessly in search of the sufficient reason for the actual existence of any member of the series, and can never in principle find it. The burden is always passed back to a prior.

It does no good to say that each one is adequately taken care of by its predecessor; that would be true only on the presumption that the latter's own being was already adequately taken care of. But it turns out that it is not taken care of by itself and requires some previous conditions to be fulfilled. It can exist only *if* these are already adequately fulfilled. It now turns out that its predecessor's conditions are not fulfilled by itself either, so the buck is passed back further. We now have the situation that each member of the series exists *only conditionally*, i.e. *if* another exists, and the latter too only *if another*, and so on without end. In other words, A exists *only if* B, B *only if* C, C *only if* D, and so on indefinitely. But from a series of all conditionals one can never get an unconditional affirmation. Yet the present being which we are trying to explain does in fact exist unconditionally. Hence somewhere along the line of its cause there must be one whose existence is affirmed absolutely, without further conditions, in a word, one that is its own sufficient reason for existing.

Our search for a sufficient explanation goes upstream in time, and once we have gone far enough back we tend to think we don't have to worry further, for every member will be taken care of by one further back. But the actual flow of being comes the other way, down from the past to the present. So unless there were a completely sufficient reason, i.e. a self-sufficient being, *already in place* in existence there would be no sufficient reason why the flow of being through the entire series ever got started in the first place or is actually going on at all (if eternal). Thus either there is a self-sufficient cause at the start of the series, which would then have a beginning, or else outside the whole series, supporting the entire being of the series all the time. The universe of Hartshorne has many partial causes of its ongoing being, one of which, God, has the sufficient reason for its own existence, but He does not provide this service fully for the contingent members. And since none of them can provide this for themselves, nowhere is there any sufficient grounding for the entire cosmic system, no matter how far back into an infinite past one goes. Thus it is not clear in his system why in fact there actually *are* any other beings outside of God himself.

Actually, why could not Hartshorne simply enrich his system and say that God is the ultimate source of the very being and creative power of all His creatures, and then continue with all the other things he wants to say, that God does not determine them fully, works with them by persuading them, etc.? I can see only two significant reasons for his not doing so, neither of them cogent. One would be if he held the position many claim is that of Whitehead, namely, that the very being, the *total being*, of any creature is *identical with its act* (its "concrescence") without remainder, so that there is no shadow of distinction whatever between the subject of the activity and the activity itself. In that case, of course, God could not be the cause of the being and power of the creature, because then He would be the cause of the very act itself, the very determiner and doer of the act; and no being, even God, can actually do, or better posit, the act of another being. Therefore the creature must be radically self-creative of its own initial inchoate being and power by which it responds to the subjective aim God imparts to it.

Some of the younger Whiteheadians, like Jorge Nobo, have argued — cogently, I think, against Lewis Ford — that not only does this not make sense in itself metaphysically (I agree), but is not the proper interpretation of Whitehead. Whitehead in many texts asserts, in addition to the creativity at work in the new actual entity's own concrescence, a transitional creative energy passing over from the perishing prior entity to the new, establishing it, with God, in its initial inchoate being, which then by its own creativity decides what to do with what it has been given — including the power it has been given. From what I can see in Hartshorne, it does not seem to me that he holds, or needs to hold, this extreme identification of the whole being and power of an actual entity with its act (the expression of its creativity). I do not see, then, why Hartshorne cannot hold that God is the ultimate source of both the being and power of the creature. And if he can, he should.[1]

II. IS GOD OMNIPOTENT?

The other reason — and I think the really central one — why Hartshorne does not go on to make God the ultimate source of the very being and power (not just the subjective aim) of his creatures is his fear that such a radical giving of being to all his creatures would imply the *omnipotence* of God. And he is absolutely adamant about rejecting such an attribute as inappropriate to God. Here is the real *bête noire*. The very term is like a red rag to a bull for Hartshorne — and for good reasons *if* the classical notion were what he understands it to be. 'Omnipotence,' for him, seems to mean that God is not only the source of all power but also *holds onto* it all, determining all actions himself, so that He is the *sole* powerful one, so to speak. This would of course eliminate all creativity, spontaneity, and freedom from His creatures, which would be more like robots or puppets than authentic agents. Such a notion of divine omnipotence should indeed be rejected.[2]

But this is not at all what the classical notion of omnipotence means, in St. Thomas, for example. This is one of the main criticisms of Thomists against both Hartshorne and Whitehead, who held much the same and declared it explicitly to be one of his main reasons against creation from nothing. In St. Thomas, for example, 'omnipotence' means (1) that God is the infinite source and fullness of all power, and (2) that He can produce or bring into being any entity that is intrinsically possible, not contradictory. It does not mean that He can do by himself any *act* or action of a being, such as, for example, drinking beer, sneezing, having sex. Above all it does not mean that He *holds onto* all the power, determining all actions unilaterally. Precisely the opposite is true. He is the one who *shares* his power most freely and generously. Every creature, as an image and participation in the perfection of God, *participates* according to its nature in the divine fullness of power, and has natural built-in capacity and positive tendency to flow over into self-expressive action. St. Thomas specifically criticizes the Arabic Occasionist philosophers, who, on the pretext of glorifying God more, reserved all exercise of power to God alone. To belittle the power of creatures is to belittle the perfection of God himself, he says, for the greater and more perfect an agent is, the more richly it can share its power.[3] God is the ultimate *source* of all power, but not the sole *holder* and *exerciser* of it. Neither Whitehead nor Hartshorne seems ever to have been tuned in to the full richness of the doctrine of *participation* in Thomistic metaphysics, especially in its application to God and the relation of creatures to Him.

Thus God is the ultimate self-sufficient source of all the being and power (or nature, as an abiding center of activity) of His creatures. He also actively works with their natures as they produce their actions, supporting both their natures and their acts in their being all the way, as the universal Transcendent Cause. But He does not determine their acts on his own. The creaturely agent itself determines, according to its nature (necessary or free), how it will let the freely offered power of God flow through it, in this particular way or that. Thus in the case of free human actions, Thomas says that God predetermines, premoves, or pre-orients the will *as nature* towards *the good* as such — which means in the concrete the Infinite Good, desired implicitly in the choice of any finite good — but man decides whether to will in act *this* or *that* good in particular. The once and for all orientation, or magnetizing, of the will towards the Infinite Good puts the will in a permanent state of actuation which virtually (or "eminently") contains within it the power to determine itself to this or that finite good.[4]

There is, I concede to Hartshorne, a more "extreme," rigorous brand of Thomism, the school of Bañez, the great Dominican commentator on St. Thomas, still followed by many — not all — Dominican Thomists, which maintains a stronger predetermining power of God over every action, though at the same time they insist God causes our free actions to be free. I am not sure I can make good sense out of this language — it seems to me more like a verbal decree than an explanation. I can well understand Hartshorne's unhappiness with this kind of Thomism, which he may possibly have taken to be essential to all Thomistic natural theology. But he should be aware that the large majority of Thomists — including all Jesuit Thomists, for example — do not hold this rigorist interpretation of St. Thomas.[5] Nor do I believe it is an accurate rendering of Thomas's own teaching. Witness the text of Thomas I referred to above about God predetermining the will as a nature to the good as such, but leaving it to the will itself to choose this or that good in particular.[6]

As I would put it myself, God offers constantly and unfailingly His superabundant power to his creatures, not yet determined in detail, and then each one determines or "steers," so to speak, this power along this or that particular line according to the nature of each, necessarily or freely as the case may be. This may be much closer to what Hartshorne is holding out for than he may suspect. But my main objection remains: he shows no appreciation of the authentic classical doctrine of St. Thomas — and of others — that of the divine omnipotence as source of all power but freely shared, participated, with all his creatures. The doctrine of participation — so central to Thomas's metaphysics as understood today — seems to be significantly missing, or hardly mentioned, throughout the whole of Hartshorne's doctrine of God, as is even more true of Whitehead's. Hartshorne does indeed divide up the total causality in the creature's activity between God and the creature's own spontaneous initiative; but the creature's own contribution does not seem to be a participation in God's own power but rather entirely self-caused, originating in a sense from nowhere.

III. PANENTHEISM

This term sums up one of the central theses of Hartshorne, namely, that the basic metaphysical relationship between God and creatures is one of *inclusion*. God and creatures cannot be "outside" each other; they must form a single all-inclusive reality, which can best be described — analogously, of course, because it is a unique case — on the model of the relation of soul to body in us. The soul guides and controls all its cells so that they belong to it and fall under its power; thus they do not have full autonomy of their own. Yet they do possess a certain independent spontaneity on their own, as do the actual entities in any nexus or society. Thus like any organism, God and His creatures form a single inclusive whole — in this case an all-inclusive whole. Sometimes Hartshorne prefers to alternate between the model of a society — in the ordinary social meaning of the term — and an organism. Still he definitely prefers and often develops uniquely the model of organism.

I would like to lodge a strong metaphysical demur to this position. The intention behind it is a good one, to insure the intimate presence of God to his creatures. But it seems to me just another perpetuation of an old metaphysical misconception founded on a misleading image. Hartshorne finds himself in distinguished company indeed, since the great Hegel falls into the same trap. It came up in medieval times, in the guise of the obvious objection that creatures cannot be distinct in being from God, if God is infinite, since God + creatures would make more being than God by himself. The classic answer seems to me decisive, yet strangely never seems to have been noticed by modern philosophers. It is built entirely on the theory of participation. As the medievals put it, God + creatures = *plura entia, sed non plus entis*. That is to say, there are more beings, more *sharers* in being, but not more *qualitative intensity* of the perfection of being itself; or, if you wish, there are *more sharers in* perfection but *no higher level* of perfection. The infinity of God is not at all to be conceived in implicitly spatial, quantitative terms, as though if there were creatures "outside" of Him His being would end here and beyond that would be further being; hence His being could not be infinite. "Outside" God in classical terminology means simply, in non-metaphorical language, "not identical with God; they *are not* God."

Thus to have more sharers in God's perfection by no means implies there is now a *higher level* of qualitative perfection. A simple example will illustrate the point. Suppose one has a mathematics teacher with a vast knowledge of mathematics, and he then shares it partially with a number of students. There are indeed now more sharers, partakers, in his mathematical wisdom, but no more (higher or fuller) mathematical wisdom around — save in the accidental sense that a human teacher may learn more in the very process of teaching. God's infinity, then, is qualitative exhaustiveness of perfection, not a quantitative or spatial inclusiveness of all other lesser spaces. It is an intensive, not an extensive concept. Thus there is no need at all that God + the world be a *single* all-inclusive reality, as Hartshorne insists, under pain of God's being limited by creatures.[7]

In addition to the fact that there is no need for this panentheistic conception of God and creatures in order to protect the infinity of God, there are serious positive drawbacks to it. The main one is this. In any genuine organism that is somehow intrinsically one — not just an aggregate of externally related members like a society — the soul (even the human soul for St. Thomas) in some significant way depends on its body (at least for its ability to operate naturally, if not for its radical existence), and of course the body in its turn depends even more on its soul. Now Hartshorne is quite willing to say that God depends on the world, but only in order to have an object to work with, to receive His gracious gifts, and also to enrich His own satisfaction. He does not depend on it for help in the actual carrying out of His own internal operations, but only as an *external* object of His gifts and a source in return of further satisfaction. But such is precisely the relation of a workman to his materials, e.g. a carpenter to his supply of wood and to his finished product as a source of satisfaction. And this is not an organic relation at all. The carpenter does not need his wood to help him carry on internally the working of his own muscles and brain in carving the wood. The carpenter and his desk in no way constitute a single organic whole, though their non-organic relation is intimate and profound.

If we turn back to God now, and insist that He is in an organic, not a craftsman relation (as the Platonic Demiurge is wisely described), then His dependence on His world must be — if the organism analogy is to retain any force — much more profound than I believe Hartshorne would be willing to accept. God would have to depend on His creatures for help in the very internal carrying out of His own causality; He could not even do "his own thing," so to speak, without the *internal* collaboration of His creatures in His own actions. This is no longer a Transcendent God in any sense of the word, merely the most powerful part of the one total organism, who would presumably need the help of His creatures even to think up the modes of possibility, just as our soul — the highest instance of organism we know, with a transcendence in being, but not in initial operation, over its body — needs its body to provide the initial phantasms for its abstractive power to work with. If God needed the world in order to carry on his own internal operations, then He and the world would constitute a mutual circle of dependence that would require some higher cause to put them together initially as an interdependent composite. For if A depends on B for its ability to actually operate, and B in turn depends on A for the same ability, then each presupposes the other already existing and operating in order for it to operate, and vice versa. In this case neither could get going unless some unifying higher cause posited them both in being as a simultaneous unitary being.

There is another, perhaps more serious, difficulty from our side of the picture. It is hard to see how there is place for genuine freedom, lucid and deliberate, for the genuine self-possession proper to the dignity of the person, if it is part of an organism. To be such a part means — if we are to give any strength to the term 'organism' — that the organism can claim all its parts and hence their actions as *mine*. That means that God would have to lay claim to all our actions, including our evil ones, as *His*. This would make Him responsible for evil, even our moral evil, which is exactly the opposite of what Hartshorne maintains with such vigor elsewhere. The responsible self-possession and independence of the free person seems to me intractably resistant to being considered as a "part" in any significant not merely societal sense of a larger whole which somehow owns it as its own, and so can say "It is mine."

Thus in conclusion it seems to me that (1) the conception of the God-world relation as panentheistic is not needed, because based on a implicit spatial misconception of the qualitative infinity of God, and (2) the conception of a soul-body organismic relation, unless one attenuates it beyond significant meaning, inevitably implies too strong a dependence between the two — more than Hartshorne himself would want. If he let go of the implicitly spatial conception of infinity and shifted to a participation model, he would not need his organic model at all. And the participation model would not necessarily imply that he give up what is most dear to him, the profound receptivity of God towards His world.

It seems to me that the terms 'in God' and 'outside of God' are both too tied to metaphor, not properly literal even in an analogous way. The spatial connotations remain too strong. More proper and precise metaphysical terms would have to be simply 'is identical with, or a part of, the being of God', as opposed to 'is not identical with, or a part of, the being of God'. If one wishes, however, to use the expression 'in God' — and it does have a venerable history, even occasionally in religious language, e.g. St. Paul's "in Him we live and move and have our being" — one can say meaningfully that all creatures are *within the field* of God's all-enveloping loving presence and power, as He constantly and attentively supports their existence and works with their natures through His power. Thus in terms of the identical reason — His omnipresence through creative and supportive power — we can say, as we wish, that God is "in His creatures" or that they are "in Him" (within the field of His power). It would seem to me that the really central concerns of Hartshorne could still be adequately taken care of within this mode of speaking.

IV. GOD AS DIPOLAR: FINITE AND INFINITE

Here we come to the heart of Hartshorne's most distinctive and original contribution to philosophical theology: his conception of God not as a simply infinite, "monopolar" Pure Act, but as dipolar in His very being, that is, *infinte* in His eternal *potentiality*, in His "existence," as he puts it, but *finite* in his concrete *actuality* as he receives through time the ever growing accumulation of the experiences of all his creatures, thus constantly enriching his own treasury of value. This is the God who is totally receptive to all that happens, the universal Effect (because affected by everything) as well as the universal Cause, the God who grows with us in his actuality through time, but is both absolutely unsurpassed by any other being and *unsurpassable* in richness of goodness, power, perfection, love, knowledge, etc. by any *other*, that is, unsurpassable by any but himself.

There is much that is truly admirable in this conception. And I think there is no doubt that Hartshorne's central description of God as the *Unsurpassable by any but himself* is indeed an original contribution to philosophical theology — and a brilliant one in its own way. The finite side of it (and the infinite as well) has its problems, as we shall see. But to my mind the central positive contribution that must somehow be integrated into any metaphysical conception of God that is compatible with our religious experience and language, at least with the image of the Judaeo-Christian God, is this: that God is infinitely sensitive to all that goes on among us in time, and infinitely receptive of our responses to His love. All His creatures, and especially His free personal ones, make a great difference indeed to God's consciousness, so that He is truly related to them as they are to Him (although in his own distinctive way).

To interpret the immutability and Pure Act of God as though nothing of what happened among His creatures made any difference at all to Him, as though He were *indifferent* to our responses, would result in a God of philosophy too alien to our religious sensibilities to be acceptable as an articulation of what is the case, or at least of what we firmly believe to be the case. Our life and our thought cannot be that far apart. And I think it is a mistake to hold, as some metaphysicians do, that metaphysics has in its own right an absolute or ultimate veto over what we can believe and live on religiously. Religion can and should have the right to challenge metaphysics to adapt, if need be, to make the fit closer between thought and life. I will also candidly admit that St. Thomas and Thomists in general — with some notable contemporary exceptions — have not said enough to make clear how this is possible in their metaphysical conception of God as Pure Act and absolutely immutable, with no "real relation" to the world. Thomists must meet head on and explicitly the challenge of process philosophy of God and in particular of Hartshorne, whose philosophical theology is so much more fully developed than that of Whitehead.

Now to my examination and critique of how Hartshorne goes about achieving this worthy goal.

God as Changing

It is clear that God's consciousness must register everything that happens in the world of creatures; it must be infinitely sensitive and receptive, if you wish, to all this is and happens. And since creation is free, this means that the contents of His consciousness must be *contingently different*, given this particular creation, than it would have been, given another creation. All Thomists, including St. Thomas, have no difficulty admitting that. It is a caricature of classical theism to claim that it holds that, since God's existence is necessary (i.e. he is a necessary being *in this sense*), therefore everything in Him, including all the contents of His consciousness, is equally necessary and could not be other than it is. That would effectively cancel all freedom in God.

But here is my key objection. To say that everything contingent in our world makes a *difference* in the divine consciousness is not at all the same as to say that it makes a *change* in God. There is no necessary conceptual implication between making a difference and making a change. Making a change in God's consciousness means that it would be *first* one way, then *later* in time another way; it would first be lacking this bit of knowledge, then later acquire it. But for St. Thomas (and on back to St. Augustine, who first made the point), the whole of time itself is part of this created world, is itself therefore created. God stands completely outside the whole realm of time. Time is not some overarching entity or framework including both God and creatures in some common measure. God is simply not in created time at all, and there is no other.

Hence God in His eternal NOW is simply present to each event in our time, neither before or after it, but simply as it actually occurs. What God knows is embedded in the flow of created time, but in no way does that imply that His own process of knowing is also caught in the same flow of time within His own being. Our flow of time is based on constant physical changes or motion in matter. It makes no sense to say that God's own inner action of knowing is locked into this process of physical (or any kind of created) motion. Whatever He knows from our world is simply registered in His consciousness in His eternal NOW, so that He is *always* the God who knows *all this*. *Eternally* His consciousness is *contingently other*, corresponding exactly to all that happens in our moving world, contingently *different*, but not first not knowing and later knowing any particular item. Total sensitivity to the tiniest event, to "every tear and every smile," as Hartshorne rightly insists must be the case, is in this divine consciousness, but not *first* absent, then *later* present.

Thus there is no need to put change, successive temporal change, in God in order to ensure the contingency of His consciousness as regards our world. The only God there actually is, or ever has been, or will be, is the God that freely decides in His eternal NOW to create this world and sensitively registers in his consciousness all that goes on within it. To be contingently different than one could have been does not imply that one is first one way and later another; that is just one mode of contingency — our earthly one, plunged in successively moving matter as we are.[8]

It is a cause of constant surprise to me that process thinkers and Hartshorne in particular never seem to come seriously to grips with this conception of contingency in God, as *contingently other* but without successive temporal *change.* (We are leaving out for the moment the question of whether God's perfection is greater because of creation than without it.). Of course, Hartshorne can answer that he has already argued the impossibility of any changeless knowledge in God, since God on this view would have to know the future from all eternity and so before it happens, and it is impossible to know the future, at least the free futures, before they happen.

He is entirely right that no one, not even God, can know the future before it happens (unless it is already predetermined in its causes), because a non-existent not predetermined by some existent is simply unknowable. St. Thomas himself is adamant that actual existence is the necessary root of all knowledge. (Hartshorne also maintains — and I have no quarrel with him *on this* — that not only free personal agents but all actual entities have some tiny degree of unpredetermined spontaneity, hence none would be fully predictable.) But St. Thomas's whole point is that God does not know what is future to Him. He knows events in time "in their presentiality to Him," as he puts it, that is, as they are actually going on in their own *present.*[9] For those down in the physical time flow, one present or "now" *excludes* all others, hence in one of our present nows we cannot know a future one. But God is not locked into any of our nows. Hence it should never be said, as a good Thomist, that God knows what is future, i.e. future *to Him*; he knows only presents, each in its own proper present.

Hence I think it is incorrect, or at least misleading to say, as so many classical theists do, including St. Thomas, that God knows the future *from all eternity* (*ab aeterno*). This gives the impression that God somehow knows the future from way back *before* the creation of the world, since He is eternally existing and immutable. This is quite false. God does not know anything before the world exists. Since time itself is created, there is no "before." God is always knowing — not from an eternal past, but *from His eternal NOW*, or, as I prefer to avoid misunderstanding, *in His eternal Now* — this world and all that goes on in it, as it is going on, but always as a finite whole, with a finite duration (at least in its beginning) if it has such. He is always present to this whole and all parts of it.

I also think it is incorrect (or at least misleading) to say, as many do, including Thomas at times, that God knows past, present, and future *simultaneously*, in a single *simultaneous* vision. The term 'simultaneous', to my mind, is extremely difficult, if not impossible, to detach from reference to our time flow, as though God knew all in one single *moment* or point of time. That would be absurd, because they are not in a single moment; neither is His knowledge-act. St. Thomas's example of a person viewing a parade all together from above as opposed to from the reviewing stand limps badly. Even from above one could not see them all passing the reviewing stand at once.

Hence I believe that the only proper way to speak is to say "God knows (timelessly, or without tense) that such and such happens at time *t*," but we cannot say *when* he knows it — today, tomorrow, or whatever. He just *knows* all events in their presentiality, in or from the vantage point of his eternal NOW. This NOW, as St. Thomas says explicitly, *includes* all our nows. Hence to try to picture it as some simultaneous "point" at which all lines from past, present and future become fused into one in God may well be a serious mistake. We just can't say how "thick" or "thin" temporally God's NOW is. It might, for all we know, be an infinitely distended motionless presence from inside of which all of history would appear just as it is in its unfolding. There would have to be indeed, in the divine consciousness, an irreversible internal order or sequence of mental contents or objects of knowledge, possibly something like an intelligible succession which would not involve physical change in God but only correlation with each point of our time — a divine "spiritual time," if you will — but not at all our time flow. We must leave the exact *how* hidden in unimaginable mystery, saying only the minimum necessary of positive things about it, and carefully avoiding saying the wrong things.

In sum, I see no contradiction or incoherence in the position I have outlined above; it takes in all the infinitely delicate sensitivity of consciousness of Hartshorne's God, but without the added baggage of change, which does import the new problem of embedding God in our physically based created time flow. There is just no one time flow for God and our world — probably not even the same one for angels (pure spirits) and our world. I will not even bring up the Relativity problem of *which* among the many relative time series God would be in, since there is no more absolute time.[10]

God as Infinite in Potentiality, Finite in Actuality

The dipolarity in Hartshorne's God consists in this: God is infinite in His *existence*, which means in His inner nature in itself considered in abstraction from the actuality of His relationships with the ongoing world; but He is finite in His *actuality*, i.e. considered in the full concreteness of His ever-changing, ever-growing relations to the ongoing world. God's knowledge of the world and His continuous receptivity, as He takes into himself all the values emerging from the experience of all His creatures, are always complete and perfect for that moment, hence always finite at any one moment, but ever expanding as present moves into future. Thus at any moment in the ongoing process that is the universe God is *unsurpassed* and *unsurpassable* by any other but himself — but *not infinite*. *All* actuality, in fact, Hartshorne tells us, is necessarily finite, because determinate.[11] And as He lives in this actuality of relatedness to us God experiences with us all our joys and triumphs and rejoices in them, and also feels our sorrows and sufferings and suffers with us in His own way as we go through them — except that He does not experience evil as such, because it is a negation, but gathers up only the positive in His eternal memory of values.

How then is God infinite? It can only be in his *potentiality*, as possessing inexhaustibly the power to deal with the world in unsurpassable wisdom and love down through infinite time. God's infinity lies in His *inexhaustible power*, not in his actuality.

In assessing this interesting and original position, let me first consider the *infinite side* of this dipolarity. I have some serious problems here. Surely the infinite potentiality of God is not just a passive empty receptiveness but an *active* power. But an active power is potential only in relation to others, to what it will or can do *for them*. Inside the being possessing this power there must be the actual presence of a perfection proportionate to the fullness and perfection of the power. A potentiality does not reside in nothing actual, just floating there somehow on its own. It must be based on something actually there in the real being of the agent. Pure active potentiality for both St. Thomas — and Aristotle before him — is a state of pure actuality in the agent, in full actual possession of the perfection from which flows its power; it is called potential only with respect to the actual communication of its power to others as its potential effects.

Furthermore, if God is the ultimate source of all being (at least the self-sufficient source of His own being, even for Hartshorne), then surely He must be an immense inner plenitude of actual being, of actual existence, which is in no way an abstraction. Having the fullness or *highest degree* of qualitative intensity of perfection, not being the *sole possessor* of it, is precisely what metaphysical infinity means for St. Thomas in the participation tradition stemming from Plotinus.[12] Is this inner actuality in God, the necessary support of His power towards others, finite or limited in perfection and fullness? If limited, by what is it limited? If limited, does this mean there is some higher qualitative intensity of inner being possible? From what source would it derive, if not from the one God? Surely not from some other.

I am troubled, frankly, by what seems to be an implicit supposition behind Hartshorne's conception of God: it is as though God's consciousness were a totally extroverted one, as though the only *life* God had, His only active occupation that fills his consciousness positively, is His relation to what happens in this world distinct from Him. Does God then have no rich inner life, no actual inner *experience* of joyous love given and received within himself? Here is where the Christian doctrine of the Trinity offers a beautiful complement to what no natural reason or philosophy can reach on its own. According to this revealed doctrine, God enjoys an immensely, infinitely rich inner life of self-communicating love, in which the Father, the Primordial Source, pours out His whole being, His identical nature, into the Second Person, the Son or the Word, in total ecstatic love, holding nothing back, and the two together then in an act of mutual love bring forth the Holy Spirit as their mutual love image.

Thus God already enjoys within himself, *actually*, an immensely rich, joyous experience of both giving and receiving love. All the very real joy and satisfaction the Triune God gets from our finite world can be but a tiny participation in this already existing fullness of experience and value. This is what God *does* inside himself/herself/themselves, and I find any serious recognition of this and its philosophical importance strangely missing both in Whitehead and Hartshorne. Now he might well answer that this is theology or faith, not philosophy. This is quite true, but at least philosophy should not deny or close the door to it prematurely, but leave the inner life of God untouched as a Mystery of *life*, actual life — allow God to have a *dipolar actual consciousness*, introvert as well as extravert. I see no good reason, then, for denying to God an infinite actuality of inner life, as well as the added finite actuality of His relations with us and our world. Otherwise the God of Hartshorne — and Whitehead — seems to be afflicted with a strange inner darkness, or unconscious state, with respect to himself, lit up only by looking down towards us and receiving satisfaction from us. Nor is it enough help to say He is occupied with thinking up all the infinite (?) possible patterns, or eternal objects, for guiding this world. This is still an exclusively extraverted inner life.

Now let us look at the *finite side* of the divine dipolarity. Here we touch upon one of Hartshorne's most basic and I think fruitful insights in philosophical theology: the divine receptivity and relatedness to the world. Place must be found for it in any adequate philosophy of God, including Thomism. I think this can be done in an alert and open-minded Thomism not rigidly wedded to its own terminology, but the chances are Thomists would not have done so except under the vigorous prodding of Hartshorne himself, for which we must be grateful. I would like to express his insight somewhat differently, in more Thomistic terms, to avoid the difficulties I see in his strongly realist way of putting it.[13]

It must be admitted that the divine field of consciousness, in its relation to creatures, is not only contingent but finite *in its content*, because dealing with a finite number of finite beings, a finite world, which has been freely created and could have been other than it is. There is then a whole dimension of the divine reality which can be called finite. This is what Hartshorne calls the "finite actuality" of God. But I would insist that this finitude — and contingency — remains restricted to the field of the divine consciousness *as relational ad extra*, i.e. as looking towards creatures distinct from His own being. This relational intentionality of His intelligence truly relates Him to all His creatures and renders Him infinitely sensitive and receptive to all that is going on, especially to the responses of His free creatures. But all this remains within the field of His consciousness as relational, in the order of *esse intentionale*, as St. Thomas would put it, or being *as known*, as existing in the mind. This does not derogate from the infinity of God in His own real, intrinsic, or absolute being, or add on by that very fact any new finite *real being* to God. Thus, just as the immense multiplicity of the objective contents of the divine consciousness as knowing creatures does not destroy or cancel the simplicity of His own real being, so too the finitude of the creaturely objects of His consciousness does not annul the infinity of His own real being in himself. Finitude in the relational field of one's consciousness does not entail finitude in one's own real being, unless one has confused mental and real being. This is entirely compatible with traditional Thomism, I believe, though it has not always been clearly said by Thomists.

Secondly, the relational field of the divine intelligence with respect to creatures is *contingently other* than it would have been if a different world had been created, and reflects with infinite sensitivity — and receptivity — every least detail in this contingent world, as Hartshorne rightly insists and St. Thomas explicitly agrees. But, as we have argued above, this does not entail that a *change*, a temporal successive change, is constantly going on in this field, in God's act of knowing the world. God in or from his eternal NOW is just directly present to each item in its place in our time flow, without being immersed in this created time flow itself. His consciousness is *always contingently other* because of His free decision in this NOW to create this world and not some other. He is *always* the God who in this eternal NOW rejoices over our responses to him in time, takes delight in the participations in His infinite goodness. There is not and never has been or will be any other real God than the one whose consciousness is contingently and finitely other because of this world he has freely decided to share His goodness with. But this does not imply a change going on in this consciousness, so that it is in its own real order first one way and then later another way, first empty of creatures then later — whatever that could mean — filled with them one by one.

Thus God in His relational conscious field, continent and finite though it be, will not be surpassed — to use Hartshorne's terminology — even by himself. But this finite field *could* have been surpassed by himself if He had decided in His eternal NOW to create differently. I see no good reason for, and many against, linking finitude and contingency in the divine consciousness, on the one hand, and temporal change on the other. Just because *we* cannot imagine what the inner phenomenology of divine knowing is like does not prevent us from affirming what it *must be* under pain of importing positive unintelligibility and incoherence into God — much worse than leaving his Mystery unpenetrated.

It will be noted, however, that I have given up the traditional Thomistic doctrine that God is not really related to the world. Although this can be defended in a very narrow technical sense, it is to my mind too misleading for the modern reader and leaves too much dangerously unsaid to be fruitful as a philosophical explanation of a religiously available God. Hartshorne himself once told me that if only Thomists would be willing to concede this point, his main battle with them would be won. I am glad to concede to him this victory. And if God is related at all to creatures, He must be, as Hartshorne rightly maintains, the *most related* of all, the *supreme Receiver* — but in the intentional order of relational consciousness, as eternally contingently *other*, not as changing.[14]

Divine Receptivity and Infinity: Are They Compatible?

We still have not met the full thrust of Hartshorne's challenge. He maintains that the divine receptivity is not compatible with His actual infinity, and holding onto the actual infinity of God is the principal flaw in classic theism, such as found in St. Thomas. For him, the *experiencing* of value *is* reality. So when God is receptive of what goes on in our world, experiences the values we produce and gathers them up in His ever-growing eternal treasury of remembered value, such experiencing means a growth in the reality of God, by the constant addition of new values never experienced by Him before. Hence, although at any one moment God's actual reality and perfection is unsurpassed and unsurpassable by any other being, still the richness of His experience and hence actual reality is constantly growing as our world advances through time, so that He is constantly surpassing himself in the sum total of His actuality. Hence the divine actuality must be *finite* at any given moment in time, but ever growing. Infinite divine actuality would deny receptivity to God, and if He is receptive then His actuality cannot possibly be infinite. One must choose; and divine receptivity is far more important for the religious conception of God than than is infinite actuality or Pure Act.

We have already seen how the contingency and finitude of the contents of the divine field of consciousness in relation to creatures, while it matches exactly every item in our time flow, does not imply that there is a time flow or change within God himself, only that his relational consciousness is eternally *different* because of all that is in our world, but not first one way and later another. We will not go back over this point.

But what about the question whether the divine actuality in God himself is greater because of His experience of our responses to Him and the values we produce? This is the core of the problem. In Hartshorne's system, where God is not the ultimate source of all being, all perfection, where the relation between himself and creatures is therefore not one of participation, and where God does not know what we are doing by doing it with us actively, this position certainly must follow. God is constantly experiencing something new coming from us that does not come from Him as a shared participation in His own perfection.

But in a participation metaphysics like that of St. Thomas the situation is not the same. God already possesses an actual infinity of inner life and joyous experience within himself. He then takes delight in sharing His own fullness of inner life of self-communicative love with the immense variety of His freely chosen creatures, and takes delight in receiving their responses — all in His eternal NOW. But all that he receives from us is only a tiny finite image or participation of his own already infinite fullness or *qualitative intensity* of joy experienced in His own inner life. So there is indeed a vast multiplicity of new finite determinations of the divine joy returning to Him from his participating images. But these never add up to anything approaching a *higher qualitative intensity* of life and perfection than the infinity He already possesses.

Even though St. Thomas himself never says this, and probably would refuse to say it, I see no really decisive metaphysical difficulty in saying that God knows, experiences, and enjoys a whole multiplicity of genuinely novel finite modalities of participation in his infinite goodness, so that God's experience is precisely *different* in His eternal NOW because of us than it would have been otherwise — different in His relational experience turned toward us, and thus richer in new *determinate* ways of enjoying new finite participations in His already infinite life and joy. But I do not see that an indefinite *number* of new sharings in God's already infinite richness of life are any threat to His infinity at all — as long as they are participations, deriving entirely from His gifts to us and His working supportively with us. Similarly I do not see that His own new determinate modalities of enjoyment from His creatures are any threat to His already infinite interior enjoyment of His own life. Infinity plus one finite, or any number of finites within the order of participation, even within God's own consciousness, does not negate either side, as long as the infinity is of a personal kind that is able to share its own riches freely and take delight in this sharing. In a word, the point is that sharing in finite modalities is no threat to the infinite fullness of Source, especially when this infinity of perfection is precisely of a personal kind, where perfection must mean in fact the fullness of altruistic, self-communicative love, where the Infinite One is an Infinite *Lover*. But that is precisely what God is.

I do not think Thomists are careful enough in pointing out that all the perfections of God, Pure Act and all the rest, must always be controlled by their central rooting in a *Personal Being*. The Pure Act of Existence, Infinite Perfection, Immutability, etc., when taken in the concrete in their *one* existing instantiation, are not to be thought of in some purely objective, impersonal way, like the smoothly rounded motionless block of matter Parmenides images as Being. They must be precisely the highest qualitative intensity of *personal life*. Being at its supreme level *is* through and through personal; that is what it means *to be* without restrictions, and the fullness of personal life is precisely the life of self-communicating love, as revealed in the Christian Trinity, a life not of static contemplation, but of infinitely intense intercommunication between persons, *circumincessio*, as the Scholastic theologians put it (a mutual indwelling and "circulation" inside each other, so to speak), in a word, the life of interpersonal love that is equally giving *and* receiving, self-communication *and* receptivity. That is what it *means* to live personally in the full sense, and a fortiori at an infinite level. Any metaphysical theory that would interpret the attributes of God in such a way as to diminish or abolish the personal character of their subject is off the track from the beginning. The person, St. Thomas says, "is that which is most perfect in all of nature"; hence it must control and adjust all the other attributes to itself — they must not dominate and distort it.

This is indeed an expansion of Thomism. But if a careful synthesis is made of (1) *difference* in the relational consciousness of God toward us, rather than change, especially in the sense of our temporal flow; (2) *participation* of all real being both in existence and power from the One Source, so that all that comes back to the Source never rises to a *higher* qualitative level of perfection than the Source; (3) the *active working of the divine power* in all creatures, doing with them all they do, knowing what we are doing by how we let His active power flow through us; (4) an *infinitely rich interior life* of His own in God in the ecstatic self-communicating love within the Trinity, so that any finite satisfaction or joy God receives from us is but a tiny participation in this already actualized inner infinity — if these are put together carefully, I say, I think we can generate a metaphysics of God and creatures that is a legitimate expansion of the key insights of St. Thomas (or what I might more safely call a "Thomistically inspired" philosophy of God). And expand in some way like this I think Thomists must, if we are to meet the profound and rich challenge of Charles Hartshorne. I am deeply moved and inspired by the basic insights motivating his dipolar natural theology; but I feel he puts it together the wrong way as a technical metaphysical system, with too many blind spots regarding change, actual infinity, and participation, resulting in too many unnecessary paradoxes.

POSTSCRIPT ON PERSONAL IMMORTALITY

Let me say just a few words on Hartshorne's view that personal immortality — an everlasting life of the individual person with God after death — is neither possible *nor desirable*. That it is not possible derives from Hartshorne's process theory of the personal "I" as not the perdurance of the same concretely identical entity, but a society of successive actual entities bound together by various bonds of inheritance, etc. I do not wish to enter here into what would have to be a long discussion. Let me just say that I, with many others, do not accept this process view, either in Whitehead or Hartshorne, as adequate to the reality we know as persons and selves. But let that pass.

What I find more interesting and challenging, with its own nobility of conception, is the idea that I should not even want or need an unending individual immortal life in personal communion with God. His treasuring up in total and unsurpassable detail all the lived values and achievement of my life, my unique personality, etc., for His glory and loving satisfaction, is all I need and should desire. Anything else would be an excessive self-centered absorption in my own little life for itself, instead of living for God and His service.

The one great and inconsolable flaw I find in this letting go of the self is this: I will never — and no created person will ever — fulfill the great unrestricted dynamism of my spirit, constitutive of me as intellectual and willing being, as a person, *to know God face to facc*, to *experience* His infinite goodness and the marvel of His self-communicating love within the Trinity, which I would so long to share — and in which He has lovingly invited me to share, according to Christian revelation. This present life in the present body is such a chancy and incomplete journey of "seeing darkly in a mirror," as St. Paul puts it, that it could not possibly satisfy this immense longing to see the Truth and commune with the Good as it is in Itself, no longer through the imperfect and irretrievably blurred mirror of finite, especially material, creatures.

Yet Hartshorne tells us that we can *never* possibly come to know what he admits should be the Great Love of our hearts, never get to penetrate within the wonder of God's providence over the universe, even the depths of the universe's own created wonder and richness — in a word, that I should be radically frustrated with no hope of assuagement in the deepest longings of my mind and heart. To this I say, "No sale." This does not appear to me as self-centeredness contrary to my nature, to the way I was made by my Creator, but the total centeredness in God for which I have been destined by the constitution of my very nature as dynamically finalized, drawn *toward* God, by Him. I cannot look on radical frustration of the deepest innate drive of my nature, of which I am not the cause, as noble unselfishness but as inexplicable, irrevocable frustration. The wondrous mystery of final face-to-face communion with God, my Source, is that the two extremes are brought together here by God: my total giving up of self-centeredness to put my true center in God turns out also to be my most authentic self-fulfillment. We are indeed finite in our actuality, and in many respects in our potentiality. But let us not set the limits of our finitude too low.

To sum up this whole paper, I have been more challenged, and learned more, from the profound and authentic insights of Charles Hartshorne than probably from any other living natural theologian; but I must disagree with many of his metaphysical formulations of these insights. They leave strewn in their wake too much priceless and irreplaceable china from the classical tradition.

122

NOTES

1. I have developed this point at greater length as applied to Whitehead in my book, *The Philosophical Approach to God* (Winston-Salem, NC: Wake Forest Univ., Philosophy Dept., 1979). Chap. 3: "Christian Theism and Whiteheadian Process Philosophy: Are They Compatible?"; see esp. pp. 67—86.
2. See, for example, Hartshorne's *Omnipotence and Other Theological Mistakes* (Albany: SUNY Press, 1984).
3. *Summa contra Gentes, Book III, ch. 68* (Pegis trans. *On the Truth of the Catholic Faith*); *De Veritate (On Truth)*, quest. 9, art. 2.
4. *Summa Theologiae*, I—II, q. 9, art. 6, ad obj. 3: "God moves man's will, as the Universal Mover, to the universal object of the will, which is the good. And without this universal motion man cannot will anything. But man determines himself by his reason to will this or that, which is a true or apparent good. Nevertheless sometimes God moves some specially to the willing of something determinate, which is good; as in the case of those whom He moves by grace, as we shall state later on." Cf. *On the Power of God*, q. 3, art. 7. ad obj. 13: "The will is said to have dominion over its own act not by exclusion of the First Cause, but because the First Cause does not act on the will in such a way as to determine it by necessity to one object, as it determines natures, and therefore the determination of the act remains in the power of the intellect and the will." See also *Sum. Theol.*, I—II, q. 10, art. 4: "As Dionysius says, it belongs to the divine providence, not to destroy, but to preserve the nature of things. Therefore it moves all things in accordance with their conditions, in such a way that from necessary causes, through the divine motion, effects follow of necessity, but from contingent causes effects follow contingently. Since, therefore, the will is an active principle that is not determined to one thing, but having an indifferent relation to many things, God so moves it that He does not determine it of necessity to one thing, but its movement remains contingent and not necessary, except in those things to which it is moved naturally."
5. Cf. Anton Pegis, "Molina and Human Freedom," in Gerard Smith (ed.), *Jesuit Thinkers of the Renaissance* (Milwaukee: Marquette Univ. Press, 1939), pp. 99 ff.; Gerard Smith, *Molina and Freedom* (Chicago: Loyola Univ. Press, 1966).
6. The finest article I know that brings out with umambiguous clarity and textual support St. Thomas's doctrine of the non-determining causality of God on the human free will — in respectful but firm opposition even to his own Dominican brethren of the Bañezian School — is that of the distinguished Italian Dominican metaphysician, Umberto degl'Innocenti, O.P., "De actione Dei in causas secundas liberas iuxta S. Thomam," *Aquinas* 4 (1961), pp. 28—56.
7. See the critique by Colin Gunton, *Becoming and Being: The Doctrine of God in Charles Hartshorne and Karl Barth* (Oxford Univ. Press, 1978), pp. 57—58.
8. I only recently discovered that the same critique of Hartshorne's position on this point has been clearly and incisively made some time ago by Merold Westphal, in his very insightful article in defence of classical theism against the arguments of Hartshorne, "Temporality and Finitism in Hartshorne's Theism," *Review of Metaphysics* 19 (1965—66), pp. 550—64.
9. *Sum. Theol.*, I, q. 14, art. 13.
10. I understand Hartshorne feels he is now off the hook on this thorny point over which he has received so many objections (including from Lewis Ford) because of the startling new development in physics deriving from Bell's theorem, showing apparently that subatomic particles, once joined together, are forever joined in complementary properties, responding to each other's changes instantaneously across space faster than the speed of light, thus suggesting that the physical cosmos is somehow a space- (and time-?) transcending whole behind the scene of space. This may help him, but it is not clear yet that there is

but one common time for this whole — it might transcend time entirely as it does space in certain limited respects.

11. See Hartshorne's *A Natural Theology for Our Time* (LaSalle: Open Court, 1967), p. 24: "Only potentiality can be strictly infinite . . . actuality . . . is finite. . . ."

12. Cf. W. N. Clarke, "The Limitation of Act by Potency: Aristotelianism or Neoplatonism?" *New Scholasticism* 26 (1952), pp. 167—94.

13. See Chap. 3 in my book, *The Philosophical Approach to God* (note 1), pp. 87 ff.

14. See the reference in note 10 above.

8. Can the God of Process Thought be "Redeemed"?

ANDRÉ CLOOTS and JAN VAN DER VEKEN

I. PROCESS PHILOSOPHY AND THE CONTEMPORARY METAPHYSICAL DEBATE

A major critique of classical metaphysics, first made by Nietzsche and echoed again and again by Continental philosophers, is that, from its very beginnings in Plato and Aristotle through its fulfillment in Hegel, metaphysics has in fact been 'onto-theology.' This means, in Heidegger's terminology, that the difference between Being and beings — the 'ontological difference' — has been overlooked, because Being (as the event of coming into unconcealment) has been reduced to *a* highest kind of Being, viz. God, who is conceived as the already available Ground of all other beings. In classical theism, after all, God is *a* Being, albeit the supreme One. He is conceived as the Highest Substance, or Ground; but the very stress on God as the Highest Being, or *Ipsum Esse subsistens*, has, according to Heidegger, obscured the real historical Event of coming-into-presence (*Seinsgeschick*, the *Mittence* of Being). Heidegger, surely one of the most influential thinkers on the contemporary European scene, writes: "Metaphysics is 'onto-theo-logic.' Someone who has experienced theology from its growing origin — the theology of Christian belief as well as philosophical theology — prefers today to keep silent about God within the reach of thought."[1] Heidegger tends to criticize not just a certain kind of theodicy, but metaphysical God-talk in general: ". . . Causa sui. That is the right name for the God of philosophy. But man can neither pray nor sacrifice to this God. Before the causa sui man can neither fall to his knees in awe nor play music and dance. This godless thinking which must abandon the God of philosophy, God as causa sui, is thus perhaps closer to the divine God."[2] Thus while one may indeed wonder what 'God' could mean for Heidegger, it clearly is not identifiable with 'Being.' The religious and the metaphysical ultimates do not coincide.

There has been and still is much criticism of Heidegger's approach to the problem of God. Recently, for example, John Macquarrie, who as a translator of *Sein und Zeit* is very familiar with Heidegger's position, has frankly written: "I think one has to say very firmly that Heidegger must not be

S. Sia (ed.), *Charles Hartshorne's Concept of God*, 125–136.
© 1990 *Kluwer Academic Publishers. Printed in the Netherlands.*

allowed to lay down what is permissible for theologians to say, or to decide unilaterally where the boundary between theology and philosophy is to be drawn."[3]

Nevertheless Heidegger has had a lasting influence on God-talk in Continental philosophy. His criticism has certainly led to more careful thinking about God and being, with philosophers now hesitant to too readily identify the two; and it has given a place of prominence to the very question whether talk about God is possible at all within a philosophical context. Whatever one thinks about Heidegger's approach, the questions he raises cannot be ignored, nor can they be settled without careful analysis. At least the classical answers are no longer as self-evident as they once were.

On the other hand, talk about God and thought about reality should not be too readily separated either. To think is to think things together. Among others, such distinguished contemporary thinkers as Henri Bergson, Werner Heisenberg, Pierre Teilhard de Chardin, Stephen Toulmin, David Bohm, and Arthur Peacock have advocated and are advocating dynamic worldviews, in which science, religion, and philosophy engage in truly creative dialogue. Much popular writing as well reflects this concern. The work of Fritjof Capra is a case in point. Such works aim to fulfill the task deemed so urgent by Whitehead of saving the very essence of culture, indeed, of ensuring sheer survival. These thinkers surely can and often do recognize Whitehead as an ally and source of inspiration. For example, while Ilya Prigogine and Isabelle Stengers are not Whiteheadians in any technical sense of the word, they do acknowledge Whitehead's influence and share many of his basic concerns. Perhaps the most striking Whiteheadian influence on a contemporary group of thinkers is acknowledged in Raymond Ruyer's *La Gnose de Princeton*. The so-called 'gnostics' consider Whitehead to be a 'pre-gnostic,' a precursor. And while Hartshorne's great stress on God may seem less congenial to these thinkers, a careful reading of his work reveals a similarity to their own monistic tendencies even greater than Whitehead's.

Also, in turning to philosophy in the strict sense of the term, and especially to those trends in Continental philosophy which do not reject metaphysics as such, Whitehead and Hartshorne seem to be a possible source for a "rebirth after the death of metaphysics" (to quote the title of an article which appeared in the *Hartshorne Festschrift* thirty years ago). But most contemporary thinkers refrain from identifying 'Eminent Creativity' with the personal God of religion. Can the religious word 'God' function within a metaphysical system? Has religion anything to do with 'metaphysical map-making'? And if God has a place within such a context, how should He be conceived; what should be His place, status, and function?

Process thought is surely one of the rare contemporary movements to talk frankly about God in a metaphysical context. But contrary to what is often thought, there are real differences between Whitehead and Hartshorne on this point. From the beginning Whitehead made a clear distinction between the religious and metaphysical ultimates, i.e., between God and creativity.

God is not creativity itself, but its 'primordial characterization.' Nevertheless God retains a central function in Whitehead's metaphysics. Hartshorne, on the other hand, brings the religious and metaphysical ultimates closer together again, owing to his concepts both of creativity and of God.

II. THE RELATION BETWEEN CREATIVITY AND GOD IN WHITEHEAD

In Whitehead's philosophy of organism all being has to do with the rhythmic process of the one and the many. "The many become one, and are increased by one." Therefore creativity, "that ultimate notion of the highest generality at the base of actuality,"[4] has two 'aspects': concrescence and transition. "For the fundemental inescapable fact is the creativity in virtue of which there can be no 'many things' which are not subordinated in a concrete unity. Thus a set of all actual occasions is *by the nature of things* a standpoint for another concrescence which elicits a concrete unity from those many actual occasions. . . ." And: "The creativity in virtue of which any relative complete actual world is, *by the nature of things,* the datum for a new concrescence, is termed 'transition' " (PR 211, emphasis added). So creativity is the principle of *activity* whereby the many and the one are linked rhythmically. And this is its primary meaning, expressing the 'nature of things.' Creativity is activity in the present and from the present to the future. Concrescence and transition are 'aspects' of one and the same activity, pervading all that is. "The creativity of the world is the throbbing emotion of the past hurling itself into a new transcendent fact. It is the flying dart, of which Lucretius speaks, hurled beyond the bounds of the world."[5]

Creativity is also the principle of *novelty*. Through creativity, in its primary meaning, another and new actuality comes into existence. But for all this, another formative element is equally necessary, viz, the primordial structuring of possibilities orienting each new occasion. Only then is definiteness possible, which in turn is the precondition for value, order, intensity, harmony, and beauty. Whitehead links this primordial structuring, this sphere of possibility, with the *religious* notion of God: "It is termed 'God' because the contemplation of our natures as enjoying real feelings derived from the timeless source of all order, acquires that subjective form of refreshment and companionship at which religions aim" (PR 31—32).

When taken into metaphysics the religious notion of God should not be identified with 'being' or 'activity' (creativity) as such, but should be associated with the definiteness achieved by that activity and, more specifically, with its direction. The universe is not a chaos but a cosmos. *Within* the creativity of the world there is an orientation to order, 'luring' towards beauty. Whitehead links the God of religion first of all with that definiteness and that upward urge. For in his philosophy God — and especially the God of the Christians — is associated with "the 'tender elements' in the world" (PR 343).

More and more, however, and especially towards the end of *Process and Reality*, the awareness grows that God is also related to that other feature of creativity, viz, time as perpetual perishing. And here the notion of the 'consequent nature' of God becomes important. Of course, there are systematic reasons for introducing God's consequent nature: to be actual at all, God should — according to the ontological principle — also be the unification of his actual world. But the introduction of God's consequent nature is first of all inspired by the problem of perpetual perishing: "This is the problem which gradually shapes itself as religion reaches its higher phases in civilized communities. The most general formulation of the religious problem is the question whether the process of the temporal world passes into the formation of other actualities bound together in an order in which novelty does not mean loss" (PR 340). Here again the image is one of 'tenderness,' the tender care that nothing be lost.

Whitehead's nonidentification of God and creativity, indeed the clear and strong distinction which he makes between the two, is deliberate. Despite the important place he gives God in his writings, Whitehead surely does not want to shower God with metaphysical compliments; but at the same time he is very sensitive to rational order in the world, and to the urge towards (and the presence of) goodness, harmony, and intensity.

Creativity as such is neutral towards order, goodness, harmony, and intensity. Things could just as well go the opposite way. Ongoingness is by no means necessarily a movement towards beauty. Creativity is activity as such, leading to chaos as well as cosmos, realizing disharmony as well as order. Process does not inevitably mean progress. The religious notion of God, however, is fundamentally linked to upward movement, to refreshment and beauty, to harmony, adventure, and peace. Therefore, when incorporated into a philosophical scheme, the religious ultimate should not be identified with the metaphysical ultimate. God and creativity do not coincide.

Not all being is good in se, and disharmony, chaos, pain, and evil are not merely the 'absence of being.' Whitehead is too sensitive to the dark side of reality to explain it away so easily. And it is precisely for this reason that he draws such a distinct line between God and creativity. In *Science and the Modern World*, when for the first time he speaks of the relation between God and the metaphysical ultimate, he writes: "Among medieval and modern philosophers, anxious to establish the religious significance of God, an unfortunate habit has prevailed of paying to him metaphysical compliments. He has been conceived as the foundation of the metaphysical situation with its ultimate activity. If this conception be adhered to, there can be no alternative except to discern in him the origin of all evil as well as of all good. He is then the supreme author of the play, and to him must therefore be ascribed its shortcomings as well as its success. If He be conceived as the supreme ground for limitation, it stands in His very nature to divide the Good from the Evil, and to establish Reason 'within her dominions supreme.' "[6] Later, as the notion of the consequent nature of God becomes more prominent, God is again dealt with in the context of the struggle between good and evil: "The ultimate evil in the temporal world is deeper than any specific evil. It lies in the fact that the past fades, that time is a 'perpetual perishing'. . . . But there is no reason, of any ultimate metaphysical generality, why this should be the whole story" (PR 340).

If God be the metaphysical ultimate with no further qualification, then the explanation of all evil, as well as all good, has to start with him. But this is hardly compatible with the intuition basic to at least the Christian faith — an intuition spread throughout the ages — that above all God is good. Hence the problem arises: if God is the creator of the world, how is evil possible? Even Leibniz's semi-deterministic 'best-of-all-worlds' needs a 'theo-dicy': God must be freed of the charge of causing evil.

To avoid ascribing evil, in one form or another, to God, Whitehead makes a clear distinction between God and creativity. God is not the only creative agent. As Hartshorne likes to put it, not all decisions are God's. Especially since the last century the awareness has grown that the finite makes its own decisions, that it is autonomous, original, and hence responsible for its own choices. Philosophically, this new sensitivity was mainly a reaction against Hegel's panlogism. Existentially, the 'Auschwitz-experience'[7] painfully sharpened this awareness. God *cannot* be responsible for all that happens; clearly this is not the best of all worlds.

This problem can be considered from another, yet closely related, point of view, viz, the problem of meaninglessness. Traditional 'theological' metaphysics searches not only for the foundation of all existence, but also for its final meaning. Since not everything that exists or happens seems to be meaningful, there is always the suspicion that in the end nothing really is. The possibility of the ultimate absence of meaning is real. A theodicy, a justification of the totality of reality, does not seem to be a viable option. The world is clearly not good enough to be *nothing other* than *God's* creation.

On the other hand, the religious intuition persists that, for all the differences between God and being, God nonetheless has to be related to all that happens. Nothing is essentially alien to God. So the problem is twofold: on the one hand, God, if He is good, cannot be responsible for evil; on the other hand, if He is to be God, He has to be related somehow to all that happens. To employ the religious notion of God in metaphysics is to attempt to do justice to the real possibility of evil, and thus to the autonomy of the finite and the contingent, while at the same time to ground the hope that ultimate meaninglessness will not prevail against His very presence in the totality of reality. All these have been central themes in recent Continental philosophical theology. Both by his conceptions of creativity and God and by his reconstruction of their relationship, Whitehead has tried to give a coherent metaphysical expression to all these modern concerns.

Whitehead's God is not 'creativity itself,' nor does He create the world; rather "he saves it: or, more accurately, he is the poet of the world, with tender patience leading it by his vision of truth, beauty and goodness" (PR

346). God is the primordial characterization, conditioning all activity. As such "he is not *before* all creation, but *with* all creation" (PR 343). "He is the lure for feeling, the eternal urge of desire" (PR 344). At the same time He is the primordial exemplification of creativity (PR 344), weaving his "physical feelings upon his primordial concepts" (PR 345). In the systematic language of *Process and Reality*, and according to the ontological principle, God is an actuality, but the only one that is not also an actual occasion: he is the only nontemporal actual entity. God is not Reality itself, but accounts for its order, rationality, beauty, urge towards intensity-in-harmony, and everlastingness.

III. FROM WHITEHEAD TO HARTSHORNE

Hartshorne's thought has always been considered to be the continuation of Whitehead's, and, in part at least, rightly so. For Hartshorne creativity is also the central notion, and the distinction between creativity and God plays an important role, generally for the same reasons as for Whitehead. Nevertheless Hartshorne's Process thought shifts considerably from Whitehead's concerning the notions of creativity and God as well as their relation.

For Whitehead creativity is foremost the principle of activity, whereby the one and the many pass rhythmically from the one to the other. Further, and to some extent derivative from this, creativity is the principle of novelty. But for Hartshorne creativity is foremost *free* activity, "productive of unpredictable novelty."[8] "To be is to create" (WP 132), which means: "To be is to be free" (WP 133). But creativity, as free activity, is relative, having an infinite range of possible degrees: an activity is more or less free or creative (WP 132). This means that for Hartshorne the notion of creativity is analogical, while for Whitehead the many become one, not analogically, but literally in the same basic way on all levels. Related to this, Hartshorne employs the notion of consciousness analogically, turning Process thought into a pan-psychism.[9] God then becomes eminently creative and eminently conscious, and, in a sense, He becomes creativity — as well as consciousness — itself.

This leads to Hartshorne's new understanding of God. Whereas for nondivine creativity, Hartshorne stresses originality and spontaneity, concerning God's creativity, he stresses receptivity.[10] The reason is clear: for Hartshorne the notion basic to an understanding of God is first of all 'all-inclusiveness.' "Cosmic Wholeness ... is the essential concept."[11] "In theistic religions," Hartshorne writes, "God is the One Who is Worshipped" (NT 3). And worship is "a consciously unitary response to life" (NT 5). Thus in order to be worthy of worship, God must be — in Anselm's terms — the not-conceivably-surpassable being (NT 17). Only then is He truly worthy of man's complete worship and love. If all things that exist are not included in the worshipped One, "then, in being even slightly interested in them (i.e., the nondivine actualities) we are doing something besides loving God" (NT 16). Thus God "is the wholeness of the world, correlative to the wholeness of every sound individual dealing with the world" (NT 6). "An individual (other than God) is only a fragment of reality, not the whole; but is all individuality . . . similarly fragmentary? Or is the cosmic or all-inclusive whole also an integrated individual, the sole non-fragmentary individual?" (NT 6—7).

In these statements the basic lines within which Hartshorne's concept of God — and his whole philosophy — moves are clearly delineated. His basic concern is not so much the rhythmic process of becoming as it is the question "is the cosmic or all-inclusive whole also an integrated individual?" (NT 7). And this is the basic concern not only of his own philosophy; it is as well, according to Hartshorne, that of religion. Therefore God is not primarily the primordial structuring of possibility linked with an urge towards beauty; that is, He is not primarily 'the poet of the world' leading the world with his vision of goodness and beauty. Rather, God is foremost the a priori all-inclusive One, the final integrative unity of reality. He is the "Apotheosis" (PR 348), rather than the "Eros" (SMW 326), of the Universe.

Consequently Hartshorne's panentheistic God is not simply the first characterization of creativity, but, in two respects, He is creativity itself, viz, connotatively and denotatively. God is said *connotatively* to be creativity itself insofar as He is eminently creative, i.e., creative in the literal sense; and He is said *denotatively* to be creativity itself insofar as all creativity finds its home in him. God is the ultimate 'locus' of all creativity, "the place of all things, and all things are, in the most utterly literal sense 'in' him" (CSPM 17). But how then can those problems that led Whitehead to distinguish God from creativity as such be avoided?

Hartshorne, like Whitehead, makes a distinction between divine and nondivine creativity — even a strong one. But his distinction is made *within* the idea of God's a priori all-inclusiveness. Nondivine creativity is not merely an 'emanation' of a fullness of being, but is an autonomous and original contribution to the whole of reality, and, as such, to God himself. Whereas in classical theism, as P. Schoonenberg points out, there are more *beings* than God, but not more *being*,[12] in Hartshorne's philosophy there is, in a special sense at least, more *being* than God. Indeed there is more creativity than God's creativity. Still this nondivine creativity is not really outside God. And even if, for Hartshorne, the autonomy of the finite and contingent must not be obscured; even if, to the contrary, such autonomy is a precondition for a coherent metaphysics; still nondivine creativity resides in God, which means, in its very being it is included by God, and whenever something new comes into existence it will be included by God.

All this implies that for Hartshorne metaphysics ultimately becomes a 'metaphysics of God.' And here too the shift from Whitehead is striking. The question 'Why is there something rather than nothing?' has been called the metaphysical question par excellence. Translated into Whitehead's philosophy, it becomes 'Why is there creativity rather than nothing?'. For creativity is the "ultimate explanation,"[13] which itself cannot be 'explained' further except in terms of 'what things are,' i.e., in terms of the 'nature of things.' All explanation finally ends 'in' creativity; nothing can exist outside it. Even God can only 'explain' or 'be a reason' thanks to the creativity of the world. For Hartshorne, on the contrary, thought is through and through God-thought: God is the beginning and the end of metaphysics. And so, translated into Hartshorne's philosophy, the metaphysical question par excellence becomes 'Why is there God rather than nothing?', which is answered by an ontological argument for God's existence. As Hartshorne writes, "It is my personal view that a metaphysics can also be integrated by taking as one's intuitive starting point, not creativity or the category of the ultimate; but deity." After stating his understanding of the ontological argument and the meaning of perfection, he continues, "One will in this way have derived the equivalent of the category of the ultimate from the religious idea alone" (WP 165).

Hartshorne's move to this concept of God as the all-inclusive unity of all there is clearly finds its foundation in his interpretation of God as panentheistic, which in turn derives from his basic philosophical and religious intuitions, viz, of the individual unity of reality and of the nature of worship and perfection respectively. Actually these two intuitions are rather two aspects of the same intuition of the unity of all in God.[14] God is Reality Itself as the all-encompassing Individual Reality: "His memory is the past, his plan the predictable future, his love is his prehension which makes the many individuals one world, his power is the realm of the possible, his enjoyment that of the actual" (WP 61).

Whether Whitehead's God is panentheistic is debatable. W. Christian thinks it is not: "For Whitehead God's prehension of the world is in God, but the world is not in God."[15] For Hartshorne, on the contrary, to prehend perfectly is literally to include.[16] With Hartshorne Process philosophy becomes not only panpsychism, but also panentheism.

IV. BY WAY OF CONCLUSION

Now the question remains: can the Process conception of God be 're-deemed'? That is, is it a viable option in these nonmetaphysical times? Can its proponents profitably join the dialogue of those who are still asking ultimate and religious questions?

First, it seems best not to identify Whitehead and Hartshorne too readily. Their differences are often obscured by their all too obvious similarities. As was stated, one of the great merits of Whitehead's metaphysics is its crisp and clearcut distinction between creativity and God. It is Whitehead's most important contribution to philosophical theology. A simpler metaphysics is conceivable, but when God is identified with the creator, in the most common sense of the word, there is no escaping His responsibility for evil as well as good. Whitehead sees the complexities of this world, which is not good enough to be the outcome of one single creative agency. Thus God and being are not equivalent, and in this regard Whitehead is clearly in line with

Heidegger. But, whereas for Heidegger God is not a being either, God is conceived by Whitehead, after all, as *an* actual entity, albeit a very special one. In this respect Whitehead seems to fall into what Heidegger calls the onto-theological structure of Western metaphysics. Here Whitehead comes close to traditional theism, even though his God is not the creator-God of traditional Christianity. But Whitehead differs decisively from classical onto-theology in that for him God is not Being itself, nor is He "subsistent Being" ("*Ipsum esse subsistens*"). Whitehead's alternative to Being is Creativity pervaded by God as its primordial characterization. But Creativity is not actual enough to be all-encompassing Reality. Whitehead's metaphysics is really a pluralism of interrelated monads, with God as the supreme Monad.

And what about Hartshorne? Under the guise of a more traditional terminology, Hartshorne represents a strong monistic tendency in the philosophy of religion. One's first impression is that Hartshorne speaks of God in a rather traditional way: God knows the world and is eminent creativity, allowing for other, lesser forms of creativity. God does not decide everything and is even a suffering God. But when pressed, the similarity of Hartshorne's ideas to those of the great idealistic tradition becomes obvious. Based on Anselm's argument, Hartshorne's God has all the hallmarks of Spinoza's 'Substance': God is necessary, all-encompassive, eternal being. In a certain sense, God is being itself and not simply *a* being. "He is the definitive, universal being."[17] All other beings are 'in' God, as the Spinozistic 'modes' are — by definition — in 'Substance.' Or in Hegelian terms, there is only one 'Absolute'; everything else must literally be in the 'Absolute.' Moreover, the 'Absolute' is the whole, and the 'Whole' alone is absolute. Hartshorne holds that Hegel wavers between pantheism and panentheism; but it is obvious that, when pressed, Hegel ends up a panentheist. Hartshorne's notion of inclusion-through-knowledge brings him closer to German idealism and its Anglo-Saxon offshoots than would ever have been possible for the empiricist Whitehead. In fact, Hartshorne *is* an idealist in a very strong sense: to know is to include, and to know perfectly is to include perfectly. The great advantage of Hartshorne's system is its conception of God as not just one individual among individuals, not one being among beings. God is "*the* being. God is the universally relevant, the definitive being, the being whose reality includes every other reality and defines its reality."[18]

How is this inclusion to be conceived? Hartshorne himself answers: "Now, I conceive inclusion in idealistic terms. To include something in the ultimate sense is to know it, to be aware of it, to have it as a content of awareness. If I knew, fully knew, the happiness of someone else, I would have that happiness, it would be mine. What we call knowledge in ourselves is an abstract, very limited thing, so that we can know other people are happy and that may not make us happy. But if we fully knew, concretely and absolutely knew, their happiness, we would have it, it would be ours; and that's the sense in which God is everything."[19] Hartshorne thus conceives this inclusion primarily in terms of knowing. God is eminently knowing, and this means that He is eminently inclusive, since to know is to include. In this way Hartshorne can say that God is Reality itself, while at the same time strongly affirming the existence of an autonomous realm of the non-divine. His key to reconciling these two affirmations is his notion of all-inclusiveness. Indeed everything hinges on the possibility of conceiving this all-inclusiveness in terms of inclusion-through-knowledge. So there is strong evidence for an idealistic, monistic reading of Hartshorne's notion of inclusion. And yet he equally seems to stress the difference between divine creativity and creaturely creativity. All things may be in God, but inclusive Reality is not simply identical to the included realities. All in all, Hartshorne seems to meet well a basic requirement of contemporary philosophy, influenced as it is by Heidegger. The charge of onto-theology leveled against traditional metaphysics does not apply to Hartshorne, as he cannot be said to have overlooked the ontological difference — and, it should be added, the ontological unity — between being and beings. And yet Hartshorne is strangely different from Heidegger: "My dad knows everything about God," to quote Hartshorne's five year-old daughter, while Heidegger knows almost nothing about Him. But Heidegger has a lot to say about Being and beings (the ontological difference). Hartshorne's God-talk, on the other hand, can easily be translated into the language of a philosophy of being. It is a rewarding exercise to read 'being' wherever Hartshorne has written 'God,' and 'beings' wherever he has written 'nondivine creativity.' Such a reading brings Hartshorne even closer to Heidegger.

The question, however, remains: should God and being be identified? There is no doubt that many of the things Heidegger says of Being have traditionally been said of God: Being takes the initiative; it reveals itself, and still it remains hidden; it speaks to those alone who know how to listen; and heeding the call of being is ultimately a matter of grace. It can well be argued that Heidegger's true inspiration is the German mystics, and that his philosophy is a thoroughly secularized form of mysticism. This has already been proposed by Karl Löwith, providing an eye-opening key for interpretation. Meister Eckhart and the Rhineland mystic Heinrich Suso (1295/1300—1366) are hidden and revealed on almost every turn of the fieldtrack.

Still the identification of God and Heidegger's Being is ill-advised and offers no solution to the problems of today's natural theology. Heidegger himself explicitly rejects such an identification. The need for a clearer distinction between God and being presents itself when both the metaphysical problematic and religious sensitivity are taken into account.

Nor should God be identified with all-inclusive creativity either. 'God' is undoubtedly a religious category, a category of interpretation. One cannot be forced to see creativity as divine creativity. Hartshorne has always admitted that there is no convincing proof of God's existence. But he surely admits that the necessary existence of all-inclusive reality can be proved. For it simply cannot not exist. Thus Hartshorne's metaphysics would gain immense credibility if it ceased to label all-inclusive reality 'God.' Should it not be left open whether all-inclusive reality can be meaningfully called God? A believer who understands what Paul says to the philosophers at Athens ("In him we move and have our being." Acts 17:28) will recognize in all-inclusive reality some features of divine care. But he recognizes it as such precisely *because* he believes. A nonbeliever recognizes in all-inclusive reality *only* the ongoingness of the universe itself.

If the God of religion is neither *a* being, nor 'Being itself,' nor even *the* all-inclusive Being, how then should He be conceived? 'God' is the philosophico-religious name given to all-inclusive reality *as qualified* by an urge towards unity, harmony, goodness, and beauty. Religious experience is precisely the hopeful recognition of that urge, which is represented by the believer as fulfilling the universe by its directedness towards values — a divine urge, more personal than man, and, although now struggling and suffering along with him, victorious in the end. Is 'agape' (1 John 4:8) not a good name for that urge?

Hartshorne labels his form of neoclassical theism 'panentheism.' But the world is *not yet* good enough to be called panentheistic. If it were, it would coincide with the Kingdom of God. A redeemed Hartshornian philosophy could rightfully be characterized as a hopeful belief in 'eschatological theo-en-pantism,' a belief not far from Paul's cry "that God be all in all" (1 Cor. 15:28).

It is so difficult to identify God with all-inclusive reality because, without doubt, idealistic inclusion is for many of us not a viable concept. Perfect knowledge may include its objects, but contingent realities are too earthly, too bodily, too 'heavy' to be included by knowledge. The dark side of existence, the sphere of nonrealized possibilities, is not merely evil resulting from cross purposes. And this is why, along with Eckhart and the mystics, Nietzsche and Dionysius are found in Heidegger's thought about being. His thought includes nonthought. Hartshorne's way of philosophizing, by contrast, seems somewhat limpid and ethereal. It is almost too logical to reflect our not-completely-logical world. It is too 'idealistic' for ordinary, not-completely-rational beings.

But for those who can grasp it — either by connaturality or conversion — Hartshorne's philosophy is a refreshing source of true metaphysical inspiration in these nonmetaphysical times. It speaks of God to an age that has proclaimed his death. It is a philosophy that has truly exhausted all the resources of one basic insight — as all great philosophy should do.

NOTES

1. M. Heidegger, *Identität und Differenz* (Pfüllingen: Neske, 1957), p. 45.
2. *Ibid.*, p. 64.
3. J. Macquarrie, *In Search of Deity. An Essay in Dialectical Theism*, The Gifford Lectures, 1983—84 (London: SCM Press, 1984), p. 162.

4. A. N. Whitehead, *Process and Reality. An Essay in Cosmology,* corrected edition, D. R. Griffin and D. W. Sherburne (eds.) (New York: The Free Press, 1978), p. 31. All further references will be to this edition, hereafter noted within the text as PR.

5. A. N. Whitehead, *Adventures of Ideas* (New York: Macmillan, 1933), p. 227.

6. A. N. Whitehead, *Science and the Modern World* (New York: Macmillan, 1933), p.258. All further references will hereafter be noted within the text as SMW.

7. In Whitehead's life, there was the experience of World War I and the death of his son in that war, which seems to have had a great impact upon him.

8. C. Hartshorne, *Whitehead's Philosophy. Selected Essays 1935—1970* (Lincoln: University of Nebraska Press, 1972), p. 132. All further references will hereafter be noted within the text as WP.

9. Whitehead does not use 'consciousness' analogically, but literally. He makes a clear distinction between 'mental' and 'conscious.'

10. Cf. C. Hartshorne, *Creative Synthesis and Philosophic Method* (London: SCM Press, 1970), p. 12: "Our new philosophical doctrine is that even God's creativity is his higher form of emergent experiential synthesis, or response to stimuli. He influences us supremely because he is supremely open to our influence." All further references will hereafter be noted within the text as CSPM.

11. C. Hartshorne, *A Natural Theology for Our Time* (LaSalle, IL: Open Court, 1967), p. 7. All further references will hereafter be noted within the text as NT.

12. "Dantur plura entia, non datur plus entis." See P. Schoonenberg, "God in relatie en in wording," *Streven* 33 (1979—80): p. 884.

13. It has been argued that creativity in Whitehead's philosophy cannot be an explanation because it is not an actual entity, and "no actual entities, then no reason" (PR 19), as the ontological principle holds. Indeed creativity is not a 'reason' in the sense of either an efficient or a final cause, as is required by the ontological principle. But as far as the most general characteristics are concerned, one cannot give 'reasons,' i.e., still more ultimate actual entities. It is 'because of' the creativity of the world that 'reasons' can play at all.

14. Or to put it in terms of the title of Hartshorne's Ph.D. dissertation, "The Unity of Being in the Absolute or Divine Good."

15. W. Christian, *An Interpretation of Whitehead's Metaphysics* (New Haven: Yale University Press, 1959, 1967), p. 392.

16. Even when, especially in the seventies, the problem of the relation between contemporaries and the problem of simultaneity arise, and when these problems seem to make a strict panentheism more difficult to maintain, Hartshorne sticks to his basic intuition: even when God does not prehend the actualities in their subjective immediacy, He prehends and includes them *once* they are and *as* they are, i.e., once they have become.

17. "A Conversation between Charles Hartshorne and Jan Van der Veken," *Louvain Studies* 8 (1980), p. 134.

18. *Ibid.,* p. 133.

19. *Ibid.,* p. 134.

9. Hartshorne's Concept of God Examined in the Light of Phenomenology and Buddhism

HIROSHI ENDO

I. INTRODUCTORY REMARKS

In this paper the phenomenological movement from Husserl to Levinas and the development of process philosophy from Whitehead to Hartshorne are comparatively studied. The aspects to be compared are: first, how universals are dealt with in both fields; secondly and mainly, in what modes the opposition between interiority and exteriority presents itself in the development of both trends. The essentials of Hartshorne's concept of God will come to the fore all the more clearly against the background of such a comparison.

My purpose is not to indicate in the final analysis the differences between Hartshornian process theology and Levinasian moral theology, but to try to find some possibility for the former to comprise the latter. In so doing, I will also show that some main characteristics of Buddhistic thought can be congenial to both theologies.

II. THE PHENOMENOLOGICAL MOVEMENT FROM HUSSERL TO LEVINAS AND PROCESS PHILOSOPHY

In order to arrive at Hartshorne's concept of God one must take note of his methodological anthropomorphism. All our best thought is anthropomorphic, argues Hartshorne, in the sense that we must take our own reality as a sample of reality in general. Moreover, we most surely and adequately know this sample not only by seeing, hearing, touching, tasting, smelling it as we can with non-human things, but also by being it.[1] Now, how do we understand our reality, so far as we see, hear, touch, taste and smell it? In the light of the fact that understanding our own reality influences the understanding of reality in general and above all God's reality, how we answer the above question is crucial. Moreover, what does it mean to say that we know our reality by being it? How are knowing and being connected with each other?

Let us enquire into the meaning of Hartshorne's argument from two perspectives, i.e., phenomenological as well as process-philosophical. Seeing,

S. Sia (ed.), Charles Hartshorne's Concept of God, 137–152.
© 1990 Kluwer Academic Publishers. Printed in the Netherlands.

hearing, touching, tasting, smelling the sample (= our reality) is experiencing the corresponding sensa. Phenomenologically, experiences usually make up the sediment of meanings which, when relevant and as needed, motivate further experiences. In Husserlian terminology, the former 'founds' (*fundiert*) the latter. Berkeley's example of hearing the rattle, with direct understanding that a horse carriage is approaching, illustrates well how sedimentary meanings motivate our experience of hearing the horse carriage rather than the mere rattle. When we look into the mirror and see our own face rather than an almost symmetrical, particular geometrical pattern, the experience of seeing is also 'founded' on previous experiences.

According to the process philosophy of Hartshorne, human consciousness is a single linear succession of states. Previous states are retained cumulatively in the present nascent state in its process of becoming past actuality.[2] And it is easy to think analogically with Husserl that previously experienced universals or some of Whiteheadian eternal objects emerge in the nascent state when relevant and as needed.

Thus far, there seems to be little disparity between experiencing our reality and being our reality, because past actuality having once been nascent present is not essentially different from the now nascent present, which is primarily our reality or, so to speak, the core of our reality.

According to Husserl, temporal modification from a present to the past retained in the new present enables the stream to constitute itself as a continuous stream. In that sense it is the ontological basis on which linear succession can be a single continuum. Thus we happen to be cumulatively our reality not as mere fact but we cannot be our reality until cumulativeness emerges.

One aspect of Husserl's concept of God is the ground of the metaphysical distance between the nascent anonymous present and the retained past therein. This distance in the non-temporal or pre-temporal "unity-in-separation" is always teleologically presupposed by and contained in the cumulation. God is operative here as concealed co-presence.

Another aspect of his concept of God is derived from his thought on platonic ideas. This is not necessarily irrelevant to cumulativeness. Husserl remains basically in his own stream of consciousness, but when in his genetic analysis of meaning he is confronted with the problem of the origin of universals, he transcends in the long run his own conscious territory and goes back to the ancients' consciousness.[3] He is entitled to do that, he would say, for the essence of consciousness does not depend upon individual conscious realization. And in the same way, he asserts, reflection does not change the essence of consciousness, so that phenomenology itself, whose method is reflection, is valid.[4] Here the universals warrant legitimacy of the transcendence from occasion to occasion. We could even say that the universals seem to maneuver teleologically in the splitting of conscious reality; otherwise, there will be no necessity for their existence. Thus Husserl's God has an aspect of pantheistic internal telos and another theistic aspect as ultimate pole-idea (Pol-Idee).[5]

The mind-body problem annoys Husserl more, since the essence of consciousness seems to give no help to the solution of it, and when bodily occasions are also taken into consideration, the above-mentioned method of identifying "experiencing our reality" and "being our reality" is no more appropriate. This is because it did not occur to Husserl to utilize a percipient occasion as sample to give analogical explanations to bodily occasions. For Husserl occasions outside the linear succession are not included in his own reality. In order that such occasions may be dealt with, Husserl brought them into the conscious society of linear personal order. One example is kinesthesia which functions as one of the clues to deal with the bodily occasions.[6] For example, when we look into the mirror, and see our face frowning, we have not only the visual experience but also the kinesthetic feeling of frowning, the former experience being 'founded' upon the latter. That is to say, in the nascent present there are innumerable past experiences passively or semiconsciously synthesized, among which kinesthetic occasions play a role to constitute the meaning of our bodily extension as well as extension outside the body.

Here the problem is that Husserl does not grasp our own reality as a nexus of innumerable contemporary occasions, cellular occasions, molecular occasions and so forth. For what interests him is only the meanings of any event whatever that are directly given to his consciousness, so that he could live through them.

It is Levinas who stands near to process philosophers not only by being sensitive to the becoming of occasions but also by accepting our whole reality as a nexus of both conscious and bodily occasions. He criticizes Heidegger, indicating sarcastically that the latter's humans do not get hungry.

Levinas says, "We live from 'good soup,' air, light, spectacles, work, ideas, sleep, etc. . . . . These are not objects of representations."[7] In comparison with 'consciousness of (*conscience de*)' in Husserl, Levinas calls 'live from (*livre de*)' a kind of intentionality, i.e., intentionality of enjoyment, in contrast with Husserlian intentionality of representation. Here the concept of enjoyment means almost the same as in Whitehead. Whitehead's enjoyment, physical prehension, is in its own nature exclusive, but derives its share of infinity from the infinity of appetition, which is in its own nature all-embracing.[8] For Levinas the essence of enjoyment is also the transmutation of the other into the selfsameness (*transmutation de l'autre en Même*). It is not the mere awareness of what fulfills life, but embraces (*embrasser*) all the content of life and living life itself. It is also said that in enjoyment, the process of constitution which comes into play wherever there is representation is reversed. That is, the intentionality of enjoyment, unlike the intentionality of representation, holds onto the exteriority, which the latter suspended. Levinas symbolically expresses enjoyment as made up of memories of thirst and quenching, just as in Whitehead the process of fulfilling physical purpose occurs repeatedly. Enjoyment is indeed such a pulsation. And for him to grasp the exteriority is to posit oneself in the world corporeally,[9] which means to enter into a relation with the earth (exteriority, others) by determining and at the same time being determined by it, like a painter taking notice of himself coming out of the picture he is painting. That is to say, exteriority rejects all the endeavors to make it completely transparent by the aforementioned Husserlian subjectivistic theories of 'foundation' (*Fundierung*) or of passive synthesis, etc. It has, as it were, its own infinite density. It is also irreducible to a system of, so-called, anonymous operational references which Heidegger's analysis of instrumentality intended to show; namely, the network of almost unconscious purposive indications.

It is said that Levinas went deeply into phenomenology and transcended it from within. What is meant by 'transcend from within'? The answer is that Levinas made thorough internalization to the very limit (i.e., in terms of process philosophy, the reduction of every occasion to the conscious society of personal order) and thereby he found on the contrary what remains always beyond his reach, the non-possessable. That is, he extended his own reality beyond Husserl's transcendental subject. Now, his reality consists of all the bodily as well as conscious occasions and yet he is confronted with unfathomable exteriority. A navigator makes use of the sea and the wind. He dominates them in a certain sense, and yet he does not thereby transform them into things, i.e., the possessable.[10]

For Levians essence is egoistic in the sense that it tenaciously retains itself through varied occasions. By means of such an essence can Husserlian reflecting ego remain the same. All the internalizations of the Husserlian and Heideggerian type are based upon that logic. We need essences, whatever they may be, in order to sustain and prolong our own endurance. For Levinas 'following the essence' never brings us to Divine presence. God does not exist even in exteriority, but beyond exteriority and that in an ethical context, which will be discussed below.

Now, the Levinasian concept of being (*être*) is hard to understand. The concept seems, however, to approximate boundlessly the Whiteheadian concept of being. Being has power to, and is ready to, draw us into its territory. Being is indeed the burden we cannot but bear. Existents emerge in the relation to being and at the same time accepting being. That is to say, on appropriating being we extricate ourselves from being into existence. When he discusses 'enjoyment' Levinas seemingly construes the unfathomable depth of this atemporal being as an inlet of exteriority.

But let us be more careful to avoid drawing a hasty conclusion. Our body contains cumulatively innumerable past occasions. In this sense being already lurks in our body. Enjoyment cannot be conceived irrespective of such being. But in addition to that Levinas must have taken hold of the contemporary nascent present of bodily occasions. Although his philosophy seems to have no essential relationship with relativity theory, he must have felt the exteriority of those nascent occasions. It seems to me this is the very reason why his concept of existence is not confined to existence of conscious occasions.[11] If so, it may be a mistake to deal with Levinas only from an existentialist perspective.

The development from Husserl to Levinas is important in the sense that the phenomenological perspective has been enlarged and the concept of exteriority brought in, though universals have been deprived of their power to be indicative of Divinity.

I once tried to show Husserl's metaphysics in his later period as a subsystem of Whitehead's cosmology.[12] The Husserlian God is shown above to have primitive unrefined dipolarity. Levinas comes close to process philosophy, but the situation becomes difficult for us to make speculations on dipolarity. Now, we shall see next the development of process philosophy from Whitehead to Hartshorne against the background of the phenomenological movement as presented above.

III. DEVELOPMENT FROM WHITEHEAD TO HARTSHORNE

We will consider the development from Whitehead to Hartshorne by taking up the problem of universals first.

As Hartshorne indicates, in Whitehead's theory of becoming there is room for suspecting that in the so-called superject nothing remains but eternal objects.[13] Let us take up this problem first. Whiteheadian eternal objects make up a hierarchy according as their abstractness increases. Located at the lowest level is for instance 'red in its particular shade'. Eternal objects of this lowest sort is problematic, incurring the above suspicion. Moreover, the queer, extraordinary atmosphere continues to envelope all sorts and all levels of eternal objects. Even God's primordial nature itself is thereby influenced.

This becomes more conspicuous when we take into consideration, how eternal objects of both subjective and objective species are transmitted to our final percipient occasions. According to Griffin's analysis, Whitehead's eternal objects as sensa are identical, only their functions are different, whether they ingress into the enjoyments in molecular occasions, cellular occasions or into the transmutation of final high-grade, conscious experiences.[14] In low-grade occasions their functions are receptions, while in high-grade occasions, they are the characterization in objectifying the nexus. And moreover by two-way functioning of them, they are plastering two occasions, one of which prehends the other. Thus, logically speaking, just as in Russell's theory of description some substratum is presupposed to exist before it appears in the given context, so eternal objects do exist to substrate both their quality and their functioning, so that they are no less individual entities than what Whitehead calls actual entities. Thus, actual entities seem to have little to add, except for removing by transmutation the difference of logical hierarchy of class and element, which is postulated in Russell's theory of types.

Thus considered, in so far as Whitehead's doctrine of eternal objects is concerned, the remnant of traditional substantialism seems still to maneuver behind the scenes.

Now, let us go to the primordial nature of God. Whitehead's ontological principle requiring everything to be in some actual entity, those substantial eternal objects are in God's primordial nature, which is itself like eternal objects an atemporal actual entity not presupposing the world and accordingly Whitehead takes it to be deficiently actual, namely, only conceptual actuality.[15] However, seen from the above argument of the vacuity of actual entities in general deprived of their positive roles, the primordial nature is, ironically enough, the typical actual entity rather than exceptionally deficient.

However, the primordial nature, although deficiently actual, fulfils the general mode of concrescence. In that sense it is aboriginal instance of creativity. Namely, God's subjective aim brings forth mutual sensitiveness among its conceptual prehensions, unifying all the eternal objects by evaluating, and so determining the status of, each in the mutual relationships of all. Thus in satisfaction of the primordial level, the barren inefficient disjunction of separate eternal objects are brought into adjusted efficient conjunction. This adjusted togetherness as an actual efficient fact constitutes all the eternal objects into relevant lures of feeling.[16] And what is important is that the subjective aim of the primordial nature being the intensification of God's formal immediacy, the lures conferred on eternal objects seem ultimately to be goads toward God's primordial appetition to intensify his own immediacy. Therefore, finite actual entities appropriate not only eternal objects but also, by understanding the status of the appropriated eternal objects, are drawn into the relevance of all the eternal objects, submitting themselves ultimately to God's primordial appetition.

Thus, although Whitehead posited the concept of God as locus for eternal objects, some minor change of ontological principle might save us from positing the concept. It may be possible that eternal objects take care of themselves in coalescing into a vast system of potentialities, because the way of coalescence itself is a potentiality among many others. And eternal objects themselves evolve, as in Peircean cosmos.[17]

Therefore, the reason why God's primordial nature is significant for finite occasions is primarily not that all the eternal objects are unified in it, but that God has appetition to intensify his subjective immediacy, to which the occasions can relate themselves by hybrid physical prehensions. Indeed we can conceptually get into such a divine realm, so to speak, which is immanent in the world and by which we are persuaded to future advances. This is very important, for otherwise finite actualities could not have appetition to prehend the eternal objects.

Now, we have come to find ourselves in a queer situation. For human existence, God plays important roles in the sense that our will to be originates from God, but not in the sense that eternal objects are in it. The above-mentioned higher order eternal objects can evolve from and within the eternal objects. Now, can this evolution itself be regarded as God's spirit? The answer is "No," because, if so, all the eternal objects are objects of conceptual prehensions or some eternal objects are subjective forms of the conceptual prehensions, and, if the former holds, evolution fails and, if the latter holds, infinite hierarchy is presupposed as is seen in Bradley's paradox. To aviod the paradox, God must prehend eternal objects without any subjective form, that is, without giving any form of unity, and equivalently after all without any evaluation, against Whitehead's original intention.

The conclusion is, actual occasions prehend God not for eternal objects but for creativity instantiated by God. Why do they not have direct contact with eternal objects and creativity? The ultimate cause of this predicament may be Whitehead's having separated the primordial nature and creativity.

Another problem of the primordial nature is that in this nature God is unconscious for want of contrast. According to Ford, Whitehead introduced the physical nature of God just experimentally in order that God might have conscious propositional feelings.[18] However, in Whitehead such God's dipolarity is not thought through, as Whitehead himself confessed in answer to Johnson's question.[19] For instance, there seems to be logical incongruence between God's primordial existence as an actual entity and God's superjective nature necessary for his everlasting consequent nature.

Now, Husserl's God is rather similar to Whitehead's in so far as the latter's primordial nature gives our reality its telos for subjective intensity and also eternal objects of higher order as pole idea. But as in the case of Husserl the concept of Whitehead's eternal object must be re-examined, so that the dipolarity of God may be put in order.

Hartshorne's doctrine of universals must now be taken up for discussion. For him universals, unlike eternal objects, are not definite or determinate, but definable and determinable, so that they will be rendered definite and determinate as they are actualized at each step in transmission. Hence, it is not the case in Hartshorne that a universal itself subsists through the process of transmission. Here it is actualization that elicits particular qualities with particular relational essences. Now there is no need to locate these universals in some actual entity in order that they may be brought into efficient conjunction, because qualitative universals are a continuum in the beginning. And God's primordial nature is the general metaphysical character of creative advance. So, there is no need for God to prehend eternal objects so as to become the aboriginal instance of creativity.[20]

My interpretation is that this thought has developed under the influence of Peirce's objective logic. Peirce advocates a topological continuum of quality with infinite dimensions, even before space and time are created, the cutting of which degrades the height of dimensions down to our world.[21] According to my understanding here firstness (potentiality) and thirdness (continuity) are yet unseparated, as primogenitor of process.

Now, we will consider the development from Whitehead to Hartshorne in the perspective of the interiority-exteriority opposition. In the beginning let us examine the status of nexus in Whitehead's metaphysics. In order to harmonize intensity of satisfaction and stability of continuous existence the structured societies, such as atom, molecular, cell, animal body, psyche with its body, etc., enhance their mentality, of which there are two modes; transmutation and acquiring novelty. Living things, in which we are interested, show both modes of enhancement. What is to be noted here is the extensiveness presupposed in both cases. For transmutation extensiveness is presupposed in presentational immediacy. With regard to acquiring novelty empty space is always presupposed. "Life lurks in the interstices of each living cell, and in the interstices of the brain." says Whitehead.[22] It is interesting to see that empty space is regarded by Whitehead as nexus. Indeed empty space is not any corpuscular society. There is no corpuscle in it. In so far as empty space is nexus, it has as its member an occasion — empty occasion, I would say — which it is possible for the living society to prehend.

Now, I would propose a tentative interpretation of this concept of empty space. And for that purpose let me refer to Nobo's doctrine that an actual occasion prehends a piece of extension as its own creative domain, before they prehend the so-called initial data.[23] This creative domain for each actual occasion is also said to be the proper region or extensive standpoint of the occasion which is, therefore, in the case of our percipient occasion a presented locus. And what is more important for our discussion to follow is the concept 'quasi-proper region,' as he calls it, which is the extensiveness for togetherness of actual occasions. Whitehead's actual world can be construed in two ways. There is the world as contained modally in an actual occasion and the world into which the actual occasion throws itself, consequently leading to the enlargement of the world. The latter with its potentiality has a quasi-proper region.

The transmutation in our percipient occasion (Whitehead argues that even in so-called inorganic occasions transmutation occurs as long as the occasion is a member of a structured society) presupposes prehension of an empty occasion i.e., presented locus in presentational immediacy. The interstice in the brain is in terms of Nobo's extension a part of a quasi-proper region. But the interstice in the brain spoken of physiologically is nothing but the interstice as is approached in the interstice of the physiologist's brain. To make a long story short, a physiologist can not see another person's brain. When he thinks he sees another person's brain, he really sees his own brain. Thus transmutation occurs in the interstices in the brain as parts of a quasi-proper region. It is by means of projection that in our proper region we see outside. Namely, Nobo's proper region is part of quasi-proper region with no homogeneity between the two of them.

Novelty comes into question next. My interpretation is that in any corpuscular society with subsidiary societies of personal order bundled together, it is hard for an actual occasion conceptually to prehend novel eternal objects, because the defining characteristics are so solid as to leave no room for novelty, in other words, it strongly coerces its order to any actual occasions to prehend its element. Therefore, the locus where novelty is internalized cannot be a corpuscular society but empty nexus. Therefore living occasions are conditioned merely by their own preceding occasions in the same linear succession, and accordingly are free to prehend novelty. However, a living occasion hybridly prehends the conceptual prehension of preceding occasion, so, as Whitehead says, living occasions are canalized in the Bergsonian sense with the result that personal order arises.[24] And Whitehead concludes finally that spirit and body go in harmony. But this seems to be a slightly hasty conclusion, for "hybrid prehension" seems to include some logical difficulties on which I do not argue for the present.

Now, Cobb rightly indicates the absurdity of this theory on interstices when adopted to the interpretation of God.[25] It really sounds strange that God should lurk in interstices of the world. Cobb says, "It would not help to think of God as flitting around in the interstices." And according to Cobb Whitehead does not make it clear why God could physically feel the extensive world, notwithstanding that God is primordially unextensive, being situated at some point of the world. I would say, this is because Whitehead put emphasis more upon actual entity than on nexus, more on becoming than on transition, more on proper region than on quasi-proper region. The same tendency has been seen more conspicuously in Husserl. But actual entity and nexus, becoming and transition, proper region and quasi-proper region, these connect each other in the way in which Wittgenstein's solipsistic subject shrinks to naught and at the same time the realistic world expands.[26] As shown above, both terms in opposition never stand side by side. The moment one appears, the other vanishes.

This situation is rightly comprehended by Hartshorne. His analysis is free from partiality. In him both terms in opposition are harmonized. For Hartshorne a psychical occasion is located not in the notorious interstices of the brain but where the brain as a whole nexus is located. In the light of Nobo's theory of extension the proper region of psychical occasion and the quasi-proper region of the nexus of brain occasions extend, so to speak, one above the other. However, there being no third extension common to both, they are in a sense independent of each other. So, there is no logical reason for psychical occasion to be situated at a tiny spatial nexus, nor at the nexus of brain occasions. And those two domains are, though not identical, immediately related to each other. This immediacy leaves no room for a logical construction of the relation.

Thus, Hartshorne's interpretation of psychical event is effective for constituting a more natural concept of God. God is, in a sense, co-extensive with the nexus of nexus of . . . of nexus of worldly events. God and the world are not located in the extension common to both, still less are they identical, and yet they are immediately related to each other.

IV. LEVINAS AND HARTSHORNE — EXTERIORITY AND MORAL THEOLOGY

In this final section we will compare the Hartshornian concept of God and Levinasian, both of which are constituted somehow in intention toward exteriority.

Here special attention must be paid to the problem of contemporaneity. For Husserl the genuine exteriority became explicit in intersubjectivity. His alleged solution of this problem is notorious. However, his God operated as savior to lay ethical foundation for the above-mentioned unity-in-separation both in the nascent present and intersubjectivity. In fact his body is controlled by 'verborgene Vernunft.'[27] In other words, he understood God as something on which both kinds of unity-in-separation are ultimately and commonly dependent. Such a way to connect the consciousness of inner temporality and intersubjectivity brought him an unhappy result, for people thought his solution of intersubjectivity was too subjectivistic. Indeed there are two opposite ways to grasp the import of the connection. To bring exteriority into the inner sphere with the result of changing exteriority into interiority, — this is the way people understood Husserl — or otherwise of finding exteriority in inner sphere. If the latter be taken into consideration, it would be possible to see an element also in Husserlian thought to induce us to go into Levinasian thought as well as process thought. Levinas went from the conscious sphere down to bodily occasions, wherein he tried in vain, so to speak, a prehensive overcoming of exteriority, by what he calls intentionality of enjoyment.

As a matter of fact, what is overcome by physical prehension, intentionality of enjoyment, is not contemporaneity. If the genuine exteriority always presupposes contemporaneity, it consists in the mutual relationship of contemporary bodily occasions. Levinas' insight falls short of this state of affairs that process philosophers accurately seized. But as I mentioned before, Levinas must have had, so to speak, intuitive comprehension of it. Otherwise he could not proceed to his theory of visage without falling into inconsistency. And it is in intersubjectivity, namely between humans as nexus, that Levinas perceived it clearly at last.

Now, Hartshorne as well as Whitehead knows well the exteriority of contemporaneity nestling deep in the body. However, Hartshornian nexus overcomes any exteriority with ease. The process of the whole nexus of bodily occasions finds no difficulty to go over the interstices in a contracted universe, the body. In this respect, Hartshorne's metaphysics is essentially different from grotesque phenomenological philosophy which ingests nutrition from the interstice itself as is most typically seen in Sartre's pour-soi. Hartshorne's panentheistic concept of God originates from positiveness in overcoming the interstices in opposition to phenomenological concept of God who supplies us with nothingness, i.e., the gap in unity-in-separation.

Therefore, it seems to me, the whole nexus of divine occasions co-extensive with the world, does not suffer from the predicament of so-called cross section of the world process, which does not really exist. Any discrepancy is enclosed and dissolved in the nexus. It is at this point that a very important characteristic of Hartshorne's God is to be indicated.

Now, an actual occasion is passive in two senses. Namely, it is coerced by what it prehends. But this can be no helpless passivity, for actual entity does prehend what it is coerced into prehending. But actual entity is absolutely passive, when it throws itself before others and even before the future occasion in the same personal order, so as to be prehended. To use Kraus's manner of speaking, the self-superjecting of an occasion is its putting itself into absolute passivity, which has nothing to do with teleological over-powering, i.e., concrescence.

Let us analyse this state of affairs in the light of creativity. As I said before, Whitehead's version of creativity includes in itself recursion, or, I dare say, self-reflexivity. "Many become one and are increased by one" is, to speak strictly, "Many become one and are increased by one, and the many increased by one are again a new many, so they become one again and are increased by one again and —" This aspect of creativity is well explained by Hartshorne's self-transcendence of God. This is a logic of transition, not concresence. The afore-mentioned absolute passivity is tantamount to this recursiveness, whose burden, the enigma of creativity, so to speak, God takes care of. Whitehead focussed on the analysis of actual entity with the result of making creativity an enigma. The problem was not solved until it was done by Hartshorne.

But does not the Hartshornian God presuppose the Husserlian God in his self-transcendence? The answer is "no". The Husserlian God is the ground of interiority, while the self-transcendence concerned is not governed by the logic of nascency. Levinas says that we must first be thorough in keeping inside, lest we should internalize anything not properly internal and take what is thus internalized for something external. This attitude of Levinas does not import the relation of presupposition but it well indicates how interiority differs from exteriority.

Now, the greatest problem is related with ethics. Levinas noticed the fatal impossibility in the genuine exteriority in the strict sense of the word in the intersubjective relationship of "face to face". His argument seems to be successful in explicating the origin of ethics. His moral theology has persuasive power because there seems to be even almost no logic in his theory-making.

Now, for Levinas visage is essentially otherness. In the rise of visage I am aroused to moral responsibility to others. The other's radical otherness implies ethical and imperative structure. The visage appears as opposition, an absolute resistance, logos of which is a prohibition, "Thou shalt not kill." This is signification without any context. If it had any context, it would follow the Husserlian logic of interiority, which Levinas rejects.

Now, for Levinas God is entirely other and the infinitely third person who is absent rather than present. He is absolutely transcendent. We can reach God only in visage as metaphysical experience. The visage is suggestive of the transcendent outside the immanent horizon of understanding, where subject-object relationship holds. Therefore, it is not I but others that open the way to God.

For Levinas a subject is not properly subject which rules over its interior territory but that which is subject to visage, and is subject also to Divinity. Now, being subject in this sense can be interpreted by the contributionism Hartshorne holds. For Hartshorne human life is of value, because it contributes to the divine life. Therefore the supreme aim for our moral life is to enrich the divine life. Thus far, Levinas and Hartshorne are close. But it is also true, for Levinas one must be, to begin with, unconditionally ethical before visage, where divinity then emerges, while for Hartshorne ethics originates in one's contribution to God which seems to take precedence over promoting good life among others.

After all, the contribution to the divine life means to become immortal in the perfect divine memory. My being as a whole throughout my life-span is not determined until my death. To speak somewhat phenomenologically, it is after my death that the meaning of my entire life, not of each part of my life, will be created in God's mind. Thus, my death is nothing but creation of my being, or I might say, resurrection. Hartshorne rightly says, "It is not my death, but God's that would make my life a mere absurdity."[28] Here the logic of exteriority and absolute passivity is well illustrated. Through my death I do not coerce, but leave myself to be recreated. It is impossible to recreate oneself, but possible to get recreated by God in the ever-enlarging context.

However, the important thing is to return from the reality in general comprehended by way of methodological anthropomorphism again to our own reality. In Hartshorne's process theology, can we be so deeply and seriously concious of otherness as in Levinas' moral theology? Indeed how can we become aware of God as absent rather than present from the Hartshornian point of view? In short, what is the existentialistic meaning of Hartshornian panentheism?

According to Hartshorne, God is generous enough to let us be free. In this respect God is to us what a parent is to a son. In Levinas' terminology God is free from egoistical structure to internalize us into his territory by his own egoistic subjective form. In Levinas essence is egoistic, because it sustains itself by holding everything for its own sake. I dare say, instead of containing, God throws off. When I feel absolute passivity before visage, I feel being thrown off. But whence comes this feeling? In so far as others are subjects like ourselves, why could they refrain from internalizing us by their egoistic subjective forms? So it cannot come from others as persons. Thus considered, could we not feel divine discretion in our being thrown off? God does not live in otherness. As Lenvias says, otherness is trace of God. Otherness does not symbolize God. God is not merely Fregean reference (*Bedeutung*). For process philosophy our reality contains innumerable contemporary bodily occasions. If we come to feel othernesses in such a body of ours, and free ourselves from Husserlian 'I can (Ich kann)' of kinaesthesia, in that passivity I feel divinity beyond otherness. And as argued in the preceding section, what is each experience of otherness but the inlet to the divine quasi-proper region which directly touches all the proper regions of finite occasions?

Thus Levinasian moral theology is comprised in Hartshornian panentheistic theology. Levinasian ethics can be derived from Hartshorne's metaphysics, under the condition that the latter thought contains as one of its aspects the absolute passivity as argued above.

Now, for Levinas existence of God need not be proved. The more deeply we feel passivity before visage the more deeply do we feel the graciousness and benevolence of God, in which God no doubt exists. On the other hand, Hartshorne tries to reexamine Anselm's ontological proof. However it seems that the proof is unsuccessful, for whatever exquisite technique of modal logic you may make use of, the problem of ontological commitment of the relevent modal system remains outside the system of proof theory.

Let me say more in detail. My refutation against Purtill's simple version of Hartshorne's proof is as follows.[29] Suppose there are three possible worlds, W, W', W''. Let W' be possible to W, and W'' be possible to W' and W. Besides, suppose $q \supset \Box q$ holds in all the worlds, and accordingly $\Box (q \supset \Box q)$ holds in W. Now, suppose in W'' proposition q holds, and by presupposition $q \supset \Box q$ holds. Here arises no contradiction. Next, in W' $\Diamond q \supset q$ does not hold and $q \supset \Box q$ holds. This is not contradictory. Since q holds in W'', $\Diamond q$ holds in W'. Therefore, in W' such a situation occurs as q does not hold, nor does $\Diamond q \supset q$ hold, but $q \supset \Box q$ holds. Lastly $\Box (\Diamond q \supset q)$ does not hold in W, because there is at least one possible world, i.e., W' where $\Diamond q \supset q$ does not hold. And by presupposition $\Box (q \supset \Box q)$ holds in W. Hence $\Box (q \supset \Box q) \supset \Box (\Diamond q \supset q)$, i.e., $(q \rightarrow \Box q) \supset (\Diamond q \rightarrow q)$ is false! The result is that one of the very important premises of Purtill's argument fails. However, if we adopt a stronger modal system S5, then the proposition concerned can be proved, because in S5 the relation between the worlds is reversible and accordingly if in W'' q and $q \supset \Box q$ hold, then by Modus Ponens $\Box q$ holds. Thus, we can go back to W' and let q hold there.

As for the original Hartshorne's argument, it presupposes Becker's postulate, which also turns out to be valid in S5, but invalid in S4, where the relation between the possible worlds is irreversible as shown above.[30] To Hartshorne's view S4 is appropriate, otherwise not only cumulativeness would be absurd, but also it would become meaningless that God transcends himself.

Moreover, from a view-point of modal predicate logic, if $(\exists x)\,Px$ means that perfect being exists, it is doubtless that both Barcan formula and converse Barcan formula hold, i.e., $\Diamond (\exists x)\,Px = (\exists x)\,\Diamond Px$ is true. And the problem will be shifted to that of transworld identity. The troublesome ontological question arises whether or not what Kaplan calls 'transworld heirlines' exist. Thus, the problem goes outside the system of proof theory. However, let me add, that the above argument is within the framework of possible world semantics.

I am rather pessimistic about logical proofs of God's existence. Hartshorne's methodological anthropomorphism has to be reversed at last. His panentheistic argument must again be exsistentialistically interpreted. I think an ethical approach such as Levinas proposed may be one of the suitable approaches.

V. ABSOLUTE PASSIVITY AND EMPTINESS IN BUDDHISM

Process thought has truly many aspects, to emphasize one of which makes it appear as a vast, immeasurable system of panpsychism which supplies innumerable occasions with freshness of mind, and to emphasize another aspect brings forth a rather negative thought which asserts that the subject of every individual perishes. And the above argument emphasized transition rather than becoming, quasi-proper region rather than proper region, nexus rather then actual occasion. As a result a sort of metaphysics of absolute passivity seems to have been derived. And this metaphysics has a certain similarity with Levinas' metaphysical basis of his ethics. Now, let us try to see further characteristics of the metaphysics in comparison with some thoughts in Buddhism.

When one takes an absolutely passive attitude before others, giving up every objectifying function, i.e., in Buddhistic expression, giving up attachment to beings, one's own subject also empties itself. In Buddhism such self-emptying is done in meditation. An attempt to seize upon emptiness renders emptiness an object, to which one is attached. According to Prajnaporamita-sutra in the ultimate reality all the objects vanish, all the things become empty and they lastly arise beyond every decision of "either-or". The concept of time is the prototype of attachment, because past, present, and future are clearly prescinded. What holds really true of existents stands off past, present and future. Therefore, existents do not become, nor come, nor go away. The genuine suchness of a multiple of existents is aloof from time.

But ontologically important is the following aspect of this sutra, namely here the transtemporal genuine suchness of all the existents is identified with the transtemporal suchness of Buddha and temporality is dealt with as if it were the locus (not in the sense of extension) where existents and Buddha encounter. Therefore, by the fact that our reality is temporal, it can be transtemporal. Self-emptying is, so to speak, going through temporality out into transtemporality. And in the light of process philosophy self-superjecting with no subjective forms nor subjective aim encounters in its absolute passivity beyond microscopic time of the past (seen in the nascent present), present and future (also seen in the nascent present) Benevolence of God. What makes a difference is how seriously one accepts contemporaneity and tries to search into the religious meaning here.

VI. CONCLUDING REMARKS

The above argument has been based upon the strict distinquishing of actual entity and nexus, becoming and transition, proper region and quasi-proper region. This distinction is itself problematic. However, if the distinction be allowed and thereby an attempt to reach some new metaphysical meaning of process philosophy be possible, then Hartshorne's process theology is the product of so deliberate, adequate speculations that it can be interpreted, as I think I may have been able to show above, as comprising Levinasian theology and some important thoughts in Buddhism. However, I would like to add that his methodological anthropomorphism, to go from human experience to speculation, must by all means be reversed, so that we could somehow find our experiential way to Divinity without being troubled with the logical proof of God's existence.

NOTES

1. Sia, S., *God in Process Thought*, 1985, Martinus Nijhoff, p. 116.
2. Hartshorne, *CSPM*, p. 123.
3. Husserl, E., *Die Krisis der Europäischen Wissenschaft und die Transzendentale Phänomenologie* (Husserliana Bd. VI), Beilage I, Martinus Nijhoff.
4. Husserl, E., *Ideen* I (Husserliana Bd. III) §77, §78.
5. Strasser, S., "History, Teleology and God in the Philosophy of Husserl", *Analecta Husserliana*, Tymieniecka (ed.), Vol. IX, D. Reidel, 1979, pp. 317—33.
6. Claesges, U., *Edmund Husserls Theorrie der Raumkonstitution*, Martinus Nijhoff, 1964, S.58.
7. Levinas, E., *Totality and Infinity* (translated by A. Lignis), Martinus Nijhoff, 1979, p. 110.
8. Whitehead, A. N., *Process and Reality*, The Free Press, 1978, p. 348.
9. Levinas, *ibid.*, p. 127f.
10. Levinas, *ibid.*, p. 131.
11. Levinas, *Le temps et L'autre*, P.U.F., 1983, p. 24.
12. Endo, H., "The Metaphysics of Time in Husserl and Whitehead" (Proceedings, International Conference (*Process and Reality, East and West*) 1984, p. 230.
13. Hartshorne, *IOGT*, pp. 269—82.
14. Griffin, D. R., "Hartshorne's Differences from Whitehead", *Two Process Philosophers*, L. S. Ford (ed.), Printing Depart., Univ. of Montana, pp. 35—57.
15. Whitehead, *PR*, p. 343f.
16. Whitehead, *ibid.*, p. 32, p. 88.
17. Peirce, Ch. S., *Collected Papers*, Ch. Hartshorne and P. Weis (eds.), Harvard Univ. Press, Vol. VI, 1935, 6. pp. 189—209.
18. Ford, L. S., *The Emergence of Whitehead's Metaphysics*, State Univ. of New York Press, 1984, p. 212, p. 259.
19. Johnson, A. H., "Some Conversations with Whitehead Concerning God and Creativity", *Explorations in Whitehead's Philosophy*, L. S. Ford and G. L. Kline (eds.), Fordham Univ. Press, 1983, pp. 3—13.
20. Hartshorne, *NTT*, p. 26.
21. Peirce, *ibid.*, 6.189—209, 6.214—6.237.
22. Whitehead, *PR*, p. 105f.
23. Nobo, J. L., *Whitehead's Metaphysics of Extension and Solidarity*, State Univ. of New York Press, 1986, pp. 205ff.
24. Whitehead, *PR*, p. 107f.
25. Cobb, J. B., Jr., "Overcoming Reductionism", *Existence and Actuality, Conversations with Charles Hartshorne*, J. B. Cobb, Jr. and F. I. Gamwell (eds.), Univ. of Chicago Press, 1984.

152

26. Wittgenstein, L., *Tractatus Logico-Philosophicus*, London, 1922, 5.64.
27. Husserl, *Ideen* II, (Husserliana Bd. IV), §62.
28. Hartshorne, "Philososphy After Fifty Years", *Mid-Twentieth Century American Philoso-phy*, P. Bertocci (ed.), Humanities Press, 1974, p. 149. Cf., Viney, D. W., *Charles Hartshorne and The Existence of God*, State University of New York Press, 1985, p. 117.
29. I found Purtill's argument in the above cited book of Viney's, Chapter IV, pp. 45—57.
30. Hartshorne, *LP*, p. 51.

10. Some Remarks on Charles Hartshorne's Conception of Theology

PIOTR GUTOWSKI

I. INTRODUCTION

The term 'theology' has traditionally served to designate: 1. an elaboration of the revelation of a given religion (e.g. Christianity), or 2. the philosophy of God. The latter is also designated by the following terms: rational theology, natural theology, theodicy, and even *sensu largo*, the philosophy of religion. The starting point for theology in the first of the above senses is the data of revelation in some concrete religion, which revelation is subject to synthetic or analytic elaboration, whether this be for theoretical, or for practical purposes.[1] The philosophy of God is a rational (autonomous with respect to faith) investigation of the existence and essence of God. It has been cultivated as a methodologically uniform discipline (either in the character of general metaphysics or in some other character), or as a methodologically complex discipline (either in the character of general metaphysics or in some other character), or as a methodogically complex discipline (constituted by problematics belonging to various philosophical disciplines, or constituted by both philosophical and non-philosophical problematics).[2]

Hartshorne's conception of theology cannot be easily situated within the framework of the above typology. It is close to the philosophy of God — Hartshorne often stresses the rational character of this discipline and its strict connection with metaphysics.[3] On the other hand, this discipline is not completely autonomous with regard to the contents of revelation, since one of its tasks is to grasp the religious concept of God.[4] The link between Hartshorne's understanding of theology and the religious concept of God means that any evaluation of Hartshorne's concept of God must be preceded by an evaluation of his conception of theology. The manner in which one approaches theology to a large extent bears upon the kind of results which will be obtained. For example, there will be one kind of vision of God in the case of a theology which is autonomous with respect to sciences and revelation, and yet another in the case of a theology which takes both of them into account.

In my essay I intend to consider Hartshorne's programme for theology. I

S. Sia (ed.), *Charles Hartshorne's Concept of God*, 153–162.
© 1990 *Kluwer Academic Publishers. Printed in the Netherlands.*

do not claim, however, to discuss this problem in its totality. Some of my questions concerning Hartshorne's conception of theology may be a result of the incompleteness of the source material with which I must deal, since the greater part of Hartshorne's works are not accessible in Poland. I hope that at least some of these questions will prove to be to the point. In keeping with the wish of the editor, I will add a short survey of Polish literature concerning process theology.

II. THEOLOGY, RELIGION AND PHILOSOPHY

When one intends to characterize some domain of knowledge, it is best to indicate those of its features which set it apart from other related disciplines. In the case of theology, one must first of all inquire into its relation to religion and philosophy.

In his *Creative Synthesis and Philosophic Method*, Hartshorne writes that any adequate theory about God is either a metaphysical theory or else nonsense.[5] Thus he rejects such a natural theology which would be composed of problematics belonging to philosophy and the sciences (unless metaphysics were to be somehow joined to the sciences). A theology based upon philosophical disciplines other than metaphysics is for Hartshorne also unacceptable.[6] What then is the relationship between theology and philosophy?

It seems that there are two main possibilities: either theology will be entirely identified with metaphysics, or it will have a starting point other than that of metaphysics, at the same time drawing from the theses and methods of metaphysics when it sets about to explain something. Both of these suppositions find confirmation in Hartshorne's works. "Neo-classical metaphysics", he writes, "when its ideas are adequately explicated is neo-classical natural theology, and *vice versa*."[7] In this case theology would be the philosophy of God, a discipline epistemologically independent of the content of religious revelation. The latter would play the role of an element which serves to test philosophical conceptions of God.[8]

In another place, however, Hartshorne writes: "If the task is to form a rational theory about the central religious idea, the idea of God, it seems proper to begin by asking religion, including revealed religion, what it means by 'God'."[9] Given such a claim, theology would be intermediate between theology as it has been traditionally understood and the philosophy of God. Its rationality could still be rescued if one were to accept that there is some universal religious experience of God (and the content of the Sacred Scriptures were to be acknowledged as the record of such an experience). In such a case, theology would be particular metaphysics. Hartshorne, however, does not accept the division of metaphysics into general and particular.[10]

Hartshorne's statements quoted above seem not to be in agreement with each other. The point in question is here the position which the data of revelation occupy in theology, if they be the starting point for theology, or they fulfill a testing role with regard to its conclusions. Either Hartshorne's position is incoherent in this matter, or it has undergone some kind of evolution, or he is speaking of two different kinds of theology, or else he conceives the relation between metaphysics and religion in such a way, that metaphysics can to some extent draw upon contents of revelation without destroying its own strictly rational character.

The above question can be left aside if we look at the religious concept of God not from the point of view of the position it occupies in Hartshorne's theology, but from the point of view of the function which it plays in his theology.[11] This function can be reduced to one of eliminating a concept of God which would not be in keeping with the basic content of religion. This process of elimination can take place at the beginning of theological considerations, in which case theology can be said to be a philosophical development of the religious concept of God, or at the end of theological considerations, in which case we are going to be dealing with the testing of the conclusions of rational theology.

Thus for Hartshorne theology is the philosophy of God cultivated, as it were, on the horizon of the religious idea of God. This does not mean, however, that the religious idea of God which is obtained from investigations upon religious experience *sensu largo* (a part of which are the data of revelation) is in his theology something less important than purely rational considerations. On the contrary, the reading out of the basic contents of religious faith is not only an intergral part of Hartshorne's theology, but it seems to be also its most significant component. It decides on the value of purely rational considerations.

The confrontations between the theological concept of God and the religious one also belongs to theology, and the emphasis which Hartshorne places upon the necessity of bringing about this confrontation seems to me to belong to the most original elements of his theological vision. Thus for Hartshorne, theology is on the one hand purely rational metaphysics (natural theology), and on the other hand, an attempt to read out the basic content of religious revelation, as well as the comparison of these two investigations.

In the starting point of theology as metaphysics, the object is experience *sensu largo*, the world of concretes, of existents.[12] It is possible, according to Hartshorne, to cultivate metaphysics without the inclusion of theistic problematics, but this means only that the theistic meaning of metaphysical concepts have not been formulated. In such a case, however, they will be vague or equivocal, and the system will be too indeterminate to withstand a rational critique.[13] The difference between metaphysics and natural theology will not lie in a difference with regard to the particular data which each has to explain, nor in different methods of explaining these data, but rather in this: the metaphysician and the natural theologian differ with regard to their respective cognitive attitudes. Metaphysics is natural theology when it is regarded from the point of view of its ideal of intelligibility, of the coherence of its system and the clearness of its concepts: "the properly formulated theistically religious view of life and reality is the most intelligible, self-consistent, and satisfactory one that can be conceived."[14]

The goals set by Hartshorne for metaphysics (and at the same time for natural theology) are both theoretical and practical. Metaphysics is the search for *a priori* truths which, when gathered together into a coherent system would adequately interpret every element of the world (experience).[15] This task is at the same time both theoretical and synthetic. The demands of coherence, adequacy and noncontradiction are here important, and they are at the same time the basis for critiques of other philosophical systems.

Apart from these theoretical goals, Hartshorne sets practical assignments to metaphysics. As well as the acquisition of knowledge (and the communication of attained knowledge), Hartshorne is also concerned with convincing or conviction: "Arguments are useful only if they convince some who otherwise would not be convinced."[16] Besides this, metaphysics must have some practical applications. Such an application is that of metaphysical categories to religion: "If a metaphysician can make sense out of this topic so much the better, but if not, why do we need his system."[17]

The application of metaphysical categories in religion is not only the goal of metaphysics, but also the test of adequacy of these categories.[18] Since this is so, there must exist some primitive and uninterpreted content of religion which will fulfill such a testing role. The reading out of this content is a basic matter for Hartshorne's theology, if every philosophical formulation concerning God is to be evaluated with an eye to whether it expresses some basic religious content.[19]

Hartshorne assumes that the religious (prephilosophical) idea of God is conceivable. In his opinion, there are two sources which contain that which is essential for the religious understanding of God. The first is revelation and the official confessions of various churches (and not only of one). The second is the particular experience of God which makes appearance in prayer, in the feeling of sin, etc.[20] This source is in many respects difficult to analyze. There are many difficulties in communicating in an informative language the content of such experience. Perhaps it is for this reason that Hartshorne refers more often to the first source. After all, it can be treated as a record of a past experience of God.

This part of Hartshorne's investigations differs from metaphysical investigations with regard to its aim and the methods applied. What is involved here is not the philosophical interpretation of the content of revelation, but the discovery of some prephilosophical concept of God. In this connection strictly metaphysical method (for example, abstraction) cannot be applied here. One must rather describe the basic content of revelation (or of the experience of God). Such a description would be either independent of metaphysics, or it would constitute an introductory stage of metaphysical investigations.

If our aim is to grasp a contentually rich (although not necessarily in a clear and distinct manner) religious idea of God, then our point of departure cannot be the totality of all religions, present and past, taken together. However, with respect to the ideal of universalism, our analyses cannot be based upon any one religion alone. Hartshorne, then, restricts his field of research to the higher religions, by which he means Christianity, Islam, Judaism, Hinduism and Buddhism.[21]

According to Hartshorne, a common and basic element of the higher religions is worship.[22] There are many different kinds of worship. By worship Hartshorne understands "The *integrity* of all one's thoughts and purposes, all valuations and meanings, all perceptions and conceptions."[23] Worship thus understood is identified with total love. Hartshorne alludes in this connection to the command of the love of God as is written in the Old Testament. Worship is tantamount to total love for God, i.e. love "with all one's being."[24] Hartshorne emphasizes at the same time that what he has in mind is not the fact of worship, but rather the idea of worship. We understand the idea of such a total love, but there are not necessarily such people who love God in this way.[25]

From such a concept of worship Hartshorne deduces the features of the object of this worship. Since worship is to be a total love, God must be the universal object of all love. He must be furthermore one and unsurpassable. Besides this, there must be a radical asymmetry between God and his worshippers.[26] Religion also describes God as unsurpassable in his goodness, power and knowledge, and, in a certain way (with respect to his happiness) dependent upon the actual state of the world. According to Hartshorne it is this understanding of God which is common to all higher religions.

The agreement of a given theological concept of God with the corresponding religious one, together with the demands of coherence, noncontradiction and adequacy are the basic criteria for evaluating this theology. Hartshorne places much weight upon the demonstration of the falsehood of other standpoints.[27] Next he points out the incoherence and onesidedness of the way in which a given question is treated, and its nonconformity with the religious idea of God.[28]

III. SOME COMMENTS AND QUESTIONS

Now that I have briefly presented some aspects of Hartshorne's conception of theology, I would like to formulate a few remarks and questions concerning it.

Hartshorne's requirement that every philosophical formulation concerning God must be evaluated with regard to whether it expresses contents in keeping with the religious idea of God, seems to me to be at best doubtful. This is not only on account of the difficulties involved in getting to the essence of religious experience, but mainly on account of the methodological problems which give rise to this postulate. Metaphysical argumentation is incommensurate with religious thought. Religion and metaphysics make use of different languages and formally refer to different states of affairs. The identification of the God of religion with the God of philosophy is possible only with respect to denotation, but not with regard to the meaning of the term used, for the languages of these two domains (faith and knowledge) are not univocally translatable.[29] Such an identification is, I think, a matter of the individual act of faith of a given philosopher, and not a problem which could be taken up by theology or philosophy as such.

The lack of coincidence between the conclusions of philosophical thought and the beliefs of religion was, I think, profitable for religion, for on the one hand, it made people realize that the anthropomorphic images suggested by certain readings from the Sacred Scriptures can be false (since philosophical investigations led to other visions of God than the religious one). On the other hand, the difference between the two concepts of God, as well as the impossibility of proving all the truths of a given religion demonstrated the limitations of human knowledge. In this way the position of religious faith was made impregnable by knowledge.

The requirement that the God of the philosophers and the God of religion be one and the same seems to me to lead either to fideism (and a significant limitation of the cognitive power of human reason) or to panlogism (and the reduction of faith to knowledge). To accept the religious idea of God as having metaphysical importance means to resign from the universal validity of metaphysical statements, or to accept the assumption that this idea is, in a sense, universally innate (if universalism of metaphysics is to be saved). Such an assumption makes possible the ontological proof for the existence of God. This assumption, however, is open to discussion.

Hartshorne's manner of resolving these dilemmas goes in the direction of panlogism (sometimes his position is described as "untamed rationalism" or "ultra-rationalism"). He refers to the content of religion, but in the final analysis he treats it after the manner of knowledge. This is testified to by the fact that he does not call into question the cognitive value and the universality of the religious idea of God, and by the fact that he treats all those religious beliefs which he regards as non-rational as if they were lacking in all value (he rejects for this reason e.g. the doctrine of a new life after death). Hartshorne in principle does not recognize the existence of any mysteries (apart from that mystery which is for us the content of the concrete aspect of God).[30] The field of faith is not very wide here. The greater part of that which is commonly thought to belong to the domain of faith is, for Hartshorne, knowledge.[31]

The description of the religious idea of God gives rise to many questions.[32] These are mainly questions concerning criteria. First of all, what are the criteria for selecting one religion and not another for analysis (in other words, the criteria of how high or primitive a given religion is)? Futhermore, there arises here the doubt as to whether among those religions recognized by Hartshorne as being "higher" there does not exist some one religion which is the highest of all. If this were the case, then the essence of religion would be much richer with respect to its content than this essence as it is accepted by Hartshorne. In such a case, the philosophical conception of God would have to take into account more elements originating from religious revelation.

If, for example, one were to take Christianity as being the highest among the "higher" religions, then one would have to count among the essential features of religion these concerning the Redemption, the Resurrection, and man's life after death. Of course, it is possible to give some interpretation of these theses within the framework of process theology, but such an interpretation would at the same time constitute a certain kind of modification (and so, according to Hartshorne one can speak of man's immortality but only in the memory of God, while Christians believe in a new life after death). If then some one religion alone were to be acknowledge as being the highest, then the concept of God proposed by Hartshorne would not be in keeping with the religious idea of God. This seems to be the reason why some theologians who are associated with certain official denominations are very cautious about the possible application of process thought in expressing the truths of faith recognized by their respective churches.

If, however, one were to agree with the idea of looking for the essence of higher religions, accepting at the same time Hartshorne's selection of which religions are to be regarded as higher, there would remain the question of how this essential ingredient is to be grasped. According to Hartshorne, analysis should be focussed upon those aspects of experience which are generally known as being religious. There are different experiences in various religions, but each religion sets the idea of God apart from all other ideas, no matter how this idea may be conceived in other religions. Thus, there must be, concludes Hartshorne, some special kind of experience which would serve as the basis for assigning meaning to the idea of God.

Such a position is not free of difficulties, for one may ask what the criterion is for regarding a given experience (a given text from the Scriptures) as being basic, and another as insignificant. In Hartshorne's writings we constantly encounter such evaluations (e.g. the commandment to love one's neighbour as oneself is regarded as being redundant in comparison to the commandment to love God, and the texts speaking about heaven and hell are regarded as false doctrine).

Now, even if one were to agree with Hartshorne that the essence of religion is worship and that this is the same thing as total love for God (as expressed in the Old Testament), his analysis of this commandment would still be debatable. Hartshorne, starting from the features of the act of love (an ideal act) makes certain inferences about the features of the object of this act. Such an inference is not, however, valid, if one does not accept some assumptions about the relation of ideas to things, and about the possibility of inference from ideas to things.

The commandment to love God "with all one's being" does not necessarily imply that God is all-encompassive and that he is the immediate object of our every act of love. The above commandment can be understood in such a way as to order obedience to God, which obedience calles for a certain effort on the part of the man who is to fulfill this commandment. Furthermore, there are some other possible ways to interpret this text, but in order to be able to select from among these interpretations, it would be necessary not to call upon some speculative analysis, but rather to apply historico-philological methods. I think that one cannot make any valid inferences about the meaning of this commandment without first taking into account such researches. A line of research whose purpose is to discover the pre-philosophical idea of God cannot use strictly philosophical methods.

IV. PROCESS THOUGHT IN POLAND

Finally, I will survey Polish literature on Hartshorne's theology and process theology in general. This literature is, unfortunately, not very extensive. The Polish philosophical and theological public has no access to any published translations of Hartshorne's works. The Polish reader can learn about process theology from translations of the works of L. Gilkey, I. G. Barbour, N. M. Wildiers and J. Van der Veken.[33]

The following Polish authors have published on process theology: K. Waloszczyk, "Myśl chrześcijańska wobec filozofii procesu" (Christian Thought and Process Philosophy), Życie Katolickie, 3 (1984) No. 10, pp. 55—60; J. Jakubowska, "Bóg, człowiek i świat w ujęciu R. Niebuhra i A. N. Whiteheade'a" (God, Man, and the World in R. N. Niebuhr and A. N. Whitehead), Życie Katolickie, 4 (1985) No. 3, s. 124—147; S. Kowalczyk, Wieki o Bogu: Od presokratyków do teologii procesu (Centuries about God: From Pre-Socratics to Process Theology). Wrocław: Wydawnictwo Wrocławskiej Księgarni Archidiecezjalnej, 1986; J. Życiński, "Filozoficzny Bóg wiary w ujęciu nowego teizmu" (The Philosophical God of Faith in the View of the New Theism), Znak, 38 (1986) No. 383, pp. 3—16; T. Szubka, "Problem Boga w filozofii procesu" (Problem of God in Process Philosophy), Znak, 38 (1986) No. 383, pp. 119—126; M. A. Krąpiec "Monizm czy pluralizm?" (Monism or Pluralism?), W kręgu filozofii i religii, M. Kiliszek and J. Leskiewiczowa (eds.), Warszawa: Kościół Swiętej Trójcy, 1987, pp. 1—70.

As can be seen from the dates of these publications, interest in process theology has arisen only in the last few years. Process thought has been evaluated in different ways by various authors.

J. Życiński, K. Waloszczyk and J. Jakubowska evaluate it positively, as they see in it new paths for theology. J. Żciński thinks that process thought permits theology to give a deeper treatment of many traditional problems than has been possible up to this point, e.g. the problem of freedom, of evil, of grace. K. Waloszczyk emphasizes the competence, erudition, and comprehensiveness of the American process theologians. In their thought he sees mainly possibilities for a new, Christian treatment of the relation of God to the world. He gives a positive evaluation of the close contact which this thought has with the world of modern science. J. Jakubowska considers process philosophy as a possible foundation for Christian theology.

S. Kowalczyk and T. Szubka point out some difficulties which may arise if process philosophy is applied in Catholic theology. According to S. Kowalczyk the way in which the personality of God, his relation to the world, and the relation of God's primordial nature to his consequent nature are treated is open to question. Kowalczyk questions the validity of many of the criticisms which process philosophers make against so-called classical theology. T. Szubka stresses the need for Polish translations of the works of process philosophers, but at the same time remarks that any use of the categories of this philosophy in Catholic theology can lead to a modification of the content of some of its dogmas.

M. A. Krąpiec, the main Polish exponent of existential thomism, evaluates process theology and philosophy in a decidedly negative way. He very strongly criticizes Whitehead's and Hartshorne's conception of God as being monistic. He objects that process theology confuses the physical and theological (and also philosophical) modes of explanation, as a result of which that which should be the explanation (God) becomes the object which requires explanation. Krąpiec situates the views of Whitehead and Hartshorne in the post-Hegelian tradition which, according to him, is based upon the acceptance of contradiction as the foundation of thought.

NOTES

1. Cf. S. Kamiński, "Metodologiczna osobliwość poznania teologicznego," *Roczniki Filozoficzne KUL*, 25 (1977), No. 2, p. 83.
2. Cf. S. Kamiński, "Filozofia religii i filozofia Boga," *Roczniki Rilozoficzne KUL*, 30 (1982), No. 2, p. 16.
3. Ch. Hartshorne, *Creative Synthesis and Philosophic Method*, London: SCM Press, Ltd., 1970, p. 40. From here on I will quote this work as CSPM.
4. Cf. S. Sia, *God in Process Thought*, Dordrecht: Martinus Nijhoff Publishers, 1985, pp. 9—12. From here on I will quote this work as GPT.
5. CSPM, p. 39.
6. Thus natural theology is not, for Hartshorne, a part of the philosophy of religion as it is commonly thought to be in the analytical tradition.
7. CSPM, p. 40.
8. CSPM, p. 39.
9. I quote according to GPT, p. 10.
10 CSPM, p. 39.
11 Consideration concerning the proper sequence of procedures in metaphysics are, I think, less important. The content of metaphysics is given to the philosopher in a certain sense "at once," it is only in view of the requirements arising from presentation that it is ordered sometimes in one way, at other times in some other way. In CSPM Hartshorne writes: "I have tried to show (. . .), how from the mere idea of God a whole metaphysical system follows; one may also proceed in the opposite direction, and show how from general secular considerations one may arrive at the idea of God and a judgement as to its validity. But the two ways of proceeding differ only relatively and as a matter of emphasis." CSPM, pp. 40—41.

12. The explication of the interchangeability of various definitions of the object of metaphysics is to be found in CSPM, pp. 24—41.
13. CSPM, p. 39.
14. CSPM, p. 276.
15. Metaphysics is *a priori* in the sense that its statements cannot be falsified by any possible experience, but this is not to say that metaphysics does not start from experience. Cf. CSPM, pp. 29—33.
16. CSPM, p. 275.
17. CSPM, p. 39.
18. Cf. CSPM, p. 39.
19. Hartshorne is not concerned about the observable *fact* of religion, but rather about its *content*, and more precisely, about its *basic content*.
20. Cf. GPT, p. 12. S. Sia emphasized that, according to Hartshorne, the idea of God makes its appearance primordially in an emotional and practical form rather than in logical or analytical one. Neither it is simple or coherent, and it is often expressed in a poetic way. Nonetheless it contains a richness of insight.
21. Cf. GPT, p. 16.
22. Cf. GPT, p. 12.
23. I quote according to GPT, p. 17.
24. The introductory condition of such worship is man's humble acceptance of his fragmentariness. Cf. GPT, p. 11.
25. Cf. GPT, pp. 12—13.
26. Cf. GPT, pp. 14—15.
27. Cf. CSPM, pp. 82—88.
28. It would be difficult to go into details here and explore the validity of Hartshorne's critiques, and so I shall go no further than to indicate the fundamental assumptions of these critiques.
29. Cf. S. Kamiński, "Epistemologiczno-metodologiczne problemy filozoficznego poznania Boga," *W kierunku Boga* B. Bejze (ed.), Warszawa: ATK, 1982, p. 89.
30. Cf. GPT, pp. 29—30.
31. This is not to say that this knowledge is always certain. According to Hartshorne "all philosophizing is risking: cognitive security is for God, not for us." Ch. Hartshorne, " The Development of My Philosophy," *Contemporary American Philosophy*, J. E. Smith (ed.), London: George Allen & Unwin Ltd., 1970, p. 215.
32. I leave aside here the difficulties involved in trying to separate religious and non-religious elements. Hartshorne is fully aware of these difficulties. Cf. GPT, p. 9.
33. L. Gilkey, *Nazwanie wichru* (Naming the Whirlwind), Warszawa: PAX, 1976; J. Van der Veken, "Bóg i rzeczywistość: Wprowadzenie do 'process theology'" (God and Reality: Introduction to 'Process Theology'), *Novum*, 1980, No. 12, pp. 82—109; I. G. Barbour, *Mity, modele, paradygmaty* (Myths, Models and Paradigms), Kraków: Znak, 1983; N. M. Wildiers, *Obraz świata a teologia* (The Vision of the World and Theology), Warszawa: PAX, 1985.

11. Continuity and Novelty: A Contribution to the Dialogue between Buddhism and Process Thought

JOHN S. ISHIHARA

I. INTRODUCTION

The observation that Buddhism and process philosophy have parallels is, of course, not a new one. Indeed, Whitehead himself noted that his own philosophy may have more obvious parallels with Indian or Chinese ways of thinking than Western.[1] In his references specifically to Buddhism, however, Whitehead is largely negative.[2] Hartshorne has seen the relationship more positively and has noted points of affinity as well as difference. This paper will look at these points and focus on two key differences. The work of two other process thinkers, John Cobb and David Griffin, who more fully discuss the relationship between Buddhism and process thought will also be summarized to clarify these differences. One difference centers upon the process intuition that sees both change and continuity as basic to a conceptuality of reality. They fault Buddhism with an over-emphasis on change, and where the tradition does address this issue, it results in a substantialization of reality and a philosophy of being rather than of becoming. The second centers on the source of novelty in the process of coming to be. In process thought, it is with God that novelty is introduced into the act of coming to be. If I am reading Hartshorne correctly here, however, he does not seem to emphasize this point as much as Cobb or Griffin. His perspective suggests a way in which novelty can be discussed without resorting to God. Thus, the two basic criticisms of process thought made against the Buddhist conceptuality of reality are the problems of continuity and novelty. In regard to the problem of continuity within change, a detailed look at the Sarvāstivāda conceptuality of *dharma* or moment of existence may clarify the Buddhist position and deflect much of the criticism that Hartshorne and others have levelled against Buddhism. As to the notion of novelty being introduced by God in the process of coming to be, as noted above, Hartshorne himself suggests a way that need not demand God. This will be explored in the larger context of a discussion of the lack of a source of novelty in the Buddhist conceptuality of reality.

On the one hand, the paper will be countering a mis-representation of an

S. Sia (ed.), Charles Hartshorne's Concept of God, 163–184.
© 1990 Kluwer Academic Publishers. Printed in the Netherlands.

aspect of the Buddhist conceptuality of reality. On the other hand, what this entails is a confrontation with the traditional Buddhist understanding of *dharma*. One cannot fault Hartshorne or other process thinkers for holding this mistaken view of *dharma* since the traditional Buddhist understanding presents *dharma* as this substantial entity. This internal Buddhist problem of how it should interpret this facet of its conceptuality of reality has significant influence on the on-going dialogue between Buddhism and process thought.

II. PROCESS CRITICISMS OF BUDDHISM

A. The general point of contact between process philosophy and Buddhism is their common stress on becoming. This is referred to in Hartshorne's discussion of the difference between classical and neo-classical metaphysics. Classical metaphysics is a metaphysics of being or substance and characterizes much of the Western philosophical tradition. "There is another form ... in some respects admirably worked out in Buddhism, but in some respects left unfinished in that tradition — the metaphysics of becoming or creativity. I call this the neo-classical tradition."[3] Specifically, he sees the Buddhist insight of no-self as a key parallel, and it is around this parallel that he discusses Buddhism. The reason he centers on this topic is that he feels that the emphasis on the substantial self has inhibited the West and specifically the Christian West in fully manifesting the commandment of love. Moreover, ethics in general has been undermined by the emphasis.

> Apart from his eternal objects, Whitehead's mode of thought is to a remarkable extent, reminiscent of ancient Buddhism, the venerable tradition which most adequately rights the balance against certain exaggerations in the Greek tradition. The Buddhists renounce the effort to explain love by self-interest; indeed they deny the ultimacy of the idea of self as capable of an identical interest through the vicissitudes of time. Whitehead once remarked, with a quizzical smile, "I sometimes think that all modern immorality is due to the Aristotelian notion of individual substance." A Buddhist would understand this remark without difficulty.[4]

This parallel between the Buddhist no-self notion and Whitehead does not mean they are identical. Hartshorne notes a vital difference between the two. In discussing the love of one's neighbour, Hartshorne notes the difficulty inherent in the classical metaphysics' position through its insistence on self-substance. Fulfilling this ideal of love is truly impossible. When one is a substantial being inherently apart from others, how can one relate to another? The neo-classical tradition with its de-substantialized notion of self can say that the relation between 'me' and 'myself' is the same in principle though not in degree to the relation between 'me' and my neighbour. This is how one can ease the excessive individualism of the West that has tended to weaken its ethics. Following this statement of the neo-classical position, he again makes the point that Buddhism has done this and therefore has not had the same tendency toward such weakness. He, however, notes the difference between the two: a vital difference in attitude toward life.

From this weakness Buddhism has been largely free. But this advantage has been paid for by a certain negativism, a certain inadequacy or at least ambiguity, in the Buddhist view of the values of existence. This defect does not derive from the fact that Buddhism is a philosophy of becoming and events, rather than of being and substances. It is connected instead with a certain radical pluralism in the Buddhist conception of event. Some Buddhists tried to defend a doctrine of the present reality of the past, but they failed to carry full conviction, and the reason may have been that they spoke in the same breath of the reality of past and also of future events. This symmetrical way of arguing the case always blurs the issues between classical and neo-classical doctrines. For if all events are real together, then the totality of events simply is, and being not becoming is the inclusive conception. The Buddhists meant to be philosophers of becoming; but they could see no way to do so except by a symmetrical denial of past and future events, leaving only the present event as real. But then all life is vain, for all actual experience is doomed to destruction. So the ethical defect which most Westerners feel in Buddhism is tied in with a metaphysical one, just as the ethical defect which Asiatics often feel in Christianity is tied in with its individualistic philosophy of substance.[5]

Buddhism's attitude toward life is negative or to put it differently its emphasis on becoming leads to a meaninglessness or futility in the face of this constant becoming. He sees this as an outcome of Buddhism's emphasis on the present, rather than of a metaphysics of becoming. This emphasis on the present leads to the ultimate evil of perpetual perishing without any hope of some form of endurance. He makes note of the Sarvāstivāda school that advocated the reality of an event through the past, present, and future. Though this may be seen as an effort to resolve the problem, its advocacy of the symmetrical reality of past, present, and future denies becoming. It makes any philosophy of becoming one of being, since if the becoming events are all real through time, they just are and are not in the process of becoming. This had to be negated, and so it led to the Mahayana emphasis on the present. It is to the Sarvāstivāda notion of *dharma* that we will turn later in this paper. Again, this will clarify the problem and deflect some of the criticism. How does neo-classical philosophy deal with this?

Western neo-classical philosophy has produced a synthetic-conservative theory of events in which the "immortality of the past" is provided for, without any relapse from the standpoint of becoming (I have so far failed to find a clear anticipation of this in Asiatic sources). Events endure — but in later events, not in any mere being. . . . Whitehead is perhaps the first clear expositor of it. It separates entirely the Buddhist insight expressed in the "no-soul, no-substance" standpoint from the negativism of much Buddhism. The resulting philosophy seems essentially Christian and Judaic. . . . By de-absolutizing self-identity, one opens the way to an ethically valuable de-absolutizing of non-identity of self with others. The only strict concrete identity is seen as belonging to the momentary self, the true unit of personal existence, as Hume and James rediscovered long after the Indians, Chinese, and Japanese. (Alas, the rediscovery included considerable repetition of the radical pluralism which plagued the Buddhists). Each momentary self is a new actuality, however intimately related to its predecessors. It is self-enjoyed rather than self-interested. All aim beyond the present is interest taken by one momentary self in others. A kind of "altruism" is thus the universal principle, self-interest being but the special case in which the other momentary selves in question form with the present self a certain chain or sequence. But this chain has no absolute claim upon its own members. Only the cosmic Life has absolute claims.[6]

The process notion of enduring objects is the key to the neo-classical solution to the problem of perpetual perishing. In short, there seems to be nothing comparable to an enduring of an event in the next event in Buddhism, and so, the negativism of Buddhism arises. Both becoming and enduring are advocated in the neo-classical formulation, while Buddhism only emphasizes change.

In discussing personal existence, Hartshorne sees both Buddhism and Whitehead as affirming becoming and non-substantiality as well as the enduring quality of the society. This discussion is in the context of a discussion of determinism.

> ... the antecedent factors do not wholly determine the becoming, yet when it occurs it is determinate. As Whitehead puts it, it is internally determined and externally free. ... Decision would settle nothing not already settled without them. Time would not even so much as 'reedit eternity'. Only Solovyov seems to see, with Buddhists, Lequier, Bergson, and Whitehead that the total concrete reality in a personal existence is new each moment. (People object that) timeless substantiality of the self is proved by experience, by our ability to know the past and the future. As if either Bergson or Whitehead or Solovyov had ever forgotten this ability, or had any special difficulty in their terms. Or even perhaps the Buddhists long ago, for that matter. (But Whitehead does more justice to the internal retrospective relationships between successive events in a single society or sequential system.)[7]

Here, Hartshorne at least sees Buddhism as giving credence to the empirical self. The problem of no-self in this instance does not seem to lead to the negativism of mere perpetual perishing. Whitehead, as noted, clearly works out the enduring quality of the sequentially related society more than Buddhism.

B. Turning to Cobb, in summary, he agrees with the above Hartshornian analysis, that is, the affinity between Buddhism and process thought is in their de-substantial view of things in general and the self in particular. Moreover, he also sees the fault that Hartshorne notes but does not describe it as negativism but rather as an ignor-ance of the particulars of the world in terms of both ethics and science. For Cobb, there is real possibility that both traditions can enrich the other. In the case of process thought enriching Buddhism, the general thrust of the discussion can be summarized by two points. Process categories can help more fully and rationalistically work out Buddhist insights, and, in regard to the above mentioned fault, it can help Buddhism see the particulars while holding on to its process or de-substantial base. Clearly these two points are interrelated since working out Buddhism in terms of process categories would entail the second point. As for Buddhism enriching process thought, the radical meaning of Buddhist emptiness can aid in more fully expressing the de-substantial nature of God and the process conceptuality of reality.

The ignor-ance of particulars is explained by Cobb two ways, the first is from a general analysis of the Buddhist position, and the other is from a Whiteheadian analysis. The first explanation sees Buddhism as advocating a turning into oneself to 'remove' oneself from the particularities of flux — to see the flux so as to 'remove' oneself from it. "Buddhism has broken the dominance of the self, or 'I' in its continuity from the past and into the future. In doing so, it has freed people from defensiveness, anxiety, and self concern. It has achieved a unique serenity and openness".[8] It is this aloofness from the flux which opens one up to this serenity and openness. Yet Buddhism itself has recognized the limitations of such a view. "The Buddhist recognizes as a limitation the lack of attention its adherents direct to particularities of the world. Buddhism has failed to nourish scientific inquiry and social ethics."[9] Even when one considers the Mahayana ideal of compassion, because of Buddhism's tendency to analyze the composite nature of things so as to be neutral toward them (non-attached toward them) there is a diffuseness about Buddhist compassion that does not take in the individuals that are the object of compassion. All impetus toward social commitment is therefore undercut since ". . . the initial analysis through which non-attachment is fostered so denies the intrinsic value of particulars that discrimination among particulars as better or worse is undercut."[10] With this radical advocacy of non-discrimination, the practical problem of bettering the present physical and social conditions is given no real basis for action. Why do something to better conditions when there really is no better or worse? Cobb does hold that a de-substantial world view coupled with attention to the particulars is possible. He, of course, works this out in process terms.

The problem, again, is the Buddhist emphasis of the present moment. This leads to merely momentary existence and no endurance. While process thought stresses the non-substantial character of things, it also stresses their empirical identity through time. This identity is real and valuable. Cobb explains the Whiteheadian reason for this dual stress and its difference with Buddhism in the following:

> Whereas Buddhist thought takes it stand within what Whitehead calls the
> process of prehensive unification or concrescence, Whitehead begins with

the analysis of the temporal process from without, in terms of transition. When in *Process and Reality* he turned to the analysis of concrescence, he adopted in part the perspective of concrescence, but his analysis through-out is informed by his prior study of transition . . . he finds among the components of concrescence other units of process. Whitehead thereby grounds within concrescence itself its temporal relation to the past, although he agrees with the Buddhist that the unit of process, the actual occasion, is not a temporal process. Apart from its inclusion of other units of process, the concrescence, is as the Buddhist affirms out of time. (He explains the Buddhist non-attachment ideal in relation to Whitehead) . . . Whitehead wants to locate within concrescence all elements needed to explain ordinary experience, whereas the Buddhist seeks in concrescence freedom from many of these elements. For example, Whitehead looks for the elements of purpose and choice in concrescence itself and accordingly identifies subjective aim and decision as universal aspects of concrescence with particularly important roles. Buddhists, if they acknowledge such elements at all, attribute to them no special importance. Whatever is there, is there, signifying nothing and explaining nothing.[11]

C. For Griffin there is a mechanistic tendency in the Buddhist conceptuality of reality that hinders any meaningful behaviour. In his analysis of *anātman* (no-self), he notes four meanings of the term that he sees being used. (1) There is no underlying, un-caused substantial soul, (2) things in general also lack a substantial center, (3) there is no 'mine' and; (4) composite entities are no more than the sum of their parts. He states that one and two would be agreed upon by process thinkers but three and four cannot. It is especially four that he focuses upon. It is a major thesis of Griffin that seeing a thing as *only* being the sum of its parts is the major fault of the Buddhist analysis. A thing is both self-made and other-conditioned.[12] Another point he makes and which is similar to Cobb's is that Buddhist non-attachment is accomplished by an analysis of the composite nature of all things leading thereby to a neutral feeling of disinterest that breaks the chain of desire. This wisdom of the way things are leads to an un-focused concern for others. Yet in Buddhism there is another method leading to concern for others which can overcome this lack of concern for the particular other. Griffin calls it the method of the unlimited and unlike the analysis of empty things, it expands the self by identifying it with more and more individuals. It is, however, the analytical method that is prominent in Buddhism.[13]

Griffin also makes the point about a thing being nothing but the sum of its parts in terms of causality. He holds that Buddhism ultimately undercuts all talk of self-causation and self-determination with its four-fold denial of causation (specifically true of Nāgārjuna). Self- and other-causation is denied, since there is no self and no other. Causation by both self and other is also denied. Finally, to say that there is no cause is denied. Griffin states that Whitehead's position is the 'both-and' alternative and Buddhism's denial of the four alternatives leads ultimately to a denial of causation. He sees in this denial the inherent Buddhist tendency toward determinism. There is no real progressive change. A thing, since it is really no more than the sum of its causes/parts, can never exhibit any kind of newness. It is what has been and will be.[14] One last point is that the goal of Buddhism, affective neutrality, poses problems. There are two main problems. The stress on the subjective form of the person divorced from the objective data which an autonomous affective state (neutrality) assumes is simply incorrect. For one thing how does one explain normal, common reactions to certain things. Furthermore, this autonomy contradicts the whole idea of being determined by one's environment. One cannot be divorced from the objective data.[15]

The central position from which Griffin seems to be speaking is his contention that causation has a bi-polar characteristic. This is the reasoning behind preferring the method of the unlimited over the method of analysis. The latter leads to a closing into oneself and is, of course, manifested by affective neutrality. The solution to the faults seems to be suggested in the following: "It seems that what Buddhism needs is a doctrine of partial determination and partial self-determination. This would allow for karmic influence, as well as the possibility of overcoming it, and for the (only) partial ability to overcome likes and dislikes, and the influence of circumstances upon one's psychic well-being".[16]

In discussing self- and other-determination, he notes that both in the actual occasion and living person there is an aspect of both other- and self-determination. In his analysis of the actual occasion he notes the following characteristics:

Each actual occasion is a synthesis of innumerable prehensions. Prehensions can be compared with Buddhist *dharmas*. However, and this is the first major point, actual occasion is not simply a term for an aggregate of prehensions. Rather, it refers to the process and result of synthesizing the prehensions. It is a unity arising out of a multiplicity, and as such is more than the sum of its elements (although it is not independent of them).[17]

In discussing the living person he notes its difference from democratic and corpuscular societies which are serially ordered but are only aggregates and not true individuals. In short, there is no over-all unit of action and reaction. In monarchical societies, however, there arises a key difference where a higher lever series of occasions of experience occur and one can speak of a soul.[18] But Griffin argues that "the main point is that, by virtue of this higher level type of actual occasion that emerges in monarchies, they are structurally different from democracies. Hence the analogy between the chariot (which is simply the sum of its parts) and the person must be rejected".[19]

D. For Griffin and Cobb, the question of real social concern in Buddhism can be partially resolved by emphasizing the 'method of the unlimited' rather than the method of analysis. To that extent, the question of particularity and meaningful behaviour is resolved by the use of this strand of the Buddhist tradition. Nevertheless, this question of the particular and meaningful behaviour will not be fully resolved until Hartshorne's concern about the lack of enduring occasions in Buddhism is addressed:

It is necessary, I believe, to connect the differences regarding God and the asymmetry of time with the Western bias toward a positive valuation of normal human living, as contrasted to the Asiatic tendency to devalue it. ... Buddha was oppressed by the universal truth that all definite things and relations are ephemeral. Whitehead agrees that the persistence of persons and things through change is in the end temporary and is only an abstract way of looking at what, concretely, is a succession of ever-new realities, each displacing its predecessors — except (for Whitehead a crucial qualification) insofar as this displacing consists in a more or less inadequate prehending ("abstractly", or by partly "negative prehensions") of predecessors, and except, further, that all actualities are prehended adequately, or in their full truth, by divine actuality. Only in this way does Whitehead think it possible to avoid the conclusion that "all experience is but a passing whiff of insignificance". To save the passing moment from everlasting nihilation, he sees no alternative to the ideal appropriation of the moment as imperishable datum in the divine experience. Such objectification as the non-divine subjects achieve is severely limited, incapable of preserving anything like the full richness and value of the data, and the objectification of an event by successive non-divine experiences tends to get fainter and fainter.[20]

We will first, then look at the Sarvāstivāda notion of *dharma* and address this problem of continuity. In the above, however, Hartshorne is quite emphatic that continuity alone is not enough but that the notion of objective immortality must be added to give real meaning to the flow of history. This whole question then of Buddhism needing finally to become theistic to resolve fully this problem must be addressed in addition to continuity in prehension. Finally, the question of determinism that Griffin so forcefully emphasizes in the above is intimately related to this theme of meaningfulness. This will be addressed and discussed in terms of the process acceptance of the 'both/and' alternative and in the larger context of the source of novelty. Let us now turn to the Buddhist notion of *dharma*.

III. AN INTERPRETATION OF 'DHARMA'

What I intend to do is look at how the Sarvāstivāda concept of *dharma* should be understood. It is hoped a better understanding of the reality that the term names will show how in Buddhism there has been a tendency, however muted, to meet some of the deficiencies pointed out in the above. This analysis of *dharma* will be an attempt to see what the term refers to in the Sarvāstivāda system. It is in this most important of the Southern Buddhist schools that *dharmas* and their analysis play a central position. Th. Stcherbatsky and Isaai Funahashi will be the main sources for the Sarvāstivāda analysis. The text source for both of these scholars is Vasubandhu's *Abhid-harmakośa-śāstra*. Though it is, strictly speaking, a Sautrantika analysis of the Sarvāstivāda position (and therefore does not reflect a fully Sarvāstivāda position), it is nevertheless, "... considered to be the most authoritative treatise of the Sarvāstivāda school".[21] However, the Sautrantika bias must be acknowledged and an effort to understand Sarvāstivāda as it is has to be carefully made. This effort is helped by the systematic nature of the text and its 'labeling' of each school's position. Before entering a discussion of the work of the above two scholars, I would like to state the standard under-standing of the Buddhist attitude toward *dharmas* and then introduce some work by David Kalupahana who develops quite a different understanding of *dharmas* as taught in the early tradition before the rise of the formal schools of Scholastic Buddhism.

A. The term *dharma* comes from the verb root *dhṛ* which means 'to hold'. It is that which holds what is real. The variety of meanings of this term develop from this basic meaning. The term can refer to law, truth, moral obligation and teachings. For our purposes, the basic meaning of the term is described in the following phrase from the *Abhidharmakośa-śāstra*: "It is called *dharma* because it can hold/maintain the characteristics of the thing". It is that basic element of a thing that is still the thing. The problem then is what exactly is meant by this element, this basic entity. Traditionally, from the Mahayana viewpoint, Buddhism until Mahayana held to the emptiness of the self and the existence, substantial existence, of the *dharmas*. With the rise of Mahayana there arose the insight that both the self and *dharmas* are non-substantial. Everything is empty. The *dharmas* are substantial entities of own-being (*svabhāva*), and it is these entities that make up the empty self. This, then, is the interpretation of the pre-Mahayana position. Most traditional scholarship seems to agree with this interpretation. Takakusu Junjiro in his basic refer-ence work holds to this understanding that in early Buddhism *dharmas* are substantial entities.[22] The reasoning for the rise of the Mahayana nonsub-stantial understanding of *dharmas* follows from the analysis of the self as empty. This reasoning is summarized by Griffin. He writes that Nāgārjuna "regarded even the dharmic events as empty of substantiality, and in that sense unreal. This later development can be regarded as an out-working of the inner logic of the earlier position (re: self), as Nāgārjuna himself claimed".[23] The explanation of the Mahayana position is very reasonable. One can very easily see the logic of the argument once one agrees that the self is empty. The trouble, and this has bothered me, is that it really is a bit too reasonable and simple. Why could not others see the obvious validity of the argument before? The groundwork was obviously laid out by the analysis of self and the claim that the self is empty. Progressive de-substantialization may be what happened in the development of Buddhist thought.

B. David Kalupahana in his work on early Buddhism argues against this interpretation. Kalupahana sees the earliest tradition as not only claiming that *anātman* referred to the self but to all entities. For Kalupahana, Nāgārjuna's negation or de-substantialization was already present in early Buddhism. He goes into a rather detailed discussion of some early texts and uses Stcherbatsky, Murti and others as antagonists representing the traditional interpretation of the early Buddhist understanding of *dharma*. He proposes to rethink this traditional understanding by a thorough and neutral reading of these early scriptures.

There are three main arguments or areas in which he proposed his new and more correct understanding of early Buddhism. The first argument is carried out by identifying *anātman* (no self) with *niḥsvabhāva* (no own-being or no substance). He shows that in the scriptures *anātman* means the emptiness of all *dharmas* not only the self. The second argument is a redefining of impermanence so as not to mean momentariness. The assertion that all is impermanent is a traditional argument for the non-substantiality of entities. For him, the assertion of momentary actuals (which is another traditional understanding of the early Buddhist position) undercuts non-substantiality. Finally, he looks at the conditioned nature of the *dharmas* and asserts that whenever one speaks of *dharmas*, causally conditioned *dharmas* are meant. Anything that is conditioned is by definition not substantial but rather empty. The arguments seem to center around the correct understanding of the three marks of existence: impermanence, suffering and *anātman*.

"The most important characteristic of *dhamma* (Pali for *dharma*) are said to be impermanence (*anicca, wu ch'ang*), unsatisfactoriness (*duhkha, k'u*) and non-substantiality (*anatta, wu-o*)".[24] This is a most basic and early formulation of Buddhist doctrine, and it is important to see that the term *anatta* (skt. *anātman*) does not refer only to a doctrine of no-self but a doctrine clearly stating that all things are empty of substantiality. The logic that Griffin grants the Mādhyamika adherents is clearly operative in the earliest tradition of Buddhism.

> Therefore, the view was accepted that just as the individual is unreal, so the component parts, the aggregates, are unreal in that they have no substance (*ātmanan-svabhāva*), being subjected to becoming (*bhūta*), composition (*sankhata*), and causal production (*paticca samuppanna*). Thus, *anātman* becomes a synonym of *niḥsvabhāva*. That the aggregates (*skandha*), taken not only in combination but also separately, are non-substantial is emphatically stated in the sūtras. (He footnotes to the *Majjhima Nikāya* 1.136, and the *Khandhasamyutta* of the *Samyutta Nikāya*). The Chinese *Āgamas* seem to go further in maintaining that even the aggregates taken separately are nonsubstantial (*wu o-anatta*) and unreal (*k'ung-sunna*).[25]

He continues his argument, "Even a later Theravada text such as the *Kathavatthu* is unequivocal in its criticism of the substantiality of *dharmas* (*dharma-svabhāva*)".[26] He goes on to repeat and note text confirmation that the earliest tradition most specifically denies substantiality to *dharmas* and equated *anatta* with *niḥsvabhāva*. "The theory of the non-substantiality of the *dharmas*, as pointed out above, was not new to the Pali *Nikāyas* and the Chinese *Āgamas*. In the Pali *Nikāyas* we find specific references to the doctrine of the non-substantiality of all *dharmas* (*dharma-nairatmya*) in the locution "*sabbe dhamma anatta*".[27] The Pali phrase means, "All *dharmas* are no-self (nonsubstantial)". He cites the *Majjhima Nikāya* 1.228; *Samyutta Nikāya* 3.133 and 4.401; *Anguttara Nikāya* 1.286; *Theragatha* 678; and *Dhammapada* 279.

In Kalupahana's analysis of the meaning of impermanence, he rejects the claim that early Buddhism even entertained the explanation of momentariness.

Hardly any evidence can be gathered from the Pali *Nikāyas* and the Chinese *Āgamas* to support the view that things were considered to be momentary (*kṣaṇika, ch'a na*). We do not come across any statement such as, "All forces are momentary" (It is footnoted that rather than that phrase, it is stated that all components are impermanent). The theory of momentariness is not only foreign to early Buddhism but is contradicted by some statements in the *Nikāyas* and the *Āgamas*".[28]

The observation that all is impermanent is purely descriptive and does not necessarily entail any assertion of momentariness. The world is looked at and the primal intuition is that it is impermanent. This is all that is trying to be said. To work it out more is to say simply that things come to be, change and pass away. This is all that is being claimed.

According to early Buddhism, things are impermanent, not because they are momentary but because they are characterized by birth (*uppāda, ts'ung ch i*), decay or transformation (*thitassa annathatta, ch'ien p'ien*) and destruction (*vaya, mieh chin*). Whatever is born is impermanent, since that which is born is sure to perish. What is conditioned or compound (*sankhata*) is also impermanent, and so is that which is subject to decay. In short impermanence is a synonym for arising and passing away, or birth and destruction. This pattern of things . . . is eternal".[29]

There is no substantial center of anything and so all pass away. This 'simple' observation of the world clearly supports the assertion that everything is without substance. The analysis into momentary existence, again, blurs the issue and can lead to a substantializing of the elements. For Kalupahana, no such concept was entertained in early Buddhism.

The third argument again centers around the correct meaning of the three marks of existence. It also concerns the difference between component existence (both as component parts and made up of components . . . *sankhārā*) and *dharmas* which as Kalupahana notes, "when applied to empirical things, is always used in the sense of 'causally conditioned dhammas' (*paticcasamup-panna-dhamma*)".[30] As the above asserted the non-substantiality of all things because of impermanence, now Kalupahana asserts this non-substantiality through the conditioned existence of all things. His analysis of a variation of the formula of the three marks of existence again shows the radical negation of substantiality that is in the early Buddhist reality view. He notes that the phrase "*Sabbe saṅkhārā aniccā, sabbe saṅkhārā dukkhā, sabbe dhammā anatta*" is found abundantly throughout the early scriptures. He cites *Majjhima Nikāya* 1.228; *Samyutta Nikāya* 3.133 and 4.401; *Anguttara Nikāya* 1.286; *Taisho Shinshu Daizokyo* 2.66b—67a, 668c and 1.9. *Saṅkhārā*, again, refers to component existence both component as part and as being made up of parts. However, the nuance of the term seems to imply a deliberately put together or organized compound and the components of such a compound. He notes that it "describes anything in which man's dispositional tendencies (*saṅkhārā*) have played a major role".[31] There are, however, things that are not as deliberately composed, that is, composite things that are more natural or 'causally conditioned'. *Saṅkhārā* then refers to this more narrow meaning of component existence, while *dhamma* (again always *paṭiccasumuppanna dhamma*) refers to a more inclusive meaning of composite existence. The phrase can then be translated as "all components are impermanent; and components are unsatisfactory; all *dhammas* are non-substantial".[32] It seems to be rather clear from this phrase that everything, causally conditioned *dhammas* and component existence, is empty and nonsubstantial. Yet, again, traditional interpretation has repeatedly understood the components as being substantial. He focuses on the treatment of *khandha*, the components of the self. There are five *khandha*. In the traditional interpretation, since the self is made up of them it is empty, but the *khandha* are not. This component of existence, according to the traditional interpretation, is substantial existence. Needless to say, Kalupahana negates such a view and cites supporting passages in the scriptures.

> . . . the aggregates (*khandha*) are considered to be causally produced (*hetum paṭicca sambhuta*). (*Samyutta Nikāya* 1.134.) The characteristics of the *dhammas* are said to be found also in the causes. They are said to be impermanent (*anicca*), conditioned or compounded (*sankhata*), and causally produced (*paṭiccasamuppanna*) and are therefore not substantial (*Samyutta Nikāya* 3.9 and 3.103).[33]

For the early Buddhists, as well as Mahayanists, everything is empty. One would have to look carefully at the sources used, but this innovative and tradition-breaking work of Kalupahana does seem to present a forceful argument against the view that pre-Mahayana Buddhism held that *dharmas* are substantial. He makes a strong case for early Buddhism. He asserts that early Buddhism holds this non-substantialist view, but the Sarvāstivāda certainly does not; and it is because of this school and its wide influence that pre-Mahayana Buddhism has been labelled with this substantialist charge. He asserts that Stcherbatsky carries over the substantialist bias of Sarvāstivāda to the earlier tradition. He therefore negates the carry-over effort of Stcherbatsky but does not reject the interpretation that Sarvāstivāda is itself substantialist. However, it is contended that looking at Stcherbatsky in particular and Sarvāstivāda in general, one can at least raise the possibility of questioning such a substantialist charge on the former and clearly see faults in the charge against the latter.

C. Kalupahana and other interpreters of the Sarvāstivāda tradition in general and Stcherbatsky in particular do not carry on the traditional interpretation of the school out of a totally mistaken interpretation of the material. Sarvāstivāda clearly lends itself to the substantialist charge. The name itself (*sarva*, all; *asti*, exist; *vāda*, view) clearly is an indication of the seeming materialistic or realistic orientation of the school. When the Stcherbatsky translation of a section of the *Abhidharmakośa* is read,[34] the word substance comes up repeatedly. The outer reality of a thing changes, but the inner substance does not change. In short, the traditional interpretation of the school and the Stcherbatsky treatment is clearly not without foundation. In Stcherbatsky, one finds clear indications that he considers *dharmas* to be substantial elements. In his provisional definition of the term we clearly see such a tendency: ". . . at present we take it to mean an *ultimate entity*, the conception of which is the domain of matter, excludes the reality of everything except sense-data, and in the field of mind, of everything except separate mental phenomena".[35] Components of existence are substantialized. There are real entities in the end after analyzing the compound existence of things. This is even more clearly expressed in his discussion of *anātman*:

> The term *anātman* is usually translated as "non-soul", but in reality *atman* is here synonymous with a personality, an ego, a self, an individual, a living being, a conscious agent, etc. The underlying idea is that, whatsoever be designated by all these names, it is not a real and ultimate fact, it is a mere name for a multitude of interconnected facts, which Buddhist philosophy is attempting to analyze by reducing them to real elements (*dharma*). Thus, "soul-lessness" (*nairatmaya*) is but the negative expression, indeed a synonym, for the existence of ultimate realities (*dharmatā*).[36]

His understanding of *anātman* is not that it expresses the non-substantiality of all existents, but that, rather, it expresses the analysis of compound existence so as to see the substantial reality of the components. Granted, he speaks only of 'ultimate realities' or entities which may be interpreted non-substantially, but the nuance of the terms clearly points to substantial realities and entities. He quotes from the *Abhidharmakośa* and expressly makes the point that these existing realities are clearly substantial: "Whatever exists is a substance. . . . An element is something having an essence of its own".[37]

There are problems, however, with the above interpretation of the Sarvāstivāda material. In the phrase above where 'soullessness' and 'ultimate realities' (*dharmatā*) are equated, Stcherbatsky paraphrases a passage from the *Abhidharmakośa*. The interpretation is problematic because of the translation of *dharmatā* as 'ultimate realities'. As Kalupahana notes, *dharmatā* does not mean 'ultimate realities' but the causal connection between two *dharmas*. Thus, as Kalupahana states, "If *dharmatā* stands for the causal connection, it cannot mean an ultimate reality (*dharmasvabhāva*)".[38] The above equation of 'soullessness' with *dharmatā* then means that 'soullessness is equated with conditionedness'. Moreover, the phrase defining an element (*dharma*) as something with its own essence is problematic. It is the *Abhid-harmakośa* phrase quoted at the beginning of this section giving the general definition of *dharma*. The key term is *svalakṣaṇa*. Stcherbatsky translates it as 'essence of its own' and my own translation is 'characteristic of the thing' (that is, self-characteristic) and Kalupahana translates *lakṣaṇa* as "causal characteristic".[39] It is simply that which makes a thing what it is. There is no sense of substantiality in the word as 'essence' conveys. Kalupahana's translation clearly goes in a non-substantial direction. There are problems, then with the Stcherbatsky understanding of *dharma* as substantial entity. The questionability of this assertion of substantiality is reflected, however, even in statements by Stcherbatsky. I do not propose that they negate the assertions of substantiality that he makes and are noted above, but the ambiguity does seem to point to a need to rethink the traditional understanding of Sarvāstivāda or at least scrutinize it a bit more critically.

A hint that a substantial realism is not advocated can be found in the following which notes that *dharmas* can be seen as constructs and thus not necessarily inferring substantial reality: "The realistic tendency of the Sarvastivadins, if there was any, consisted in constructing some realities corresponding to our ideas or habits of speech".[40] This also offers a hint at why Sarvāstivāda arose. There is that other basic intuition that things endure. To counter the early Buddhist emphasis on impermanence alone, the Sarvās-tivāda insight tried to speak to that common sense intuition that things also seem to be substantial or enduring. Yet substantial reality cannot be asserted if *dharmas* are viewed as a construct. In short, the Sarvāstivāda built its system not on the basis of the substantiality of *dharmas* but on the basic Buddhist premise of the non-substantiality of *dharmas*. A discussion of two characteristically Sarvāstivāda topics — momentary existence and the existence of past, present and future will clarify the ambiguity of the Sarvāstivāda position.

Though Kalupahana, as noted above, holds that momentary existence can lead to an assertion of an enduring substratum and therefore a philosophy of being, the Sarvāstivādin notion of momentary existence indicates non-substantiality along with an inherent abidingness. As Stcherbatsky notes:

> The elements of existence are momentary appearances, momentary flash-ings into the phenomenal world out of an unknown source. Just as they are disconnected, so to say, in breadth, not being linked together by any pervading substance, just so are they disconnected in depth or in duration, since they last only one single moment (*ksana*). They disappear as soon as they appear, in order to be followed the next moment by another momentary existence. Thus a moment becomes a synonym of an element (*dharma*), two moments are two different elements. An element becomes something like a point in time-space. . . . The idea that two moments make two different elements remains. Consequently, the elements do not change, but disappear, the world becomes a cinema. Disappearance is the very essence of existence; what does not disappear does not exist. A cause

for the Buddhists was not a real cause but a preceding moment, which likewise arose out of nothing in order to disappear out of nothing.[41]

If there is substantial existence in these moments of existence, it is difficult to discern. The Humean parallels are disconcerting, however. Stcherbatsky in an earlier section seems to pull back from this Humean position.

Although the separate elements (*dharmas*) are not connected with one another, either by a pervading stuff in space or by duration in time, there is nevertheless, a connexion between them; their manifestations in time, as well as in space, are subject to definite laws, the laws of causation. These laws bear the general name *pratitya-samutpada*. We have seen that the connotation of the word *dharma* implies the meaning of elements operating together with others. This concerted life of elements (*samskrtatva*) is but another name for the laws of causation ... the combined origination (*sam-utpada*) of some elements with regard (*pratitya*) to other elements. Thus it is that the fundamental idea of Buddhism ... the conception of a plurality of separate elements ... includes the idea of the most strict causality controlling their operation in the world process.[42]

We see in the above quotations a clear indication of the non-substantiality of the *dharmas* with an assertion of connectedness or continuity among them.

The following re-inforces this notion of the non-substantiality of the *dharma*-moment:

The Sarvastivadins construe the theory of the momentary character of the elements in the following manner. Every element appearing in phenomenal life is affected simultaneously by four different forces (*samskaras*), the force of origination (*utpada*), decay (*jara*), maintenance (*sthiti*), destruction (*anityata*). These forces affect every element at every moment of its existence, they are the most universal forces, the characteristic features or the manifesting forces of phenomenal existence (*samskrta-laksanani*).[43]

In the one *dharma*-moment, there is birth, decay, endurance, and death. No time elapses, yet there is this process of arising and passing away. This dynamic quality of the *dharma*-moment clearly points to non-substantiality. Yet does this radical momentariness not lead to what Hartshorne has correctly seen as negativism? On the contrary, each *dharma*-moment is an integral whole that has fully fulfilled its potentiality. "The reality moment is the moment of action, of its being achieved, 'We call a moment', the Sarvastivadins maintain, 'the point when an action is fully achieved' ".[44] The *dharma*-moment is indeed empty, yet it achieves a wholeness and integrity that goes beyond its momentariness. This aspect of the Sarvāstivāda is more fully seen in its characteristic assertion that things exist, are real, in the three periods of past, present and future.

The term Sarvāstivāda is applied to this school precisely because of its unique insistence on the *dharmas* being existent in the past, present and future. It is also this insistence that marks this school as advocating a philosophy of being: there is a substantial existence that endures the passage of time. Is substantial existence really being asserted?

As stated above, the Sarvastivadins maintain that all elements exist on two different planes, the real essence of the elements (*dharma-svabhava*) and its momentary manifestation (*dharma-lakshana*). The first exists always, in past, present, and future. It is not eternal (*nitya*) because eternality means absence of change, but it represents the potential appearances of the element into phenomenal existence, and its past appearances as well. This potentiality is existing forever (*sarvada asti*). The future potential elements are, indeed, divided in this school into two different sets, those that will appear (*utpatti dharma*) and those that are suppressed and never will appear (*anupatti dharma*). Since the moment (*kshana*) is not something different from the element (*dharma*), time in general is not different from the elements taken collectively, as far as they have not lost their capacity of appearing in phenomenal life. In fact, 'the times' is one of the synonyms used to designate collectively the elements appearing in ordinary life. But the term (*kala*) implying the reality of one time, is carefully avoided; it is replaced by the term 'transition' (*advan*). When the Sarvastivadin maintains that "everything exists", it means that all elements exist, and the emphasis which is put on the reality of elements refers to the conception that their past as well as their future transition represents something real. From this fundamental tenet the school derives its name. Since the conception of an element answers rather to our conception of a subtle force than of a substance, the reality, i.e. effectiveness of the past is not so absurd as it otherwise would appear.[45]

While at the beginning he talks of the "real essence of the element", at the end he denies the idea of substance and substitutes "subtle force". The above passage states the ambiguity of the Sarvāstivāda position quite clearly. It wants to maintain endurance yet can really never assert real substantiality. What is also important to see is that what Sarvāstivādins want to emphasize is that the past has effect on the present and that the present is open to affect the future. That really seems to be all they are asserting by their insistence on the reality of past, present and future. In other words, though moments appear only to disappear there is a retention of their influence through time (the next moment). However, substantiality is really never asserted.

D. Funahashi Issai is a noted expert of Sarvāstivāda. He states that the Sarvāstivāda did not hold a substantialist view. Let us look at some related terms and their original Sanskrit. "*Hottai* (*dharma-essence*) is the rendering of *svabhāva* (and also *dravya*) which is usually translated as *jissho* (own-nature, own being), however even though '*own-nature*' and '*dharma-essence*' are used, they definitely do not indicate a substantial (*jittai-teki*) thing".[46] The basic reality of all of Buddhism, according to Funahashi, is that 'all things are impermanent', and so there can never be substantial existence asserted. When the Sarvāstivāda says that the 'three periods are real and the *dharma-*essence is always existent', it does not mean to declare an enduring substantial existence. Rather the 'always' in the above phrase really should be understood as 'at any moment'.[47] There is no underlying substratum of substantial reality that flows through the three periods. The momentary existence at any moment is real but as the above quotation states the *dharma*-essence cannot be seen as something substantial. There is no substantial *dharma*-essence and there is no substantial substratum flowing through time, yet at any one moment the *dharma*-essence is real. The *dharmas* arise to disappear. The essay ends with this quizzical remark, "Compared with the *svabhāva* that the Nāgārjuna of the *Mādhyamaka śāstra* rejects and negates, is not this one (the Sarvāstivāda *svabhāva* that is being put forward) quite different?"[48] This is the point: the traditional interpretation of the Sarvāstivāda is this Mādhyamika opponent that upholds substantial existence. Yet as Funahashi notes, and I hope this section makes clear, what indeed is being so fully rejected? The Sarvāstivāda does not uphold substantial existence. It too stands on the reality of non-substantiality and tries to build a system that is more fully aware of that other basic intuition of endurance. *Svabhāva* may be upheld, but it certainly is not substantial existence. *Dharmas* are real actualities but they are clearly not substantial existence. The question naturally arises, what was Mādhyamika so aggressively negating?

IV. CONTINUITY AND NOVELTY

A. The traditional understanding of the gradual de-substantialization of Buddhism's view of reality from a no-self to no substantiality of all things had always bothered me. The logic of the jump from no-self to emptiness of everything was just too obvious. As was asserted above, Buddhism began with that basic intuition of impermanence and the non-substantiality of all existence. The Sarvāstivāda arose to express more fully the equally basic intuition that things endure. As Whitehead notes, however, the two intuitions cannot be separated. The Sarvāstivāda never abandoned that most basic of Buddhist intuitions. It just tried to give voice to the other intuition which was also inherent in early Buddhism but perhaps never fully voiced. Mādhyamika arose to counter what it saw as too much of an 'endurance' tendency. Yogācāravijñaptimātra arose to counter the negative tendency of Mādhyamika. So we see in the history of Buddhist thought the see-saw endeavour to give voice to both basic intuitions. What is important to see is that all of Buddhism holds to non-substantiality and impermanence and all of Buddhism holds to the reality of endurance (even Mādhyamika but it is indeed hard to see). It is interesting to note in this regard that while Mādhyamika in its treatment of the self is quite negative about giving any reality to an enduring quality of the self, Sarvāstivāda as seen in the *Abhidharmakośa-śāstra* quite readily refers to the continuity or stream of existence of the self. The phrase *hsiang hsu* (there is continuity but no substantial self) occurs prominently in the beginning of the *Abhidharmakośa-*

śāstra chapter on the self.[49] Thus, this tendency in Sarvāstivāda to 'substantialize' the intuition of non-substantiality is true. Yet it never denies either the non-substantiality of the self or *dharma*-moments. It is in the Sarvāstivāda effort to 'substantialize' the notion of continuity, i.e. the influence of a *dharma*-moment on the next moment, that it counters the charge of meaninglessness. Except for the matter of novelty, the development of the mental pole and the problem of self-determination in general, the Sarvāstivāda *dharma*-moment parallels Whitehead's actual occasion quite closely. It is in this Sarvāstivāda *dharma*-moment that non-substantiality is upheld and an enduring quality asserted. Perpetual perishing is true, but there really seems to be partial immortality in the subsequent moment.

The question of continuity within a non-substantial context is resolved in the above interpretation of the Sarvāstivāda notion of *dharma*. The completeness of the *dharma*-moment does not merely perish without a trace but lives on as it affects the next *dharma*-moment and thus achieves a form of immortality. This partial endurance does not, of course, resolve the entire problem of meaninglessness, since, for Hartshorne, objective immortality in the mind of God is the ultimate and complete means by which an actual occasion is preserved. The retention of a perishing *dharma*-moment in the subsequent moment is always imperfect and incomplete and in itself is not enough to preserve it in anything close to its entirety. God then is necessary in its activity through its consequent nature to give full meaning to all that has come to pass.

B. Without God, the only thing one has is this imperfect and partial retention of the past in subsequent moments. Buddhism is indeed limited to this form of immortality. Is it all that bad, however? The fullness of each moment is realized in the now, and yet there is no attempt to deny the continuity of that now-moment with previous and following moments. There seems to be a real balance here with a realization of the horizontal and vertical dimensions of time. There is meaning in this. The emotional problem of confronting life as a fading memory is there, yet I see nothing in life that can deny this hard fact. To hope for something more is human nature, but that does not mean that it is true.

This denial of objective immortality is a basic position of all of Buddhism. Yet, there are some suggestive elements in the tradition that may approach this notion of objective immortality. Zen Buddhism often speaks of reliance upon the awakening experience of previous seekers and of course places great emphasis on the awakening experience of Śākyamuni in opening up the path to enlightenment for all. This can be interpreted in various ways. What is suggested by this is a notion of a storehouse of benefit or enlightening grace through which all who practice gain enlightenment. Enlightenment and enlightening activity seem to have an immortality that goes beyond mere retention in subsequent moments. The soteriological context of what is retained and what is imparted limits the specific content of immortality, but nevertheless something indeed is retained and it seems to be retained beyond just the fading retention in subsequent moments. the notion of a storehouse of enlightenment is not foreign to Buddhism, and so an idea of a receptacle of these enlightenment events in the wholeness of reality (God) cannot be simply ruled out. Those opposite events of non-enlightenment (all other events) would also have to be included. Enlightenment takes on its full meaning only in relation to these non-enlightened events. This notion of non-enlightened events being received by the wholeness of reality is more emphatically articulated in the Pure Land tradition and centers on the actively grace-full figure of Amida, the one who imparts enlightenment. It is in Amida that the un-enlightened ones are received and without a negation of un-enlightenment, a transformation of the un-enlightened to enlightenment takes place. Amida's primary characteristic as that receptacle of enlightenment is that it receives the un-enlightened. Thus, all events are found in this receptacle of enlightenment that is Amida.

The above is speculative and I am honestly not sure that I can fully endorse it. I do think, however, that this view of objective immortality is in the common practice of Buddhism. There is firm belief that one remains forever in the mind of Amida as one enters into his land of enlightenment (Pure Land). It is best to think of this birth in the land of Amida in terms of objective immortality. For our purposes, now, a discussion of subjective immortality would be pointless. So, the notion of objective immortality in the mind of Amida is a viable one and can be seen as the Buddhist attempt to make meaningful the perpetual perishing of all events.

C. The second issue of determinism and the lack of a source of novelty mark obvious differences with a process view of reality from that of Buddhism. It is Griffin's critique that most explicitly cites this deficiency in the Buddhist analysis of reality, but I believe his view states a real hestitation on the part of both Hartshorne and Cobb in fully endorsing the Buddhist position. On the one hand, it is quite simple to counter Griffin's objection centered on the analysis of the self based on the chariot metaphor. There is an integrity or wholeness of the self that is recognized in Buddhism. The Prajñāpāramitā emphasis on the such-ness of existence speaks to this issue. The self is obviously more than just the sum of its parts, it is the such-ness of itself as well. I do not know if that explains the self any worse or better than saying that it is a serially-ordered monarchy. On the other hand, the matter is complicated, however, by the rhetoric of Buddhists in saying that the unenlightened state is total conditionality and the enlightened state is total freedom from conditionality. It is this rhetoric that denies the 'both-and' option of process thought that simply speaks about the conditioned quality of existence. The point is that a thing is its environment and what it brings to its environment (the many becoming one and is increased by one). From the process perspective, it makes no sense to talk about any element of reality as being either totally conditioned (determined) or totally free from those conditions. Buddhism should take this concern seriously.

Simply put, the rhetoric of 'all and none' is metaphoric. Common sense perception of reality shows that the 'both-and' alternative is valid. One is not totally determined by one's environment, since one brings something to one's environment, however little. It is true that the un-enlightened in their ignorance of the way things are, ignore the conditionality of their existence and are, paradoxically, more tied down to this conditionality to the point that it approaches almost total conditionality. Enlightenment, among other things, wakes one from this stupor of ignoring the conditionality of one's existence so that this knowledge and acceptance allows one to act more freely *in* this conditionality. One cannot literally transcend this conditionality. The quizzical definition of karma by D. T. Suzuki when he said karma is that the arm bends inwards and not outwards points to this inability to literally transcend the limits of conditionality. Coming to see this truth about one's arm frees one to do the most with one's arm and thus metaphorically frees us from this limitation. It is obvious, however, that such insight will never literally free us from the fact that one's arm bends inwards and not outwards.

Moreover, it is precisely this rhetoric of the enlightened being able to transcend the conditionality of one's environment totally that allows Buddhists to ignore the elements of conditionality in which all of us find ourselves. The analysis of the conditionality of economic and political oppression, racial discrimination and sexism are all things that are finally unimportant to a Buddhist because he or she can supposedly rise above them in enlighten-ment. This 'all and none' rhetoric of Buddhism has prevented Buddhism from completely coming to terms with the implications of the conditioned structure of one's existence. Here, process thought has much to offer Buddh-ism in renewing its focus on the conditioned quality of existence.

As for the question of the source of novelty through God's introduction of the subjective aim to all entities in the process of coming to be, both Cobb and Griffin find this to be a principal difference between Buddhism and process thought. In the following, Hartshorne shows his difference with Whitehead and suggests that Buddhism and indeed process thought need not have this element.

It may surprise some that I have not mentioned the Whiteheadian doctrine of "eternal objects". In one phase there was, I gather something of the sort in early Buddhism. It dropped out, and I personally think that this doctrine is a dispensable element of Whitehead's system. If he needs it, then so and for the same reasons does Buddhism. But I fail to see the necessity on either side. Creativity, momentary actual creatures, and a form of creativity (and corresponding actuality) able to prehend all actuality adequately and cosmically, are the essentials. Creativity itself (the determining of the antecedently indeterminate) simply as such, is merely a concept of productive becoming general enough to span the differences between the various levels of non-divine and also divine productive becoming. It is said not to be an actual entity. The actual entities (including God) are all creatures, in thinking about which we may abstract various aspects. They are also all "self-creative" and influential in the becoming of others. God is in a unique sense Creator, since the divine form of creativity is cosmically relevant, has always had and must always have instantiation in actuality, and by its ordering influence gives the cosmic process a coherence or order (allowing for quite real but limited aspects of disorder arising from the self-determinations of the creatures) which could not otherwise be explained.[50]

Novelty arises out of the process of coming to be in the sheer activity of creativity. In Buddhist terms, the process of conditioned arising includes this element of newness and novelty without the introduction of the subjective aim by God. God is not absent, obviously, for Hartshorne. In terms of being the repository for the eternal objects, God is not necessary. However, as that cosmic prehending entity and as the principle of order and becoming God is necessary. Can something like this be seen in Buddhism? We have already tentatively posited a prehending one in terms of objective immortality; and it does not seem to be far-fetched to look at conditioned-arising as that principle of order and becoming. This principle of order and becoming in no way dismisses chance and disorder, the sheer wonder of indeterminacy, for as Hartshorne notes, "For Whitehead there is no strict natural or moral causal law which holds absolutely of any part of reality. 'Disorder is as real as order.'"[51]

NOTES

1. Alfred North Whitehead, *Process and Reality*, corrected edition, David R. Griffin and Donald W. Sherburne (eds.) (New York: The Free Press, 1978), p. 7.
2. *Ibid.*, pp. 244, 342, and 343.
3. Charles Hartshorne, *The Logic of Perfection and Other Essays in Neo-classical Metaphysics* (Lasalle, Ill.: Open Court Publishing Company, 1962), p. ix.
4. Charles Hartshorne, "Whitehead's Novel Intuition", *Afred North Whitehead: Essays on His Philosophy*, George L. Kline (ed.) (Englewood Cliffs, N.J.: Prentice-Hall, Inc., 1963), p. 25.
5. Hartshorne, *Logic*, p. 17.
6. *Ibid.*, pp. 17—18.
7. *Ibid.*, p. 273.
8. John B. Cobb, Jr. *A Christian Natural Theology: Based on the Thought of Alfred North Whitehead* (Philadelphia: The Westminster Press, 1965), p. 208.
9. *Loc. cit.*
10. John B. Cobb, Jr., *Christ in a Pluralistic Age* (Philadelphia: The Westminster Press, 1975), p. 210.
11. John B. Cobb, Jr. and David Ray Griffin, *Process Theology: An Introductory Exposition* (Philadelphia: The Westminster Press, 1976), p. 139.
12. David R. Griffin, "Buddhist Thought and Whitehead's Philosophy", *International Philosophical Quarterly*, 14: 3 (1974), p. 284.
13. *Ibid.*, p. 263.
14. *Ibid.*, pp. 264—266.
15. *Ibid.*, p. 268.
16. *Ibid.*, p. 267.
17. *Ibid.*, p. 270.

184

18. *Ibid.*, p. 271.
19. *Ibid.*, p. 272.
20. Charles Hartshorne, "Whitehead's Differences from Buddhism", *Philosophy East and West*, 25: 4 (1975), p. 408.
21. Issai Funahashi, "*Abhidharmakosa-sastra*", *Encyclopedia of Buddhism*, Malasekera (ed.) (Government of Ceylon, 1961), p. 59.
22. Junjiro Takakusa, *The Essentials of Buddhist Philosophy*, 3rd edition (Honolulu: Office Appliance Co., Ltd., 1956), pp. 57—73.
23. Griffin, *op. cit.*, p. 264.
24. David Kalupahana, *Causality: The Central Philosophy of Buddhism* (Honolulu: University of Hawaii Press, 1975), p. 69.
25. *Ibid.*, p. 78.
26. *Ibid.*, p. 80.
27. *Loc. cit.*
28. *Ibid.*, p. 82.
29. *Ibid.*, p. 84.
30. *Loc. cit.*
31. *Ibid.*, p. 85.
32. *Loc. cit.*
33. *Ibid.*, p. 86.
34. Th. Stcherbatsky, *The Central Conception of Buddhism and the Meaning of the Word Dharma* (Calcutta: Susil Gupta Ltd., 1961), pp. 66—70.
35. *Ibid.*, p. 5.
36. *Ibid.*, p. 22.
37. *Loc. cit.*
38. Kalupahana, *ibid.*, p. 49.
39. *Ibid.*, p. 75.
40. Stcherbatsky, *ibid.*, p. 34.
41. *Ibid.*, pp. 31—32.
42. *Ibid.*, pp. 23—24.
43. *Ibid.*, pp. 33—34.
44. *Ibid.*, pp. 34—35.
45. *Ibid.*, pp. 35—36.
46. Issai Funahashi, *Go no Kenkyu* (*A Study of Karma*) (Kyoto: Hozo Kan, 1954), p. 376.
47. *Ibid.*, p. 377.
48. *Ibid.*, p. 380.
49. *Taisho Shinshu Daizokyo* XXIX, pp. 152b and 304a.
50. Hartshorne, "Whitehead's", p. 409.
51. *Ibid.*, p. 413.

12. A Jewish Perspective on Charles Hartshorne's Concept of God

WILLIAM E. KAUFMAN

Charles Hartshorne's major philosophical preoccupation has been the problem of articulating a tenable conception of God. The question, as Hartshorne expresses it, "is whether and how God can be conceived without logical absurdity, and as having such a character that an enlightened person may worship and serve him with his whole heart and mind."[1] Hartshorne's formulation of the problem echoes the first paragraph of the Jewish *Shema* prayer: "Thou shalt love the Lord thy God with all thy heart, with all thy soul, and with all thy might."[2] Hartshorne has these words in mind when he defines worship as loving God "with all one's heart and with all one's mind and with all one's soul and with all one's strength."[3] Hartshorne's definition of the issue indicates one of the criteria to be utilized in analyzing his concept of God from a Jewish perspective — namely, adequacy to the basic religious insights of Jewish monotheism.

In his book *God in Process Thought*, Santiago Sia states that "believers will have to judge for themselves whether they find in process thought a fuller and more faithful representation of their basic insights compared to, say, classical theism."[4] An examination of Hartshorne's conception of God from a Jewish perspective, therefore, must address the issue of the adequacy of his process thought to the basic insights of the Jewish believer.

A second criterion to be employed in a critical examination of Hartshorne's idea of God is inner consistency. Harry A. Wolfson has underscored the importance of inner consistency in Jewish thought, illustrating its role in the Talmudic method of study:

Confronted with a statement on any subject, the Talmudic student will proceed to raise a series of questions before he satisfies himself of having understood its full meaning. If the statement is not clear enough, he will ask, What does the author intend to say here? If it is too obvious, he will ask again, It is too plain, why then expressly say it? If it is a statement of fact or a concrete instance, he will then ask, What underlying principle does it involve? Statements apparently contradictory to each other will be reconciled by the discovery of some subtle distinction, and statements apparently irrelevant to each other will be subtly analyzed into their

S. Sia (ed.), Charles Hartshorne's Concept of God, 185–195.

186

186

ultimate elements and shown to contain come common underlying principle. . . . And there is a logic underlying this method of reasoning. It is the very same kind of logic which underlies any sort of scientific research, and by which one is enabled to form hypotheses, to test them, and to formulate general laws. . . . Just as the scientist proceeds on the assumption that there is a uniformity and continuity in nature, so the Talmudic student proceeds on the assumption that there is a uniformity and continuity in human reasoning.[5]

It is this assumption of the uniformity and continuity of human reasoning that is the basis of the criterion of inner consistency in Jewish thinking.

A third criterion that has functioned in Judaism is pragmatic relevance. The assessment of the consequences of an idea, practice or law has been a factor of major importance in Jewish life. Witness, for example, the recurrent Talmudic dictum — "examine what the public is practicing." Another example is afforded by a statement from the Jewish book of practical wisdom known as *Ethics of the Fathers*. In answer to the question concerning what the proper way of man is, Rabbi Simeon said: "Considering the consequences of one's actions" (*Ethics of the Fathers* 2:13).

Utilizing these criteria of adequacy, inner consistency and pragmatic relevance, we now examine Hartshorne's concept of God from a Jewish perspective.

I. ADEQUACY

Hartshorne's aim is to develop a philosophical concept of God that is also in consonance with the religious idea of the Deity. In fact, Hartshorne wants to show that Pascal's famous dichotomy between the God of the philosophers and the God of Abraham, Isaac and Jacob holds only for the classical, but not for Hartshorne's own neo-classical idea of God. Hartshorne claims that a truly philosophical idea of God must be rooted in the religious dimension.

Hartshorne holds that the essence of religion is worship. Religion as worship involves two elements: total love for God and man's acceptance of his fragmentary nature. Hartshorne defines worship as "the integrating of all one's thoughts and purposes, all valuations and meanings, all perceptions and conceptions"[6] in response to God as the worshipful One, who is all-inclusive, one and unsurpassable in his goodness, knowledge and power, but whose happiness is affected by others.

Hartshorne's notion of the basic religious intuition finds resonance in some aspects of the Jewish tradition but is in tension with other elements in the Judaic religious writings. Surely, his emphasis on the integration of all facets of the self in the service of God is echoed throughout the Jewish tradition, epitomized in the Biblical injunction: "Thou shalt be wholehearted with the Lord thy God" (Deuteronomy 18:13). Moreover, his emphasis on the reciprocity of the relation between men and God is reflected especially, in Judaism, in the relationship between God and the Jewish people, as in the Biblical verse "And I will walk among you, and will be your God, and you shall be My people" (Leviticus 26:12). Also, Scripture portrays God as affected by the actions of human beings. Notice, for example, the passage from Genesis describing the Lord's grief over man's abuse of his freedom: "And the Lord saw that the wickedness of man was great in the earth, and that every imagination of the thoughts of his heart was only evil continually. And it repented the Lord that He had made man on the earth, and it grieved Him in His heart (Genesis 6:6). Finally, Hartshorne's panentheism, according to which God includes yet transcends the world, is anticipated in the Rabbinic comment that "God is the place of the world, but the world is not His place" (Genesis Rabbah 68:9).

However, there is an aspect of Jewish worship which is in tension with Hartshorne's basic intuition. This is the element of man's total dependence and submission to the will of God. Evelyn Underhill emphasizes this aspect of worship, quoting a verse from the Hebrew Scriptures, from Psalm 145: "The acknowledgement of our total dependence on this free action of God immanent and transcendent, is therefore a true part of worship. . . . In fact the trustful and childlike demand is itself an act of homage, in so far as it has the color of adoration. 'The eyes of all wait on thee, O Lord, and thou givest them their meat in due season.' "[7] Total dependence upon and total submission to God are an essential component of the classical Jewish religious consciousness. Underhill explains: "Indeed, among all the religions of antiquity Israel's alone is based upon that confident dependence on the Unseen which is the essence of the theocratic life, and directed toward the sanctification of conduct and its total submission to the rule of God."[8]

To be sure, we have seen that according to Jewish sources, God is affected by what man does. The theological doctrine in Judaism of the partnership of God and man implies, as the Jewish theologian A. J. Heschel has asserted, that "God is now in need of man, because He freely made him a partner in His creation."[9] Hartshorne's notion of God's sympathetic dependence or "omniscient sympathy, which depends upon and is exactly colored by every nuance of joy or sorrow anywhere in the world"[10] is in consonance with the idea of the partnership of God and man and God's need for man as His covenant partner in Judaism. But it must be emphasized that man in classical Judaism is a "junior partner", for in the final analysis man is radically dependent upon the will of God for his welfare. This does not mean that God predetermines all events. The classical Judaic theological doctrine is that God has bestowed free will upon man, and He rewards righteous behavior and punishes wickedness. Clearly, the empirical evidence of the suffering of good people counts against the truth of this doctrine, and the Biblical book of Job is precisely a challenge to it. Job, an innocent man, suffers and challenges the justice of the Divine decree. God acknowledges that Job's suffering is not a consequence of sin. Thus in the book of Job we see the evolution of the Jewish religious consciousness beyond a naive doctrine of reward and punishment. Yet at the conclusion of the book, God is still very much in control, and Job, in utter abasement, responds that the ways of God are beyond comprehension.

Hartshorne challenges this notion of man's total dependence on God. He states: "The properly constituted man does not want to rely upon God to arrange all things. . . . God is to be relied upon to do for the world all that ought to be done for it."[11] What God does, according to Hartshorne, is to set limits to chance and to set up a favorable ratio of risk and opportunity. "Providence," says Hartshorne, "is not the prevention of chance but is its optimization."[12]

Hartshorne's doctrine of Divine providence is worlds apart from the classical Judaic notion that "the eyes of all wait on thee, O Lord, and thou givest them their meat in due season,"[13] the verse cited by Underhill as support for the idea of the Jew's total dependence upon God. On the other hand, what Underhill fails to reckon with is the evolution of the Jewish religious consciousness. *The issue is the extent to which Jewish theological thinking can evolve and still remain in continuity with classical Judaism.* The interaction of Judaism with Hartshorne's thought nicely concretizes the issue. The crux of Jewish monotheism is not only the unity of God but also the supremacy of God's will and the belief that nothing happens "outside of" or beyond the scope of His governance of the universe. This does not mean that in classical Judaism God contrives all events. Man is given freedom of choice, and his destiny is in part a consequence of his use or abuse of his freedom. But human destiny is *ultimately* in God's hands. In classical Judaism, the notion of chance was regarded as heretical, and associated with Epicureanism. In fact, the Hebrew word for heretic is *Epikoros*, after Epicurus. However, the effort to maintain God's ultimate supremacy over human destiny in our time has given rise to a major theological problem in contemporary Jewish thought — namely, what can the Jew believe about God after the Holocaust? If God *is* in control, why did He allow millions of innocent people to be mercilessly exterminated? No morally sensitive person can regard this catastrophe as a punishment for sin, especially when one considers the little children who went to their death. So we are either left with recourse to mystery — that God had His reasons for allowing it which we cannot understand — or we are forced to "reconstruct" the classical idea of God.

This is precisely what the contemporary Jewish thinker Mordecai M. Kaplan has done, creating a modern American movement in Judaism known as Reconstructionism. The basic thrust of this movement is that Judaism is the evolving religious civilization of the Jewish people. What is constant in Judaism is the *people*, not the doctrine. Thus the doctrine can evolve. Kaplan proposed a radical reconstruction of the Jewish idea of God. He maintained that "it is sufficient that God should mean to us the sum of the animating, organizing forces and relationships which are forever making a cosmos out of chaos."[14]

By admitting chaos, Kaplan is making room for chance factors in the universe. Those who disagree with Kaplan argue that he has compromised Jewish monotheism. Those who agree hold that it is better to believe in a God who is, in part, finite and limited rather than an omnipotent God who could have acted to prevent the Holocaust but didn't.

To summarize: In contemporary Judaism, those who agree with the legitimacy of reconstructing Jewish doctrine would find Hartshorne's philosophical theology an important theological option for the contemporary Jew. On the other hand, Orthodox Jews, who hold a monolithic conception of Jewish doctrine — that the classical conceptions of God's omnipotence and man's total dependence are dogmatically fixed and final — would not be open to Hartshorne's revisionary concept of God, and the role that chance plays in his philosophical theology. In short, the adequacy of Hartshorne's basic insights from a Jewish perspective depends upon how open a particular adherent of Judaism is to the concept of the evolution of Jewish theological concepts and their contemporary reconstruction.

II. CONSISTENCY

We now evaluate Hartshorne's philosophical theology from the standpoint of inner consistency.

Hartshorne criticizes classical theism for its "monopolar prejudice." Hartshorne here is referring to the practice of putting God on only one side, or one pole, of a pair of metaphysical contraries. Thus, according to classical theism, God is absolute, creator, infinite and necessary while the world is relative, created, finite and contingent. Hartshorne maintains that this view is too simple. He holds that God is both absolute and relative, creator and created, infinite and finite, necessary and contingent. Hartshorne refers to this double predication as the principle of dual transcendence: it takes both sides of metaphysical contraries to characterize God. Thus Hartshorne envisages God as dipolar: He has a necessary pole and a contingent pole, an absolute aspect and a relative aspect.

Hartshorne's dipolar theology seems vulnerable to the charge of inconsistency and self-contradiction. Hartshorne attempts to avoid contradiction by distinguishing various aspects of the predication of Divine attributes. He maintains, for example, that God is not necessary and contingent in the same respect. Although the Divine existence is necessary, the particular manner in which His existence is actualized is contingent. Hartshorne thus distinguishes existence from actuality. The fact that God exists is necessary, but that He exists with just the knowledge, feeling or value that He has is contingent upon the state of the universe at a particular time. Thus there is potency in God in the sense that God grows with the world; He has an infinite capacity to adjust to any world-state that becomes actual.

Does Hartshorne in fact avoid contradiction on this point? Hartshorne, as we have noted, does not see any contradiction involved in ascribing opposing metaphysical categories to the same reality provided they refer to different aspects of that reality. According to Hartshorne, the law of non-contradiction is incorrectly formulated as "no subject can have the predicates p and not-p at the same time."[15] What needs to be made clear is that they cannot be applied in the same respect. Thus a person can change in some respects without changing in every way. As Santiago Sia points out, the universe keeps changing, yet we can refer to its changeless activity; namely, the fact that it never ceases to change. Similarly, Sia indicates that for Hartshorne God can be regarded as immutable in his ultimate purpose but mutable with respect to new specific objectives in response to His creatures. God may also be said to exist necessarily in terms of His essence but contingently with respect to his inessential qualities. The upshot of the matter, Sia comments, is that the predication of contrasting attributes in God is not on the same ontological level, since one set refers to the concrete aspect, while the other refers to the abstract.[16] Hence, Hartshorne is not guilty of contradiction because the contrasting attributes he predicates make reference to differing ontological levels of the Divine being.

Another apparent inconsistency in Hartshorne's philosophical theology concerns the relationship between God and the world. According to Hartshorne's panentheism God depends on the world and is therefore inclusive of it; but in another sense, He is independent of it and consequently transcends it. This seems to be inconsistent with Hartshorne's contention that a world necessarily exists. If a world necessarily exists, it would appear that 'God' is not independent of 'world'.

Writing about 'the logic of panentheism' in *Philosophers Speak of God*,[17] Hartshorne defines the meaning of the term 'cause' in theology as "something whose existence is requisite for, implied by, inferable from, the existence of its effect."[18] Hartshorne goes on to ask whether there is a converse relation between cause and effect — namely, if the effect requires the cause, does the cause also require the effect? He notes that the main theological tradition denies this of God, holding that God is independent of the world and could have been Himself, without any world whatever. This is the view of classical Jewish theology. As discussed in my paper delivered at the 1986 Conference on Judaism and Process Theology in New York, the author of the Hebraic hymn, "Adon Olam" (Lord of the Universe) clearly had no difficulty conceiving of a Supreme Being without a world, when he wrote the words:

Lord of the Universe, He reigned alone
While yet the universe was naught,
When by His will all things were wrought,
Then first His sovereign name was known.[19]

Hartshorne criticizes this type of classical theology as follows: "This makes God different in principle from what is ordinarily meant by a cause. From a cause one expects to derive consequences, make predictions; but from God, it seems, nothing follows. He has 'made' the world, but, if he had made a different world or none at all, he would yet have been exactly what he is. Thus his effects do not seem to follow from their cause."[20] In contradistinction to this classical understanding, Hartshorne cites the view that in current science the cause necessitates the occurrence of some effect or other within a specified range of variability. Building on this view, Hartshorne argues for a formal analogy between Divine and other causation, maintaining that "God's existence would make it inevitable that there be a world but only possible that there be just this sort of world. Deity would be independent of (would not require or necessitate) any particular world, but he would not be independent of world-as-such."[21] Summarizing Hartshorne's view of the relation of God and world, Santiago Sia writes: "In Hartshorne's metaphysical system then God is not and never was without a world. There is a certain necessity in creation since God could not have been without some kind of world . . . God does not choose to have a world; he has to have one.[22]

The crux of the matter is that the Hebrew Bible, in its account of creation in Genesis, depicts God as a free personality who does not act by necessity and who does not have to create, but chooses by simple divine fiat to create. As one Biblical scholar expresses it: "The clear line of demarcation between God and His creation was never violated. Nowhere is this brought out more forcefully than in the Hebrew Genesis account. Here we find no physical link between the world of humanity and the world of the divine. There is no natural connection between the Creator and his handiwork. . . . The God of Creation is eternally existent, removed from all corporeality, and independent of time and space. Creation comes about through the simple divine fiat: Let there be."[23]

Here, then, is a clear and evident contrast between Hartshorne and Judaism on the relation between God and the world. In Judaism, God chooses to create; according to Hartshorne God *has* to create a world.

Metaphysical speculation was foreign to the Bible. But in medieval Jewish philosophy, the concept of creation was crystallized in the doctrine of *creatio ex nihilo* — creation out of nothing. In contrast, Hartshorne holds that total chaos or nothingness is inconceivable. He maintains that our conceptual machinery breaks down in trying to explicate the idea of pure nothing. Hartshorne also holds that the world is part of God: the cosmos is the body of God. In contrast, the classical Jewish theist has no difficulty in conceiving of an incorporeal God without a world or universe of any kind.[24]

What we are dealing with here are competing intuitions. Hartshorne admits that "all proof rests on intuition somewhere."[25] Whereas Hartshorne holds that God is inconceivable without a world, the classical Jewish theist maintains that God *is* conceivable without a world. The issue therefore is that of conceivability. Whether or not one will agree with Hartshorne or the classical Jewish theist on this issue depends upon the view one takes of the limits and nature of what can be conceived by the human mind.

III. PRAGMATIC RELEVANCE

As has been indicated, the classical concept in Jewish monotheism of God as an omnipotent, perfectly good Being is shipwrecked on the problem of how such a Being could tolerate the monstrous evil of the Holocaust without intervening to stop it. An adherent of Judaism who accepts as valid the principle of the reconstruction of Jewish theology will find Hartshorne's idea of God pragmatically relevant in some respects, but not in all aspects.

Hartshorne's concept of God is pragmatically relevant for his new idea of Divine providence. We have already noted his statement that Providence is not the prevention of chance, but is its optimization. He continues: "And no longer do we face the cruel alternative: either no divine control or the deliberate contriving of all our woes. The details of events — and our sufferings are among the details — are not contrived, or planned, or divinely decreed. They just happen — period. What is decreed is that it shall be possible for them to happen, but also possible for other, and partly better, things to happen. And the reason their possibility is decreed is that, in view of the state of things, as already determined by past decisions, divine and not divine, no other range of possibilities would involve a more favorable ratio of risk and opportunity." [26]

This description by Hartshorne of adequate cosmic divine power — the power to do for the cosmos all desirable things that could be done and need be done by one cosmic or universal agent — is pragmatically relevant to a reconstructed Jewish theology. Hartshorne has exposed the inadequacy of the traditional notion of Divine omnipotence as that of a cosmic power that determines all decisions. He comments: "The notion of a cosmic power that determines all decisions fails to make sense. For its decisions could refer to nothing except themselves. They could result in no world; for a world must consist in local agents making their own decisions." [27] Hartshorne has replaced this idea with a more reasonable view of a Divine power which is the greatest possible, but still one power among others. Hartshorne's concept of Divine power restores to us the idea of a Being worthy of worship, One who could not have intervened to prevent the Holocaust rather than the idea of a Being who for some mysterious reason chose not to intervene.

The liberal Jew, I believe, can accept Hartshorne's notion of Divine power. But I contend that he would have difficulty with Hartshorne's intuition that the world is the body of God. A basic principle of classical Judaism is the incorporeality of God, that God should not be conceived of as having a body. The medieval Jewish philosopher Maimonides stipulated the incorporeality of God as one of his thirteen principles of the Jewish faith. He interpreted the various descriptions of God's acts in Scripture as anthropomorphisms to be interpreted figuratively, not literally. Although I believe that other traditional attributes of God in classical Judaism, such as omnipotence, can be revised without endangering continuity with the past, I do not believe that the concept of God's incorporeality can be thus reconstructed.

The reason for this is Jewish theological modesty and reticence regarding the essence of God. I believe that, as a Jew, I can revise my understanding of God's *modus operandi*. But I do not believe that, as a Jew, I can acquire any insight into the essential structure of Divinity.

In contrast, Hartshorne maintains that he can describe the Divine essence as it really is. Hartshorne's inquiry into the inner structure of God is informed by Christian understandings. Quite revealing on this point is a comment by Hartshorne on his conception of what Whitehead referred to as the consequent nature of God:

> Any essence is abstract, and the Consequent Nature is simply the abstract principle that there must always be for each new state of the world process a new Consequent state of deity by which the world totality in question is prehended or possessed. Thus there is no one entity called God *qua* consequent, but an endless accumulation of consequent states of deity, each of which sums up all its predecessors. *This has some similarities and some differences with Trinitarian doctrine, and in my view implies that God is a personally ordered society.*"[28]

The above statement indicates that, from a Jewish perspective, one can agree with Hartshorne's modification of our understanding of God's *modus operandi*, but one must exercise caution in adopting his understanding of the inner structure of the Deity as consisting of an abstract and a concrete pole. The reason the Jew must exercise caution here is that Hartshorne's doctrine reflects a Christian motif of the possibility of envisaging the inner complexity of God's nature. This does not mean, however, that a Jew must revert to notions of *Actus Purus* and Divine simplicity, with their attendant difficulties, that Hartshorne has so cogently underscored.

For my part, I agree with Hartshorne's insight that the nature of God is complex, but as a Jew I must refrain from adopting his, or any individual's understanding of that complexity. It is instructive in this regard to contrast Hartshorne with Mordecai Kaplan. Kaplan undertakes to define the meaning of the term 'God', whereas Hartshorne is attempting to describe God as He really is. Thus is underscored a difference between two theological approaches which may very well be grounded in the nature of the respective religious backgrounds of each thinker. For the Jew, the essence of God is beyond human understanding. Scripture states regarding Moses' request to see the Divine essence: "Man shall not see Me and live" (Exodus 33:20). Although I find the categories of Hartshorne's process theology relevant toward attaining a new understanding of God's interaction with the world and man, as a Jew I must bracket his claim to know the inner structure of God. To be sure, Hartshorne recognizes the mystery in God, locating it in His concrete actuality; that is, he maintains that we have only an infinitesimal knowledge of what it means for God to know. But Hartshorne does claim that God's abstract essence is knowable. A Jew following in the tradition of Moses and his inability to penetrate the Divine essence can appreciate Hartshorne's metaphysical insights, while bracketing this thinker's specific conclusions about the inner nature of God. On this issue even a reconstructed Jewish theology must reckon with Underhill's assertion that "it is a mark of Israel's spiritual genius that from the first the Jew placed Reality within mystery: and here, perhaps, is the source of his intense aversion from all images of the Divine. It was in a thick darkness that Moses spoke with God; and the Holy of Holies made, as it were, an enclave for mystery, in the midst of the drama and clamor of ceremonial worship."[29]

From a Jewish perspective, then, we can affirm Hartshorne's understanding of the inner logic of worship, his critique of the classical idea of God's omnipotence and his resultant neo-classical concept of God's *modus operandi*. But the inner structure of God's being, to the Jew, must forever remain mysterious.

NOTES

1. Charles Hartshorne, *The Divine Relativity* (New Haven: Yale University Press, 1948), p. 1.
2. Deuteronomy 6:5, incorporated in *Weekday Prayer Book* (New York: Rabbinical Assembly, 1974), p. 47.
3. Hartshorne, *The Logic of Perfection* (LaSalle, Illinois: Open Court Publishing Co., 1962), p. 40.
4. Santiago Sia, *God in Process Thought* (Dordrecht, The Netherlands: Martinus Nijhoff Publishers, 1985), p. 112.
5. Harry A. Wolfson, *Crescas' Critique of Aristotle* (Cambridge: Harvard University Press, 1929), pp. 25, 26. For further elaboration of these criteria from a Jewish point of view, see William E. Kaufman, *Contemporary Jewish Philosophies* (Lanham, MD: University Press of America. 1985).
6. Hartshorne, *A Natural Theology for Our Time* (LaSalle, Illinois: Open Court Publishing Co., 1967), pp. 4, 5.
7. Evelyn Underhill, *Worship* (New York: Harper Torchbooks, 1957), p. 11.
8. *Ibid.*, pp. 196, 197.
9. Abraham J. Heschel, *Between God and Man: An Interpretation of Judaism*, ed. and introduced by Fritz Rothschild (New York: Free Press, 1965), p. 141.
10. Hartshorne, *The Divine Relativity*, p. 48.
11. *Ibid.*, p. 24.
12. *Ibid.*, p. 137.
13. Psalm 145:15.
14. Mordecai M. Kaplan, *The Meaning of God in Modern Jewish Religion* (New York: The Jewish Reconstructionist Foundation, Inc., 1947), p. 76. For further information on Kaplan and Reconstructionism, see my *Contemporary Jewish Philosophies*, Chapter 9.
15. See Santiago Sia, *op cit.*, p. 49.
16. See *Ibid.*, pp. 43, 49.
17. *Philosophers Speak of God*, edited by Charles Hartshorne and William L. Reese (Chicago: The University of Chicago Press, 1953).
18. *Ibid.*, p. 500.
19. Cited in my paper "The Critique of Divine Omnipotence in Process Philosophy" delivered at the 1986 Conference on Judaism and Process Theology at the Hebrew Union College-Jewish Institute of Religion in New York.
20. *Philosophers Speak of God*, p. 500.

195

21. *Ibid.*, p. 501.
22. Santiago Sia, *op. cit.*, p. 86.
23. Nahum M. Sarna, *Understanding Genesis* (New York: McGraw Hill Book Co., 1966), pp. 11, 12.
24. This is the contrast brought out in my paper "The Critique of Divine Omnipotence in Process Philosophy."
25. Charles Hartshorne, "Could There Have Been Nothing? A Reply", *Process Studies* I, (Spring, 1971), p. 27.
26. Hartshorne, *The Divine Relativity*, p. 137.
27. *Ibid.*, p. 138.
28. Charles Hartshorne in *Philosophical Interrogations*, edited, with an introduction, by Sydney and Beatrice Rome (New York: Holt, Rinehart and Winston, 1964), pp. 323, 324, italics added.
29. Evelyn Underhill, *op. cit.*, p. 205.

13. Process Thought and Some Biblical Evidence

MARTIN McNAMARA

I. INTRODUCTION

For years I have been teaching the Bible, principally the Old Testament, and in recent times my interest has been getting ever keener in the development of biblical thought and in the probability of the existence of a certain biblical metaphysic or ontology; that is, a certain understanding of reality underlying biblical teaching. These are points that need to be worked out in greater detail and not in isolation but in dialogue with students of the development of human thought. The present essay may serve as the first one for me in this direction.

There seems to exist a special kinship between process thought and the Bible and students in this field readily refer to the biblical evidence, or at least remark on the need of having the relevant biblical evidence examined. One reason may be the current emphasis on defining the meaning or explaining the meaningfulness of the term 'God',[1] on which matters there is ample evidence in the Bible. Another reason may be that some of the central issues for process philosophers and theologians are also items on which the Bible is by no means silent, or on which it may have much to say, for instance God's perfection, God's knowledge, God's power (creativity), the problem of evil, immortality.[2] The coincidence of interests is probably not accidental in view of the tremendous influence of the Bible and of Bible-generated theologies and philosophies on western thought down the centuries. One would probably have to concentrate on the religious thought of the Far East in a quest for concepts of God and religion without influence from biblical teaching.

The earliest examination of the biblical evidence on God from a stand-point similar to that of process thinkers was probably that made by Abraham Joshua Heschel in his doctoral dissertation submitted to the Department of Philosophy at the University of Berlin in 1933. This appeared in print in bookform under the title *Die Prophetie* in 1936 and was elaborated in English nearly three decades later (1962), but much more comprehensively, in Heschel's book *The Prophets*.[3] Heschel's positions were examined and

S. Sia (ed.), *Charles Hartshorne's Concept of God*, 197–218.

strongly criticised in a lengthy essay by Eliezer Berkovits two years later,[4] but have been more recently been staunchly defended by John C. Merkle.[5] Some proponents of process thought on the other hand have seen the need of an examination of the biblical evidence from a process perspective. Writing in Preface I to a collection of essays on Process Theology published in 1976, the editor H. J. Cargas has this to say:

> Process theology is increasingly among the important contemporary attempts to present the New Testament claim to modern man. . . . At this point, it seems to me that there are three kinds of homework necessary for carrying the movement further. The first of these is the development of a biblical theology. Whiteheadian thought needs a Bultmann. There have been some significant explorations of such a theology. There has been excellent dialogue between the Society for Process Thought and the Society of Biblical Literature. But there is not yet a comprehensive, exegetical *Process theology of the New Testament*.[6]

Shortly afterwards Lewis S. Ford published an entire work on the topic, under the title: *The Lure of God: A Biblical Background for Process Theism*.[7] Two chapters of this work are of special interest: Chapter 2: "Divine Persuasion in the Old Testament" and chapter 3: "Divine Sovereignty". (In this essay only the first will be examined.) Some years later (1983) a work was published by Royce Gordon Gruenler criticising the use of the biblical evidence by process thinkers: *The Inexhaustible God: Biblical Faith and the Challenge of Process Theism*.[8] Gruenler's study is an indication of the extent to which process thinkers and biblical scholars are already in dialogue. This seems set to continue, hopefully to the benefit of both the presentation of the biblical perception of God and the development of process studies. In this initial essay I do not intend to enter in any great detail into such modern studies. Instead, for the greater part I intend to limit myself to a number of biblical themes, making liberal use of Santiago Sia's *God in Process Thought: a Study in Charles Hartshorne's Concept of God*.

A point that makes the bearing of the biblical evidence on this subject all the more interesting is that Charles Hartshorne's own approach to the question of the concept of God provides what appears to be a basic principal for an analysis of the very biblical evidence. For Hartshorne the starting point for the investigation of the concept of God must be religion, not philosophy. His position is summarily presented by Sia:

> Hartshorne himself regards religion as the starting point and the frame of reference of the philosophical stand he has taken and developed while persistently claiming that classical theism has misrepresented religious insights. One must, therefore, start with the source, i.e. religion, rather than with its philosophical development.

> Religion, he declares, is intuitive in origin and the philosophical task is to find appropriate logical patterns to express this intuition. For Hartshorne then the religious idea of God is an intuitive or pre-philosophical grasp of who God is. But one is immediately aware of difficulties attending

such a claim. Religion is very much associated with philosophy and its development is, to some extent, due to that discipline. Hartshorne himself points out that high religions came into maturity only after the rise of philosophy. Nevertheless, it is possible, so to speak, to push aside as far as we can philosophical trappings so as to examine the claims of religion in their non-philosophical or pre-philosophical state.[9]

If we replace "philosophical" in this quote with "reflective" we have a principle that holds equally well for biblical teaching on God. Israelite and Jewish belief in God did develop from some undefinable initial stage right down through the time span we define as the biblical period. The concept of God further developed during the New Testament period. Like all development, this took place through reflection, although not in what is commonly regarded as the philosophical sense. It would not so much be the analysis of concepts as reflection on the God of the fathers as revealed through the events of history. This reflection and development would be on the part of certain individuals, the most outstanding of which for the Old Testament period are commonly known as the classical prophets. But it was by no means restricted to these.

II. SOME PRELIMINARY CLARIFICATIONS

There is need for clarification on certain points before we proceed any further. The first concerns what we mean by 'Bible': is it the Hebrew Scriptures, i.e. the Hebrew (and Protestant) Canon, to the exclusion of the books which by some are called the Apocrypha (including Sirach, the Wisdom of Solomon), by Roman Catholics in general as the Deuterocanonical Books? Does it include the New Testament (or, "The Second Covenant" as some now prefer to write)? In the present essay I shall include the larger canon for the Old Testament, and the New Testament writings as well. I use the broader canon since what we are really interested in here are genuine and broadly-based Israelite and Jewish concepts of God, not just those of certain books regarded by all as canonical. In fact, some of the clearest presentations of the doctrines in question are found in the later deuterocanonical books (or the Apocrypha if one prefers). I include the New Testament since this too provides evidence for doctrinal development, and this for the greater part within a Jewish ambient, culturally speaking.

Another matter to be borne in mind is that this body of literature spans a thousand years or so, and has a prehistory that is older still. When we seek the 'biblical' position on a given point we must be prepared for differing answers with regard to different periods — just as is the case for Greek philosophy. Examples for this could be multiplied: afterlife or the resurrection in the Pentateuch, Isaiah 26:19, Daniel 12, 2 Macc 7 (or later between the Sadducees and Pharisees); the 'eternity' of matter or creation out of pre-existing material or *creatio ex nihilo*, as evidenced by the Yahwist in Gen

2:4b—7; the later priestly writer in Gen 1:1—2 or the much more recent authors of 2 Mac 7:28, Wisd 11:17, and Heb 11:3.

It is presumed that by 'biblical' religion is meant the beliefs and practices which are presented as the accepted and the normative ones by the authors of the biblical books recognised as canonical. It is the religion as developed, formulated and presented by authorized persons, some of them known, many of them not known to us. Persons such as Moses and the prophets played a major role in the understanding and formulation of this religion, which we must admit often differed widely from the practices (and at times the beliefs) of the masses. The first and second commandments on Israel's obligation to worship one God and him alone is a cardinal tenet of this 'biblical' religion. Yet in pre-exilic and early exilic times it was far removed from practice. Hosea preached to a people whose deity was Baal rather than Yahweh, the God of Israel, or if Yahweh not to the exclusion of Baal and his divine consort Astarte with whose worship prosperity and the fertility of the land was regarded as inextricably linked. The same held true for the age of Jeremiah, while the Deuteronomic theologians and writers inveighed against the cult of more recently imported Assyrian gods and goddesses and their Canaanite counterparts or equivalents. In Jer 44:16—19 we have a pathetic confession of faith on the part of the inhabitants of Judah who had fled from devastated Palestine to Pathros in Egypt. Their wives had honored the Babylonian-Assyrian goddess Ishtar ('the queen of heaven', the star Venus), and they addressed the prophet Jeremiah as follows:

> As for the word which you have spoken to us in the name of the Lord, we will not listen to you. But we will do everything that we have vowed, burn incense to the queen of heaven and pour out libations to her, as we did, both we and our fathers, our kings and our princes, in the cities of Judah and in the streets of Jerusalem; for then we had plenty of food, and prospered, and saw no evil. But since we left off burning incense to the queen of heaven and pouring out libations to her, we have lacked every-thing and have been consumed by the sword and by famine.

III. PHILOSOPHIES AND THE BIBLE

Occasionally we hear voices being raised against the recasting of 'biblical' faith or beliefs in non-biblical (e.g. Greek) categories, against what is called the hellenisation of Christianity, of the faith, or of the biblical message. The transmutation of the images, and the recasting of the massage into the categories of Greek or western thought, is what is most universally lamented. This, however, has been going on for more than two thousand years, and is almost inevitable.[10]

The limitations inherent in any translation cannot be ignored, particularly in the matter of translating or transferring the concepts of one world-view into those of another which might be quite alien to it. These limitations of translation were already clearly perceived by the grandson of Sirach when, some time after 132 B.C. he translated the Hebrew text of his grandfather into Greek. In a prologue to the translation he begs the reader's indulgence in these words:

> You are urged therefore to read with good will and attention, and to be indulgent in cases where, despite our diligent labour in translating, we may seem to have rendered some phrases imperfectly. For what was originally expressed in Hebrew does not have exactly the same sense when translated into another language. Nor only this work, but even the law [= Pentateuch] itself, the prophecies, and the rest of the books differ not a little as originally expressed.

Having said this much, however, we must recognise that within the collection of books known as the Bible there is no one philosophy or theology, even though there are central, direction-setting truths, or rather the central reality of God around which the entire Bible gravitates. Underneath the biblical reality there lie centuries and worlds of culture and world-views, with the consequent variety of perception and expression that every now and then surfaces. The variety must be part of hidden origins and developments. We ar ill-informed on the precise ethnic composition and historical background of the people presented to us in the biblical narrative as 'Israel', Jacob or the tribes descended from Jacob. They must, however, in the main have been Semitic. From the Semitic races they would have inherited such primitive beliefs as that of the Holy War, making mandatory the annihilation in certain circumstances of all enemies designated as *herem*, anathema. From them, like their Mesopotamian cousins, they would also have inherited certain beliefs concerning otherworldly existence after death, possibly certain traditions regarding an immortality lost for man at the beginning of the human race, even traditions on the very formation of the world. They would also have had lore in common with Canaanites.

Nor were they aliens to world-views more properly at home in Egyptian civilization. It has been noted that the meaning of 'cosmic order', 'divine plan within creation' borne by the biblical personified Wisdom (*hokmah* in Hebrew) is strikingly similar to that of *maat* in Egyptian civilisation. It could well be that the ancient Hebrews were conversant with this Egyptian concept, or set of concepts, and took them over to express their own view of the created order. It is beyond doubt that Israel's Wisdom Literature is closely related to the corresponding literature of Egypt. Direct Egyptian influence may have come through chance connections in the time of David or Solomon, although it could well be older. Treaties were part of the Mid-Eastern political scene from the fifteenth century B.C. at latest. They seemed to have formed part of its literature too. Our earliest known ones come from the Hittites and the Egyptians. In later centuries the practice and genre were taken over by the Assyrians, who used the treaty as a vehicle for establishing and consolidating its grip on vassal states. These documents on the mutual relations of vassal to overlord must have been well known to Israel and Judah. Traces of their influence can be seen in the Hebrew prophets. The presentation of the relationship of Yahweh and his people as a covenant one probably arose in the theological circles of Israel and Judah under the influence of international treaty literature — further evidence for the ongoing presentation of theological issues in language and concepts more comprehensible to contemporaries. This theological presentation of Israel's relationship with Yahweh is found particularly in the book of Deuteronomy and in the related deuteronomic writings (Joshua, Judges, Samuel, Kings, portions of Jeremiah), representing the reflection and writing of the seventh and sixth centuries.

The transcendence and immanence of God were issues that these same deuteronomistic theologians are at pains to defend and clarify. Exile in Babylon brought Israel and her theologians into direct contact, and possibly conflict, with a theology of the Babylonian god Marduk, to whom were attributed traits and actions which Israel had reserved for Yahweh, her God alone. It was probably due to the new circumstances that Israel's implicit monotheism was made explicit in exilic theologians, such as Deutero-Isaiah. Both the exilic and post-exilic period called for new definitions, syntheses and presentations of the ancient faith. New theological issues arose. Persian influence probably gave rise to a developed theology of angels. Later Greek domination brought in Greek philosophical concepts. A combination of these new circumstances gave rise to a new form of literature known as apocalyptic, probably dependent on very ancient traditions as well as much more recent concepts. In some such an ambience, probably around 300 B.C. or later there emerged a more refined view of the afterlife and in due time of the resurrection of the dead. The national religious tradition had now to be presented, defended and even presented in new guise in the lands of the dispersion. This led to further acceptance of Greek thought, concepts and vocabulary. From the very end of the Old Testament period, and about 30 B.C. or so, in the book entitled the Wisdom of Solomon, written originally in Greek we have a magnificent new presentation of the older tradition, but in the language and developed thought-forms which was considered suitable for the changed circumstances. In the New Testament we have the new event of the coming of Christ presented as the fulfilment of the promises made of old.

I give this all-too-brief summary of the movement of biblical thought in order to indicate the complexity of the collection of writings we know as the Bible. In these books we have not one view, one theology. Rather are they witness to the self-articulation of a central tradition, an articulation arising from a sense of fidelity to belief in the God of Israel as his nature and his election of Israel became ever clearer in the vicissitudes of her history.

IV. GOD AS PERSONAL, ANTHROPOMORPHISMS, ANTHROPOPATHISMS

Central to Hebrew belief stands the perception that Yahweh her God is a living God, a person. The Israelite encountered God as a person, not as some blind force in nature, but a Being endowed with intellect and will; furthermore, as One who made absolute demands on the allegiance of each and every individual, a jealous God who would not countenance a call for allegiance by any other, a God who was transcendent and holy but who had entered into a special relationship with a people, who controlled the destinies of this people as he did of each individual and all mankind. These central truths are given flesh in a variety of ways in the Bible, as was required by human nature. The criterion for the validity or non-acceptability of any particular designation or manner of speech seems to have been the manner in which it served to express and defend these central tenets or were a disservice to them. In fact, far from being frowned on, the application to God of human forms and human passions was used by Israel's great theologians and prophets. As W. Eichrodt says in the course of his discussion of the matter:

> An unprejudiced evaluation of the Old Testament's humanizing of the deity leads us to see . . . that in fact it is not the spiritual nature of God which is the foundation of Old Testament faith. It is his personhood — a personhood which is fully alive, and a life which is fully personal, and which is involuntarily thought of in terms of human personality. There can be no doubt that among the mass of the people, and especially in the earlier period, the deity was frequently conceived as restricted to physical modes of living and self-manifestation. They understood the anthropomorphic expressions in a quite literal and concrete way, and so managed to acquire a most inadequate conception of the divine supremacy.
>
> It is, however, obvious that this deficiency was not regarded by the leading spirits in Israel as particularly dangerous. It is precisely the prophets who use such an abundance of anthropomorphic and anthropopathic expressions for God's activities, that anyone trained in philosophical thinking cannot but be constantly scandalized. . . . It is hardly surprising that the anxious formalism of later Judaism and Alexandrian philosophy was unable to come to terms with such boldness of speech, and sought to render it innocuous by means of allegorical interpretation. In this regard, some have even flatly asserted a kind of carelessness on God's part as to the manner in which he is revealed; and indeed, it is patent that those whose task it was to proclaim the divine will regarded it as far less damaging that men should have to grope in the dark on the subject of Yahweh's spiritual nature, than that they should remain unconscious of the personal quality of his behaviour and operations. A doctrine of God as spirit in the philosophical sense will be sought in vain in the pages of the Old Testament. Not until John 4.24 is it possible to declare: 'God is a spirit'.[11]

A little further on, discussing the evidence from the prophets, the same writer speaks in a similar vein:

> For it is obviously not practicable to portray a personal conscious life in popular speech without having recourse to the common imagery of human psychical experience. The living movement of God's dealings with men disappears when philosophical abstraction dictates the language to be employed. The prophets are concerned to portray the personal God, who

woos his people with love, and cannot be indifferent or cold to their rejection of him. Hence they speak frequently and emphatically of his anger and jealousy, his love and sorrow; and it is easy to see that the values which lie hidden in such language can never be abandoned.[12]

He goes on to give a citation from H. Schultz:

The repentance of God . . . grows into the assured conviction that human development is not for Him an empty, indifferent spectacle, but that it is just this inner immutability of His being, which excludes that dull, dead unchangeableness which remains outwardly the same, however much circumstances may change. . . . His jealousy is meant to express that he is not an unconscious natural force, which pours out its fullness in utter indifference, but that human love possesses real value in his eyes. His fear indicates that He is a God who sets a definite aim before Him, who constantly keeps the development of the world within the limits of His eternal decrees, and that His wisdom does not tolerate the self-assertion of short-sighted man. God's wrath and hatred . . . are standard expressions for the self-asserting majesty of his living essence.[13]

Eichrodt himself resumes after this citation with the statement of some principles which I regard as highly important for what is to be discussed below:

For this reason, God's kindness which bestows and blesses life can always stand side by side with his jealousy, the unchangeableness of the divine decree with his repentance, God's triumphing over the raging powers of this world with his fear, his beneficent power with his wrath. To draw all one's conclusions about the idea of God from one class of statements only, without taking into account the other, would be manifestly mistaken; but it must be admitted that this is a mistake which Old Testament studies have not always managed to avoid.[14]

It might be observed that both these writers seem to work within the classical framework of divine immutability, and for this reason not quite on the same wavelength as process thinkers.

A writer on biblical matters much nearer to these latter is Abraham J. Heschel. He makes a strong case against conceiving the God of the Bible, and principally of the Prophets, in the categories of Greek philosophy and for the recognition of pathos and emotion in God.[15] In a section on "The Ontological Presupposition" of pathos he writes: "Pathos denotes a change in the inner life, something that happens rather than an abiding condition. Since to the Greek philosophers the Deity was immutable, remaining absolutely and forever in its own form, it could not be susceptible of pathos, which would contradict the transcendence, independence, and absoluteness of the Supreme Being. Indeed, to attribute any pathos to God, to assert that he is affected by the conduct of these he has brought into being, is to reject the conception of him as the Absolute. Pathos is a movement from one state to another, an alteration or change, and as such is incompatible with the conception of a Supreme Being Who is both unmoved and unchangeable.

The static idea of divinity is the outcome of two strands of thought: the ontological notion of stability and the psychological view of emotion as disturbances of the soul."[16] He further notes that the Greek concept of being represents a sharp antithesis to the fundamental categories of biblical thinking. The biblical man does not begin with being, but with the surprise of being. The biblical man is free of what may be called the ontocentric predicament. Being is not *all* to him. The act of bringing into being, creation, stands higher in the ladder of problems than being. Creation is a mystery; being as being is an abstraction.[17] He notes later that a major motive for the rejection of pathos has been the fear of anthropomorphism, by which we mean the endowment of God with human attributes.[18] In his treatment of this problem he distinguishes between anthropomorphic conceptions and anthropomorphic expressions. The use of the latter does not necessarily mean belief in the former.[19] The prophets (and, we may add, other biblical thinkers as well) accommodated words to higher meanings. Words of psychological denotations are endowed with theological connotations. There is divine pathos as well as human. The nature of the divine pathos is a mystery to man. What Isaiah (55:8f.) said concerning the thoughts of God may equally apply to His pathos: For My pathos is not your pathos, neither are your ways My ways, says the Lord. For as the heavens are higher than the earth, so are My ways higher than your ways, and My pathos than your pathos.[20] "*All expressions of pathos are attempts to set forth God's aliveness*. One must not forget that all our utterances about Him are woefully inadequate. But when taken to be allusions rather than descriptions, understatements rather than adequate accounts, they are aids in evoking our sense of His realness."[21]

I have already noted Eliezer Berkovits's critique of Heschel's theology of pathos.[22] In Merkle's words, the essence of Berkovits's criticism is that the theology of pathos presupposes an analogy between the divine and the human which is an alien and objectionable concept from the Jewish point of view; thus a God of pathos "is a God shaped in the image of man."[23] Berkovits claims that Heschel's affirmation of divine pathos is based on a fallacious line of deductive reasoning and a literalist interpretation of biblical texts. He has the following to say on Heschel's line of reasoning:

The logical deduction runs like this: According to the Bible, the greatness of God is seen in the fact that "man is not an abstraction to Him, nor His judgment a generalisation." God knows man, the individual human being, and judges him as an individual. "Yet in order to realize a human being not as a generality but as a concrete fact, one must feel him, one must become aware of him emotionally." This would make sense if God's pathos could be explained logically. But since what we gain by the argument must be called a mystery, why don't we call for a mystery a step sooner? Why not reason in the following manner: It is inconceivable that the Supreme Being could be passible. Therefore, there could be no such thing as divine pathos. . . .[24]

Merkle gives a detailed exposé of Heschel's position and an analysis of

Berkovits's critique, coming out strongly in favor of Heschel's as the more faithful to the biblical evidence.[25] He cites approvingly the view of Fritz Rotschild that "Heschel has propounded a truly revolutionary doctrine, challenging the whole venerable tradition of Jewish and Christian metaphysical theology from Philo, Maimonides and Thomas Aquinas to Herman Cohen, Etienne Gilson and Paul Tillich."[26]

To my way of thinking Heschel's presentation of the evidence, and both the critique and defence of this, serve only to highlight the inherent difficulty of grasping properly the biblical presentation of God, indeed of the difficulty inevitably present in any human understanding of the divine. The different positions on the matter may be less contradictory than at first appears.

Heschel's comment on the evidence (as given above at the end of the citation from his work) could be regarded as a plea for the need of analogy for an understanding of God and of the biblical language on God. In the final analysis there is not that much separating Heschel from the earlier citations given from Schultz and Eichrodt. Nor need there be any real contradiction between these newer presentations and that of classical theism. The biblical evidence, both of the Old and New Testaments, requires that we regard the God of revelation as a person, living and concerned God, a God who cares, a God who acts. It seems to me that the central question is how to choose concepts and terms to do justice to all the relevant evidence. To profess faith in God as a *living* God requires, it would appear to me, the denial of divine passivity and inactivity. If, however, we say that God is changed by human behavior, or the behavior of created beings, we must be prepared to take the consequences of such a principle: Is he changed to be sad and glad at once?; by millions of different beings daily and over the years of unending time? A more acceptable description of God than *Actus Purus* may be found, although I presume that this designation was intended to exclude the opposite of *actus*, i.e. potency, rather than minimise faith in the Living God, Father of all, full of grace, truth, love, compassion.

V. DOES GOD CHANGE?

We now move into an area closely related to the topic just considered, and one of greater concern to process thought; in fact of concern to many theologians who would not necessarily subscribe to all the tenets of that particular school. As Gerry O'Hanlon observes: "It has been an axiom almost from the beginning of Christian theology that God is immutable, unchanging and unchangeable. . . . Recent and contemporary theological thinking challenges this traditional image of God. More and more there is an attempt being made to do justice to the element of reciprocity in the relationship between the world and God, and, in particular, to stress the suffering, and thereby liberating, involvement of God with his creation and its history."[27] Despite this contemporary rethink on the notion of God's immutability, no consensus has been reached.[28] It will be for theologians and philosophers to continue in their examination of this problem. In what follows we shall consider some biblical evidence and ask ourselves whether it is more consonant with the categories and contentions of process thought rather than with the construction put on it in the traditional synthesis. It should be obvious by now that the interpretation of the biblical evidence in such delicate areas is highly complex. It is not uniform in itself to begin with. We must have regard for the varying presentations and syntheses of at least the major biblical theologians and writers: the Yahwist, Elohist, Priestly Writer, Deuteronomists, major writers in the prophetic tradition as Deutero-Isaiah. Since the mode of biblical discourse is different from ours, if we are to reconstruct the thought patterns, or underlying ontology or lack of it of an individual writer, we must compare his statements among themselves. Then, among other things, we must pay attention to development of doctrine during the biblical period.

If we were to take many of the Yahwist's presentations of God we might be led to think that he believes God changes. He is made to appear to man under different guises: he molds man out of clay, he closes the door of the ark from the outside on Noah, he comes down from heaven to see the city and the tower the men of Babel had built (Gen 11:8). However, it requires but little knowledge of the overall theology of the theologian we know as the Yahwist to see that he is very much aware of divine supremacy and divine transcendence. His anthropomorphisms are more in the expression than the conception. This theological presentation may have been acceptable in Judah of the tenth century B.C.

The Elohist section of the Pentateuch has a different conception and approach: God is revealed in dreams rather than in human form. The Deuteronomists give heaven as God's abode. His presence on earth is through his Name (in the Temple, in the place he himself chooses). In some texts God may have been anthropomorphically represented as man. Categorical assertions in other passages that he was far removed from the human safeguarded against possible misunderstandings. Thus, through the mouth of Balaam: "God is not *man*, that he should lie, nor a son of man that he should repent" (Num 23:19; in Hebrew with verb *naham*). Or again through the prophet Hosea in a passage of exquisite anthropopathism, showing how God finds it almost impossible to punish the Northern kingdom of Israel (here also personalised as Ephraim) (Hos 11:8—9):

How can I give you up, O Ephraim! How can I hand you over, O Israel! ... My heart recoils within me, my compassion grows warm and tender. I will not execute my fierce anger, I will not again destroy Ephraim; *for I am God and not man*, the Holy One in you midst, and I will not come to destroy.

Num 23:19 denies that God could repent (Hebrew verb *naham*). This would be human. And yet 'repentance' is repeatedly predicated of God. God is presented as relenting, changing his mind, not carrying out plans he had

208

announced. The same Hebrew word *naham* is used to express divine regret
for actions performed by God himself. He regretted that he had made
mankind (Gen 6:7), the evil that he had brought on Israel (Exod 32:14; 1
Sam 15:25), that he had chosen Saul as king (1 Sam 15:11, 35). And yet,
despite what has been said concerning the divine choice of Saul, Samuel can
say to Saul in 1 Sam 15:28f.: "The Lord has torn the kingdom of Israel from
you this day . . . And also the Glory of Israel (i.e. the Lord) will not lie or
repent (verb *naham*); for he is not a man that he should repent." Dire threats
of chastisement to Israel through the prophets were often given in absolute,
categorical from: Israel or Judah would certainly be punished. Yet repentance on the people's part made God 'repent', withhold the threat. Belief in
this principle probably stood behind the threats of earlier prophets such as
Amos, even though they appear as prophets of doom, holding out no hope of
a future. It is presented as a principle of divine behavior in Jer 18:7—11: "If
at any time I declare concerning a nation or a kingdom, that I will pluck up
and break down and destroy it, and if that nation, concerning which I have
spoken, turns from its evil, I will repent (verb *naham*) of the evil I intended
to do to it."

The principle is illustrated by the story in the book of Jonah and his
preaching to Nineveh.

With regard to all this we may ask the question whether we are dealing
with a real change in God, or rather with an expression employed in the
interests of divine pedagogy, to make the revelation of the divine will the
more effective. The latter seems to me to be the case. We are moving in the
realms of language rather than in that of metaphysics, of ontology, of
teaching on the nature of God.

A further example of a possible change in the divine nature or mind might
be Exod 20:5, Deut 5:9 when compared with Ezek 18:2— 4; Jer 31:29—30.
In the former texts God says he is a jealous God, visiting the iniquity of the
fathers upon the children to the third and the fourth generation of those who
hate him. The principle seems to have been acceptable for centuries, until a
heightened awareness of the individual in the time of Jeremiah and Ezekiel
queried the justice of punishing children for sins they did not commit. God
then declared that each individual would die for his (or her) own sins, not
those of the forebears. We are hardly to take from this that God changed his
ways. It seems once again that we are in the presence of divine dialogue with
the awakening conscience of his people.

The prayer of petition in the Bible (and elsewhere) would seem to
presuppose a change of divine attitude towards the sinner or sufferer, a
change from one of anger to good pleasure. Jesus has told us that God
rejoices more over the return of a sinner to him than over many holy people
who have no need of penance. A question that remains here too is whether
we are in the presence of language that expresses realistically God's real
concern for mortals rather than of a theology on God's real nature. God is
the Father of lights with whom there is no variation or shadow due to change

(James 1:17). I doubt if support could be drawn from the Old Testament record for the position of process thought on change in God. This in itself does not prove that particular philosophy or theology false of course. There could be reasons other than biblical for a particular system of thought.

VI. GOD AND CREATION

An entire range of questions of interest to process thought deals with God's relation to creation. One is God's connection with the origin of matter or of the universe.

The Bible did not have to originate speculation on the origin of the universe. Traditions and myths on the matter existed before Abraham was. Those of Canaan and of Mesopotamia (that best known of which is *Enuma Elish*) conceived cosmic and human origins as involving a battle between a deity and chaos (figured as a monster or serpent). Before cosmos there was chaos.

The second biblical account of creation (Gen 2:4b—7), from the Yahwist, seems to accept the existence of matter before God's work began. It is debated whether the first account from the Priestly Writer is to be construed in the same way. Gen 1:1 can be construed in either of two ways, depending on how one vocalises the Hebrew consonants *br'*. Thus: "In the beginning God created (*bara'*) the heavens and the earth. The earth was without form . . .", or: "In the beginning of God's creating (*bero'*) the heavens and the earth, the earth was without form . . .". The debated question need not detain us here, apart from noting that the traditional rendering is very much in keeping with the Priestly Writer's style. An initial struggle at creation between Yahweh and the dragon or monster, however, is embedded in Hebrew poetic tradition (cf. Ps 74:13f.; Isa 27:1), possibly part of the legacy of Canaan. There are other forms of biblical tradition on the matter besides, e.g. cosmic origins presented as childbirth. In some cases Yahweh is presented as existing before creation: "Before the mountains were brought forth, or ever thou hadst formed the earth and the world, from everlasting to everlasting thou art God." Whatever of the rendering of Gen 1:1, the Priestly Writer has an exalted concept of creation of the universe. It came about by a divine word, at a simple command, without any opposition from another force. Creation by God's word is found in other passages also, e.g. Ps 33:6; Wisd 9:1; Sirach 42:15.

Whatever of the question of creation out of nothing, the Bible is eloquent on Yahweh's total mastery of creation. He preserves it in being. The favored place of his activity according to the Bible, however, is history. He controls the destinies of humans and through them shapes the course of history as a potter shapes his clay (cf. Jer 18:1—4). He controls not merely the destiny of his people Israel, but that of all peoples. He brought the Philistines from Caphthor and the Aramaeans from Kir (Amos 9:7).

VII. DIVINE PERSUASION

L. S. Ford, devotes chapter 2 of his book *The Lure of God: A Biblical Background for Process Thought*[29] to consideration of "Divine Persuasion in the Old Testament". At the outset he notes that Whitehead personally seems to have felt little affinity with the Old Testament. Psalm 24, for instance, might be "magnificent literature", but this "worship of glory arising from power" could only be based on "a barbaric conception of God." By contrast Whitehead greatly admired Plato's conviction "that the divine element in the world is to be conceived as a persuasive agency and not as a coercive agency. This doctrine should be looked upon as one of the greatest intellectual discoveries in the history of religion."[30] Ford cites some examples of the belief in divine coercive power from the Old Testament, e.g. the prosecution of holy war in defence of the tribal amphictyony, then against the enemies of the Lord's anointed (Psalm 2), the expectation of the destruction of all powers oppressing Israel on the last day. "Does evil befall a city, unless the Lord has done it?" (Amos 3:6b). God has all power, both to create and to destroy, and that destructive power could also be turned against Israel itself (cf. Mal 4:6). Ford also notes, however, that divine power in the Old Testament was interfused with moral purity (cf. Isa 6), and no matter how august, how holy, or how destructive God's power might be, it was always experienced as the expression of a divine will in personal interaction with his people. Ford continues:

> That context, however, is no longer our context. The history of God's dealings with Israel can no longer serve as the all-embracing horizon for our understanding of God, which must be correlated with a greatly expanded world history, a scientific understanding of nature and man, and a drastically altered social and ethical situation. It would appear that only a philosophical structure can provide a sufficiently inclusive context suitable to our needs. Therefore the hermeneutical task calls for the translation of Israel's experience into a contemporary systematic and conceptual framework, one that can do justice to its historical concerns . . .[31]

He notes that process theism involves the persistent effort to conceive God's activity primarily in terms of persuasion. It firmly opposes those views which from its perspective imply certain kinds of coercion within divine power.[32] He notes that, on its own terms, classical theism is hardly coercive, given its understanding of the nature of freedom. "If, however," he comments, "freedom is precisely that which cannot be derived from any external agency, including God, because it is the intrinsic self-creativity of each occasion, then divine efficient causality may be perceived to be coercive. Here we are comparing alternative metaphysical frameworks."[33] He returns to the position of Plato and Aristotle who proposed that God acts upon the world by persuasion,[34] but this suggestion was not picked up by the early Church. Christian theology, he remarks, would be vastly different if the Church fathers had done so instead of adhering closely to the Greek idea of perfection as immutability. As a result the biblical tradition has rarely been interpreted in terms of divine persuasion. Yet there are a good many biblical themes that the concept of divine persuasion can appropriate and illuminate, particularly themes which are a source of embarrassment to exponents of classical omnipotence. Divine persuasion, he states, responds to the problem of evil radically, simply denying that God exercises full control over the world.[35] God's dialogue with his creation is not limited to man, but manifest in the entire evolutionary process.[36] Conceived in terms of persuasion, creation is the emergence of that which is genuinely new, requiring the new initiatives God is constantly introducing. Creation is the fusion of novel form with inherited matter by the self-creative decision of the emergent creature. It cannot be simply conceived in terms of a creation out of nothing (first mentioned in the apocryphal 2 Mac 7:28), not insisted on in the Old Testament accounts (Gen 1, 2, 2 Isaiah, Job, Psalms). Divine persuasion, we further read,[37] illuminates our understanding of the creative Word. Classically, the divine Word in John's prologue is the Logos, that basic structuring principle whereby the world is a cosmos and not a chaos. It is the same Word spoken in creation that addresses us now, for the same purpose, which is the evocation of ever-increasing fulfilment of creaturely possibility.[38] Israel's emergence and continued existence depended upon the conjoint presence of the divine Word and its own faithfulness to the Word, and this may serve as the paradigm for understanding creation.[39] From the standpoint of divine persuasion, providence is simply another way of looking at God's guidance of the historical process already manifest in creation.[40] The apocalyptic expectation of a new world, brought about by God independently of the course of creaturely activity (and "determined from the foundations of the world") is rejected by process theism, because it sees the future as organically growing out of its past.[41]

He goes on to briefly consider the problem of biblical authority. He writes:

As we all know, the God of the philosophers is not the same as the God of Abraham, Isaac, and Jacob. But why is this so? I think that classical theism found no really satisfactory answer to this question insofar as it maintained that all of God's attributes are strictly necessary. If God's control over the world is absolute in that it is independent of all creaturely contingencies, then God's activity may flow directly from his unchanging nature which was deemed wholly necessary and self-sufficient.[42]

He goes on as follows:

But it is the business of philosophy to ascertain that which is purely necessary and universal, and any limitation placed upon philosophical reason ultimately appears to be arbitrary.

Classical theism has a penchant for universality, thus encroaching upon the proper domain of philosophy, which has its own specific procedures and canons for evidence. Yet classical theism is acutely aware of its divergence from most philosophies. We are urged to believe various doctrines concerning the incarnation, the atonement, and the resurrection of Christ for which philosophical evidence or argument is quite inadequate, on the grounds that in these religious matters human knowledge can never suffice.[43]

After some further words on the biblical record he says: "Process philosophy can complement this biblical recital by providing a description of the necessary conditions whereby such contingent divine activity is possible, just as the biblical recital can complement this abstract philosophical outline by giving it specific, concrete historical contours."[44] A little further on, towards the end of this chapter, Ford writes: "Our justification for the appeal of divine persuasion is broadly philosophical: its inherent reasonableness, its applicability to all we know about the world we live in, and its consonance with our best ethical and religious insights. As such, it is at least a partially alien criterion by which to appreciate biblical traditions, since their understanding of divine power is rather different. . . . We can recommend process theism, however, for the hermeneutical task of translating these traditions into a systematic context appropriate to our contemporary situation, without thereby losing Israel's peculiar witness to the action of God in history," noting even that "that historical involvement may also shape the concrete actuality of God himself."[45] He concludes this chapter with the following words: "If our retelling is selective, being told in systematic terms appropriate to our own age, we are only following the practice of the judges and the prophets themselves."[46]

Royce Gordon Gruenler in his book *The Inexhaustible God: Biblical Faith and the Challenge of Process Theism*[47] has, as noted at the outset, presented a critique of process theism (in general) as a hermeneutic for biblical interpretation (chapter 7), and a specific critique of Ford's volume in chapter 8: "Process theism as a biblical hermeneutic". The interested reader can turn to this for specific criticisms. Here I would like first of all to make observations on some biblical evidence which I believe could have been considered and then make a few remarks on some basic principles on the manner in which biblical evidence is used or omitted. At the outset of this paper comment has been made on the use of biblical evidence concerning the nature of God in particular. Ford cites Whitehead's words on "the barbaric nature of God." That there are elements of such a conception in the Old Testament record cannot be denied. But this conception is not the only one and any presentation of the biblical evidence would need to take the entire record into account — including the New Testament, with the presentation of God as loving Father. Within the Old Testament record, the evidence of the Wisdom Literature has been ignored as far as I can see. This is to be regretted since I believe that here there is material which should prove of great interest for process thought. Together with the traditional meaning of 'wisdom' as the art of knowing how to get things done well, how to achieve success, etc. we have in the Bible, as already noted, another meaning of wisdom as a personification or some such like. In this sense wisdom is "something like the 'meaning' implanted by God in creation, the divine mystery of creation,"[48] "a divine principle bestowed upon the world at creation,"[49] "a rationale inherent in the world,"[50] "the primeval or cosmic order."[51] This Israelite concept may bear a relationship with the *maat* of ancient Egyptian religion. This Israelite personified wisdom (*hohmah* in Hebrew) was with God at the beginning, when the world was being fashioned (Prov 8:22, where Yahweh is said to have created her, or more probably come into possession of her). The Lord himself created (or: 'came into possession of'?) her, he saw her, apportioned her, *and poured her out upon all his works* (Sirach 1:9). This divine wisdom, this plan of God, is within the created order, calling our on humans to find it and live by it. Her delight is to be with the children of men (Prov 8:31) calling out to them to seek her and find her, to follow her ways rather than those of her rival, Dame Folly (cf. Prov 8:1—2; 9:13 etc.). In one sense this Wisdom is hidden from men (cf. Job chap. 28; Baruch 3:29—31), but is also revealed because God has made himself known. In the Israelite Wisdom tradition the human confronts creation as a given, the inherent meaning of which he or she must come to understand. In this Wisdom presentation reality and life are not static, but rather something of mystery before which humans stand in admiration. Reality, God's creation, is self-revelatory. While this is not the place to develop the matter further, I believe that an examination of this Wisdom tradition from the standpoint of process thought should prove rewarding. And to repeat a point made earlier in this essay, the Wisdom Literature I have in mind comprises the later deuterocanonical (or apocryphal if one wishes) Book of Sirach and the Wisdom of Solomon as well as the earlier sapiential writings of the Hebrew Canon.

A second observation I have to make has a direct bearing on Wisdom Literature and a central position of Ford and, undoubtedly, many other modern writers on such matters. I refer to the relative status of the living God, his accredited witnesses and of human thought ("philosophy" if one wills) in the interpretation of the divine will, in the recasting or reinterpretation of the older religious tradition. In the earlier stages of the Wisdom literature in Israel, wisdom was regarded as a human attainment, or sometimes as a God-given human endowment. Wisdom seems to have had a connotation of 'craftiness' and the term was not applied to God. Humans were wise; God was not said to be so. The king's counsellors were drawn from the ranks of the sages, and on occasion the sages could be held in as high a regard as the prophet, if not higher. Kings could have the temptation to follow the advice of their wise counsellors rather than the word of God coming through a prophet. Matters seem to have come to a head in this regard in the time of the prophet Isaiah. King Ahaz would have followed his advisers, trained in the Wisdom schools, rather than the word of the Lord coming through Isaiah himself. Isaiah condemns such worldly wisdom. It will prove false (cf. Isa 29:14; see also Jer 8:8). Isaiah goes further; he now attributes wisdom to Yahweh; he is excellent in wisdom (Isa 28:29). The prophets have access to the mind of God, they stand in his counsel. To them there is revealed a mystery which is kept hidden from others. It is in the strength of this conviction that they can interpret and recast the earlier tradition.

This belief holds good for Jesus and the New Testament Church much more so than for ancient Israel. There are mysteries of the kingdom of God revealed to believers, but hidden from others. Salvation through Christ is perceived as divine wisdom through the gift of faith, not through human wisdom. In fact to a human way of thinking, the mode of this saving work is weakness to the Jew and foolishness to the non-Jew (cf. 1 Cor chap. 2).

This principle, I believe, holds good for the subject under consideration: the human science of philosophy is not the discipline to set the central norms for determining what in earlier biblical tradition is relevant for contemporary man. Despite the many positive insights and valid contributions of process philosophy and theology, I believe that the principle stated by Ford in this matter cannot be accepted. Consideration of many other points in his essays is here excluded by the limits set for this essay.

VIII. GOD'S KNOWLEDGE:

A belief that there is in God or the gods a knowledge of future events, even those dependent on man's freewill, would appear to have been widespread in ancient religions. It seems to underlie prophecy and divination of various kinds. The same holds true for Israel, only to a far greater extent. In 1 Sam 23:10—12 David asks Yahweh for an answer as to what certain persons are freely to do, and receives it. A typical case of enquiry to a court prophet as to future events is 1 Kings 22, with the answer that the king's armies are to be victorious, or defeated. In fact, one of God's great gifts to Israel was that of prophecy, which included the ability to foretell future events. Yahweh's knowledge of future events is used to great effect in Second Isaiah (e.g. Isa 41:21—29) to make manifest the difference between the Living God and dead idols. God's knowledge of the individual and of all creation, Sheol included, is the theme of Ps 139. "Thy eyes beheld my unformed substance; in thy book were written, every one of them, the days that were formed for me, when as yet there were none of them." (v. 16). Yahweh's knowledge of the future is closely connected with his nature as creator of this same future, creator of human history in particular. A theme intimately connected with this is that of the divine plan,[52] the mystery hidden to earlier ages but revealed in Christ and through the Church. The divine foreknowledge is implicit in the biblical doctrine of predestination. Those whom God foreknew he predestined, leading to ultimate glorification (cf. Rom 8:28—30). Writing from the New Testament perspective of fulfilment, Eph 1:3—12 looks at the entire process having being foreseen and predestined by God for eternity: before the foundation of the world God the Father destined (or predestined) the faithful to be God's sons through Jesus Christ (1:5), destined and appointed to live for the praise of his glory. The divine knowledge, and the implications of belief in this, have presented problems for philosophers and theologians down the centuries and continue to do so. They were not, however, problems for the biblical writers, although what they have said on the matter must be taken into consideration by theologians of all ages as they grapple with the question.

IX. THE LIVING GOD AND INDIVIDUAL IMMORTALITY

Belief in individual immortality emerged as a formulated doctrine rather late in Israelite history. From the beginnings it would appear that there was a belief in the survival of something of the person, a shade among the Rephaim in Sheol. Life for the Hebrew belonged to God and to mortals before death. It was not something to be predicated of the dead. Sheol was the negation of all that was meant by life. These concepts Israel held in common with her Mesopotamian cousins. She can be presumed to have known the quite different beliefs of the Egyptians concerning the otherworld. These, however, she refused to accept. The Ancient Near East knew of man's quest for immortality, for life without end. It is the theme of the Gilgamesh Epic. Mesopotamian tradition knew of only one mortal to be endowed with the gift of immortality, Utnapisthim the hero of the flood. Not even the superman and demigod Gilgamesh attained it. When he went in quest of it he was constantly reminded: "The life thou pursuest thou shalt not find. When the gods created mankind, Death for mankind they set aside, Life in their own hands retaining." The myth of Adapa tells how the god Ea sent to Adapa the bread of life to eat and the water of life to drink. Because Adapa did not consider the offer as serious he did not partake of them and was told that he had forfeited eternal life. In the Ugaritic legend of Aqhat, the maiden Anath asks Aqhat to ask her for eternal life and she will give it to him; she will make him immortal like the god Baal. Aqhat's reply is: "Fib not to me, O Maiden, For a youth thy fibbing is loathsome. Further life — how can mortal attain it? How can mortal man attain life enduring?"

The Israelites can be presumed to have known these stories and the Bible itself has a narrative on man's loss of eternal life offered to him at the beginning. The absence of a belief in an afterlife where good would be rewarded and guilt punished left the Israelites with a limited field for a full theodicy. It must also have created problems arising from belief in a living God intimately united with his worshippers in this world. It was probably reflection on the appropriateness of eternal union with the living God, after earthly death as before it, coupled with what seemed to be the demands of divine justice that finally led to belief in an afterlife and a bodily resurrection. We have early intimations of this perpetual union with God in Ps 49:15; 73:24. Belief in the resurrection may be read, possibly, in the somewhat late text (ca. 400 B.C.?) Isa 26:19. It became a clear doctrine in Apocalyptic writings, as in Dan 12:1—4 from about 165 B.C. from which time onwards the question of an afterlife, with or without inclusion of bodily resurrection, was center stage in Judaism, even if denied by the Sadducees.

The introduction of the concepts of Greek philosophy, such as *psyche*, 'soul', very probably made it easier for the Jews to articulate their belief in a point that was calling out for clarification. The doctrine of an afterlife is fully developed by the author of the Wisdom of Solomon, written in Greek in Alexandria about 30 B.C., who may well have drawn on Epicurean concepts and vocabulary to set forth his teaching. The ground was already prepared for the New Testament where the resurrection of Jesus stands at center, and with it the new life and resurrection promise for all who believe in him. Jesus points out to the Sadducees their error in not seeing a basis for the resurrection belief in the Pentateuch, in Exod 3:6: "I am the God of Abraham, and the God of Isaac, and the God of Jacob," a text which he cites (Mk 12:26f.; Mat 22:31f.; Lk 20:34—38), with the comment: "He [i.e. the God of Israel] is not the God of the dead, but of the living," to which is added in Luke: "for all live in him." The God of Israel, the God put before us in the Bible, is both living and life-giving, in this world and in the next. It was probably a latent metaphysic or ontology of this sort that had the central tradition in Israel reformulate its ancient faith to express belief in eternal life, and for most Jews this was seen to include belief in bodily resurrection as well.

X. CONCLUSIONS

In this essay I have touched on some of the principles which I believe must be borne in mind in any use of biblical evidence in questions of theology, philosophy or in any other science. After this I have examined some of the questions which I take to be of interest to students of process thought. With what success I have done this I am unable to say. In a sense, on my part it all represents a first attempt at such a dialogue.

The more I study the Bible, the Old Testament in particular, the deeper do I perceive it as a divine dialogue with mankind, one whose mode of discourse is heavily determined by man's ability to grasp a message about God and less concerned with the inner nature of divinity. Before his departure Christ told his disciples: "I have yet many things to say to you, but you cannot bear them now" (John 16:12). It was a central tenet of Old Testament religion that a human could not see God and live (cf. Exod 33:20; Isa 6:5; Judg 13:22, etc.). The mode of biblical discourse is very much determined by the desire to get certain central truths concerning God to his covenanted people. Starting from a point where Israel had pre-Yahwistic and pagan concepts of the divine, there began a journey during which these were purified of what was erroneous and developed in what was genuine. By reason of their purpose, the presentation of truth concerning God in the Bible are many and varied. How much we can pass beyond these presentations made at various times and in many ways to the inner nature of God is something that can only be discussed in any meaningful way for each individual case. My own impression is that the inner nature of God will continue to elude us. The vastness and depth of the mystery involved, however, is an invitation to further probe rather than evade the issues. Through dialogue between philosophers, theologians and biblical scholars it may be possible to work out a meaningful biblical metaphysic, in the sense of the biblical view of God and creation underlying the divergent presentations of the different biblical writers. As is the hope of proponents of process thought, such dialogue should enrich both process thought and the issues confronted by biblical writers.

NOTES

1. On this see Santiago Sia, *God in Process Thought: a Study in Charles Hartshorne's Concept of God* (Martinus Nijhoff, 1985), p. 1.
2. See the table of contents in Sia, *op. cit.*
3. Abraham Heschel, *The Prophets*, part 2 (Harper and Row, 1962).
4. Eliezer Berkovits, "Dr. A. J. Heschel's Theology of Pathos," *Tradition: a Journal of Orthodox Thought*, 6 (1964), pp. 67—104.
5. John C. Merkle, "Heschel's Theology of Divine Pathos," *Louvain Studies*, 10, 2 (1984), pp. 151—165.
6. Harry James Cargas and Bernard Lee (eds.), *Religious Experience and Process Theology: The Pastoral Implications of a Major Modern Movement* (N.Y.: Paulist Press, 1976), p. ix.
7. (Philadelphia: Fortress Press, 1978).
8. (Grand Rapids, Michigan: Baker Book House, 1983).
9. Sia, *op. cit.*, p. 9.
10. See, for instance, Heschel, *op. cit.*, pp. 27—58 and 247f.
11. Walter Eichrodt, *Theology of the Old Testament*, vol. 1 (London: SCM Press, 1961), pp. 211f.
12. *Ibid.*, p. 216.
13. *Old Testament Theology*, Engl. trans. of 2nd ed., vol. 2 (1898), pp. 109f.
14. W. Eichrodt, *op. cit.*, pp. 211f.
15. See, A. Heschel, *op. cit.*, pp. 27—47, 48—58.
16. *Ibid.*, p. 40.
17. *Ibid.*, p. 43.
18. *Ibid.*, p. 49.
19. *Ibid.*, p. 51.
20. *Ibid.*, p. 56.
21. *Ibid.*, p. 57.
22. E. Berkovits, *op. cit.*
23. Cf. *Ibid.*, p. 94.
24. *Ibid.*, pp. 81—82 in J. Merkle, *op. cit.*, pp. 161—162.
25. Merkle, *op. cit.*, pp. 160—165.
26. *Ibid.*, p. 160.
27. Gerry O'Hanlon, "Does God Change?: H. U. von Balthasar on the Immutability of God," *Irish Theological Quarterly*, 53 (1987), p. 161.
28. *Ibid.*, p. 178. See also *God and Change* Special Issue of *New Blackfriars* (May 1987) and Santiago Sia (ed.), *Process Theology and Christian Doctrine of God* Vol. 8 of Word and Spirit (Petersham, Mass.: St. Bede's Publications, 1986).

29. (Philadelphia: Fortress Press, 1978).
30. In Ford, *op. cit.*, p. 15.
31. *Ibid.*, p. 16.
32. *Ibid.*, p. 17.
33. *Ibid.*, p. 18.
34. *Ibid.*, p. 19.
35. *Ibid.*, p. 20.
36. *Ibid.*, p. 21.
37. *Ibid.*, p. 22.
38. *Ibid.*
39. *Ibid.*, p. 23.
40. *Ibid.*
41. *Ibid.*, p. 24.
42. *Ibid.*
43. *Ibid.*, pp. 25—26.
44. *Ibid.*, p. 27.
45. *Ibid.*, pp. 27—28.
46. *Ibid.*, p. 28.
47. (Grand Rapids, Michigan: Baker Book House, 1983).
48. Gerhard Von Rad, *Wisdom in Israel* (London: SCM Press, 1972), p. 148.
49. *Ibid.*, p. 441.
50. Bruce Vawter, *The Path of Wisdom: Biblical Investigations* (Wilmington, Delaware: Michael Glazier, 1986), p. 161.
51. Dermot Cox, *Proverbs, with an Introduction to the Sapiential Books* Old Testament Message 17 (Wilmington, Delaware: Michael Glazier, 1982), p. 161.
52. Pierre Gelot and André-Alphonse Viard, "Plan of God," in X. Léon-Dufour (ed.), *Dictionary of Biblical Theology* (London: Chapman, 1967), pp. 382—385.

14. Rigor, Reason and Moderation: Hartshorne's Contribution to the Philosophy of Religion and Philosophical Theology

DAVID A. PAILIN

At the start of the "Preface" to *Man's Vision of God* Hartshorne points to the "mountainous — I had almost said, monstrous — mass of writings devoted to 'philosophical theology'" and asks what there is left for him to add. His reply is "exactitude, logical rigor."[1] What he claims here "simply, if without apparent modesty," has been one of the major characteristics of his publications in the succeeding half-century. Whereas, for instance, it may not be possible to arrive at "a trouble-free interpretation" of Whitehead's theological views (and, according to Hartshorne, Whitehead himself "said once that he felt that his thought about God was 'very vague,' but that others would be able to clarify the matter"[2]), Hartshorne has made important contributions to theistic thought by discriminating analyses of the contents of such notions as those of the divine necessity, perfection, relations, power and awareness. In this respect he has considerably clarified the concept of God not only for process theology but also for theological understanding generally.

Although there are many fundamental links between Whitehead's ideas and those of Hartshorne, it is a mistake to think of the latter as simply or even primarily a disciple and developer of the former's notions. While Hartshorne is a 'process philosopher' or 'neoclassical metaphysician' whose understanding has, as he freely admits, been considerably influenced by Whitehead's, he justifiably protests against being described as "a Whiteheadian."[3] He acknowledges that Peirce has also had a substantial influence on his understanding and that other notable contributions come from a wide range of thinkers including Emerson, Royce, Bergson, James, Leibniz and Plato.[4] In the end, though, Hartshorne is an independent and original thinker who pays attention to the thoughts of others so far as they seem able to contribute to the development of insight. He particularly consults the works of Whitehead and Peirce because he judges that they "surpass previous writings sufficiently to merit careful consideration."[5]

The determining factor in Hartshorne's thinking is his commitment to the canon of reason. At the age of seventeen, he reports, he decided "to trust reason to the end." His publications support his claim that from that time he has sought to make his thinking about religion and other matters "good

220

thinking" — *good*, that is, "by the proper criteria of thinking." In accordance with this aim he rejects in principle the view that fundamental questions are beyond the limits of reason and intelligibility; on the contrary he bases his own work on the conviction that "the ultimate concepts have a rational structure, lucid, intellectually beautiful."[6] A second characteristic of his religious understanding, then, is its rationality. In attempting "to introduce more strict modes of thought into philosophical theology,"[7] he recognizes no authority but that of rational justifiability.

The title of Hartshorne's latest book ('latest', that is to say, at the time of writing — born in 1897 he is still adding to his list of publications!), *Wisdom as Moderation: A Philosophy of the Middle Way*,[8] points to a third characteristic of his thought. This is its mediating and reconciling quality. It finds expression in various ways. It is seen, for instance, in his application of Peirce's rule, "think in trichotomies not mere dichotomies, the latter being crude and misleading by themselves."[9] Accordingly he seeks to perceive how the positive truths discerned by allegedly contradictory positions such as monism and pluralism[10] can be coherently reconciled in a third way. So far as the concept of God is concerned, this is exemplified in his recognition of 'panentheism' as a third possibility beside classical 'theism' and 'pantheism', and in his appreciation that an adequate concept of the divine involves *both* a necessary/absolute/abstract aspect *and* a contingent/relative/concrete aspect rather than demands an *either/or* choice between them.

Through his mediating analyses Hartshorne seeks to delineate a middle way for theistic understanding between the extremes of atheism and of theism as traditionally understood. The former denies "that there is any radically pre-eminent being" whereas the latter asserts "a pre-eminent and *in all respects* perfect reality, . . . conceived as an exhaustive actualization of *all* possible good properties." Hartshorne holds that there is "a mean between" these positions. This mean makes it possible to affirm in a self-consistent way both the reality of "cosmic Power and Perfection" in a significant sense and, by also acknowledging "the genuineness of ordinary localized or imperfect forms of power and value,"[11] the real significance of human being. His theistic understanding thus avoids the error of holding with Nietzsche (and such current popularizers of the misunderstanding as Cupitt) that a proper recognition of the divine perfection entails a total devaluation of the human as well as its obverse, namely, that the significance of human being can only be affirmed by denying the reality of the divine.

In applying rigor, reason and moderation to "reflection upon the religious object,"[12] i.e., God, Hartshorne does not recognize any normative authority in references to religious experiences, divinely revealed insights, traditions, scriptures and institutions. Furthermore, in his commitment to reason as the only proper warrant for theological claims, he regards it as essential in some cases and as preferable wherever else it be possible to use *a priori* modes of argument. In *A Natural Theology for Our Time*, for instance, he argues that in the case of divine existence it strictly follows from the concept of it as being essentially necessary, and from the divine interaction with the non-divine as essentially universal, that "there cannot be empirical proofs"[13] — at least, that is, not in the "sharp sense" that Popper identified according to which only what "some conceivable experience would falsify can be claimed to be empirical."[14]

The significance of this for arguments about the existence of God will be considered shortly. What is immediately of interest is the form of *a priori* argument which Hartshorne prefers to use in meeting this requirement. In a list of what he regards as his "special contributions" to process philosophy he outlines this method as one of "doctrinal matrices: the method of decision by elimination from exhaustive divisions of the doctrinal possibilities."[15] What it consists of is the discernment of what are considered to be all the possible solutions to the question under discussion, and then a critical analysis of each of these apparent options in order to show that all but one of them is untenable, ideally because on inspection all but that one are found to be self-contradictory. If, then, the initial list of possible answers is complete and if no such objections can be validly raised against the remaining one, the latter must be held to be necessarily true. (If convincing reasons can be raised against each option without exception, the conclusion must be that the original question is unanswerable and hence itself intrinsically incoherent.)

In *Man's Vision of God*, for example, Hartshorne summarizes his thesis by listing the possible ways of conceiving the definitive perfection of the divine in terms of whether God is to be thought of as being unsurpassable, either solely or in combination, in all, some or no respects. The conclusion which is held to follow "unambiguously" from the examination of these notions in the preceding chapters is that the conception of the divine as "unsurpassable by anything, even by self" in *some* respects *and* as "unsurpassable, except by self" in *all other* respects is the only member of this "logical schema" against which there are no "decisive objections." Hence this way of conceiving of God's reality "as an existent being" is held to be "self-evidently true"; the other conceptions are to be discarded as "at best superfluous."[16]

This mode of argument "by elimination" is also used in the chapter on "Ideas of God" in *Creative Synthesis and Philosophic Method*. Here Hartshorne presents "an exhaustive division" of the divine reality in terms of the qualities of necessity and contingency in both their "eminent or transcendent" and their "ordinary or non-eminent" forms. Having compared the possible combinations with five "principles of criticism", he concludes that the "reasonable requirements are fully met only by" one of those combinations.[17] A similar method of proof is used in the following chapter where he gives six arguments for the existence of God — ontological, cosmological, design, epistemic or idealistic, moral, and aesthetic. In each case he maintains that there are only four options to choose between, one of which involves the affirmation of the existence of the divine, and that inspection shows all the non-divine options are "not only unacceptable as true but absurd, not genuinely conceivable." Thus he concludes that the other option, that which affirms the existence of deity, is "necessarily true."[18]

One value of these arguments — and it is a considerable one — is that they clarify what is involved in the question of theism. Those who deny theism are committed to upholding one or other of the options which Hartshorne criticizes as rationally unsustainable. On the other hand, such arguments may not be as completely convincing as at first appears.

It may be questioned, for instance, whether the list of options is complete or, where it is formally complete (as in the case of the options all, some, or none), whether the material concept is totally appropriate to the divine reality. To argue, for instance, that the divine must be conceived as loving (or knowing or seeing . . .) *all* since the alternatives — of loving *only some* or of loving *none* at all — are not credible ways of considering the divine as the perfect leaves open the question of the fundamental appropriateness of attributing love (or knowledge or sight . . .) to the divine. Whereas the argument may seem acceptable in relation to the divine as loving, it is not so clear that it is so in the case of the divine as 'seeing' (from what perspective, at what scale, in what form?) and even less so in the case, say, of 'smelling.' (Is it appropriate, for instance, to argue from the universality of divine awareness that the divine experience must include appreciation of the odor of roasting meat and of the stench of rotting carcases?[19]) While theism may not be vacuous since some material notions are justifiable as symbolic expressions of aspects of the divine reality, doubts may arise about whether these notions fit that reality sufficiently closely to be the reliable basis for *a priori* arguments. Countering the apparent rigor and decisiveness of such reasoning and so qualifying confidence in its conclusions, is Whitehead's suggestion that "weakness of insight and deficiencies of language" are likely to prevent philosophers from ever achieving a final formulation of their first principles.[20]

Furthermore, while Hartshorne is convinced of the rationality of ultimate concepts, doubt about *a priori* arguments may focus on their presupposition, namely, that reality itself is correspondingly rational. While, that is, *a priori* arguments may be held to show in what ways we are inescapably committed to thinking about reality, those influenced by Kantian or Wittgensteinian analyses of thought or by other post-Enlightenment notions of the cultural relativity of ideas may point out that it does not necessarily follow that reality must correspond to our ways of understanding it. A comparison of Hartshorne's views with those of Anselm is illuminating in this respect. In the *Proslogion*, for instance, Anselm considers — presumably according to his intellectual formation by his culture — that the definitive unsurpassability of the divine unquestionably includes impassibility. In Hartshorne's judgement, in contrast, this is not only far from self-evidently so: the opposite attribution (eminent passibility) is self-evidently the correct way to understand the divine reality. [21] Similarly Hartshorne comments on Anselm's *Cur Deus Homo* that "a weakness in Anselm's thinking is in the 'human-all-too-human' valuations on the basis of which he applies" the definitive formula for the divine.[22] The inescapability of such anthropological conditioning of theological judgements, however, means that all *a priori* arguments about the divine are somewhat suspect on their own, including those that Hartshorne presents.

When pressed to the extreme, basic doubt about rationality threatens the legitimacy of all attempts at understanding and ultimately leads to a state of intellectual anarchy. In practice, however, while experience may be considered to indicate that rational reflection is reliable enough in the case of the practical issues of secular life, it is not so obviously warrantable in the case of attempts to determine the nature of ultimate reality. Confidence in *a priori* arguments needs to be tempered by a recognition of the implications of such facts as that Anselm and Hartshorne regard opposite qualities as self-evidently entailed by divine perfection.

In this respect, as in many others, Hume reflects the suspicions of common-sensical, empirically-minded, practical people when he states that "the argument *a priori* has seldom been found very convincing" to people at large. Whereas the metaphysically inclined may transfer habits of "abstract reasoning" to inappropriate subjects, other people "feel always some deficiency in such arguments, although they are not perhaps able to explain distinctly where it lies."[23] For those who find abstract thought difficult to follow, the arguments appear too neat and clever to be completely trustworthy on their own. What is needed is some significant way of moving from purely *a priori* reflections to discerning what Whitehead speaks of as "renewed observation rendered acute by rational interpretation"[24] and I. T. Ramsey calls the "empirical fit" between the thought by which we try to understand reality and things as they are experienced — bearing in mind that what we perceive to be the case is always to some extent moulded, both naturally and culturally, by our modes of conception.

Hartshorne's views on arguments for the existence of God — and particularly those on the ontological argument — must next be briefly considered since they provide important insights both into the nature of divine existence and into the logical status of claims about it.

It is interesting to note that the fundamental point of J. N. Findlay's well-known attempt to disprove God's existence by reference to the supposed intrinsic absurdity of the concept of it[25] was anticipated by Hartshorne in *Man's Vision of God*. In the latter's discussion of the ontological argument it is maintained that "necessity of existence is essential" to an adequate concept of the divine. From this it follows that *either* the conception of necessary existence is "sheer nonsense" and "we must admit a negative ontological argument, in disproof of God" (which was to be Findlay's argument), *or* it is wrong to hold in principle that in all cases "essence cannot imply existence."[26] Claiming that the former alternative (which he calls "positivism"[27]) is to be rejected, Hartshorne has persistently (it might even be said 'notoriously') argued in various ways[28] that "the perfect cannot be conceived not to exist" and hence that perfection (i.e., the divine) "cannot have the modal status of contingency."[29] Accordingly, on the grounds that the proper definition of God's existence means that it must be considered to be "necessary" absolutely, God "must be."[30] Three points need to be made here about Hartshorne's views on this matter.

The first is to note that Hartshorne shows, as Findlay himself later acknowledges,[31] that there is sense in the notion of necessary existence. In opposition to those who assert (in Hartshorne's judgement, more as a result of blinkered dogmatism than as a product of rational reflection) that necessity is attributable only to a logical relationship between propositions and that whatever is conceivable as existing must also be conceivable as not existing, Hartshorne expounds what he regards as Anselm's horrendously neglected insight — "a stroke of genius if ever there was one." This is that in the case of God alone existence is properly predicable in a "unique and superior form," namely, that of "existence *without conceivable alternative* of failing to exist" or "self-existence."[32] Talk about the existence of God, that is, connotes a mode of being which is otherwise describable as that form of existence which is uncaused (*i.e.*, never was brought into being by anything that is prior to it), omnitolerant (*i.e.*, is compatible with all that is actual and with anything that is possible and so could never be brought to an end by anything that could occur), everlasting (*i.e.*, never had a first moment when it began to be and will have no final moment), and independent (*i.e.*, is "entirely neutral as between alternatives of particular existence other than its own").[33] By such analyses of the notion of divine existence Hartshorne has both helped to clarify the unique character of that existence and has identified a coherent ontological meaning for the phrase 'necessary existence.'

The second point is that while Hartshorne's understanding of 'necessary existence' illuminates *how* God is to be conceived to exist (*i.e.*, the kind or manner of existence that is appropriate to God alone), it does not show *that* God exists. Hartshorne himself rejects this interpretation of his argument. He maintains that the ontological argument, especially in the so-called 'second' form which is based on the definitional requirement that *necessary existence* be attributed to the divine, confronts us with the choice between "positivism" which holds that " 'God' is without coherent meaning" and "theism" which holds that "divinity exists necessarily."[34] There seem, however, to be no convincing grounds for holding that the concept of God as perfect is not coherently conceivable. Hence, he argues, it follows that because God is to be conceived as existing necessarily, God must be held necessarily to exist. The ontological argument "furnishes a valid proof of theism."[35]

In spite of Hartshorne's frequent claims to the contrary, this argument is fallacious. That necessary existence must be attributed to God does not show that God in fact exists. What it does show is that *if* God exists, then God exists *necessarily* — i.e., as one whose *mode* of existence is that of necessary existence (as one, that is, whose existence is uncaused, omnitolerant, everlasting, independent and so on). Hartshorne claims that such a conclusion is self-contradictory since the 'if' implies a contingency which the 'necessarily' denies.[36] This is not so. The notion of necessary existence refers to the (unique) character or mode of divine existence, not to the fact[37] that God is. Because necessary existence must be predicated of God, it does not follow that God must (and so does) in fact exist. The concept of a subject may entail that a certain quality must be predicated of it but this does not show that any actual entity in fact instantiates that conception and so has that quality. It does follow, though, from the conception of the divine as having necessary existence that reality as a whole and in all its parts must *either* be theistically grounded (because God exists) *or* be utterly without any theistic quality at all (because God never has existed nor ever can exist). This alternative does not mean that God, whose only mode of existence is that of necessary existence, is to be conceived as existing contingently (a notion which Hartshorne justifiably condemns) but that there are two absolutely distinct possibilities in the case of the nature of reality — theism (which holds that reality is ultimately a meaningful whole) and ontological positivism (which sees the universe as randomly pluralistic).

Thirdly, though, while Hartshorne's work on the ontological argument does not prove that God exists, it makes a fundamental contribution to understanding the logical character of claims (both positive and negative) about the existence of God. Hartshorne himself states,

I do not think the question of whether God exists is logically in the same class with any historical or scientific question. To conceive God is not to conceive what might exist, but to conceive what existence itself fundamentally is, and what any discussion of existence always presupposes. The cause of possible (contingent) existence is itself more than merely possible — it is necessary.[38]

This logical oddity does not mean that appropriate claims about the existence of the divine are exempt from all rational rules. Such an implication would make the notion of God nonsensical. What it does mean is that such claims are not subject to rules that apply only to contingent realities. They are, though, subject to the universal rules which apply to all reality, necessary and contingent.[39]

Since God's existence is to be conceived as necessary — in the way that Hartshorne uses that term with reference to existence — it follows that affirmations of God's existence must consider it to be true whatever else happens to exist. Reflection on this suggests that God's existence has to be regarded as inexplicable, a state of affairs for which no reasons can be given beyond reference to the intrinsic nature of Godself. It simply is what is the case.[40] It is true of reality just as an *a priori* truth is true of the system which embodies it. In Hartshorne's judgement, as was mentioned earlier, the necessary existence of God also means that no *empirical* arguments can demonstrate either that God exists or that God does not exist — where 'empirical' is meant in Popper's sense as referring to what would be falsified if some conceivable events occurred.[41] Because, that is, statements about the existence of God, as the necessarily existent, refer to a state of affairs which is conceived to be compatible with all other actual and possible realities, they can neither be verified nor falsified empirically. Hence Flew's famous application of the 'Falsification Principle' to theistic belief is fundamentally mistaken so far as claims about the *existence* of God are concerned. To demand that theistic believers must be able to conceive of something as happening which would disprove such claims if they are to be regarded as claims which "provide explanations or express assertions,"[42] is to make a demand which fails to recognize the proper logic of statements about divine existence. While this demand is appropriate in the case of claims about what is contingent, it cannot be applied to the necessary existence of the divine. The ontological argument thus shows that "mere empiricism" is inadequate "to adjudicate the theistic question."[43]

Claims about God's reality have little material significance, however, if they are restricted to statements about the bare existence of the divine; they are necessarily meaningless, furthermore, if examination shows that the concept of God is intrinsically incoherent because it inescapably contains mutually contradictory elements. The most important of Hartshorne's contributions to philosophy of religion and to philosophical theology — and, indeed, to theological understanding generally — is to have shown how certain basic difficulties in the theistic notion of God may be overcome. By perceptive analyses he has produced fruitful and original insights into the logical character of the concept of God and into the nature of the material attributes of God. The result is a way of thinking about the divine which is religiously appropriate and theistically significant as well as rationally coherent.

In dealing with the notion of God, most theologians and philosophers have considered that God is primarily to be conceived as absolute, necessary, perfect and unchanging. Such a position is readily defensible. A being that is not absolute, not necessary, not perfect and not immune from alteration appears to be unable to satisfy the religious requirement that God be the totally adequate object of worship, the theological requirement that God be thought of as essentially 'that than which a greater cannot be conceived,' and the philosophical requirement that God be understood to be ultimate in being, value and rationality. On the other hand, while the resulting notion of the deity as an 'Unmoved Mover' may meet a number of intellectual needs, it seems to be irreconcilable with theistic affirmations of God as purposive and graciously active. If, that is, the divine reality is conceived as being essentially and in every respect absolute, necessary, perfect and unchanging, it is considered to follow that that reality cannot without contradiction be conceived as having the self-conscious intentional agency and reciprocal 'I-thou' relationships which theistic believers also consider it to be essential to predicate of the divine as a personally living mode of reality. The God who is wholly absolute, necessary, perfect and unchanging, then, is the God of "the philosophers and scholars" against which Pascal protested; it is not the "God of

Abraham, God of Isaac, God of Jacob."[44] Hartshorne's considerable achievement is to have perceived how the concept of God may be understood in a self-consistent manner so that it does meet the demands of the believers' faith and worship, of the theologians' systematic reflections and of the philosophers' principles of ultimacy.

The key to Hartshorne's concept of God lies in his 'dipolar' distinction between 'existence' and 'actuality' and his perception that in the unique case of the divine the formal, definitive characteristics of the former (*i.e.*, the divine existence) are not the same as those of the latter (*i.e.*, the divine actuality) but are their polar opposites. While, however, Hartshorne urges "all philosophers" — and, we may add, theologians — to recognize "the manifest difference between *existence*, the mere abstract truth *that* an abstraction is somehow concretely embodied, and the *actuality*, the how of the embodiment,"[45] a number of readers have clearly failed to follow Hartshorne's understanding of this matter. It is important, therefore, to outline its basic structure. This should prevent such accusations as that Hartshorne is trying to have his philosophico-theological penny as well as his religious bun by presenting a series of pairs of mutually contradictory ideas in a logically sophisticated disguise — a charge made, for instance, by one British theologian who, when challenged to justify the criticism, admitted that he did not grasp Hartshorne's fundamental dipolar distinction.

Hartshorne expresses the difference between existence and actuality thus: " 'existence' merely a relation of exemplification which actuality (any suitable actuality) has to essence."[46] To hold, that is, that something definable as having a particular essence 'exists' is to hold that somewhere something actualizes that particular essence in some appropriate from. Consider, for instance, the statement, 'A dog exists in the next room' — a statement which would normally be expressed by saying something like 'There is a dog in the next room.' Leaving aside as irrelevant for the present discussion the reference to when and where this dog is located (*i.e.*, 'in the next room'), this statement asserts that 'in the next room' there exists an object which is properly to be identified as a 'dog' (*i.e.*, an object which instantiates the essence of 'being a dog'). If, therefore, the statement is true and if we went into wherever is 'the next room,' we would find there something which is (or has been) organically living, animal, four-legged and with some form of the other essential attributes of being a 'dog'. That is what is meant by saying that a dog 'exists' there. What this statement gives us, though, is only the specification of various ranges of possibilities within which the particular case of the dog that is 'in the next room' will be located. From the statement, for example, we cannot tell what breed of dog it is (a chow or a collie or a mongrel or . . .), how large it is (as great as a Saint Bernard or as small as a corgi or . . .), what physical state it is in (emaciated or overfed or healthy or . . .), what kind of temperament it has (bouncy or snappy or calm or . . .), how trained and obedient it is, whether it has a tail or not and how vigorously it wags it, and so on. So far as we only know that 'a dog exists in the next room,' we only know that there is something in the next room which in some specific way appropriately realizes one point in each of these ranges of possibilities. The 'actuality' of that particular dog is constituted by the combination of these specific realizations.

In every case of a non-divine object, its existence is relative, contingent, changing and finite. Such an object, that is, exists only as something whose bare being (*i.e.*, 'existence') is determined by its relations to other objects, is dependent upon some prior objects for having brought it into being and is liable to be destroyed by other objects, is subject to radical change in that it came into being and eventually will cease to be, and is limited to a particular spatio-temporal location. Furthermore, since the *existence* of all non-divine objects is relative, contingent, changing, and finite, *a fortiori* their actuality must also be similarly conditioned — for their actuality is their particular instantiation of qualities which fall within the range of possibilities appropriate to their existence.

In the unique case of God, however, the divine existence "is to be thought of as *inevitably* actualized somehow, that is, in some suitable concrete reality."[47] As was noted earlier, the appropriate mode of *existence* for the divine is describable as that of necessary existence. It is also absolute, unchanging and infinite. The existence of God, for instance, is not determined by God's relations with the non-divine: rather God exists as the totally independent ground of all others (*i.e.*, 'absolutely'). Likewise, God exists 'necessarily' — as dependent on nothing other than the divine, as the omnitolerant whose existence was never brought about by another, is not threatened by any other, and will never be brought to an end by another. Similarly the divine existence is unchanging — God never began and never will cease to exist; it is also infinite — God is co-present to all moments in time as they occur and to all points in space.

Hartshorne's crucial insight, however, is to have perceived that the divine *actuality* is not identically qualified. On the contrary, it is to be understood to be relative, contingent, changing and finite. Although, then, unlike everything other than God, God's existence must be considered to be necessary (*i.e.*, according to my understanding of the implications of the notion of the 'necessary' character of divine existence, if reality is theistic, then the divine must always be instantiated in some appropriate form), the particular manner in which the divine reality is 'actually' realized depends both upon divine decisions and upon the character of the non-divine. For example, while God necessarily exists as the creative ground of all that is, the actual character of the divine creativity in practice may be held to depend upon the divine decision to create this present rather than some other possible cosmic order.

Accordingly, whereas theologians in the past have generally assumed that because God must be conceived as being absolute, necessary, unchanging and infinite, the divine must be considered to be so qualified in every respect, Hartshorne has shown by means of the dipolar "logic of ultimate contrasts"[48] that it is coherent to maintain that in certain respects it is appropriate to conceive of the divine as having relative, contingent, changing and finite aspects. Consider, for example, the nature of divine knowledge. On the one hand, *in principle* God must be held to exist as one who knows absolutely, necessarily, unchangingly and infinitely all that there is to be known.[49] A being whose knowledge is or might be less than perfect, who is or might at some time be ignorant of some things that are occurring, who has forgotten or who might forget some past events, or whose capacity for awareness is restricted, is not the proper object of worship who is 'that than which a greater cannot be conceived.' God, that is, must be conceived positively as "absolutely cosmic or universal in his capacities."[50] On the other hand, *in practice* the actuality of the divine knowledge is relative to what is there to be known (God, for instance, cannot be aware of me at this moment as wearing a tie if I am not wearing one), contingent upon what is actually the case (God cannot know as actual at this moment my grandchildren if I have not at this moment got any grandchildren), changing (what God knows to be the case 'now' alters as different things come to be 'now' the case) and finite (what God knows as real is limited to what actually is real). Accordingly, since to be real is to be in a temporal process and since the relationship of past and future to the present is asymmetrical, God's perfect knowledge at any moment must be of what is then "the past-and-definite *as* past-and-definite" and of what is then "the future and partly indefinite *as* future and partly indefinite."[51] From this it follows, as Plato and Aristotle both recognized but many theologians have not, that in order to be able to know a changing world, the divine must be able to change. There is no justifiable way of making the divine an exception to "Aristotle's principle that in knowing it is not the known but the knower that is influenced."[52]

Similarly while in principle the formal qualities of being absolute, necessary, unchanging and infinite are to be predicated of the *existence* of divine love, in practice the *actuality* of that love is relative, contingent, changing and finite. In principle, that is, God as the proper object of worship and greatest conceivable must be conceived to exist as one who has without possible limitation the highest benevolent concern for all: God "loves or cherishes all creatures for their actual and potential qualities."[53] In practice, though, the actual implementation of that love is limited by what entities are there to be loved and by what, in view of the present circumstances and future possibilities, God perceives to be the best for each entity in relation to what will produce the highest satisfaction overall.[54]

On the basis of this dipolar understanding of what is to be attributed to the divine existence (*i.e.*, to the divine reality in principle) and to the divine actuality (*i.e.*, to what God is in practice), Hartshorne has notably clarified theistic understanding of the nature of divine perfection and of the relationship between God and the world. In the case of the former, Hartshorne rejects the view that God's definitive perfection must be regarded as a wholly static mode of being, an absolute state which cannot in any way change and in which all possible values are actualized (*i.e.*, an *ens realissimum* and *actus purus* view of the perfection of the divine reality). One reason why Hart-shorne rejects such a view of divine perfection is that it is incoherent. It implies that "that are no incompatible yet genuine value possibilities, and that potential value could be exhaustively actualized." This is contrary both to reflection (for certain values are non-compossible) and to experience (which is that every determination of being this rather than that involves the denial of certain possible values).[55] Another reason is that it assumes that the maximum of concrete value is a fixed value like the top of a finite scale. The *ens realissimum* and *actus purus* view of divine perfection is thus held to be based upon an inadequate analysis of what it is to be perfect — an inade-quacy which produces a fundamentally mistaken perception of the nature of perfection. How, then is God's perfection to be understood?

In a properly organized test of observation of the objects on a tray, for example, candidates would score 100% (*i.e.*, a perfect score) if they recorded all the objects that were on the tray: they could not score more than 100%. The only possible variations from 100% accuracy of observation would be towards the relative imperfections of 99%, 98%, 97%, ... Theologians have generally considered that God's perfection is to be understood on this kind of model. They have regarded it as a kind of fixed 100% which cannot change in any way because they have assumed that any change must be for the worse. As essentially perfect, therefore, God is judged to be incapable of change in any way.

In so far as this judgement recognizes that God can never be other than perfect, it is correct. If the divine is to be a proper object of worship and 'that than which a greater cannot be conceived,' God cannot even be envisaged as being capable of being other than perfect, let alone ever in the past actually having been or in the future becoming less than perfect. On the other hand, when the temporal aspect of reality is taken into account, it becomes apparent that the past, present and future constituents of contingent (*i.e.*, non-divine) reality are not simultaneously present like objects on a tray. What is contingently present has come to be actual out of the indetermina-tions of what was previously future; on becoming actual it then perishes into the pastness of the totally determined to be succeeded by novel occasions of self-determination. Hence a perfect observation of the constituents of the temporally-ordered processes of reality, if it is to remain perfect, involves changes in the contents of what is observed as being present and continual increment in what is remembered as having once been observed as being present and has now become past.

In the light of such considerations — which apply *mutatis mutandis* to other material attributes of the divine — Hartshorne fruitfully suggests that it is essential for a satisfactory notion of divine perfection to distinguish in a dipolar manner between the abstract existence and the concrete actuality of that perfection — between, that is, what God's perfection entails in principle and what it involves in practice. To return, therefore, to the example of divine knowledge, if it is correct to hold that reality is in process and that divine perfection entails among other things that God knows all that there is to be known exactly as it is, it follows that in order to be perfect the contents of God's knowledge of the actual (both past and present) must increase as each new event occurs. Accordingly, while God is to be conceived as being in principle unchangeably perfect in that it belongs to the perfection of the abstract existence of the divine that God knows always whatever is knowable, in practice the actualization of that perfect knowledge means that what God is aware of as having become determinate will be continually augmented as new things come into being in the processes of reality.

In the light of this analysis of its characteristics, Hartshorne speaks of God's perfection in general as a matter of "modal coincidence."[56] In that the divine awareness embraces all reality, it is to be held that:

Any actual thing God enjoys actually; any possible thing would be his actual possession were it actual for anyone. From this . . . it follows that though God can increase in value, he can be surpassed by no other than himself. For any increase anywhere is *a fortiori* increase in him.[57]

Consequently Hartshorne describes the formal nature of divine perfection as one of "dual transcendence" — a formula which he claims to be his own.[58] On the one hand, God is unsurpassable by others. God's perfection means that no being can even rival God, let alone be greater than God. In principle God transcends all. On the other hand, God's later states surpass God's earlier states in terms of their incremental value since in the intervening period novel entities have come into being and hence their value has been incorporated into the divine reality. Take, for example, two points in the temporal order of reality, t_1 and t_2. At t_1 God incorporates and enjoys the value of all that has come to be and is now the case. At a later time, t_2, though, God will not only incorporate and enjoy the value of all that was incorporated and enjoyed at t_1 but also of all that has come to be in the interval between t_1 and t_2.

Hartshorne has also used the dipolar conception of the nature of the divine to clarify the concept of the relationship between God and the processes of reality. In the past it has been generally assumed that this relationship must be either one of fundamental identity, as in pantheism, or one of complete distinction, as in traditional forms or theism. The former position, pantheism, is radically unsatisfactory because its understanding of the absoluteness of the divine leads it to deny a proper degree of autonomy either to God or to the world. If their fundamental identity does not mean that the world *is* the activity of God (and hence that the supposed autonomy of creaturely agents within the world is an illusion), it entails that 'God' is but a cipher for the aggregate of worldly agencies and refers to no purposive activity over against those agencies. The latter position, traditional theism, is equally unsatisfactory. It is a monopolar position which assumes that the divine perfection and ultimacy entails that God must be held to be in every respect absolute, necessary, and unchanging whereas the non-divine is in every respect relative, contingent and changing. On this basis it is maintained

232

that God must be regarded as impassible and without potentiality. The consequence of this is that God is so divorced from the world that neither can anything that happens in the world affect the divine nor can the divine respond to events in the world in a particular and purposive manner. As Hartshorne notes, the result may be a picture of God as "eternally and immutably" as well as "completely blissful" but it is "ludicrous" to speak of such a "benefit machine" as loving — for *loving* involves caring about one's influence upon others and being affected by those others.[59] So far, then, as theological and philosophical appreciations of the essential nature of the divine are considered to require either a pantheistic or a monopolar theistic understanding of the relationship between God and the world, they entail an understanding which contradicts any affirmation of the personal, gracious and purposive interaction between God and the world which is at the heart of theistic religious faith.

Hartshorne's notable achievement in this respect is to have perceived, on the basis of his dipolar analysis of the divine attributes, that a third option is not only assumed by theistic religious faith but also is rationally coherent. This position he calls "panentheism", a term earlier used by K C F Krause. According to this position the divine is totally aware of the world and hence embraces all the events that come to be in the world within the divine reality. God is thus said to be "the Whole in every categorial sense," embracing "all actuality in one individual actuality, and all possibility in one individual potentiality."[60] Since, then, every event that occurs is completely embraced within the divine reality, its value is forever thereafter part of that everlasting reality. To some extent, therefore, non-divine agents have a part in producing God's concrete state.[61] At the same time, God is not just a cipher for what results from the decisions of non-divine agents. As "the supreme whole" God's "whole-properties are distinct from the properties of the parts."[62] God has a distinct self-consciousness and independence of the non-divine agents. This means that the former can intentionally seek to influence the decisions of the latter. By 'panentheism', then, Hartshorne states that he "affirms God as containing both an all-independent all causative factor *and* the totality of effects."[63] God's causal influence on others, though, is one of persuasive luring rather than the exercise of coercive might. Accordingly it presents no threat to the proper, if limited, autonomy of creaturely agents.

In developing his dipolar panentheistic concept of God Hartshorne makes persistent and perceptive criticisms of the doctrines of divine impassibility and omnipotence. The former doctrine, at least according to certain interpretations, denies that God can be affected in any way by what happens in the world. As has already been noted, this view of the divine as an unmoved mover, acting (if at all) as an oblivious final cause, not only makes a nonsense of any serious attempt to regard the divine as totally aware and personally loving; recognition of the dipolar character of the divine also shows that such an understanding is not required by a proper appreciation of the absolute, necessary and unchanging character of the abstract aspects of the divine reality. According to Hartshorne, the relationship of God to the world must, rather, be conceived as one of eminent passibility: in principle God is absolutely, necessarily and incessantly (*i.e.*, unchangingly) affected by whatever happens in the world, and in practice God embraces all that does actually happen in the divine reality. God, therefore, is not to be conceived as a being "whose life is sheer joy and beauty" but as "the cosmic sufferer, who endures infinitely more evil than we can imagine ... God is the concrete unity of the world, not the selected catalogue of its good aspects."[64] This image clearly disturbs many people since it contradicts both their fantasies about the untrammelled bliss of the perfect state and the Aristotelean-inspired notion of the divine reality traditionally dominant in Christian theology. It should not, though, be surprising, even less objectionable, to Christian theologians whose understanding of the concrete character of the divine is to be formed in part by reference to images of Jesus as loving and suffering.

In the case of the notion of omnipotence, the error in the traditional understanding of divine power, according to Hartshorne, is not that it holds that God "must in power excel all others" but that it fails to consider clearly what is to be envisaged as "the highest conceivable form of power."[65] The notion that God is to be worshipped as "a cosmic power monopoly" is a fundamental error: "sheer monopoly of power or decision-making in one agent is a nightmare — strictly speaking an absurdity — not an ideal."[66] It is an "absurdity" because power is essentially relational. To refer to "power" is to refer to the ability of one agent to affect another. The other agent only exists, however, so far as it is itself at least a locus of some power to be what it is and to resist threats to its being such. A being that had an absolute monopoly of power would in effect have no power for there could be nothing at all on which or over which to exercise (*i.e.*, actualize) that alleged power. The notion of divine power as a cosmic monopoly, furthermore, is a "nightmare" both because it perceives God as a tyrant who decides everything (and hence is totally responsible for all the evils which occur) and because it treats human beings (and everything else) as without any power of self-determination and so as utterly valueless.[67] Hartshorne describes this notion of divine power as "a hopeless misconception of the divine 'majesty' " which "betrays a pitiful human weakness."[68] It is the inverse projection of the human sense of frustration rather than the product of correct insight into the nature of God's creativity.

As the creator who respects and enjoys the products of all the decisions of non-divine agents, God must instead be seen as exercising a power which "influences all that happens" (for the divine scope is universal) "but determines nothing in its concrete particularity."[69] In *The Logic of Perfection* Hartshorne suggests that while God seeks to check, encourage and redirect the impulses of our wills, "he cannot wholly initiate or absolutely control them." This is not because God is "limited in his power to do what he wishes to do" but because God "is not so confused as to wish to destroy the very nature of being."[70] God's power is the implementation of the divine purpose as Creator for the emergence of morally free and creative individuals. It is a power, then, which is best perceived as actualizing itself in "the appeal of unsurpassable love."[71] As with Hartshorne's notion of divine passibility so too with his notion of divine power, the insight into the nature of the divine may contradict some long-established theological prejudices but it harmonizes with the image of God perceived in Jesus as one who sought — and seeks — to attract all people to himself by his acts of limitless love.[72]

How, then, is Hartshorne's contribution to the philosophy of religion and philosophical theology to be summed up? Primarily he is to be seen as a philosopher who has used rigorous analyses and rational reflection to develop a concept of God which accords with the intentionally active divinity that is the object of theistic faith. As a metaphysician, though, he is interested in determining what is necessarily and universally true of the ultimate reality rather than concerned to reach insights into the concrete actuality of God's activity in contingent situations. His vision of God is accordingly cosmic. Occasionally this leads him to conclusions which may seem to be quixotic but which on reflection pose intriguing questions about the justification of certain theistic beliefs about the divine. He holds, for instance, that "it is a formal requirement of the idea of deity" that God "must always relate himself to absolutely all creatures." God's care about "weal and woe" applies impartially to all. Hence we must beware of the temptation to think anthropomorphically about God. God must be considered to wish "all creatures well" without exception. This may seem unexceptionable until it is noticed that Hartshorne concludes from this that it is basically mistaken to hold that "God can wish well to the sick child in such fashion as literally not to care about the woes of the bacteria causing the sickness."[73] Those, though, who wish to deny his conclusion must find reasons to justify their position.

Hartshorne recognizes that people would like to know how God does in practice respond to particular situations. How, for example, is the divine care for the child balanced against the divine care for the bacteria? What is the "particular concrete way" in which God's perfect love is presently actualized in relation to my being? To attain such knowledge, however, we would have to be able to grasp "the contingent valuations of a radically-superior mind."[74] It is a knowledge to which, in Hartshorne's judgement, metaphysicians should not presume to be competent to aspire.

Some believers and theologians maintain that important insights into the active actuality of the divine are attainable through divine self-revelation — for the Christian faith particularly through the divine self-revelation in Jesus who is the Christ.[75] It is a position which Hartshorne does not share. Once, in conversation about an attempt which I had made to outline an understanding of Christology in accordance with process thought, he told me that in his younger days he had made attempts to make sense of the doctrine of the person of Christ but each time his father (who was an Episcopalian clergyman versed in canon law) told him what heresy he was committing.

Eventually he gave up. In answer to a question about the place of Christ in his thought, he is recorded as having said this:

> I don't think in a metaphysical system you can bring in an historical character. This is mixing history and metaphysics. . . . I have never been able to do that. . . . You can always say that the life of Jesus as portrayed in the Gospel is a symbol and probably a unique symbol of religious faith. I've always found it difficult to go beyond that.[76]

Nevertheless, while Hartshorne leaves to 'theologians' the task of trying to identify the contingent actuality of God's activity in relation to the processes of reality,[77] he presents an understanding of the divine which is fundamentally in harmony with the notion of God that is at the heart of theistic (and hence of Christian) faith and practice. Sensible of the definitive characteristic that God be conceived as the totally adequate object of worship, the rigor, reason and moderation which characterize his thought have enabled him to make major contributions to the way in which the divine is to be understood. In particular he has drawn attention to the meaning and implications of the 'necessary' existence of God and shown, by his dipolar panentheistic model, how to overcome many of the hoary problems of reconciling the God of the philosophers with the God of theistic faith in a coherent concept. These are major contributions. It is right that their fundamental importance be recognized.

NOTES

1. Charles Hartshorne, *Man's Vision of God and the Logic of Theism* (Hamden, Connecticut: Archon Books, 1964), p. vii. (This work was first published in 1941.)
2. Charles Hartshorne, *Whitehead's Philosophy: Selected Essays, 1935–1970* (Lincoln and London: University of Nebraska Press, 1978), p. 145.
3. Charles Hartshorne, *Insights and Oversights of Great Thinkers: An Evaluation of Western Philosophy* (Albany: State University of New York Press, 1983), p. ix; cf. Charles Hartshorne, *Creative Synthesis and Philosophic Method* (London: SCM Press, 1970), p. xv.
4. *Insights and Oversights*, pp. xiiif.
5. Charles Hartshorne, "My Neoclassical Metaphysics", in *Whitehead's Legacy*, P. Jonkers and J. Van der Veken (eds.), (Leuven: Center for Metaphysics and Philosophy of God, 1981), p. 26.
6. Charles Hartshorne, *The Logic of Perfection and Other Essays in Neoclassical Metaphysics* (La Salle, Illinois: Open Court, 1962), pp. viiif; cf. *Man's Vision of God*, pp. 126ff.
7. *Man's Vision of God*, p. xix.
8. Charles Hartshorne, *Wisdom as Moderation: A Philosophy of the Middle Way* (Albany: State University of New York Press, 1987).
9. *Creative Synthesis and Philosophic Method*, p. 100.
10. Cf. *Wisdom as Moderation*, p. 6.
11. *Ibid.*, pp. 26f.
12. *Man's Vision of God*, p. vii.
13. Cf. Charles Hartshorne, *A Natural Theology for Our Time* (La Salle, Illinois: Open Court, 1967), chapter 3.

236

14. *Ibid.*, p. 67.
15. Charles Hartshorne, "Ideas and Theses of Process Philosophers", in *Two Process Philosophers: Hartshorne's Encounter with Whitehead*, Lewis S. Ford (ed.) (Tallahassee, Florida: American Academy of Religion, 1973), p. 102 (# E5); *cf.* Charles Hartshorne, "Postscript" in Santiago Sia, *God in Process Thought: A Study in Charles Hartshorne's Concept of God* (Dordrecht, Boston, Lancaster: Martinus Nijhoff, 1985), p. 119.
16. *Man's Vision of God*, pp. 342ff; *cf.* pp. 8f.
17. *Creative Synthesis and Philosophic Method*, pp. 263f, 266.
18. *Ibid.*, p. 281.
19. *Cf.* Genesis 8, v. 21; Isaiah 5, v. 25 and Nahum 3, v. 3.
20. Alfred North Whitehead, *Process and Reality: An Essay in Cosmology*, corrected edition, D. R. Griffin and D. W. Sherburne (eds.) (New York: The Free Press, 1978), p. 4.
21. *Cf.* Anselm, *Proslogion*, chapter 8; Charles Hartshorne, *The Divine Relativity: A Social Conception of God* (New Haven and London: Yale University Press, 1964), *passim* and especially pp. 54f.
22. Charles Hartshorne, *Anselm's Discovery: A Re-Examination of the Ontological Proof for God's Existence* (La Salle, Illinois: Open Court, 1965), p. 136.
23. David Hume, *Dialogues Concerning Natural Religion*, N. K. Smith (ed.), (Oxford: Clarendon Press, 1935), pp. 235f.
24. Whitehead, *op. cit.*, p. 5.
25. *Cf.* J. N. Findlay, *Language, Mind and Value: Philosophical Essays* (London: George Allen & Unwin, 1963), pp. 96ff.
26. *Man's Vision of God*, pp. 76f.
27. *Cf. Anselm's Discovery*, p. 3.
28. *Cf.* David A. Pailin, "Some Comments on Hartshorne's Presentation of the Ontological Argument" in *Religious Studies*, 4 (October 1968), pp. 103ff; David A. Pailin, "An Introductory Survey of Charles Hartshorne's Work on the Ontological Argument" in *Analecta Anselmiana*, Band 1 (1969), pp. 195ff.
29. *Logic of Perfection*, p. 73.
30. *Ibid.*, p. 53.
31. *Cf.* J. N. Findlay, *The Transcendence of the Cave* (London: George Allen & Unwin and New York: Humanities Press, 1967), pp. 89f; J. N. Findlay, *Ascent to the Absolute: Metaphysical Papers and Lectures* (London: George Allen & Unwin and New York: Humanities Press, 1970), pp. 90ff.
32. *Anselm's Discovery*, pp. 33f.
33. *Logic of Perfection*, p. 80; *cf., ibid*, pp. 75ff.
34. *Ibid.*, p. 70.
35. *Ibid.*, p. 33.
36. *Cf. Anselm's Discovery*, p. 34.
37. 'Fact' is used here to refer to 'what is the case' generally. The term is not restricted to its root sense (*cf.* 'factum') as referring to 'what has been made' and so is essentially contingent. According to the sense intended here, both what exists necessarily and what happens to exist contingently are 'facts'.
38. Charles Hartshorne, "God and the Social Structure of Reality" in *Theology in Crisis: A Colloquium on the Credibility of 'God'*, (New Concord, Ohio: Muskingum College, 1967), p. 27.
39. *Cf. Anselm's Discovery*, pp. 65ff.
40. It is important to note that when Hartshorne speaks in *Anselm's Discovery* of "an *absolutely* inexplicable brute fact" (p. 70), he is using the phrase to refer to a mode of existence which is "through and through *pure* chance." For God to exist according to such a mode of existence would be for that existence to be "a wholly and simply irrational contingent fact." In other words, it would be to hold that "God exists, He might not have; He does not exist, He might have — whichever is true, there can ... be no aspect whatever of reason in its being true." Hartshorne points out that this is not Anselm's

position — nor is it Hartshorne's own position — since it conceives of the divine existence as absolutely contingent. What Hartshorne maintains is that "God *is* states the only possible truth about the divine existence; hence there can be no question of why, or how it came about, that God does, rather than does not exist ... The sole and sufficient reason is that it must be so; there being no possible alternative ... " (*Ibid.*, p. 70f) It is in this latter sense, namely, that the divine reality contains — or, rather is — its own reason for existence, that is intended in the text when it is stated that God's existence is an inexplicable state of affairs.

41. *Cf. A Natural Theology for Our Time*, pp. 66ff.
42. A. Flew in "Theology and Falsification", printed in *New Essays in Philosophical Theology*, A. Flew and A. MacIntyre (eds.) (London: SCM Press, 1955), p. 106; *cf.*, pp. 96ff.
43. Charles Hartshorne, *Aquinas to Whitehead: Seven Centuries of Metaphysics of Religion* (Milwaukee: Marquette University, 1976), p. 20.
44. The quotation is from a record of a religious experience which was found sewn into Pascal's jacket. The text of the record is printed *inter alia* in David E. Roberts, *Existentialism and Religious Belief* (New York: Oxford University Press, 1957), pp. 20f.
45. *Wisdom as Moderation*, p. 81.
46. *Anselm's Discovery*, p. 131.
47. *Ibid.*, p. 38; *cf.* pp. 38ff.
48. *Cf. Creative Synthesis and Philosophic Method*, pp. 99ff.
49. *Cf. Aquinas to Whitehead*, p. 15: "The necessary being, God, has ideally complete knowledge of the world."
50. *A Natural Theology for Our Time*, p. 136.
51. Charles Hartshorne, *Omnipotence and other Theological Mistakes* (Albany: State University of New York Press, 1984), pp. 26f.
52. Charles Hartshorne, "Can We Understand God?" in *Louvain Studies*, vii/2, (Fall, 1978), p. 78.
53. *Creative Synthesis and Philosophic Method*, p. 261.
54. *Cf. Logic of Perfection*, p. 109.
55. *Creative Synthesis and Philosophic Method*, p. 229.
56. *A Natural Theology for Our Time*, p. 20.
57. *Ibid.*, p. 72.
58. *Omnipotence*, p. 45; *cf.* pp. 44ff; *Creative Synthesis and Philosophic Method*, pp. 227ff.
59. "God and the Social Structure of Reality," p. 22.
60. *A Natural Theology for Our Time*, pp. 20f.
61. *Cf. ibid.*, pp. 113f.
62. Charles Hartshorne, "Epilogue: The Logic of Panentheism", in Charles Hartshorne and William L. Reese, *Philosophers Speak of God* (Chicago: University of Chicago Press, 1953), p. 511.
63. *Ibid.*, p. 505.
64. *Man's Vision of God*, p. 331.
65. *Omnipotence*, p. 10.
66. *Creative Synthesis and Philosophic Method*, p. 292.
67. *Cf. Omnipotence*, pp. 11ff.
68. *Creative Synthesis and Philosophic Method*, p. 292.
69. *Omnipotence*, p. 25; *cf. A Natural Theology for Our Time*, p. 97 where Hartshorne points out that "Ruling is interaction, not mere [*sc.* one-way] action" and Charles Hartshorne, *Reality as Social Process: Studies in Metaphysics and Religion* (Glencoe, Illinois: The Free Press and Boston, Massachusetts: Beacon Press, 1953), p. 40.
70. *Logic of Perfection*, p. 203.
71. *Omnipotence*, p. 14.
72. *Cf.* John 12, v. 32.
73. *Logic of Perfection*, p. 142.
74. *Ibid.*, p. 109.

238

75. *Cf.* David A Pailin, "The Incarnation as a Continuing Reality" in *Religious Studies*, 6 (December, 1970), pp. 303ff; *Man's Vision of God*, pp. 67f.
76. Reply by Hartshorne in "Questions Addressed to Professor Hartshorne", in *Theology in Crisis: A Colloquium on the Credibility of 'God'*, pp. 48f.
77. *Cf.* David A. Pailin, *God and the Processes of Reality* (London: Routledge, 1989) for discussion of aspects of this relationship.

Critical Response by Charles Hartshorne

1. Walker on Afro-American and African Theology

In replying to individuals, I begin with four whose essays raise ethical and political questions. I begin with them in honor of the principle enunciated by Theodore Walker that God is on the side of the oppressed. Remembering also the Scriptural saying, "The last shall be first," I reverse, in these essays only, the alphabetical order followed in the remaining replies.

How adequately Walker represents "Afro-American or native African systematic theologians" I have little basis for judging. I have read Cone, and I once talked a little with an African theologian who, like me, was a member of a committee of the General Council of Churches to draw up a statement on "God and Nature;" but my present memory of these exposures to the subject Walker deals with so lucidly is faint. I am deeply pleased to find how well Walker understands my thought and how fully, even more so than he quite realizes, I find it harmonious with my beliefs.

Throughout my career I have been distressed by the fact that so few blacks (to use an expression that I like as little as I do 'whites' — the Amerindians' term 'palefaces' seems to me more apt) have taken my courses. I have never been anti-black or anti- any other skin-color (or anti- any other near or remote geographical origins) where human beings are concerned and have tried to argue against such prejudices. It does not follow that I have done all that was desirable to help in this sad, tragic matter.

One of the many reasons why I am proud of being the son of Marguerite Haughton Hartshorne is that when a woman in our church in a small Pennsylvania town told her that one does not use titles, Mr. or Mrs., with negroes and that "first names are enough with them," she closed the discussion by the simple declaration: "I am accustomed to calling her (a woman who did our laundry) Mrs. Smith. I think I will continue to call her Mrs. Smith." She treated a Chinese laundryman we also dealt with as a fellow human being to whom respect was due. I recall a beautiful present, something Chinese, that he gave her.

I regard Howard Thurman as one of the finest preachers to an educated audience that I have been privileged to hear. (Benjamin Mays was another.) It happens that I once had, with a small and nonpoisonous snake, an experience

S. Sia (ed.), Charles Hartshorne's Concept of God, 241–321.
© 1990 *Kluwer Academic Publishers. Printed in the Netherlands.*

which I interpreted, broadly speaking, somewhat as Thurman did his experience. The snake at sight of me began sliding away. I began running after it — perhaps to see what it would do. For a moment I lost sight of it, then suddenly there it was, close and facing me. It seemed even to be threatening me. "So," I thought, "the other animals, unlike some human beings, seem always to make the best of circumstances. If running away does not work, they try the remaining possibility: to frighten off the enemy by appearing as formidable as possible." At the present time perhaps the way blacks can do this is by voting in much larger numbers. Two otherwise admirable Afro-Americans I know, one of each sex, have told me they did not think it "makes any difference" who is elected. Perhaps it would be better to try and see. The little snake was in no danger from me; but it could not know that and did its best. Our foresight in political matters is limited; we can do our best and hope for the best.

Walker's account of my theism contains no definite error that I detect as such. His nearest to it is the apparent failure to see that my or Whitehead's objective immortality is intended to include what some call "social immortality," and this involves the "collective immortality" of Mbiti as well as his "living-dead," or preservation in the consciousness of relatives or friends. I agree that I was wrong in taking the ancient Jews as the only ones that accepted death as the ending of the career of a human individual if the tradition Walker describes goes back to pre-Christian times. I find it very interesting that the Africans lacked the to me at best superfluous myth of transmigration, pre-existence or post-existence of persons in other animal, human or nonhuman, bodies. I also appreciate the absence in this account of any mention of heaven or hell. I am deeply committed to the view that we exist to contribute to creaturely happiness between birth and death in this world, and at present on this planet (not in some mythical place such as Dante or Milton gave verbal pictures of) and to make this contribution as an enrichment of the Life that has had no beginning and can have no end.

2. Phan on Liberation Theology

Professor Peter Phan compares two forms of theology, showing, so far as I can see, excellent understanding of both. I have rather neglected the literature of the liberation doctrine; but, as Phan knows, many of my students and readers have not neglected it. It is interesting to find that classical theism, in both its Catholic and its Protestant forms unsatisfactory to most North American philosophers, has been perhaps still less helpful to South Americans.

Two Europeans known in Latin America may have influenced thought in the process direction. Ortega-Y-Gasset believed in freedom and indeterminacy as cosmic principles, and so did Bergson. Mary Markovski, a former student of mine, and an authority on Bergson, is dedicated to the liberation cause. That we must move away from some mistakes of the Middle Ages in theology need not mean (and the examples of Russia and China support the view that we had better not take it to mean) that we must move away from theology itself. The vision of God need not (aside from the question of cosmic epochs) be a vision of some other world; it can be a nobler vision of this world, one in which the young look not for the excitement of drugs, or of wholesale smashing of their social order, but for the challenge of new knowledge, or courageous application of old knowledge (improved, expanded versions of the Peace Corps, perhaps), to the bettering of our human condition on this astronomically isolated planet, in which our single animal species has so much power for good as well as for ill. It is scarcely my future advantage that is at stake, but that of my (in the near future) almost certainly younger readers and my or their children and grandchildren, or readers and readers' readers. It is our species' future — and, let us not forget, that of huge numbers of other species as well — that is in question.

For the virtues professed by the "moral majority", belief in the literal truth of every sentence in a certain book is not only not necessary, but may no longer be helpful. The prior question is whether in this vast cosmos there is or is not a cosmic mind. This question was simply put and vividly answered by Francis Bacon when he said that he would rather believe all the superstitions of several religions "than that this universal frame is without a mind."

He probably did not believe those superstitions but did believe in cosmic mind. Surely grown men and women can see the difference between cosmic mind and what some members of a single species of animals on a single planet, out of billions of probable planets, have written on a number of pages. As someone has said, the claims now made *about* the Bible (by some of those who did not write or translate it) exceed considerably the claims one finds definitely made about itself *in* the Bible. And in any case, there are many allegedly sacred writings. What kind of conceit is sufficient to bolster the claim, "I know that one, and I know which one, of these writings is the absolute truth while the rest are more or less erroneous"? If this is modesty, what would conceit in this matter be like?

A "creation scientist" has argued that evolution is not a scientific fact but a philosophical speculation, a mere theory. Suppose he is right. He still must explain why, of the hundreds of philosophers and scientists whom many of us know about, not one percent, virtually none, stand up to say that nothing like evolution has occurred. Similarly he must also explain why millions of mainline religious people accept evolution and regard the Book of Genesis as poetry not science, and as expressive of the best that could be done before there was any organized science in the world, or anything that is now meant by 'philosophy' as a discipline. Even the theistic question itself should not be answered dogmatically. If we are not respectful of carefully-arrived at beliefs of persons whom we have seen, how can we claim to love God whom we have not seen?

Kant was at his best when he said that the starry skies and ethical principles are the two great religious clues. We seem almost to see God when we look through a great telescope, since we see much of the field of action, which is analogous to the body, of the inclusive mind, if there is inclusive mind. And what kind of evidence could there be that there is *no* inclusive mind? This is not at all like questions about demons or fairies. Only two possibilities: there is or there isn't cosmic (or super-cosmic) mind. Mystics think they have direct positive evidence, multitudes think they have indirect positive evidence. Examine unbelievers and you will often find them focusing on some more or less antiquated, discredited form of theism, not theism simply as such. Often they are rightly rebelling against some tyrant view of deity that insults or belittles human capacities and makes God far from the most lovable of conceivable beings.

Perhaps we cannot ever agree, one way or the other, about the besouled or soulless cosmos. In any case we can only show our love to God, if we can believe in God, by respect for God's creatures, or our respect for our fellow creatures, by respecting their belief or unbelief in God. Whatever our beliefs, we have to live with one another. War and the police are less and less attractive as means for settling religious disputes. Religious wars never did make much sense. Now they seem really crazy, at least for the great powers. Whether or not we can all achieve orthodoxy, we had better try, in Phan's words, to achieve orthopraxy.

All my adult life I have made efforts to come to a worthwhile position on ethical and religious aspects of economic problems. For an even longer time I have wrestled with the question of war and peace, first without the revolutionary implications of nuclear explosives, and then, since the first atomic explosion revealed that these were to be henceforth available, and as, through association with one of the achievers of this fearful power, Leo Szilard, I became aware of what it was likely to mean with respect to the two great powers (only third-rate scientists had any doubt that Russia would acquire the technology before long), I have tried in various ways to think what philosophers can do to help. The results of all these efforts are, I fear, not much. Of course I did know that the talk in the early Reagan years of winning a nuclear war was ignorant or irresponsible. It was less clear what other response to the challenge made sense. General MacArthur, in his way a genius, went to the heart of the matter. "This is our last chance." In other words, no superficial remedies will do. Formerly, peace through strength seemed a definite goal: to make war unattractive to enemies but still, if they chose to run the risk, not unendurable for one's own country. But now we have weapons whose use looks about equally suicidal for both sides. Nuclear explosives give a monstrously paradoxical kind of "strength." Whom do they threaten? Everybody in the world, including those who invent and control them! In what sense then, are they weapons?

Reagan argued, influenced by the physicist Edward Teller, that each new weapon elicits a new kind of defense. Until now this proposition has been borne out by facts. But what Reagan or Teller failed to add was that, even with the new defenses — for instance, shields, armour, steel-clad battleships, you name it — in spite of all counter measures, wars become more and more terrible in their effects. Some eighty years before the nuclear age began, its basic danger was predicted by T. L. Peacock, satirical novelist of England, not by any scientist, philosopher, or statesman! Writing about the negative results of (applied) "science," Peacock listed "explosions, rockets, rifles, cannon, poisons," all getting ever more various and deadly, and came to the conclusion, "I almost think it is the ultimate destiny of science to exterminate the human race." We now have (or does it have us?) the ultimate explosive, poison, weapon. That is where we are.

It should humble all of us that only one Nineteenth-Century writer thought so rationally about the history of scientific technology and war. How wise is anyone of us when the world problems are to be dealt with? The experts are baffled. However, many scientists saw from the beginning of the nuclear age that the new power was an extremely ambiguous possession. Oppenheimer saw, Szilard saw, Einstein saw. But Edward Teller seems not to have seen. And he it was who misled Reagan in his Star Wars plan.

In World War II an English scientist misled Churchill, and some American statesmen as well, about the military value of population bombing. Many men and materials were wasted in bombing Dresden. Other scientists knew better — Seversky for one. Of course these are controversial matters; and I am not an expert. But I think I can sometimes form a reasonable judgment of character. There are more reliable people in science than Teller. What one reads about his career gives some of us pause.

As Eisenhower warned us, the military-industrial complex can warp and poison our judgment. Scientists are only human if they are sensitive to the temptation to enjoy the research money that the Pentagon has at its disposal. Civilian control of the military is a phrase it is easy to pronounce but — well, we do what we can. As Reinhold Niebuhr used to say, man is a cunning animal. Perhaps we can make it for some centuries more. We have to hope so.

Why did no scientist or philosopher predict what Peacock virtually predicted as an all too conceivable result of science? I see as one reason the lack of any widespread, vigorous belief in freedom as fundamental principle of life and reality, and of the relation of freedom to real chance, partial disorder. It was thought that with God, or with natural or human laws substituting for God, the increase of power coming from science need not mean increase of danger, or risk, but only of opportunity. If freedom means partial disorder, and if science increases the scope of our practical freedom, it increases risk as well as opportunity. Peacock did not believe in determinism, made hilarious fun at its expense; and his character, The Rev. Dr. Opimian, called science an "edged tool, with which men play like children and cut their own fingers." The doctrine of compatibilism (that significant freedom is possible without chance and disorder) opened the door to a onesidedly optimistic view of progress. We have had science too little aware of its risks.

That we are so ill-prepared for the present dangers by our intellectual leaders is, I submit, definitely connected with the still popular view to which the Peirce-James-Whitehead (also almost Bergsonian) doctrine of universal tychism as the negative side of universal freedom is the most fully worked-out alternative. This alternative has yet to elicit its literary fruits. Mark Twain, Thomas Hardy, Ambrose Bierce, Nietzsche, Robinson Jeffers (whose determinism is unambiguously expressed in his poetry), and many others have yet to be comparably counterbalanced in novels or poetry.[1] Except for Sydney Lanier's poetry, whose belief in at least human freedom is also unambiguous, the metaphysics of freedom still lacks its literary expression. So much the worse for us all. The harmlessness of determinism is a myth, itself far from harmless.

As for the poor, the suffering, the oppressed, we have them even in North America. Our economic inequalities are far too great; the poor are much too poor and the rich too rich. I will change my mind about this when more of the latter stop acting as though the most important thing is how many hundreds of thousands millions, or billions their income or fortune is. My favorite story about a truly great man is about Beethoven. He and Goethe knew and admired each other, the great musical composer and the great poet of their time and country. One day, as they were walking together, they met a member of the nobility. Goethe, who had a shrewd sense of the power even stupid but fortune-favored individuals can wield, bowed low to the Honorable so and so, while Beethoven kept on walking. When the poet had finished greeting his highness and caught up to Beethoven, the latter said, "There are two of us. There are thousands of them."

At present the two great powers seem in a process of learning to understand that military power has become bafflingly ambiguous and that they have common need to find non-military solutions for their conflicts. In neither of them is there adequate sensitivity to the real needs of the poor countries. Our recent attempts to deal with Latin Americans have failed badly. A president who seems scarcely to know much about the poor and oppressed in his own country is not likely to grasp what is needed in Middle and South America. Recently, before the administration began to talk loudly about getting Panama's Noriega out, three of the surrounding countries were quietly acting to persuade him to leave. Ignoring this, our representatives began unilaterally to use our economic power to force him out. Our traditional image of a bullying great power seems to have given Noriega what he needed to withstand us.

The so-called "contradictions" of capitalism seem matched by the perhaps even more glaring contradictions of communism. We are all more or less baffled by the complexity of the world economy. We had better take more seriously the dangers of economic imperialism and the present imperative to find ways of moving away from "standards of living" that cannot be universalized for the planet because of the finitude of fossil fuels and other resources. We need to think about C. P. Snow's proposition that it cannot continue indefinitely that many in some countries live so extravagantly while much of the world's population *at best* barely avoids starvation, more and more forests are destroyed, agricultural soil is washed into the sea, and air and water polluted. A world emergency seems in the making. Even our huge national debt must not prevent us, if we have any sense and decency, from trying to help less fortunate neighbors: Mexico for one, and Canada, whose forests we are destroying by acid rain from our smokestacks and cars. Meanwhile, populations multiply faster than supplies.

Phan's magnificent essay prompts me to try to make amends for a defect in my previous writing. I have stressed the idea of divine love and objected to what has sometimes been meant by divine "justice," taking this word in its legal sense of rewards and punishments. I still say that God does not punish and is not a judge passing sentence. The divinely decided orderliness of nature does bring it about that actions have for the actors agreeable and disagreeable consequences through the partly chance intersections of creaturely freedoms. The details of these consequences, however, come (so far as we can know) only from creaturely, not divine, decisions. Except on the human level, and often on that level, these decisions are largely unconscious, effected by what Peirce called the "spontaneity of feeling," and not made with reference to ethical principles. As President Carter, a religious man, put it, "life is unfair." The Book of Job is about this truth.

Yet there is a sense in which God is supremely fair and just. Every form of life is basically good and largely symbiotic with every other, including parasites. Although universal freedom is the essence of life as such, both vegetarian and carnivorous animals primarily enjoy themselves while they live, and their death pangs are mostly brief and comparatively insignificant compared to the prevailing harmony they enjoy as functioning psychosomatic organisms. Moreover, their joys and sorrows are fully shared by divine sympathy and are as real as the animals feel them to be. God intends their welfare, I believe, in every case. As Tom Paine put it long ago, the creatures can give God nothing but their own and their offsprings' or companions' (or other creatures') happiness. And this gift is indestructible, once achieved. As for their unhappiness, God does not reject that as unworthy of attention. Moreover, life as such is never a net loss. When neither we nor our cells derive any satisfaction from life, we are no longer alive. I cannot convince myself that life is anything but a good, in itself. Schopenhauer was essentially wrong. Hitler's life was a terrible evil in its effects on others, but just in itself it was better than sheer nothing. And so were the lives of his victims while they lasted. Even in Auschwitz, what kept the poor sufferers alive was not the suffering, but some relics of good.

What I have said far too little about, however, is that we all share responsibility for *optimizing* the chances, not only of our own welfare and happiness, but also the happiness of those affected by our actions. The ghastly evil of slavery in our past, from which our Afro-Americans still suffer dismal consequences, is a shadow on all of us. Our economy may also have been harmfully exploitative of countries in the third world to the South of us. Richard Hartshorne, a famous geographer, once told me he wondered which was worse: economic imperialism or military imperialism. He was thinking of Cuba (and perhaps Haiti).

At this moment it is not clear which population is most miserable — in Nicaragua where we weakly support the insurgents, or El Salvador where we strongly support the government? Perhaps we need to learn to act less unilaterally and more internationally. Our misplaced faith in military overkill and deficient faith in cooperation between mutually respectful countries may be making us too much "part of the problem" and too little "part of the solution" in our dealings with our Southern neighbors. If we scold the British for India's troubles, we perhaps should ask ourselves whether the Philippines, in whose affairs we have for ninety years intervened with a sometimes heavy hand, is at present doing very well economically by comparison — considering the vast complexity of the Indian linguistic and religious problems and the frightful monsoon climate (heat, fearful drought, and fearful and uncertain wetness). The East Indians learned a lot from the British. Have we done better with our colonies? Our whole country is a colony — for the Amerindians.

I have to hope that Phan and the other liberationists will help in the grim situation we seem to face in our hemisphere. Perhaps, too, we need our own Gorbachev or national reformer. Our reflective animal species has to live by hope. Mere despair is sinful, as I was taught to believe.

One more question I shall try to deal with here is, "Why have so many been able to think that we must believe in determinism and therefore must believe that it does not prevent us from doing what we want to do and from being free in that sense?" Determinism is the simplest way to assert the principle of causality that is obviously necessary to science and to a viable philosophy. We seek and must seek simplicity in our thinking, and the reason for Whitehead's warning that we should "distrust" the simplicities we think we find is less obvious. Since variety (and unexpectedness) is "the charm of life" and life is the secret hidden in the so-called "inanimate" world (where science has been slow to find it), many centuries were required to understand that order is not the unqualified principle of reality; rather, creativity is that principle. Nineteenth- and early Twentieth-Century clinical psychiatrists were deterministic; but, as several of them whom I know have said in recent decades, the idea of creativity has in this century been coming into its own.

There is another cause of confusion. The situation is not that one might clearly and consistently believe in determinism. As Popper has said, only physicists achieve anything like clarity in thinking about this topic. To quote Peirce and J. L. Austin, talk about determinism is only talk, not genuine expression of belief, comparable to our belief that we will die sooner or later. But the matter is obscure enough so that we can think we believe, and this pseudo-belief does real harm. It shields us from facing honestly the dangers in principle of the life and mind we share, though in enhanced degree in our case, with other animals, single animal and plant cells, and still simpler self-active agents.

Not only does our pretended belief in strict determinism, or dogmatic generalization of micro-indeterminism to determinism (in any other than trivial aspects) on the macroscopic or human psychological levels, bar the path of inquiry into the realities of the human situation even apart from religious questions; it also and above all tends to falsify theological thinking as though the beneficent-tyrant idea of God (or the empty idea of sheer infinity) were the only alternatives to agnosticism, or to the virtual deification of our species as the locus of all value. The notion that God *either* decides everything, *or* decides to allow freedom with its risks, stacks the cards against a sound philosophy of religion. Supreme creativity has no option between producing some world or other every single agent in which is "self-moved" in some degree, and not producing any such world. The idea of wholly unself-moved, unself-creative creatures is null and void. Besides freedom in its supreme or divine and its nondivine forms there cannot be anything at all. "There is nothing but freedom" is a statement I did not invent; I heard it from the geneticist Sewall Wright (who did not quite believe in *supreme* freedom). I take it to rule out any theism radically other than the one I believe in.

There is a "catch" in the definition of freedom as doing what we want to do. Suppose what we want to do is to add to the definiteness of reality; to resolve indeterminacies; to do on a lesser scale and fallibly what God as Creator does cosmically and infallibly; make decisions that are not fully determined by any other deciders, or any combination of factors other than one's *present* self. This is what Epicurus wanted, James wanted, Bergson wanted, Iqbal (of Pakistan), my father, and my teacher W. E. Hocking wanted, and at heart probably we all want — to be creators, even though with a small *c*.

Universal freedom as inherent in life and activity as such makes the verbally conceivable notion of a world without risk of conflict and suffering a pseudo-idea. Does freedom equally exclude a world wholly without malice, deliberate causing of suffering, sadism, or masochism? The answer seems to be, "No, except on condition that life and mind are present only in God and in forms of mind devoid of high levels of consciousness capable of criticizing motives in the light of ethical ideals or principles." Such a world, it seems, was our world in early stages of the Big Bang and before advanced stages of planetary formation. The development of the *Homo sapiens* brain perhaps marked the transition on this planet from non-moral to immoral as well as moral behavior. As a student of animal behavior for almost eighty years, I find the notion that even ideal or divine power could make such a transition occur with no risk of wickedness, genuine immorality, uncontrollable hatred, selfish greed, and the like, implausible. I admit, however, that I find equally implausible the idea that, supposing many planets with high forms of life, they are all disgraced by vigorously thinking or "sapient" species as wicked as our species has been. This seems an unduly gloomy view. Surely some of these species must be or have been more truly sapient, more ethical, than we are or have been. To this extent there may have been a *Fall*. Anyhow, repentance for our individual shares in this may be in order. Oppressions have indeed occurred, and notably in this century. They are occurring.

3. Morris on Political Philosophy

Randall Morris's excellent essay is the only one I recall about my contributions, such as they are, to political thought. Where he thinks Whitehead, Green, Mill, or some other liberal does better, he may be right. I make no boasts as a philosopher of politics. It has long seemed to me that the difficulties of human political decisions surpass all others and make metaphysics easy by comparison. After all, the human psycho-somatic system is the most complex organic system we know, short of the entire cosmos; and human societies are the most complex quasi-organic systems. Over and over again in voting, I find myself unsure that the person or the procedure I vote against is really less promising than the one I vote for.

Probably I have overemphasized the competitive and underemphasized the cooperative aspect of individual values; but I am sure I have never intended to say, without qualification, that "individual goods are mutually exclusive." As a philosopher, enthusiast for and part-time practitioner of several of the arts and sciences, I know that, for instance, finding truth as an enjoyable value need not prevent, but may help, others to enjoy this value. My writing itself is a search for the common good. Not only science but also philosophy are essentially cooperative. On the other hand, we all know that whatever goods are in limited supply — and the finitude of the earth (and our solar system and galaxy) means that some goods will, for the foreseeable future, be so — there will be some competition for these goods.

I am a biologist as well as philosopher in my thinking. Animals use animals or plants for food. Males of many animals compete for food, for territory, or for mating with a certain female, or a certain group of females, and human sexual customs do not eliminate competition in this area. I personally have not had to suffer from this kind of competition. That is one of the ways in which I have been fortunate. Nor have I suffered seriously from the competition for academic promotion or salary; but this, too, is my good fortune. For one thing I began my career with some moderate but seriously helpful inheritances, and have never known real poverty or the threat of it. I also loved and married a woman with various marketable skills. What I have somewhat known is the way friendships with other philosophers have in a few instances been troubled by inability on my part (or the other person's part) to like the friend's thought as well as I (or the other person) liked the friend himself. This was not, even for me, altogether mitigated by the fact that it was in some cases I who enjoyed wider response to my writing. It still made trouble for both.

Perhaps the chief thing to say about my stress on incompatibility is that, in my belief, the most influential cause of atheism or agnosticism is the problem of evil seen as insoluble; either because divine power was taken to have deliberately caused what happens in the world, or because freedom or moment by moment self-determination was taken as confined to the human species, or to the higher animals; or, rather than taken as present in some degree above zero in every truly singular unit-actuality that there is or could be. In other words, the old formula, one's own freedom so far as compatible with the freedom of others, was not seen, as I see it, as applicable to reality in general. Combining this with the social structure of all life, mind, awareness, the interdependence of individuals, and the inseparability of freedom and chance (first proclaimed by Epicurus and Lucretius and rediscovered by Peirce and James), the classical problem of evil is shown to have arisen from a misuse of the word omnipotence, or perfect power. In a metaphysics of freedom, providence logically could not exclude chance, but can only optimize the ratio of risk and opportunity.

As Morris realizes, the foregoing does not tell us just how great the risks must be. I have always been haunted by the socialist ideal. As the economist Henry Simons said (alas, he died prematurely), socialism is fine "as a description of heaven" on earth. If we were all angelic, perhaps it would work. But unangelic parents and teachers make angelic children and pupils unlikely. There are perhaps some angelic parents and teachers; but how many unangelic ones! So — we do what we can.

Morris does not mention the sexist or feminist aspect of political problems. This is my chief regret about his essay. The problem is hardly metaphysical; since reality in general is, on the radically subhuman and the radically superhuman or divine levels, asexual. However, our language about God is sexed, and wrongly so. Only in recent decades have I stopped using masculine pronouns for deity. I take as significant the fact that the ignorance until recent times of the role of female ovaries and egg cells, fully matching if not definitely surpassing the role of the male organs in transmitting the nobler or formal element in generation, was unknown. Think of Aquinas defining feminity as the "inability to secrete semen!" This, wrote he, is "what makes a woman a woman." Defining the sex by a negation! It seems to me scarcely forgivable, since it was based on sheer ignorance, and there was no clear reason to suppose that the truth about the functions of the ovaries and the reason for menstruation was known. (Besides, why talk as though womb and breasts are of no importance?) Aristotle, of course, was responsible for this mistake. Male chauvinism was surely involved. But for the spokesman of a great church to proclaim such an insult to half the species! "Oh well," as Peirce said on some such occasion.

Of living philosophers who have dealt with political questions, I see Mortimer Adler as among the most helpful. In his *Common Sense of Politics* he argues that we must choose between improving our mixed economy (with some socially-owned elements, but others left to free enterprise and the market) and trying to change it to what he calls "universal capitalism," in which ideally everyone has part ownership in the means of production. What Michael Harrington calls "democratic socialism" is also attractive, though I have not adequately studied his writings. In John E. Roemer's *Free to Lose* I find the most impressive argument I know of for the Marxist charge that capitalism is exploitative. Partly as result of Reagan's relative catering to the rich and remarkable forgetfulness or ignorance of the poor, it is becoming obvious that in this country we cannot reasonably continue to take the increasing gulf between the dismally poor and the fantastically rich with complacency. The history of feminism (even in the very country of John Stuart Mill, who knew better), shows how stubbornly those who have unshared with those they have been taking advantage of. The French ideals of Liberty, Equality, Fraternity all have their validity; and we should never Liberty, Equality, Fraternity all have their validity, and we should never abandon any of them. As Adler says, no society has as yet attained an adequate degree of the first two, not to consider the third.

To be an individual animal is to have some power and need to decide its own behavior; to have the degree of conscious rationality of normal mature human beings greatly intensifies this power and need. Genuinely feeble-minded individuals form a special case, as do infants, and the violently or hopelessly insane. The primates and whales, especially the latter, are hard to classify in terms of rationality, but seem at most comparable to small children unable to mature further. Various other mammals are less comparable to us, but still superior to fish and reptiles. In their family life, birds are more like us than are most mammals, in that male birds mostly take part in care for the young. Many bird species show a primitive form of musical sense, as does one species of whale and one primate, also wolves (in their howling), some Lemurs, and, in extremely meager form, some insects, frogs, and toads.

Human beings, who can symbolize universals fluently, and therefore are less narrowly restricted than other animals to particular modes of behavior (and can even generalize the idea of loving other creatures to the point of viewing all of them as objects of concern by the Universal and All-Surpassing Individual) must have greater capacity for making proper use of freedom than other earthlings. Alas, they also have greater capacity for making improper use of freedom.

Equality is important because friendship is a universal value among the highest animals, and certainly among human beings. The ideal of friendship includes equality. A friendly society is equalitarian rather than hierarchical or caste-ridden. The partriarchal idea of marriage was natural enough when high death rates made it necessary (if populations were to be maintained or increased in an uncrowded world) for women, on the average, to bear many offspring and also caused many mothers to die before offspring were able to care for themselves. It is less natural under present conditions. The silver lining is that marital love can now be a supreme form of friendship. In our sixty-two years of marriage, Dorothy Cooper Hartshorne and I have never made decisions by one of us issuing commands to the other. In all that time neither of us has had any other friend comparable as such. In the one case close to that the man was also one of my best friends, and neither he nor my wife dealt with each other by commands. They respected each other as equals.

In degrees of talent or skill neither innate nor cultivated equality is to be expected. However, there are degrees and kinds of inequality that are undesirable and in our society greatly overvalued. Fantastic conspicuous waste in the use of limited resources, enormous political power through financing of officials and legislators, in a world in which, in some countries outright starvation, in many, including our own, severe deprivations (including political helplessness) of large portions of the populations are ugly aspects of the current scene.

As for fraternity, we are all interdependent members of one species, one superfamily, the only planetary species upon whose behavior the future of animal life on this planet largely depends. Whatever our constructive value, our destructive or "nuisance" value, to ourselves as well as to others, is so great as to render the other species negligible by comparison. As Ben Franklin said, if we do not hang separately we may all hang together.

The unique power or value we have as species is not something that men have and women do not, something whites have and blacks do not, something Westerners have and Asiatics do not. It is also not something that every human individual has. No infant has it, no fetus has it, no small child has much of it (compared to gorillas, for example). It is our symbolic power, shown in language, including musical notation (which many women and nonwhites master and I do not), mathematical notation (ditto), use of graphs and other kinds of diagrams. No race or sex is known that cannot master such skills, but many individuals cannot, and many that could fail to.

In the previous paragraph I stated no mere opinions, but rather facts now known with reasonable certainty. The specifically human skills are not matters primarily of skin color, geographical origins, or sex. They vary immensely among individuals; but among large groups identified by color, sex, nationality, or other crude criteria, the differences are by comparison small, constantly changing, and for all we know largely dependent upon circumstances and socially provided or not provided opportunities. The Stoics saw this long ago. Sadly, one reflects, many fail to see it now!

Besides Adler another philosopher with Jewish background, Paul Weiss, in *Toward the Perfected State*, has dealt extensively with political problems. I have studied this book too little to judge it, but suspect that it embodies much shrewd grasp of human nature. On one subject it disappoints me. Nuclear fission, as making major wars look more and more like species suicide, is not adequately taken into account. Kant was right when he took the war-peace problem to be our hardest. Richard McKeon, another philosopher with (in this case partial) Jewish background, took peace as the central philosophical goal of our century. I cannot quarrel with this, and I wish I had done more to further that objective.

In this context Adler confesses his inability to deal effectively with the divisive influences of fundamentalist religions. Here, too, I feel a kinship with Kant in his search for a religion of reason. Religion has been divisive partly because of an unreasonable trust in our human ability to arrive with ease at absolute truth, whether by rational methods or intuition; and, whether the reasoning or intuition is our own or that of some prophet or élite class, this excessive trust alternating with unreasonable distrust in human reasoning or intuition. Extreme deconstructionism is unreasonable distrust. Medieval theologies and later Protestant Biblicisms (idolatries of book worship), with their Inquisitions and religious wars, were examples of unreasonable trust.

Kant's own theism was insufficiently deconstructed medievalism. Before Darwin, Kant was anti-evolutionary in an unreasonable way. He also indulged in the intellectual idolatry of taking past phenomena as omnipotent to determine present and future phenomena, substituting tyrannical natural laws for the benevolent tyranny of the all-determining deity. There was, too, the subtle idolatry of worshipping timeless and spaceless eternity and disparaging spatio-temporal actuality — as though there could be freedom without an open future, or social relations and the values of friendship and love without distinctions between here and there! Kant also retained the medieval idea of posthumous careers for human individuals, and looked down upon the ancient Jews, who nobly sought to serve God without hope for heavenly rewards, or fear of hellish punishments. The Enlightenment was still, in more ways than even its critics usually envisage, in the medieval prison.

However, Kant's ideal of a reasonable religion and a reasonable science [both modestly held] is mine, and I do not apologize for this. I appreciate the stimulus of Morris's essay.

4. Davaney on God, Power, and Liberation

In my long career I have of course read many essays, other than my own, that were unpublished at the time I read them. Of these, I recall none that gave me more satisfaction than this one by Sheila Greeve Davaney. Not a single sentence seemed to call for correction as interpretation of my thought. None seemed lacking in clarity or readability. Indeed, I feel proud to have furnished an occasion for so admirable a statement of the feminist cause. It is a cause I have favored since before the beginning of my college junior year, and before I knew much about the history or present state of philosophy.

In my book on American philosophy, I quote Emerson's incisive and whole-hearted endorsement of a list of women's rights drawn up by an American feminist group in 1848: "If the women demand ... political equality, refuse it not. 'Tis very cheap wit to find it so funny." Whitehead's defense of women's suffrage that I read only a week or two ago for the first time was similarly vigorous and to the point, though more carefully argued. Long ago I heard a radioed lecture pointing out that George Meredith's *The Egoist* was really a devastating criticism of Victorian male chauvinism. I reread the book, which I had read in 1917, and found this to be the case. A famous modern Japanese novel, *The Sisters*, and a classical Chinese novel *The Dream of the Red Chamber*, both by men, convey a picture of women as fully as interesting as men but less fortunate as society treated them.

However, the earliest novel of high quality in world literature, Lady Murasaki's *Genji Monogatari*, was by a woman in eleventh century Japan. Theodore Dreiser's *Sister Carrie* was a wonderful test case for male literary critics, some of whom couldn't "take it" that it was the man, not the woman, who came to grief from an illegal and not particularly ethical affair. That the book was a masterpiece struck me as so obvious that only arbitrary bias could explain failure to see and admit its merit.

Since I agree with the feminist points that Davaney makes, and since she states many of them better than I have done, I urge the reader to give her essay careful reading. For the rest I shall supplement her account by giving a quite personal testimony of my observations of both sexes supporting the proposition that we should move farther away from the old patriarchal stereotype of the family and of society than we have yet done.

(1) Most of my students have been men, yet it is to suggestions of women that I owe two definite constituents of my philosophical scheme, whereas I am not sure of any equally definite debts to the male students while they were students. One constituent came from a woman whose name and appearance I cannot recall, beyond that it was a she. I had been quoting Anselm's definition of God as "that than which nothing greater can be thought." Her suggestion was, insert "except itself" after *greater*. God cannot be surpassed by conceivable *others* but is in principle all-surpassing in the mathematically strict sense that includes self-surpassing. It was perhaps later that I came upon Fechner's phrase, "God continually surpasses God," long anticipating the process view that divine perfection is unrivalled not by being timelessly the exhaustive actualization of all possible positive values (a contradiction or sheer nonsense since, as Whitehead notes, there are incompossible possibilities for positive value), but by having an all-surpassing *manner of increasing* in value.

The other conceptual constituent that I owe to a woman is to one I could name; but as she is no longer alive, is not known as a philosopher, and for still other reasons, I shall not name her, except as Kay. I had been talking about the idea of Max Dessoir that beauty (like virtue in Aristotle) is *between extremes*, these being the merely pretty at one pole and the sublime at the opposite pole — in other words slight or superficial harmony at one extreme and great or profound harmony at the other. However, Dessoir had a two-dimensional diagram representing the two extremes just mentioned horizontally while in the vertical dimension *beauty was at the top* and ugliness at the *bottom*. My student, an artist, said that in the vertical dimension, too, beauty should be in the middle. If ugliness is at the bottom, as Dessoir had it, the top is something as distinct from beauty as ugliness is. Ugliness involves an aspect of disorder, but so does beauty. Pure order, unrelieved by any aspect of tension, uncertainty, or surprise, is monotonous, boring. Beauty is unity in variety; unity temporally is partial repetition or fulfillment of expectation, variety temporally is partly unexpected contrast and can be delightful surprise.

Any artist can avoid disorder. Just draw a circle; in no way can a more unified line be represented. But so what? It took an artist to realize that, as Kurt Sax put it, once for all, "aesthetic order is the vast realm between mechanism and chaos," sheer order or unity, in contrast to sheer disorder or multiplicity. So I can claim, thanks to Kay, that I am probably the first in all history to say of beauty what Aristotle said of virtue, that it is the central value, and this in two dimensions, between the sublime and the pretty, as well as between the ugly or incongruent, and the merely neat or too unqualifiedly ordered.

Beauty is a circle inside a greater circle. Outside the greater circle is the hopelessly superficial (at the right) or the hopelessly profound (at the left) and the hopelessly unvaried at the top and the hopelessly ununified at the bottom. "Hopelessly" means, "not really experienceable." Even the ugly is not valueless; the strictly valueless is what is not even noticed because there is no

258

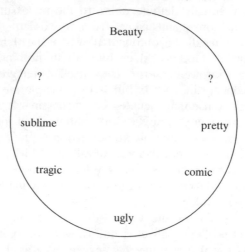

Max Dessoir's Aesthetic Circle
(according to my memory)

Revised Aesthetic Circle (with thanks to Kay)
mere unity, order, mechanism, monotony

mere variety, disorder, chaos
Outside the circle, no aesthetic value.
Everywhere inside, some value.

intrinsic reward in doing so. Life is enjoyment essentially, not suffering. Only failing to live provides the absolutely negative. No animal has to live. Living is basically voluntary. This is why the doctrine of eternal suffering in Hell is really nonsense. It is sadism or masochism carried to the contradictory extreme. Of all the things to be afraid of, it is the least fearful, from my perspective. My pious parents did not, according to my memory, even talk about it in the least.

Those who say, as Croce did, that all positive aesthetic value is beauty (so that the inner circle is not needed and the outer circle is beauty) are making one choice, but not the best choice, in word usage. Ordinary language is wiser. As Bosanquet showed long ago, ugliness, as we normally use the word, is not absolute lack of harmony or concord but is a bearable deviation from harmony, or the ideal of aesthetic order. Literally unbearable deviations, and this is tautology, are simply not born! They are mere limits of thought that can be approached but not reached.

Probably some male students also gave me incisive help that escapes my memory. But that two women did give it is evidence that blanket disparagements of womanly cultural capabilities are unacceptable. They have always been so, as Socrates, Plato, and the Stoics knew and said; but Aristotle did not know or say. So much the worse for us all, because the Middle Ages followed Aristotle on this topic. Far too many modern philosophers have done poorly on it, too. Schopenhauer and Nietzsche are outstandingly poor, but until recently few have been very good. Emerson and Whitehead stand out as exceptions. I think C. S. Peirce does too, on the whole. William James, I am sorry to say, is not of much help here. His lack of interest in child psychology is one aspect of this.

(2) Two historical points seem to me important, more important perhaps than either men or women in general realize.

(a) Before the existence and function of the female egg cell was even guessed by scientists or philosophers, it was probably not in human nature to avoid attempting to turn this ignorance into a supposed knowledge that there was no such entity or function, and that, as Aristotle at his worst asserted, the female parent provides only the ignoble "matter" while the male furnishes the nobler "formal" element of the offspring. I say that (apart from male bias) this was not an educated or shrewd guess, but *at best* just a guess, a leap in the dark. Granted the two principles, form and matter, there is nothing in this assumption from which it can be validly deduced that one sex must provide only one element and the other sex the other element. Indeed it is logically possible, and in fact true, that both sexes provide particular examples of both elements. The formal inheritances, the genes, come partly from both parents, and at least as much from the mother as the father. The genes are the formal inheritances, yet they are material if anything is. There is one essential kind of gene that comes *only* from the mother. The sex-determining gene comes from the human father. Obviously from the father comes only a very small amount of physical stuff and from the mother a great deal, both from the womb and the mammaries. This is Aristotle's reason, or rather excuse, for jumping to the conclusion that the male contributes nothing physical that is needed and the mother nothing formal or non-physical. If all this is not poor reasoning, what would be that in an, in general, very clever person?

In the foregoing I have far from exhausted the gaps in Aristotle's reasoning, not just in his knowledge, in this socially important subject. It is a topic for research: how far other prescientific prejudices against women are based on a similar confusion between a deficiency of knowing and knowing a deficiency.

It seems a fair presumption that this played a world-wide role. Apart from scientists and philosophers at their best (Newton, Peirce, Popper, for example), we tend to lack the Socratic wisdom of acknowledging our abysmal ignorance.

(b) The other historical point is the effect of applied science in reducing the death rate, and therefore, in the long run, the desirable birth rate, so that, instead of the species having a need for women on the average giving birth to n children, this number should be reduced to one half or one third of n. Moreover, the mother will have an average life span which entails that a much smaller percentage of her life will need to be devoted to child-bearing and child-caring. What is she to do with this much enlarged later portion of her career? I wonder if even feminists have sufficiently reflected on this change in what is desirable in women. It is mathematically demonstrable that not even our galaxy is large enough for the offspring if population growth were to maintain its recent rate for a not very large number of centuries. Either fewer babies will have to be born or more premature deaths must occur. Is it the latter that ultra-conservatives want? Will there someday be a Pope or statesman who will actually face this issue fairly and squarely? Meanwhile, it is time to face the truth that the basic cultural handicap of woman is not in what she lacks but in what she has — and, for the sake of the species, must in most cases use.

As Marxists rightly insist, large quantitative changes always constitute also qualitative changes. Feminism in this sense was predictable, had men paused to consider the matter with care. Not many, it seems, did so. Thus Kant said women should not vote because they lacked economic independence. Suppose this reasonable, why did Kant not go on to ask, "Must it always be so? Must women always be only wives and mothers and nothing else of recognized importance?" I am sure he thought science would lower the death rate. So . . .? Hegel was both a racist and a sexist. The Stoics and also Epicureans, however, to their honor, said that of course women have the ability and right to cultural achievement.

There are unreasonable extremes of feminism. I have even encountered, to my sorrow, two women who embodied an extreme of anti-feminism. In my book *Wisdom as Moderation* I argue for the doctrine that basic values in general, including not only Aristotelian virtues, temperance and many others, but also beauty, and truth in various forms, are to be found in the middle ground between false or vicious extremes. Every movement or social cause has a fanatic extreme. A theologian I have known liked to say that there is "always a lunatic fringe that needs, now and then, to be snipped off."

If sexism is a social ailment, so is racism. One can argue historically in a similar way for either of them. What have women, or Africans, done culturally, where among them have been the great philosophers or scientists? Here, too, science and technology have changed things. The quantitative results are obviously great, the qualitative changes are less obvious and hard to measure. The biological necessity for women to do what men cannot do is not matched by any known biological necessity in the case of blacks, Hispanics, and other ethnic minorities; but the difficulties of overcoming the historical results of slavery and many other occurrences are nevertheless great. It never did make sense to deny the full humanity of women or any of the races. The crucial marks of the human species are not skin color or any other obvious physical details of this kind, but the fluent use of language and of manipulative hands, and neither sex nor any race is incapable of either. Shakespeare knew this.

Davaney emphasizes aesthetic values. In my aesthetic classes I tried to communicate my belief that the supreme and inclusive art is the art of life itself, including above all the arts of friendship and love in various senses, including cultivating the sense of divine love. For this sense motherhood is, quite obviously — if one looks straight at the facts — a better symbol than fatherhood. We males must make the best of our second rank. Bravo for the sociologist Ashley Montague, who knows the score here! The female is not a parent (actual or potential) comparatively lacking something; the male *is* a parent lacking a good deal. We can both make the best of our respective statuses, allowing for the fact that some males are not very masculine and some females not very feminine. Indeed, above all we must never forget that *individual* differences exceed *by at least a hundred times* sexual (or racial) differences when it comes to abilities other than the physically sexual. Compare a low-grade moron (of either sex) to Jane Austen, Edith Wharton, or Madame Curie.

Concerning my rationalism, I agree that, like words in general, *reason* or *rational* must be used with care. Also, 'correspondence' as key to the meaning of '*truth*' gives no absolute power by its mere use. I add, however, that merely refusing to use it also gives no such power. There are many ways of spelling out what *kind* of correspondence there can be between symbolic arrays and what is symbolized. I go with Tarsky and Karl Popper here. Absolute lack of correspondence does seem to me to throw no light whatever on what science or metaphysics are trying to do; and I believe that "coherence" (in the sense Whitehead gives the word) constitutes truth on the highest level of metaphysical generality and includes correspondence in the limited sense required for truth on that level, that is, *necessitas de dictu* corresponding to *necessitas de re*. In metaphysics the former necessity is in what we must say if we want to make sense (consistent and positive sense) in interrelating our *most general* conceptions, while the latter necessity is what never could fail, or have failed, to obtain in reality, not only in reality as in our cosmic epoch but reality in any genuinely conceivable cosmic epoch, and with no matter what genuinely conceivable natural laws. I use "fact" to refer to contingent truths, and for them coherence does not suffice to establish correspondence. Just this is the difference between metaphysics and physics, or any natural science, or history.

Concerning naturalism I once called myself a "theistic naturalist," but have given this up because it tends to blur the distinction between metaphysical and empirical statements. In making such distinctions I claim no infallibility. I do claim that I have never intentionally denied the full humanity of women or ceased to find laughable or deplorable all denials (alas, not always by males) of their rights as members of *homo sapiens*.

I end with a perhaps unkind remark: Why, oh why, have so many women followed men in one of their greatest and most absurd mistakes, exposing their bodies to the harmful fumes and the poison of tobacco? This is one of the subjects on which I think of Nietzsche's "Human, all too human."

5. Arabindu Basu on Indian Thought

Whether or not it is quite true that I am never dogmatic, I appreciate Professor Basu's saying this. I could say similar things about him. He is for me a superb embodiment of Hinduism, as such somewhat unique in my experience, although I have spent some months in India and known some fine Indian philosophers there, as well as some outside India. His essay presents a problem common in our profession. It raises the question, how far are philosophical differences more than verbal and how far are they differences only in words or verbal rituals? Many of the phrases in his essay, where Basu seems to state views he prefers, I can interpret as ways of stating my beliefs about God. I do not see all of them as the best ways to say what I believe, and I fail to see that all of them are mutually coherent. Also, there are some aspects of my thought that scarcely find expression in Basu's exposition of that thought. One is the distinction between change and impermanence. By Whiteheadian "objective immortality" nothing is literally impermanent, for actualities "become and do not change." Change in actualities is essentially creation, always in part self-created, and I hold with Bergson as well as Whitehead that "becoming is creation *or nothing* (emphasis added)." There is no destruction of actualities. Above all, divine change is solely in the form of enrichment, increase. I find this in Sri Jiva Goswami, founder of the Bengali School of Hinduism. "The cup is full — but behold, it grows without ceasing." Also "God is more than the Absolute." For me this is not contradictory, giving Absoluteness a clear and coherent meaning.

I would not say that there is not a "transcendent reality having no relation with the world," but I do say that this reality is abstract, and is *less* than the transcendent reality having relation to the world. Reality is whatever there is truth about, or that which is what it is no matter how particular subjects think about it. Particular subjects here are not individuals but are more concrete than individuals, for instance my-experience-now. My experience yesterday was a different subject but its individuality was also that of Charles Hartshorne. I miss in Basu any clear notion of concreteness, or of "actual entities." Before Whitehead the Buddhists came closest to this idea. It, and the idea of *prehension*, "the most concrete form of relatedness," imply a philosophical revolution, even relative to Buddhism and to Hinduism in all its forms, so far as I know them.

I have in Berdyaev precedent for saying that the basic question about *Immanence* is not, "Is God in the world?", but "Is the world in God?" God as concrete is God *having some world or other*. "*The* world" is a radically ambiguous formula. Each moment there is a slightly new world; and I accept Whitehead's "cosmic epochs" different even in their laws. So God is the God of innumerable worlds, all but one from the divine perspective previous to our world.

I miss in Basu any clear reference to my or Whitehead's "reformed subjectivism" or psychicalism, according to which no actuality is entirely devoid of subjectivity, minimally feeling of (others') feeling; that is, sympathy. Basu does hint that the so-called "inanimate world" may not be strictly inanimate. The world of mere common sense, or any particular stage of physics, need not be entirely real, it may in part be Maya. Reality is what divine prehensions (not our human prehensions) fully and directly disclose it as being.

In the saying that the self of you or me is identical with Brahman, "identity" cannot, so far as I see, have the strict meaning Leibniz gave to this term. This Advaita identity seems to me more a verbal ritual than a concept. On the other hand, of course nothing is simply "separable from God." *Nonidentical with* and *inseparable from* are not equivalent expressions. Note, however, that "X inseparable from God" is not equivalent to "God inseparable from X." On the contrary, God could be (and in the ultimate past once was) separate from any X you please — unlesss X stands for some-world-or-other.

I do not now call Shankara's view pantheism, but "acosmism." It is one of sixteen logically possible views (they could be held, but only one could be true) about God, including atheistic views. I am not sure that Buddha was atheistic. I recall a text, "There is an eternal being, unborn and undying; if this were not so, we could not ourselves escape from birth and death." Suzuki, Zen scholar, thinks Zen is not unambiguously atheistic. It is certainly not theistic in the sense of medieval or reformation theism, but neither am I. I am glad to be confirmed in my impression that Hinduism is uncommitted to personal immortality in the sense of Islam, some forms of Judaism, and most medieval and reformation Christianity. "Objective immortality" can accept death as the termination of the series of experiences of any person other than God; however, the actualities forming the experiences of the person and of its singular bodily constituents are everlastingly prehended by God. The series of experiences has its final member before death. In this sense we are temporally as well as spatially finite, indeed fragmentary. Only divine finitude is non-fragmentary, all-inclusive. To include is one thing; to be simply identical with is another thing. I cannot find conceptual coherence in blurring this distinction.

In one respect I, but not Whitehead, accept and emphasize an aspect of

Platonism that has been seriously neglected or misused by most Western philosophers: the view of God as the Soul whose body is the cosmos of the creatures, not forgetting the cosmic epochs, in a sense successive worlds.

Another linguistic trouble between us is that I am not satisfied with the formula "God self-limited-as-having-a-world," as though that were to be less than God alone. For me God is essentially world-creative, just as world is essentially divinely created. With the tradition in the West I agree that there is an unmoved mover and it is the necessary essence of God; however, *necessary* contrasts with *contingent* and the contrast is essential to both terms. A mere essence is an abstraction, less not more than the concrete actuality. Necessary and contingent are not value terms, and by themselves do not distinguish between divine and worldly. My doctrine of dual transcendence, mentioned by Basu, is relevant here. It is symbolized by NC.cn, capital letters standing for divine and lower case letters for worldly attributes. The value difference between God and world is only hinted at by this visual difference and the reversal of order between CN and nc. Tradition oversimplified the problem at this point.

The word *consciousness* I use (as Whitehead does) for a high level of soul or mind. Low levels involve feeling and only minimal levels of thinking. Divine consciousness is radically superhuman, most forms of mind in nature are subhuman. The zero of soul or mind is the zero of concrete actuality. There is no mere, dead, simply insentient matter. That we do not all know this is because our perceptions blur the fine structure of nature. What seem inert are really hosts of self-active singulars invisible and intangible one by one to us. Groups of such singulars are what we misperceive as single physical objects. Even with growing trees and such, what we see are not the active singulars doing the growing, for that action is the invisible small cells multiplying. Common sense merely as such has no access to the active constituents of inanimate or merely vegetable nature. Philosophers for nearly twenty centuries failed to guess this truth, until Leibniz did guess it; but, alas, he spoiled his stroke of genius by his excessive rationalism, his principle of sufficient reason which deprived his monads of freedom! He even called them "spiritual automatons," really a stark contradiction.

Considering intercultural differences, and the radical contrast between being human and being divine, it is not surprising if our mutual understanding about God is imperfect. Certainly Basu has made a noble effort to understand me.

6. Bracken on the God-world Issue

Father Joseph Bracken's remarkable essay puts me "on the spot." I feel painfully my inferior knowledge of physics when discussing cellular and subcellular structures. There is, I have long been aware, a passage in Whitehead in which he seems to deny personal order to a cell. In addition I have never wished to deny entirely the relevance of trinitarian speculations. (Here I may shock some Unitarian friends. I have discussed this topic in a now no longer available early book.) However, such speculations should not be used to justify the idea that God could perfectly well have created no world of non-divine things. What religious concern can there be for a deity to which the world, any world, is simply superfluous and does not, in Berdyaev's phrase, "enrich" the divine life? Besides, freedom is positive; there can be no such thing as freedom to do nothing, except in the sense that the nonliving do nothing, and that only God, among the living, exists necessarily. Also, if Trinitarian ideas mean that perfect persons might exhaust reality, then indeed we should abandon them. There must be something perfect and something imperfect (in both the absolute and the relative senses I assign these words) something all-surpassing and something not all-surpassing; such ultimate contrasts lose their meaning if either side is denied application.

My contention about the soul (or mind) and body analogy has been that Whitehead's own system is more coherent if the analogy is accepted. So far as I grasp Bracken's meaning, it is less incompatible with the analogy than he seems to think. I, too, would say that an animal's body is the field of most direct action (indeed interaction) of that animal's mind. I do see the point about a society's being its "own reason." I have not intended to contradict Whitehead on this, far from it.

It is true that a human experience is somewhat localized in the brain, whereas divine actuality must be ubiquitous. Plato was precisely the one who first said, in the *Timaeus*, that the divine body is in the divine soul and was clear that this makes a difference in principle between God and all else. *This* uniquely excellent soul has *no* external environment, large or small.

The issue between Brachen and myself (or Cobb) on whether "If a nexus of actual occasions behaves as a unitary reality, a higher-order occasion must be present" is somewhat complicated. I have indeed said that "what acts as one feels as one." However, there seem to be degrees of acting as one. A termite colony or swarm of bees may seem to act as one; but I do not concede that it feels as one. My device for dealing with such cases is this: a single termite acts as a single agent much more strictly than its colony. It has more integration. In a tree the cells multiply, and we say the tree grows; but I say that this growth of the tree simply is the multiplication of the cells. There need (*contra* Fechner) be no feeling by the three as one. In contrast, when I do a voluntary act with a feeling of doing it, it is not my cells that do this feeling. They make it possible; but in my view, they are only necessary, not sufficient, conditions for its being felt as I feel it. Each experience is partly self-created, as Whitehead holds. My brain does not *exactly* determine any of my feelings. My puzzle is, how far is the difference between what I say and what Bracken says more than a difference of words? This is not a merely rhetorical question. I am less than entirely clear about this.

It must be partly my fault that certain differences between me and Whitehead are overstated by many. I agree with Whitehead that some concepts refer to eternal aspects of reality. Metaphysical categories by definition do this. As Aristotle said, only the eternal can be (unconditionally) necessary. The series of whole numbers I take to be necessary and, therefore, they are, so far as I can see, eternal objects of divine concepts. Only the primordial nature of God can be their locus, to speak figuratively, or their "repository." So God is necessary even for this reason. By the "dispensability of Whitehead's eternal objects" I had in mind his including among such objects qualitative universals like "blue" (his own example) or other sensory or affective universals. Because of Peirce's doctrine of the continuum of qualitative possibilities, I see such a term as blue as without any single unitary meaning, analogously to Whitehead's own doctrine that space is not a collection of points. For me as for Whitehead, apart from God there could not only not be any world, there could not be any eternal aspects of the possibility of worlds. Only through a not *merely* temporal or *merely* contingent reality could there be timeless truths, such as we have in mathematics and seek in metaphysics.

I do not reject Whitehead's idea of God's function of helping us to produce novelty. We are creative if we are anything; but apart from God we are nothing at all. 'Apart from God' is an illicit formula in this system. We are *self-creative creatures*, with God as our required (conditionally necessary) Creator, as Lequier implied. Any "initial subjective aim" offered to us by God is necessary but not sufficient condition for our final or fully concrete subjective aim. The initial aim cannot be as rich in determinations as the actual concrete value realized. 'Self-creative' must be taken to mean, "with the help of antecedent acts of creativity," divine acts always included.

In giving us this help, God need not use only eternal concepts but can also use emergent ones, as (but infinitely less adequately) we can. Given the distinctions stated, I do not see this doctrine as contradictory. If I have stressed the necessity of divine ordering of the world rather than the role of God in making novelty possible, this is only a matter of emphasis, not of doctrine. *Mere* novelty would imply unlimited possibility of disorder. *Mere* repetition would imply an aesthetically impossible extreme of monotony and boredom. I agree with Whitehead that God "saves the world" from both of these extremes. God, and more or less unconsciously all creatures, seek and value beauty: harmonious intensity of experience.

Perhaps difference of emphasis is not quite the only way Whitehead and I differ on this topic. The universality of creativity seems to exclude mere repetitiveness, but how can it exclude hopeless lack of sufficient repetition to make harmony, aesthetic value possible? I deeply agree with the idea that monotony is a great evil which at the limit is unendurable, life-destroying; nevertheless the need for God, supreme freedom, to save the creatures from chaos does seem the more obvious one. With freedom there will be, if anything, variety and unexpectedness, with or without the rule of one. But, without supreme freedom, will there be sufficient unity and order? Even a committee needs a chairman.

Whitehead's greatness is seen particularly in his insight that the mere abstraction, orderliness, is not sufficient to entail a definite type of cosmic order, or system of natural laws. God is needed not simply to decide, "let there be order in a universe of freedom," but to choose *what* order out of logically possible ones. The final variety is in the diversity and unpredictability of cosmic epochs. Even God (and higher levels of creaturely consciousness, perhaps) must not be bored by endless reiteration of one type of cosmic order. So the supreme artist (which, as Randall has shown, is Plato's idea of God) produces endless variety of cosmic art-forms, not just many examples of one such form. Neither Plato nor Whitehead seems to have fully thought out this sublime idea. And Peirce opted for the alternative notion of the emergence of more and more nearly absolute orderliness out of an aboriginal chaos. Since Peirce held, rightly, as did John Dewey, that absolute order would stifle individual awareness, the Peircean scheme seems ultra-pessimistic if not contradictory in an idealist ontology like Peirce's. What he wanted was to make a closed, though infinitely large, circle out of becoming. This recalls the ancient pseudo-idea of the most perfect curve.

We have here one more example of our situation today in metaphysics: that the chief logical possibilities for theory on the most general level have, with something like completeness, been explored. Our job from now on is more to decide among views already set forth for reasons already largely given than to create views and arguments to the extent the ancient Greeks, Chinese, and East Indians did long ago. We have, whatever Thomas Kuhn may say, what they lacked, a vastly increased command, however approximate and tentative, of the truly non-metaphysical, empirical, contingent, factual truths about our cosmic situation and the nature of our species among the planetary animals.

7. Clarke's Thomistic Critique

Fr. W. Norris Clarke honors me and Aquinas by taking us both, separated by seven centuries, so seriously. He thinks I do not do full justice to Thomas's system. In this he is surely right. To do full justice to any great thinker's thought exceeds the power of human language; and certainly nothing like it can be done in anything less than a full book on the subject. I add, however, that Clarke has not done full justice to my system, hard though he has tried to do so.

In spite of my book title terming *omnipotence* a mistake, the discussions in the book qualify this charge somewhat. If the word means not-conceivably-surpassable or ideally-great power over all, then I affirm this. No being other than God has *ideal* power over anything, and no other has power over *all*. In these two senses I agree with the tradition. Furthermore, I agree with the proposition that God can do anything the doing of which by an *all-good* and *all-wise* being is *self-consistent*. It is, however, contradictory to fully determine the *free* act of another. I have repeatedly said that these are the only limitations on what God can do. One belief that separates me widely from the medieval writers and early modern thinkers in this context is that, with Peirce, Whitehead, etc., I hold that every *single* creature (in contrast to collectives) has some freedom. Hence *no* portion of nature is fully determined by divine action.

As I have somewhere pointed out, "sufficient" reason or cause is ambiguous. It might mean, sufficient to make possible; it might mean sufficient to make actual. It is modal absurdity to identify these two. Without God, nothing is possible; indeed "without God" is nonsense or contradiction in my thinking (and this whether or not "with God" makes coherent sense). I see only a rhetorical difference between what I say here and what Clarke wants me to say. Only with God, not merely with my nondivine predecessors, was I possible — or was anything at all possible, even the pseudo-thing of sheer "nothing." So I don't see what beyond words is lacking. Divine power is presupposed by any lesser power. Remember that God is primordial and therefore, somewhat as every whole number is preceded by an odd number, so some divine state or other precedes any and every state of other powers.

Divine essence-and-existence, as noncontingent, in unimaginably rich divine actuality (contingent in specifics), has always been there, no matter how far back we go.

I am glad my critic agrees with me that Thomas conceded, though Clarke is not sure he should have conceded, the logical possibility of a beginningless past of the creative process. My objection to creation *ex nihilo* is that if God created me out of nothing, then our human idea of power lacks all basis in experience. Surely God used my parents, not just nothing. And, as Clarke notes, a first state of creation is paradoxical. An actual infinity is unimaginable by us, but there is no agreement that it is really contradictory.

Why are there other beings each additional to God as previously actual? There are plenty of reasons. To speak of ideal power is to imply the contrast with non-ideal power. The "principle of contrast" is axiomatic with me. Also, the notion of a supreme form of creativity creating nothing seems an absurdity. Something is always better than sheer nothing. To impute to God the "ability" to do nothing seems to me no praise of deity. I have read Thomas and find his language taken at its best ambiguous rather than clear, as to God's power. The theologian James Ross has also read Thomas and interprets him as attributing to God power to deliberately bring about any conceivable state of affairs. True, Ross also holds, as I do, that *eternally conceivable* states of affairs are not fully definite. They are not possible worlds composed of fully definite individuals. From the standpoint of eternity, Ross said (in my presence) not even animal species can be identified. I agree. However (in his philosophy of religion book) Ross fell into the absurdity of solving the problem of evil by saying that if Shakespeare was not wicked in creating the extremely wicked Iago, then God was not wicked in creating, say, Hitler. As though Iago really did wicked things. Iago was an image of a wicked person, not a wicked person. If only Hitler had been but an image!

I have no adamant objection to saying that God is the ultimate "source" of all power. But words mean what we make them mean, "paying them extra" (as the incomparable Lewis Carroll says) when we impart a somewhat new sense to them. I, too, say that we are images of deity, as, in dilute sense every creature is. Of course we participate in divine power. I have been aware — though sometimes I forget — that Jesuits are not determinists, as Janzen and Pascal, Luther, and, I think, Augustine were. But if Thomas was trying to say what I say about freedom in relation to divine power, then I cannot think he did a good job at that point.

Clarke in one passage seems to imply as my view that a creature is, in its freedom, entirely self-caused. This only shows how difficult philosophy is. Plato said it first: what has soul is self-moved; but he failed to add what he must have known, that soul is also moved by others. Even knowing others is already that; one cannot know something if it is not there to be known.

Alas, there is more than a rhetorical difference between Clarke and me concerning panentheism. I cannot possibly accept the idea that the cosmos adds numerical plurality but not quality or value, to the divine life. Nothing is more important to me theologically than our being able to genuinely "serve God" by increasing the aesthetic richness of the divine awareness. To call this a "limitation" in the divine perfection I take to be a definite mistake. As Whitehead saw, and Leibniz should have seen — since there are incompossible values — *no conceivable perfection could*, in every dimension of value, be the greatest possible.

Why else should there be a world, if it adds no value to God? Nor does the mathematician-pupil example support Clarke's point here. The mathematician may know all the mathematics the pupil can learn, or he may not know it; but in either case the pupil gives to the teacher the value which experiencing an interesting human being, unique in all history, can give. Similarly (although I incline to attribute to God complete mathematical knowledge without help from us) God is surely interested in, or enjoys, incomparably more beauty than that of mathematical abstractions. As for greatest possible or "absolute" beauty, that is a formula the meaning of which no one (Leibniz tried) has been able to tell us. I think the aesthetic dimension of value has no logically possible maximum. This still leaves an infinite, not a merely finite, gulf between us and deity; for God ideally enjoys all so-far-actualized aesthetic values in the present and preceding cosmic epochs. Long ago I distinguished between absolute perfection, A, a real maximum, and relative perfection, R, surpassing that of all actual others, and attributed both A and R to God.

Alas, again, I do not ses clear logic in the workman analogy. The workman indeed uses the wood as mere means, but God enjoys us for our *intrinsic* values, *our* enjoyments, *our* aesthetic values. God also suffers in prehending our sufferings. In trying to show that this makes God and world so interdependent that all transcendence is lost, Clarke leaves me well behind, unimpressed, except that it reminds me again of how easily we are carried away by words. "Give a philosopher an inch," wrote Peirce, "and he will take a million light years." More simply, we (like politicians) are constantly exaggerating against each other.

As for freedom in the members of an organism, I am reminded of my own frequent pronouncement: Show me a wrong view of God and I am likely to discover in it a wrong view of the basic example from experience to which God is being compared. In our bodies, I, of course, hold, there is no complete "organicity." If a cellular process somewhere in the body produces effects on such process elsewhere, this is not instantaneously, and there is no reverse action on the state of the *previous* process causing these effects. There is partial freedom and real distinction between cells. Whitehead takes the neural conditions of our sensations to be similarly prior, and any effects of the sensations will be on a later phase of neural process — later actual entities, in other words. Similar distinctions preserve the freedom of God and of creatures relative to each other. In short the view of organism used by the critic is for me a myth, and not included in my theory. I also reject the idea that "included in God" entails "identical with God," and if it is said, "at least identical with a part of God," then I say that 'part' has several meanings. In knowing, the items known are parts of the knowing; but this is very different from a brick being part of a wall, or a finger part of a body. The subject-given-object inclusion is the most concrete form of inclusion; in the ideal case yielding to the subject the entire intrinsic value of the given.

Plato said that the cosmic soul includes the cosmic body. I agree and fail to see that this spatializes the relation. On the contrary it is psychical ideas of relations that explain space. Prehension, intuitive inclusion, is, as Whitehead argues, the reply to Hume on causality. And space-time is the system of possible and actual causal relations. Of course subjects depend on objects. But for me, differing here from Whitehead, God is not a single subject in the most concrete sense; God is a person — that is, analogous to a personally ordered society of actual entities dominantly related to a nonpersonal society of subhuman actual entities.

Whitehead and I are entirely serious in taking prehension as "the most concrete form of relation." I prehend the brain actualities more adequately than they prehend each other. But they do prehend my experiences in their deficient way. So I am in them as well as they in me, but I am, as a single subject or society, incomparably more dominant than any one of them is. In God is the ideal form of all this, and it differs infinitely, not merely in degree, from the nonideal form. Plato saw (but the world partly missed the point) that the divine body differs from all others in the absolute sense that it has *no* external environment. Plato drew some of the right conclusions from this. We can draw some he could not, since he did not even know the function of the brain, or the mythical character of the notion of inert matter.

As Rabbi Kaufman tells me, long ago it was said that "the world is not the place of God, rather God is the place of the world." How we are in God is the most concrete way to be in anything. Perhaps I may be forgiven for pointing out that to interpret the way we are in God (according to St. Paul) by the "field of God's action", to speak with Fr. Bracken, is to use a spatial metaphor. God prehends us, and this means that God's actuality (not mere existence) includes ours. I take as axiom that if for X to be without Y is logically impossible, then any description of X without mention of Y is incomplete. If God prehends us, then the divine actuality that does this prehending is incompletely described if we are left out. The metaphor "field" seems to me an inferior way to put the matter. If some prefer Brachen's language, good luck to them. But how far are we arguing about more than words here? The substantive issues seem to me more on my side, or Whitehead's.

Clarke is far from the first who has tried to get from the metaphysics of the Thirteenth to that of the Twentieth Century in a few small steps. If this is not possible, it is not only because much has happened between that time and ours. Scholasticism was, in my view, somewhat *regressive* in relation to the best thought in Plato, Aristotle, and Epicurus; and not only that, but also in relation to the best in the Old and New Testaments.

It is pleasant to read the commentator's eloquent account of the divine sensitivity to all that passes in the world, and the great difference the creatures make to the divine consciousness. So we are indeed far from Aristotle's doctrine of the unmoved mover — or from Pure Actuality — by any reasonable use of words. The contents of divine awareness must be contingently otherwise than they might have been. This means that divine potentiality is as real as divine actuality. So why the "pure?" I have taken that literally. So did Spinoza, to whom it meant, no contingency.

I have read Augustine on time (seventy years ago) but was not convinced by him, though I did agree with him that time makes no sense apart from mind, the psychical. But I also agreed with Hume long ago that a purely timeless mode of experiencing is "language idling" — to borrow a phrase from Wittgenstein. With Aristotle I agree heartily that "eternal" entails "necessary," and "contingent" entails "not eternal." Accidents happen not in eternity but in some analogue to what we call time — if you like, in the unsurpassable form of "existential time" (Berdyaev). One could give a long list of writers (including Karl Barth) who have struggled with the idea of all time being included in or known by something unchanging and have concluded that it lacks coherent sense. It spatializes time (Bergson, preceded by Lequier in different words); space being the symmetrical or directionless, and time the asymmetrical or directional, order of dependence and independence.

I wonder if, at this point, I am not more Thomistic than Clarke. For the great Medieval scholastic (as I, and not only I, read him) contingency, potentiality, and change belong together. The Socinians dealt carefully, knowing what they were doing, with this problem and came to the same conclusion as Bergson or Whitehead. So did my teacher W. E. Hocking, who convinced me on the point before I knew the other thinkers just named. Many things could be said against the idea of all time as a completed whole. I am as surprised by Clarke's idea that there is no hopeless difficulty but only mystery in this, as he is by my position. Just take one point. If we *now* are right in saying that God knows all tomorrow's happenings as definite items, then it is now and not merely eternally true that this is so. I argue, as the Socinians did, that there can be truth about tomorrow's happenings only *when* there are such things as tomorrow's happenings. And if there eternally are these things, then everything is as eternal as God.

I take the *merely* eternal to be what all times and changes have in common, and distinguish divine everlastingness: and primordiality, or undying and unborn existence, plus uniquely adequate retention of value or actuality once achieved, *both* from the merely eternal *and* from *our* way of being temporal — infinitely different as that also is. To assert time*less*ness of God's full actuality adds only a negation, and one that seems to cancel out concreteness altogether. It is abstract truths that can be timeless, like those of arithmetic. "Highest degree of intensity perfection" assumes that this phrase describes something conceivable positively without contradiction. How do we know this? I incline to think we face an open infinity here with no highest degree possible.

Does God have a rich inner life? I certainly think so. But note that I take even our inner life to consist not only in our perceptions of others but in our present memories of *our own past* experiences — not just their data but themselves. Introspection is not timeless, but (as Ryle says, and also Peirce and Whitehead as I read them) is a form or use of memory. Experiences prehend not themselves but their predecessors; some of these predecessors are one's own past states, that is to say: members of one's own "personally-ordered" society. Thus with new creatures there are *new divine subjects* intuiting, enjoying, their predecessors. There is no need for each new actual entity (divine or not) to prehend itself, it *is* itself with all its value.

Remember, too, that God enjoys not only all of our cosmic epoch but an infinity of others that in divine time preceded them (somewhat as in Origen's view). So our inner life is *almost* nothing compared to God's as aware not only of all past objects of divine prehensions but of all past divine prehensions of these objects. This is a to us unimaginably vast fullness of experience. Again, how substantive rather than verbal are our disagreements?

Here is another difference that I cannot interpret as Clarke does. I deny absolutely the notion that the unqualifiedly simple can embrace or possess anything complex. What is consistent is to say that the simple can be embraced by an actuality that is complex. (XY includes X.) The divine simplicity, like the divine, eternal and necessarily existent essence, is an abstraction that is divinely, as well as humanly, prehended and so, in the most concrete sense of inherence, is *in* the divine consciousness — which is the most complex of all actualities. This complexity is ideally integrated and reintegrated with each new divine prehension. The divine personal order is not interrupted by dreamless sleep, insanity, multiple personality, as ours is. Nor are its intuitions indistinct as to particulars and inadequately preservative of vividness.

Not only are the contents of God's worldly prehensions finite and contingent, so are the already actualized of these prehensions as subsequently divinely prehended. Knowledge of the finite cannot be simply infinite, just as knowledge of the contingent cannot be simply necessary. As the Greeks suspected, the finite is not less than the infinite but more, for only the definite, *this* rather than *that*, has beauty in the primary sense. Clarke does not mention the mistake I see in taking finitude as the mark of our inferiority in principle to God. *Fragmentariness*, being but a *part* of the finite, is the mark. God is non-fragmentary; his is the all-embracing finitude. This is incomparably more than the merely infinite. Similarly, divine relativity is the inclusive divine attribute, not absoluteness. The Hindu Sri Jiva Goswami, or one of his followers in the Hindu Bengali school, virtually said this long before I was born.

Sorry, I am aware of but reject the doctrine of intentionality as in Thomism. According to it, God knows the world because of the divine self-knowledge: the divine essence is cause of all things and in knowing the cause one knows all its *possible* effects. Yes, but possibility is incomparably less rich in definiteness than actuality. Ross, mentioned above, seems to know this; how it fits into his view of Thomas I do not know. To unqualifiedly know something is to possess it in all its qualities or values. Most of *our* knowledge is intentional only, and not possessive. That is how we are not divine. Husserl went badly wrong here, blurring the distinction between having as given and merely intending what may or may not be. When we (or anyone) prehend, the prehended must be; however, all nondivine prehension is indistinct, excludes most details from definite awareness. Only God can see that they are there even in us. The indistinctness is a Leibnizian doctrine, but his "no windows" means, no prehensions except those whose data are one's own past states.

If the past of creation is beginningless, then, although the divine actuality, like all actuality, has a certain finitude, it is *not in all dimensions finite*. But neither is it in all dimensions, or absolutely, infinite. It is not the actualization of all possible value. Each moment free creaturely (and divine) choices exclude forever values that the creatures, and *a fortiori* God prehending the creatures, could have had.

No less than Bertrand Russell agreed with me that the following is logically possible: Numerically there are, in the objectively immortal past, an infinity of achieved actualities; yet each moment there are additional actualities. Nothing has been taken away, something has been added. There must, in some sense, be *more*. Aesthetic richness need not mean the same as classification as to order of multiplicity. Each new state of the world is felt by God in contrast to all values already possessed. I find no benefit in giving up the idea that we increase the divine beauty or joy comparable to that of keeping the idea.

The reason I have not emphasized terms like "source," for the divine preëminence is that historically they went with underemphasis upon certain other terms. Causation is not handing out something already there; it is always *creative* and always receptive of past creativity — above all, divine creativity. The truly absolute infinity of the divine *potentiality* for value distinguishes deity from humanity by a more than finite difference, yet all actuality is, by definition, finite in some way. To be finite is to leave unactualized some of the absolute infinity of possibilities. The point of actualization is the gain in definiteness. Spinoza tried to make God *wholly*, or "absolutely" and in actuality, infinite and therefore denied contingency: his God is and has all that God could be or have. By admitting contingency in God, Clarke compromises his denial of change and finitude to God.

Clarke talks about "activities" in the Trinity without enabling me to see any reason why they could occur with no analogy to time. It is time that provides a real distinction between what might have been and what is, or what may yet be and what is. To say that God does X and might *have done* (note the words) something else instead implies, as Spinoza says, that we can conceive God as first not having done X and then as doing X. As Peirce says, time is "objective modality." 'Without time yet with modality' is a leap in the dark. I see no worse paradoxes in my view than in the Thomists'. And the new paradoxes may turn out to be more soluble than the older ones. (For instance, the Trinitarian "circulation," "giving and receiving," in mere eternity.)

That my view is not free from paradoxes as it now stands, I grant. Bell's Theorem in quantum physics may perhaps not help. I know too little of physics to be confident in such topics. As my first teacher in philosophy, Rufus Jones of Haverford, said, "There is an *impasse* in every system somewhere." Whitehead says similar things. If there were no difficulty in our understanding of God, it would not be God we were understanding. But when I compare my opportunities to think adequately with those of any Thirteenth century writer, especially one with so short a life as Thomas's, I think I must be stupid if I have done no better than he. Considering my childhood and youthful experiences of a very intelligent and highly-trained father, the seventy years and more that I've been thinking about the theistic problem, the many teachers of distinction I have had, the resources in comparative religion and comparative philosophy, and so on, it seems clear I have had many advantages. Therefore, with great assistance from many, including Clarke with his stimulating essay, I just may have gone farther than he quite sees in the process of improving upon classical theism. Improvements are sometimes painful; new linguistic habits come less easily with age. My father had a teacher, and I had many teachers, who deliberately broke with classical theism. I did not have to unlearn thinking in that way. I did have several Thomistic teachers here and abroad. And some of my most enthusiastic pupils or readers have had such teachers.

As I said in the beginning, I feel honored by the serious, and I now add the generous, way Fr. Clarke compares two forms of philosophical theology. Old as I am, my linguistic habits should, and perhaps, will change some, thanks to his essay.

Since writing the foregoing paragraph I have indeed acquired a new linguistic habit or two which I believe will constitute a marked improvement or addition. I thank Norris Clarke for this.

The medieval synthesis bequeathed to us a number of extreme, and as they stand unintelligible, dualisms, mitigated somewhat by hints that and how they can be reduced to moderate, more intelligible dualities. For a duality on the most general level to be intelligible, one pole of the contrast must furnish the positive explanation of the other. It must include or possess it in a more than spatial sense. (That "in" or inclusion is not exclusively spatial is shown by the truth that minutes are in hours as truly as inches are in feet! Also a multitude of 3 includes one of 2. Inclusion, in its reasonable general meaning, is far from a mere spatial or temporal metaphor.)

Among the medieval dualisms, not intelligible as they stand, are: mind and (mere) matter or subject and (mere) object; dependent and (entirely) independent; relative and (entirely, exclusively) absolute; soul and body or psyche and soma; value-maximal and nonmaximal (surpassable — by self? others? both?). Medieval hints as to how to reduce these unintelligibly extreme to legitimate dualities include the following. The Scholastics agreed with Aristotle that in all other cases knowing depends on the known, they should not have said the opposite about divine knowing. Indeed, it is clearer that infallible knowing must correspond or conform to the known than that what is called knowledge in us must do so. Since, then, God knows all things, God must in some way depend on all things, whereas we, knowing far from all things need not (and indeed cannot) depend in any such way on all things. God must have an infinitely excellent form of dependence as well as an infinitely excellent form of independence. Moreover, what God knows must in some genuine sense be in the divine knowledge, which must in some genuine sense be in God. We should recall what the Scholastics forgot or never knew, Plato's double proposition that bodies are in souls more truly than souls in bodies, and that the divine or cosmic soul contains and possesses its cosmic body. Also the mind-body relation in this case is obviously a one-many relation, and there are many souls in the cosmic body. Taking into account the cellular-molecular-atomic-particle structure now known of animal bodies, Plato's theological analogy becomes more definitely relevant than it could be in ancient times. We should also recall the medieval doctrine of *transcendentals*, or super-categorial ideas which apply to God as well as to all creatures. The neoclassical form of this doctrine is that the difference between the essential divine attributes and the universal creaturely categories is that the latter are the by-others-surpassable and the former the not-by-others-surpassable forms of knowledge, love, power, goodness, and the like. Diminish the divine attributes to allow for this difference in principle, not merely in degree, and you have what all singular creatures have in degree above zero. Bonventure seems to hint at this more than other Scholastics, and some renaissance thinkers (Campanella, Cardanus) make the principle more explicit. God is eminently powerful, knowing, loving; even the least creature has in some degree all of these qualities or capacities.

Leibniz achieved a partial further clarification by reducing, in minimal cases, knowledge or love to simple sensings or feelings (*petites perceptions* or *sentiments*). In this way the material or physical is the class of most primitive and widely distributed forms of the psychical; and the mind body relation is a relation between two or more levels of mind; it is a *mind-mind* relation, and in principle intelligible. This can, as I argued in an essay on "A World of Organisms," enable us to generalize beyond hylomorphism to psycho-soma-ticism, and this to a transcendental such that even God is psycho-somatic, and not simply "disembodied" mind or spirit.

It seems odd that it could be thought that deity might be incarnate in a single animal (a single human being) named Jesus but not in the cosmos as super-animal, as Plato implies in the Timaeus. The duality wave-particle can, in principle, I surmise, be treated as one aspect of the psycho-somatic duality without implying anything like the stark dualism of Descartes' inextended but

278

thinking substance or process and extended but not even sensing or feeling substance or process. Quantum physics in this aspect concerns processes so minute and rapid spatio-temporally as to be radically inaccessible to mere common sense.

I have shown elaborately in various writings that being absolute does not exclude being temporal, if absolute means independent. I am strictly independent of my remote descendants (if there ever are any) but they must be dependent on me for their existence — which does not mean that they will have no genuine freedom. On the contrary, if I strictly depended on their future existence and actions, then *they* would have no freedom. Determinism destroys freedom in both temporal directions. "Necessary and sufficient condition" as classically used is a symmetrical formula, meaning necessity in both directions. That is enough to condemn it as a literal truth. Hence I am unimpressed by Clarke's emphasis on the latter part of the formula. Leibniz's principle is too strong and excludes freedom, as Crusius wrote long ago. Kant, who reported this (causing me to look it up in Crusius), failed to see the point and hence had to resort to the absurdity of a wholly noumenal, timeless freedom for his ethics. How absurd it is was shown by his admission: "we do not even know that there are many rather than only one noumenon."

The moderate dualities appear in the way creatures, too, have some strict absoluteness (or independence) of successors born after their death and (apart from some extremely subtle, limited, and practically irrelevant, quantum phenomena) even of remote contemporaries, whereas all creatures depend for their very existence on their predecessors. On the contrary, God does not depend for very existence upon any definite existent or set of existents, but does depend for some contingent qualities upon every past existent in this and all so-far actualized cosmic epochs, and will depend for some future contingent divine qualities upon *every* creature that ever comes to exist, from none of which (if it comes to be after our deaths) will you or I get anything at all. Thus the ways we differ from God both in our absoluteness and in our relativity are more than differences of degree, they are differences in kind, infinite differences. So to the charge that I diminish divine transcendence I cannot respond otherwise than by saying that I think I make deity more intelligibly transcendent than classical theism or pantheism do. The "logic of ultimate contrasts" is the key.

By admitting contingent divine qualities and intrinsic relations to the world, Clarke opens the door to this logic, then tries to close it with reference to change. The neoclassical view affirms of God not just any kind of change but change only in the form of increase in aesthetic enrichment. To exclude this seems to me arbitrary logically, though it may seem unshocking because there is so much precedent for it. But I can cite many precedents on my side, both Greek and Biblical, and much support from changes in science since the Middle Ages. We now know how deep into reality becoming, or coming to be, goes, All natural science now is a kind of natural history. And many theologians imply and some clearly state something like a divine history.

Niebuhr spoke of "beyond history" but his approval (in print and conversation) of my view was too cordial to harmonize easily with the notion that he meant more than worldly history in the quoted phrase. Nor did he reject, although he stopped short of accepting, my view, which is Whitehead's, of objective immortality as sufficient overcoming of death. He preferred, he said, to leave the matter open, or a "mystery."

It is those who claim to *know* about our survival in other than divinely objective form that I wish to challenge. Also, those who insist that the survival must be forever. I deny that they can know this, and wonder if it makes sense. "Forever" is easy to say, but not so easy to really think, and it is difficult enough to justify thinking it of God without requiring believers to think it of themselves or ourselves. It is time now to stand by theism without adding all sorts of other ways of transcending what science can definitely test for its truth. My religion is belief in God and our ability to love God; the rest follows from that. I love myself and my friends, relatives, and readers as *finite, nay fragmentary*, spatio-temporally, apart from God's weaving all that we are between birth and death into imperishable wholes, everlasting but not timeless, in the everlasting but not timeless divine experience.

That divine temporality and worldly temporality (as grasped in my feeble understanding of physics, a science undergoing considerable change and expectations of more change) are not easily combined seems to me a serious but not a decisive objection. To understand deity without diminishing it to our level may not be any less difficult than this particular problem suggests it is.

For many years I have been aware of Fr. Clarke's critical comments on neoclassical theism and find it fitting that I have been at last put in the position of having to reply to them. In these difficult matters disagreement need not be looked upon as lack of respect. To judge from the account given of it by Frederick Ferre in his *Philosophy of Technology* (Englewood Cliffs, N.J.: Prentice Hall, 1988), Professor Clark's essay "Technology and Man" (see Mitcham and Mackey, eds., *Philosophy and Technology*, N.Y.: The Free Press, 1972) is a valuable contribution to our thought about its subject.

8. Cloots and Van der Veken on Panentheism

I came to know Drs. André Cloots and his teacher Jan Van der Veken well in Leuven and have admired them ever since. Cloots wrote his dissertation in Flemish on my philosophy, with an English summary. He concluded that Whitehead's system was more important than mine for theology, a comparison with which I have no quarrel. I rate Whitehead the most important metaphysician of this century. I add, however, that Whitehead himself told me three things that are relevant here: (1) he said that he would like to see a "conflation of his view with a more monistic one" [and the Cloots-Van der Veken essay terms my view more monistic than Whitehead's (hereafter W)]; (2) his idea of God is vague and needs clarification; (3) he rather expected me to be among the clarifiers.

I find CV (as I shall call this joint essay) mostly an admirable statement of my differences from W, although, as seems almost always to happen in this comparison — so difficult is it to avoid misunderstanding in interpreting and ambiguity in writing philosophical essays — I find some exaggerations in the contrasts drawn between myself and W. I am not aware of having used 'consciousness' differently from W. Nowhere, I think, have I ever said that atoms or even one-celled animals are conscious. They do have feelings. Also, I have repeatedly questioned if even infants are conscious. My universal analogical term is feeling, not consciousness, and the same is true of W. By 'psychical' I do not mean conscious; for that means, not only sentient but with a somewhat high level of "intellectual feelings," that is, thoughts. This is W's usage, except that he uses 'mental' analogically to cover also forms of thought too primitive to rate as conscious but yet with minimal feelings of open possibilities for the immediate future. To be conscious is not only to feel but to *think* that and what one feels and to think about thinking. I may not have drawn the line here exactly where W does; but we both treat consciousness as a high level, not the only level, of subjectivity. W's "reformed subjectivism" is my panpsychism or psychicalism. I see no important difference.

Concerning God as *causa sui*, W says that *all* actualities are partially *causa sui* and that God as consequent is in part created by others. Quoting Jules Lequier, I take the same line. I think W is somewhat wavering or inconsistent in his way of relating God to temporality. His "God is in a sense temporal" is also my view; but I insist on it more and try not to contradict it. I do not deny that there is an eternal aspect of possibility; but it is less definite than Whitehead's eternal objects. There are for me no definitely singular, hence no definitely plural, *qualitative* eternal essences, such as exactly blue, rather than blue-green, lavender, or bluish. Peirce here for me corrects W.

My view of God as creator is scarcely distinguishable from W's of God as "poet of the world," persuading it, luring it toward harmony and intensity. The poem, so far as divinely written and humanly knowable as such, includes the pattern of natural laws characterizing our cosmic epoch. The poem as finally filled out concretely is partly written by the creatures. The idea of a composer-director of a symphony is better. The performers make their own decisions as to just how to follow their instructions. Or, if God is the writer of the play, the actors and actresses *ad lib* at least a little *all* the time. W and I agree that words have to be "stretched" somewhat to do the job meta-physics requires. Language can hardly have developed primarily to make metaphysics easy.

My sharpest difference from W about God is that I think "*an* actual entity" cannot be any closer to an adequate classification for deity, if as close, as "a personally-ordered society" of actual entities (and here I seem less monistic than Whitehead) with all nondivine societies and actualities forming the divine body. God is not *an* individual, but *the* individual, the only one *ideally* self-creative as well as partially-by-others-created, inclusively and ideally prehending all, which means feeling the feelings of all, measuring and summing up all actual values and therewith all actualities. *To be is to be for God.* Since God is also for all as well as for self, God is, in this triadic sense, being itself. I sharply disagree with Heidegger here. Since I affirm universal freedom even more insistently than W, it is difficult to see how my treatment of evil differs from W's. If there is an "author of the play" it is only in the sense of producing an outline, vague as to all particular details, with no guarantee that the details will all be unimportant, but with a guarantee that there will be a performance and that the risks of creaturely freedom are justified by its opportunities. (I emphasize the goodness and ideal persua-siveness or power of God as much as W does.)

I must mention the fact that I never use *Absolute* as synonym for divine, but strongly object to this usage. *The Divine Relativity* tries to show that God's absoluteness is merely an aspect of God's ideal relativity to whatever worlds are actual or possible. And I do not primarily start with God's inclusiveness or wholeness and try to deduce divine love, or human love for God. Rather I start with human love for God and other persons, and (with help from Plato and Whitehead) for the singular members of one's own body, and the commandment to love God with *all* one's being, and then argue that one cannot so completely love anything but an all-loving being. In this last point I am my father's disciple. Also Paul Tillich's. I do not start with mere knowing but with love as the concreteness of knowing ("to know is to sympathize" wrote Carlyle). W's "feeling of feeling," as the only concrete form of prehending or intuiting, supports this. So does his reformed subjectivism. These also support my adoption of the Platonic analogy of the World Soul. W rejects this analogy but gives no indication of having considered how his own modern scientific construction of the mind-body relation removes the worst difficulty that analogy had in Plato's time, when *no one* knew how to overcome a hopeless mind-body dichotomy.

"His thought includes non-thought." So does my thought include it. 'Feeling', with extremely minimal 'mentality' in W's sense, is also to be taken into account. Above all, collectives, even trees, are not, as units, sentient; only their microconstituents are.

I regard Heidegger's sweeping rejection of traditional metaphysics as arrogant and ignorant. What metaphysicians since Hegel did he know? Did he know about the Socinians (long before Hegel), about Fechner, Lequier, Peirce, Montague, Whitehead, and many others? Gadamer admits that his teacher's view of Plato was "eccentric." I do see a point in Heidegger's view that classical theism was "Plato for the masses," except that it was a seriously onesided Platonism as well as an incongruous version of Aristotle, plus misinterpretation of the books of the Bible (as Spinoza said).

C and V are right in suggesting that I have learned from Spinoza. However, I never accepted the latter's definition of God as the absolutely infinite substance, nor his deduction therefrom that not only does God exist necessarily but that all the things and ideas which form modes of God are also necessary. Nor did I accept his preference of space over time as attribute of deity. I never accepted his concept of substance as having only necessary properties, a concept found also in Leibniz and only by inconsistency ostensibly reconciled with freedom in the creatures. Another important difference is that I assert and Spinoza denied that God loves the creatures. In view of these differences, the statement that my view of the divine whole has "all the marks of the Spinozistic substance" is decidedly incorrect. As is well known, modal concepts are central in my thinking. Spinoza had no reasonable theory of modality, just as the Stoics did not. Only *one* of my Harvard teachers (R. B. Perry) was a determinist to the end, and he was a secular humanist and anti-idealist whom I took seriously primarily as counterbalance to Hocking's idealism. William James convinced me early that determinism cannot be true of human actions, and Peirce, that it cannot be true of any singular agents in nature. Hocking convinced me that God cannot be immutable or without an open future. (He learned this from James, I imagine, though he had arguments of his own for it.)

It seems that continental thought cannot easily escape from Heidegger's influence. And certainly it is felt in this country. As a critic of much of the older metaphysics, Heidegger makes some valid points; but his selection of examples is heavily biased toward the Germans, to the neglect of British, French, Italian, and American thinkers. On some issues he thinks as I do, thus he opposes the exaltation of eternity, necessity, mechanism, materialism, in contrast to the temporality, becoming, contingency and freedom, of life and mind as we experience them in ourselves. His distinction between *Umwelt* and *Mitwelt* is useful; but, if fully generalized, "Mitwelt" can be shown to embrace the entire "Umwelt," provided we take seriously the view of the microscopic and submicroscopic, as described in cell theory and atomic theory.

9. Endo's Comparative Study

Hiroshi Endo's essay is a courageous attempt to cross cultural, regional, linguistic, boundaries and compare several thinkers who are rather widely dissimilar. One of them, Levinas, has had no influence on my thinking, though I know how highly some regard him. Others will have to judge Endo's uses of his writings. Although I was exposed directly to Husserl's influence by hearing, reading, and talking with him, the phenomenological aspects of my philosophy are derived more from Peirce, James, Bergson, and Whitehead than from Husserl (or Heidegger, whose lecturing I heard even more extensively). I found Husserl at fault in two major respects: he had no adequate theory of the difference between intentionality, as referring to realities that may or may not exist, though the intending of them does, and having as given or what Whitehead calls prehending, the data of which are independent realities and are necessary for the prehending to occur. Objects require subjects, but not the particular subjects that prehend them. Peirce and Whitehead, independently, are both realists in this sense. In Peirce, this is what is meant by Firstness and Secondness.

If one has a second child, then one has had a first child; but one's first child may be the last. Thus numerical relations illustrate dependence and independence.

I revise Peirce's Thirdness so that the point is not that with Thirdness there are exactly three entities, one of which is dependent on the other two; but rather, in addition to dependence and independence, there is a third relation, illustrated by the mathematics of chance, that is, the theory of statistical order or probability, Peirce emphasized this type of order but did not use it in his theory of categories. He did use it in his theory of becoming or temporality. If of two events one succeeds the other, the successor will depend upon, be second to, and presuppose the other. This is the necessary connection that Hume failed to find in experience and assigned to animal faith. But in memory we intuit secondness, being dependent upon previous experience. Surprise is one of Peirce's examples. At least two experiences are required for surprise, one of previous expectation and the other of retrospective conflict or at least contrast of the unexpected with the remembered expectation. Or take the experience of struggle. It cannot be a relation of an experience with itself.

Peirce emphasizes immediate memory, as later did Whitehead independently. The notorious mistakes of memory, both thinkers saw, had misled countless philosophers into an absurd scepticism. What are called such mistakes are not really mistakes of memory in the primary, most immediate sense, but of several other relationships. In remembering a just previous sensation a tenth of a second ago, say a previous tone as heard, or a twinge of pain as just felt, what room for mistakes is there? How one verbally describes the content of the memory, its pitch for instance is clearly more than mere memory. If the question is, "Did not the British King who had not been at the Battle of Waterloo nevertheless remember being there?" My theory is, "He remembered *imagining* being there and, since imagining has similarities to perceiving, it is reasonable to suppose that he misinterpreted his actual memory of his previous imagining as remembering a previous *perceiving* of the battle." If one is careful on these two points much confusion will be avoided. I defy anyone to prove that there are *any* memories that are mere present experiences devoid of any genuinely past experiences as contents.

Consider the first feeling with which an embryo or fetus begins its sequences of primitive feelings. In the first such feeling there can be no past experience of that individual animal to remember. There may still be some given past experience, but it must be that of cellular members of the fetus's body which in its first weeks is only a cell colony.

Whitehead's view, which there is no reason I know of to think Peirce would have had to reject, was that *all* experience has the immediate past for its most direct datum or given. When we look at a star the past we see is not the star as it is now but as it was long ago. What we call memory is more informatively classified as personal perception of the personal or individual past; what we call perception is more informatively called (as I like to call it) memory of the unindividual or impersonal past, the environment's past. Here one's body forms one's most intimate environment, especially the nervous system's immediate past.

This is a clean-cut realism with respect to the data of our most direct intuitions or prehensions of the past. Past events were not dependent upon their particular successors, but they were, and all events are, dependent upon their particular predecessors. Time is cumulative creation of events, "the past is the sum of accomplished facts." When there are new accomplishments of facts there will be to that extent a new past, but by addition, not by reaching back and altering the earlier facts. We conform to our ancestors, we cannot conform them to us. Changing our thought or feeling about them will not give them any new thoughts or feelings but without them we would not have existed at all.

Here is another point that Husserl misses: we do not know other minds than ours *only* by observing behavior in other animal bodies analogous to our own behavior. When we feel pain or physical pleasure we experience a feeling, an obviously mental process; but it is just as obviously physical, since it is spatial (some pains are point-like and some massive) and it is located in space as intuited. Moreover, we feel pain when some portion of the body is being injured. When shaving, this becomes clear enough. Either there is no feeling in cells, or they cannot enjoy being injured. I have yet to be told how we could ever know that there is no feeling in cells or atoms. To explain why we suffer when our cells are injured, the simplest account is clearly to say that the mind-body relation just is a relation of sympathy: hurt my cells and you hurt me; cause my cells, some of them, to suffer and then, under suitable conditions, for instance with no anaesthetic, you cause me to suffer; for I care instinctively about (some of) my cells, I literally feel something of their feeling. If my cells generally are in healthy condition, and themselves have good feelings, then I have a pervasive feeling of well-being also. They can give me feelings for they have feelings. Sadism and masochism are not hopelessly difficult to understand. The emotional complexity of human experience is considerable.

My conclusion from the above, and many other lines of inquiry, is that so far from the truth being that we cannot directly experience "other mind," the truth rather is that we *cannot not* experience other mind, provided we allow for mind on radically subhuman levels.

Richard Zaner has shown that Descartes himself knew that his dualism of mind and mindless matter was untrue. He said of pain, it is clearly mental and yet it is clearly physical (with location and volume). How differently theorizing about materialism and dualism might have developed if this discovery by and about Descartes had been clearly made and assimilated in Descartes's time. As Leibniz did see, materialism is groundless, since the concept of mind*less* matter is a negation that no experience could justify. Stones do not feel, for what feels acts, and stones are inert; but atoms and molecules are by no means inert. To say the stone moves when it falls is only to say that its vast collection of molecules or atoms moves as a group. That the single stone moves is shorthand for the way members of the collection change locations. Each of them moves, not by mere falling, but also with *individual* to and fro movements consituting their heat energy.

Epicurus *knew* that there is no inert matter, if to know means to believe with good reason, but he did not, it seems, even imagine the Leibnizian attribution of primitive forms of the psychical ('*petite perceptions*') to atoms. Yet, never forget, he did imagine little bits of freedom in them! Why not feeling as well? Here Peirce and others took the final step. I did so before I knew any of these philosophers, on the basis of my phenomenological awareness that our sensations generally (not just pains or physical pleasures of obvious kinds) are feelings, values — not neutral qualities. They are intrinsically elements of our enjoying-suffering the world. Eventually I learned that Croce had become an idealist in a similar way. The writers who helped me most in all this were Emerson, Wordsworth, Shelley, Coleridge, and the novelist H. G. Wells (stimulated by William James) and James on religious experience. These are people who knew more about feelings than some scientists, psychologists, or philosophers ever will.

If I understand at all what Levinas, according to Endo, means by "visage," or face to face encounter with others, as leading us to God via ethics, it has some resemblance to what two other writers with whom I feel basic agreement have written. Consider the following passage from Whitehead's *Modes of Thought* (Lecture 5, Sec. 8). True, Whitehead seems to go from the sense of deity to the sense of our human fellows, or more generally of our fellow creatures. But the main point is the togetherness of the two senses.

Deity . . . is that factor in the universe whereby there is importance, value, and ideal beyond the actual. It is by reference of the spatial immediacies to the ideals of Deity that the sense of worth beyond ourselves arises. The unity of a transcendent universe, and the multiplicity of realized actualities both enter into our experience by this sense of Deity. Apart from this sense of transcendent worth, the otherness of reality would not enter into our consciousness. There must be value beyond ourselves. Otherwise everything experienced would be merely a barren detail in our own solipsistic mode of existence. We owe to the sense of Deity the obviousness of the many actualities of the world, and the obviousness of the unity of the world for the preservation of the values realized and for the transition to ideals beyond realized fact.

Thus Space, Time, and Deity are general terms which indicate three types of reflective notions. The understanding of the nature of things in terms of such concepts is what distinguishes the human species from other animals. The distinction is not absolute . . .

Our sense of space is our sense of not being alone, of coexistence. It is how we have neighbors with whom, as Peirce said, we intimately react. Without space we could have only ancestors and descendants, but no neighbors. *The intuition of space is the refutation of solipsism.* I reached this conclusion early in my intellectual Odyssey. "I am here, some others are there" is a given, not a mere hypothesis. Heidegger's "being in the world" (which I encountered later) is correct and Husserl was to this extent a poor phenomenologist, as he also was in not realizing the affective content, the enjoyment-suffering aspect, of sensation.

In one of the two greatest mystical passages in Wordsworth, beginning "Brook and road" (and sometimes put into collections of poems as a single poem, though it is just a portion of the *Prelude*), the poet comes remarkably close to saying what Whitehead says in the above quoted passage. Though the poem is without the words space, time, or deity, all three ideas are obviously there. Seldom has language reached such heights as in either of the two cases I am comparing with what, I gather from Endo, Levinas has to say.

For Whitehead, there is indeed an intimate connection between our sense of responsible, ethical mutuality and our sense of deity, and it seems Levinas thinks something similar. A number of writers support the view that what distinguishes us from other animals is that we can think such abstract notions as space, time, and deity — not that God is a mere abstraction, but that the defining characteristics of *divineness* (such as all-others-surpassing knowledge, power, or love) transcend in principle the *spatial, temporal* and other limitations of our knowledge, power, or love, and that we have an idea of this difference. The English theologian John Oman made much the same point early in this century. By animals generally, as Reinhold Niebuhr liked to say, the world is felt from the animal itself as center; we too, as animals, *feel* the world in this way; however, we *think*, if we are rational, that no animal is the center. Our ability to be more or less objective in this intersubjective sense makes us images of deity, and our realization that we remain animal fragments of reality gives us the idea that the truth has its seat in God not in us. We get glimpses of it and can serve God by contributing to the future of life as adequately cherished by and its satisfactions retained in God.

I have no quarrel with those who believe in God without making use of arguments for doing so. I do hope, however, they will examine carefully just what notions of God they entertain. I also think it important that there be reasonable grounds for religious belief since the fact, if it could be a fact, that all possible arguments for belief are fallacious would be, for some, a cogent argument *against* belief. So many arguments in the past have been fallacious that I have felt it necessary to revise these arguments. The revisions include improvements in the concept of deity, also in more careful distinctions or relations between essence, or defining traits, existence, and concrete actuality, and a careful distinction between existing necessarily and having exclusively necessary qualities. Not the dichotomy essence-existence suffices here, but only the trichotomy essence, existence, actuality. The third item deals with the question, existing just how, or in what state?

I agree with Endo and many logicians that possibility is the key to modality, necessity being what all of the relevant set of possibilities have in common. I object, however, to "possible worlds" as at best ambiguous, or, if given the classical Leibnizian meaning, simply the metaphysical absurdity of "possible individuals." If possibilities were fully individuated and particularized, there would be no point in actualizing them. The problem is not how we can, from our actual world, have "access" to individuals in purely possible worlds; the problem is the meaning of actualization if it is not individuation and particularization. It is in *our* world that potentialities, real possibilities, function every moment to furnish the difference between the settled past and the indeterminate but to-be-determined future. Becoming is *creation* of particularity and individuality, not mere selection among possible individuals or particulars. As Aristotle said, "an existing man is simply a man." There are no definite '*a's* or *an's*' in mere possibility. Futurity and possibility are two aspects of one feature of reality, and both are essentially nonparticular. Only past facts are fully definite and qualitatively complete. Before I existed there was, and in pure eternity there is, no single possibility or set of possibilities duplicating my qualities.

Leibniz's extreme view of individual identity, which excluded genuine freedom from the creation, misconceived the significance of what Whitehead called the "defining traits" of self-identity. The fully particular realities are not individuals but states (experiences), which "become but do not change." Even speaking of "possibilities" in the plural is somewhat misleading. As Leibniz assumed in dealing with spatial plurality, *where there are definite plurals there are definite singulars.* This applies to temporal as well as spatial pluralities. The successive states of individuals or substances are the final subjects of predicates, the final monads; not I or you, but I-now or you-now. These do not preexist as possibilities. Peirce, Bergson, James, Dewey, G. H. Mead support this position as well as Whitehead; indeed *he* seems sometimes to deny it.

Endo thinks that Whitehead should not have "separated" the general nature of creativity and the primordial nature of God. In a sense I agree with this. Primordially and everlastingly there are partly self-creative creatures *with* the self-creative and, in a sense, all-creative deity. What Whitehead was trying to do by distinguishing divine from creaturely self-creativity, and therefore from creativity as such, was to avoid the idea of creatures as mere puppets making no decisions additional to those made by God. Not all self-or-other creating is divine. Yet all of it becomes everlasting possession of deity through divine prehensions whereby creatures are made part-creators of the divine life. As so often, the difficulty here is partly verbal, to escape ambiguities that are all too likely to be resolved in the wrong way.

I appreciate Endo's distinctive perspective on metaphysical problems.

10. Gutowski on Philosophical Theology

Piotr Gutowski's questions are searching. My doctrine of God as dually transcendent is not an elaboration of the revelation of a given religion but is a doctrine of general metaphysics. However, since we are not God, and the existence of our species or of our world is a contingent, not a metaphysical, truth, the metaphysician should not pretend to be uninfluenced by his or her historical situation, exposed as we all are to the influence and challenge of one or more religious or anti-religious traditions. Although I hold, with Karl Popper, that metaphysical truths, whether or not we find them, are not strictly speaking testable empirically, I also hold with Popper that science (and common sense) cannot (and should not try to) divest themselves entirely of metaphysical commitments. In addition, I hold that the great advances in science tend to bring about metaphysical advances and are also in part brought about by these advances. It never was good metaphysics to suppose the absolute continuity of becoming (that nature makes no leaps) or that the heavenly bodies do not change, or that species do not. Absolute changelessness can only be abstract, that which is common to all change, or to all change after a certain time. This applies to God.

Epicurus as metaphysician, whose atoms were not entirely without freedom, anticipated Peirce and Whitehead by more than two thousand years; but it was easier to see the point when science had discovered the statistical laws of gasses, and easier still after quantum theory had gone as far as Heisenberg and the half-life laws. Since atomism meant a kind of spatial discontinuity, something like a quantum theory of becoming might well have been considered (and indeed by Buddhists was considered) long before Whitehead and Von Wright, two mathematical logicians, offered formal arguments for the metaphysical necessity of temporal discreteness.

Pure infallible rationality is not a human possibility. I argue that Peirce's excessive continuity-ism (his Synechism) was irrational on his own principles, but his father's fascination with continuity misled him. He should have anticipated Heisenberg in principle (not in the quantitative sense) by admitting that nature must make leaps and that his tychism or chancism is justified by the way nature combines both potential continuity and actual discontinuity, rather than by continuity (spatial and temporal) alone.

Another example of metaphysical progress is that the circular view of planetary orbits — on the ground that a circle is the "most beautiful" curve and that God will prefer the more beautiful — was (we can now see) mistaken, not because of the assumption about God aiming at beauty but because a circle is by no means the most beautiful curve. It is only the most simple, in a rather trivial sense. Any artist can make a reasonably perfect circle, but so what? Whitehead's "seek simplicity, and distrust it" is perhaps the most powerful light ever cast in as few words on intellectual history. People sought simplicity and were too easily and for too long satisfied with the first form of simplicity that occurred to them. It is the business of rational thinkers to know in principle what, for all they are in a position to know in particular, they may be missing.

The first rule in metaphysics, I rather think, is, "Consider what your affirmations deny; are you in a position to deny it?" Leibniz said, but did not consistently act upon, the proposition: "Metaphysicians err in what they deny, not in what they assert." Yet he denied creativity or genuine freedom by his extreme principle of sufficient reason. Then he had to sneak freedom in to cover God's action in choosing the best possible world and to dispose of the contradiction by the frivolous distinction between metaphysical and moral necessity, despite the truth he also affirmed or implied that God's moral as well as cognitive perfection is deducible from the concept of deity, as also is the existential necessity of God as defined.

Perhaps Gutowski does not distinguish sufficiently between theology as theory of deity and theology as doctrine about religion as concerned also with the human response to God in organized religions. The latter is not merely metaphysical but involves contingent historical facts of various kinds. Various religions make claims of this kind. Evaluating these involves scientific problems, and indeed many forms of empirical knowledge. Only very abstract aspects will be metaphysical. For instance, in what sense, if any, *could* God be uniquely incarnate in one otherwise non-divine individual?

Bultmann once answered the question about the difference between the God of philosophy and the God of religion by saying, "The first is the God of anyone, the second is your God and my God." I would say, rather, the first is the God of any creature whatever. In process philosophy, as Whitehead and I, with many others, conceive it, every actual entity prehends God, in most cases not consciously so. It feels God but may not be able to think God. It follows from my theory of the relation between experience and what it experiences, its given data, that these data are whatever the occurrence of that experience required as pre-conditions. With Whitehead I hold that the divine existence is one of these required conditions of any and every actual entity. Every single actual entity at least feels God. Only somewhat high forms of actuality think God.

I learn from Peirce, Husserl, Heidegger, Whitehead, and still others that metaphysics must look to direct human experience for its samples of categorial terms such as existence, actuality, dependence, independence, concrete, abstract, subject-object (in the sense of the given, not in the sense of the merely intended). I learn from Peirce, more than from Whitehead, Husserl, or Heidegger, that one should look to extremely simple mathematical truths and elementary truths of formal logic for help in finding the most universal aspects of experience as such. Peirce's Firstness, Secondness, and Thirdness, somewhat revised, come in here. *Firstness* is the independence of the present from the details of the future (there are no such details while the future is merely future); *Secondness* is the dependence of the present on the past in both memory and perception. Whitehead's prehension helps here. *Thirdness* is the mixture of dependence and independence that relates the present to the future. There are things that definitely will be, but the future involves also what may or may not be, granted the present actuality. The proposition that whatever happens was already "going to happen" long before is an attempt to coerce reality by a verbal formula, not an expression of knowledge. Similarly the proposition that causation essentially means both necessary and sufficient conditions for exactly what happens is a purely verbal argument for determinism. Nicolai Hartmann relied on this argument. By such procedures one can prove so much that it is reasonable to say they prove nothing. Quantum indeterminism only strengthens the case for partial indeterminacy; there never was a strong case for complete determinacy. It was always a leap in the dark and in an unwise direction. Peirce and some other physicists and philosopers saw this before Heisenberg. Indeed, Epicurus saw it.

I have certainly never said or intended anything like "contradiction is the foundation of thought." In method I am not Hegelian (or Marxian). Metaphysical thought is indeed the search for the consistency of the most universal categories, but scientific thought is the search for empirically, that is perceptually testable, explanations of contingent facts. It is incomparably richer than mere metaphysics. A complete philosophy of religion is much more than a theory of knowledge; it is a theory of our human condition, and its focus is on love not mere knowing. It explicates our love for God, God's love for us, and our love (and hate) for fellow creatures. In addition, since concepts derive their meaning from perception and from behavior, questions of consistency are significant only when we know, from perceived and pragmatically elucidated examples, the positive meanings of our terms. Error in metaphysics is shown not merely by contradiction but by failure to provide any definite and positive as well as consistent meaning for our assertions. Did Spinoza have such a meaning for "modes"? I am far from being the only one who thinks that he did not. Did Hegel have a clear meaning for "contingent"? Did Plato have such a meaning for 'absolute beauty'? I think not. Leibniz tried to help him, but unsuccessfully.

In metaphysics we are looking, as mathematicians look, for logical relations of consistency, dependence, and logical independence, but we are looking for these logical relations among ideas other than those of elementary formal logic. The idea of God, which (here I unhesitatingly disagree with Heidegger) is, in one of its aspects, the central ontological idea, but it is not itself a "logical constant." However, tradition has used terms like "knower of all," "lover of all," "cause of all," "independent of all," "all-surpassing," as definitive of the term *God*. "All" is certainly a logical constant. So, in one meaning, is *independent*. My strategy has been to look for elementary logical truths relevant to the idea of God, as well as to the idea of self-identity of things or persons through change, also the idea of causality, and to relate these truths to the extra-logical ideas of *value* involved in the all-surpassing status of deity.

I think I have shown, if anything philosophical can be shown, that traditional metaphysical controversies greatly oversimplified problems. God as *causa sui* is a typical half-truth, as is God as *first cause*. It is, I hold, just as true that God is causally influenced *by* all as that God *influences* all (neither statement would be true of you or me). I have shown that debates between theists and theists, or theists and atheists, have used concepts that involve a choice of one among precisely 16 possible conceptual "combinations" in the mathematical sense, and that most of these 16 were not clearly in the minds of the disputants. Nine of the 16 could be called theistic, especially 6 of these, and 4 are clearly atheistic. The one I favor can be read into Plato but otherwise for nearly two millennia it was ignored or misinterpreted (Philo Judaeus), it reappeared somewhat clarified in the Socinians, and finally, in Fechner, Whitehead, and others, it has been further clarified and developed.

11. Ishihara on Buddhism

I cannot do any justice to the complex subtleties of the history of Buddhism. My present plethora of tasks imposes limits additional to those set by lack of knowledge. Dr. John S. Ishihara has somewhat clarified a topic I have long wondered about, the extent to which we can trust Tscherbatski's statement that Buddhism in the Southern form was an extreme (Hume-like) pluralism while in the Northern form it became an extreme monism. However, I still think that the Buddhist ideal of finding a middle way between extremes was not fully realized. Nor did the West fully realize this ideal. In *Wisdom as Moderation* I make the attempt to help in this endeavor.

In my view the subtle details of the long Buddhist development are of limited importance for the West, and perhaps even for the East. Our practical and scientific problems today are so complicated, and some of them, like that of nuclear annihilation, so pressing and threatening, that we may have little time and energy for such controversies. These were natural enough when there was almost no hard science able to say, even in broad principle, what matter is and what human bodies are (and no mathematics adequate to deal with the structures of physical reality), but they are less opportune now that we have some knowledge of physical reality and know (from what Peirce called "exact logic") the difference between loose and rigorous reasoning better than was, in my view, possible in the prescientific past.

What we need to learn from Buddhism is above all the theoretical basis for the doctrine of universal compassion. Christianity taught this, but had no metaphysics that made sense out of it. "I love myself because I am myself, but I may not love you in the least because I am not you" expresses a superstitious absolutizing of the notion of self-identity. (Various Westerners have seen this, but until recently little attention was paid to their remarks on this topic.) Moreover, the universality of death shows (as Peirce, when a young man, said) that our aim should transcend our own future advantage; also, we should love the neighbor "as the self" because both of us are, in the end, but contributions to future life. I came to a similar view at the beginning of my adulthood. In my view medieval Christianity made a tragic mistake in so viewing our destiny as to make it appear that self-interest (including the desire to escape Hell and attain Heaven, was the only rational reason to act ethically. Bishop Paley makes this idea explicit, and Aquinas is not very different. So one loved the neighbor above all as means for fulfilling self-love. This is not love but supposedly expedient selfishness. I see only bad psychology, and bad ethics and theology, in this. I would think more highly of Buddhism, to be frank, if it had rejected the notion of transmigration. At least (in most of its forms) it did not make posthumous careers final ends. Yet it also failed to make clear what else positively is the final end. "Escape from birth and death" and "from suffering" is a negative goal. Surely the goal must be positive.

I grant that Amida Buddhism is in some respects close to Western theism, but it is too otherworldly to give me much comfort. Like some of the founders of Judaism I believe strongly that our business is in this world and in this, for each person, single life span. We should indeed live for the future of life during all the future, but I find a false rationalism in the notion that what we suffer or enjoy between birth and death is somehow proportionate to, and explained largely by, what *we* did in previous incarnations. Chance is inherent in freedom and simply without freedom there is nothing, bare nothing. Put positively, freedom (and with it chance) is everywhere.

It is sometimes said that reincarnation helps us to feel our kinship to the other animals since they may be or have been in previous phases human beings. For me the evolutionary view of creation, theistically interpreted, will in a scientific age do all that is relevant in such uses of transmigration.

Ishihara does not mention vegetarianism. Although I do not go all the way with this doctrine, I have deep respect for it and believe that the West needs to cut down drastically on its indulgence in wasteful indirect ways of producing protein (in far greater than needful amounts) via animal bodies themselves produced by much more consumption of vegetable protein than would otherwise be required for direct human nourishment. In the long run the human species cannot be maintained by this inefficient method. It results in overgrazing and destruction of nature.

Buddhism should also be honored for its much better record than the theistic religions, so far as I read history, in the war-peace problem, which is the most immediately threatening one of all thanks to nuclear explosives. At their worst, Christianity, Islam, and atheistic communism seem to have been partly, but significantly, responsible for the great genocides of recent history. The most recent was in Cambodia. Sartre disciples are said to have been responsible for that. Buddhism has made a more effective separation between the attainment of Nirvana and militaristic nationalism than believers in God sometimes have made between divine glory and milltary prowess. This, however, is a matter in which a philosopher remains, with human beings generally, in danger of talking nonsense.

I have yet to see that anything profound can be said by talking of emptiness that cannot be at least as well said in another way. That nothing in the world is entirely independent of all other things and in this very special sense has no "self-being" is true. But that experience of beautiful music is a positive value is not in the least cancelled out by its having been made possible by composers and performers. Nor do the causes of suffering cancel out the suffering. I prefer William Blake's language:

He who bends to himself each joy
Doth the winged life destroy;
But he who kisses each joy as it flies
Lives in eternity's sunrise.

Here is the positive meaning of non-attachment. Life is a gift, and the gift can be returned to the giver, whereby "our fleeting days acquire abiding significance," as a Jewish ritual has it.

The contributor will I hope not mind if I say that he blows hot and cold on the question of whether there is ultimately any permanence of value-achievements. He says that this is a question of fact, and we must be able to face things as they are, whether or not they meet our wishes. He also says that for Buddhism there is a treasury of values. Here I go with Albert Schweitzer. "Wishful thinking" is a weakness if it means insistence on *contingent* values, regardless of empirical evidences of their attainability. However, if there are beliefs without which in the long run life is "a tale told by an idiot, full of sound and fury, signifying nothing," so that our decisions and choices have no rational aim or criterion of comparative importance and add up to nothing good, then I hold with Schweitzer that the very act of living contradicts us if we renounce such beliefs. It cannot be rational to deny the possibility of a rational aim. The will to live has its own implications. Animal life is voluntary, mature human animal life is reflexively, consciously voluntary. I sometimes think of religion as the means whereby a vigorously thinking animal re-achieves on a conscious level the faith in life's value that the other animals have on an emotional level. Bergson, in his *Two Sources* book, gives a brilliant development of this theme. For me, he and Schweitzer settle this issue. Peirce had similar ideas. There are fatuous pessimisms as well as fatuous optimisms, and our attitude toward them is no mere question of fact. Thoughtful life that negates life itself is an absurdity. "Life is absurd" is an absurd proposition, in spite of Camus and Sartre. I deny that they make their case. Talking one way, they live another. Similarly with Schopenhauer and Leopardi.

Buddha found orthodox Hinduism unconvincing and unsatisfying; Sartre and Camus found classical theism similarly not to the point. Heidegger rebelled against his theological training, and retained of deity only a vague poetic residue. Wittgenstein found himself lacking in faith in the theological schemes he knew about. I remark that, for all we know, none of these people knew much about the forms of theism that have been emerging in the last few centuries in various parts of the world, and that are critical not only of classical theism but of classical pantheism, as well as of Advaita Vedantism, usually considered the orthodox form of Hinduism. Even in France, although

Bergson's philosophy points in the direction of the neoclassical (or dually transcendent) way of conceiving deity, Bergson failed to work out the implications of his best insights. In my country Dewey never even gave noticeable consideration to his colleague Montague's version of process theism (derived from Peirce rather than Whitehead).

"Refutation by neglect" has a certain justification and it can produce results, but it is surely a hit or miss, highly fallible way of disposing of theoretical possibilities. I think there has been too much casual guessing as to what is worth looking into in the philosophizing of this century. What did Heidegger know of Whitehead's or my theism, or of . . . I could go on? Ditto for Wittgenstein. How much did Russell know when he finally settled his accounts with religion? Santayana? He read *Process and Reality* and hated it. But this was long after he was still psychologically capable of learning new ways of thinking or feeling religiously.

Richard Rorty was my student for a year and did do some studying of Peirce and Whitehead. Yet in his remarks about religious questions he makes no use of my way of thinking or Whitehead's, and disposes of the idea of God by a scornful reference to the simple equating of 'divine' with 'infinite', an equation that (as he must, it seems, know) neither I nor Whitehead, (and not Berdyaev, Bergson, Peirce, Socinus, Lequier, etc.) accept. God is to be thought of as, equally transcendently, infinite *and* finite.

I end by quoting a remarkable Buddhist text, which I dare to take with some seriousness: "There is an eternal being, unborn and undying; were this not so, we could not ourselves escape from birth and death." How is this compatible with the total impermanence emphasized by Ishihara? Note too that the quotation explicates 'eternal' not as denial of all change or novelty, but rather as denial of a complete beginning or a complete ending in the life of the Supreme form of individual identity. I sometimes think of the Western absolutizing of personal identity as an expression of the unconscious wish (which Reinhold Niebuhr attributes to us human beings) to *be* God, rather than the localized and fallible fragments of life that we in fact are. I am glad that I was brought up to be content to worship, and not to rival, the deity. If "That art thou", the Vedantist saying, means, "That should be what thou carest about," I understand it, but I fail to see the identity of what I am with what I care about. Even God cares not just about God, but also about you and me and the sparrows. At its best theism is a genuine, though not one-sided or extreme, realism and pluralism, as well as a kind of monism and idealism.

In an issue of *Japanese Religions* (18, No. 2) are four essays comparing Christian theology and several Japanese forms of Buddhism. Certain common elements are found. In one respect I think T. G. Hand's "Mahayana Consciousness and the Christian Doctrine of the Personal God" is subtly misleading. I quote: "As Yamada Mumon experienced, the more he used names for the absolute, the farther away God became." In this use of the term "absolute" I see a confusion common to Hand and classical theism. The

298

trouble with 'absolute' is not only that it stands for a concept but that it stands for two radically distinct concepts, confused together. If *absolute* connotes the contrary of *relative*, then some of us hold that to identify God with *the absolute* is a piece of idolatry. (It is just as true, and if possible more important, that the God worthy of worship is relative as that God is absolute.) The other meaning of *absolute* is value-superiority in comparison with all others. To be relative or nonrelative are not unequivocally valuational terms. There are good and bad, inferior and superior ways of being relative, and the same with being nonrelative. After all, we can say, "absolutely false" as well as "absolutely true." The Buddhist suspicion of concepts is historically explained partly by the failure of theists for many centuries to find the best concepts for explicating the idea of worshipful superiority.

Hand has much to say about "relational" ideas of deity, but without distinguishing sufficiently sharply between internal or constitutive relations and external or nonconstitutive ones. There is also talk about the subject-object relation as one to be transcended. Perhaps before transcending it we should try to understand it. Obviously "dependent origination" is a relational idea. However it tends to blur the difference between temporal and spatial relations. Also the "mind only" principle common to Buddhism and much Western thought implies that objects, if concrete, are themselves subjects, instances of the psychical. In memory my (or your) present self is aware of my (or your) past self. From the "no soul or substance" doctrine we infer that the self is not a single definite entity identically there from birth to death (or beyond) but a succession of momentary selves or states of the person's awareness.

Hand also seems to exalt what is strictly common to or identical in all of us, the universal self. This sounds like Advaita-Vedantism. I agree that what we have strictly in common is not a person to whom I can be related and you also can be related, or who can be related to both of us. The divine person is ideally integrated as no human person can be, but even the divine person is not simply or merely identical throughout change. Also my God is not simply your God, or simply the God of Abraham. *That* God did not know me or you. To conceptualize deity is indeed a subtle and not without limit possible task, and this imposes difficulties upon atheists as well as upon theists.

As indicated at the beginning of this reply, I am not the ideal person to respond to Ishihara's learned essay. Fortunately I am not the only person who will read it and profit by it, as even I, in my own way, have done. His is in some ways the greatest of the international religious traditions.

12. Kaufman on Judaism's Idea of God

I am pleased that Rabbi William Kaufman sees as much common ground between Judaism and my metaphysics as he does. On some topics there is, I believe, more and on some less agreement than he finds. The differences are partly verbal, as is usually the case in religious and philosophical issues. Our "total dependence on God" is one of my affirmations, subject to no qualification not deducible from the definition of 'God' and the proposition that the creatures (again by explication of a metaphysical concept) all have some freedom. This freedom does not mean that we could exist or be anything at all "without God." 'Without God' is an ill-formed formula in my scheme; meaningless or self-contradictory. "Thou givest them their meat in due season" I regard as somewhat ambiguous, but capable of a good meaning. God makes it possible for multiple creaturely freedom to constitute a viable world such that the risks of freedom (that is, of life or mind as such) are justified by the opportunities. Animals do normally get their food, and divine action was necessary for this to be possible. (Animals, however, do sometimes starve, as when usual rains do not fall and an area becomes desert. Freedom and chance are inseparable, and moreover there must, in any viable world, be some degree of predictability, some sort of natural laws, and this renders problematic the desirability of divine intervention in details of worldly happenings.)

I disagree somewhat with Kaufman's interpretation of the end of the Book of Job. God is in command in some sense of this metaphor, but the voice from the whirlwind tells Job that he does not well understand what it means to say that God "creates" the world. Not simply divine justice is beyond our understanding, divine power is (perhaps even more) beyond us. Is it like, but incomparably more than, that of the power of a King or patriarchal father? Surely not much like it. Is it like that of a potter with clay? In my opinion this is an extremely poor analogy, and it contradicts freedom. In fact we now know scientifically that the real constituents of clay have (for all we can ever know at least) their own trivial freedom, so far as the laws of nature are concerned, and that no potter can simply determine their activities. We need not quarrel with ancient peoples, Jews and Greeks (though Epicurus shrewdly guessed it) because they did not know this truth, but we should face it now that we do know it.

Perhaps more important still, we should note the stroke of genius of Whitehead in his doctrine of the objective immortality of all experiences in subsequent, especially divine, experience. The ultimate providence is that each creaturely actuality is imperishable in the divine prehension. This divine inclusion of our actuality is detailed, fully particular, hence personal, and unfailing. The Afro-American song about "the whole world in his hand" is in this fashion utterly true.

Does it compromise God's "independence" to say that God cannot be without some world or other? I see only a worship of a *word*, independence, in the classical doctrine here. If God *wanted* to exist without creating a world but could not, this might be a weakness, a deficiency of divine power. But why should God want this? Freedom to make no positive use of freedom seems nonsense to me. God creating nothing would be God only potentially not actually creator. And if the choice of inaction were voluntary, it would be a volition of the lesser not the greater good! Please note too that there is no reason, in the theory of dual transcendence, for holding that the divine need for some world or other is only contingently satisfied, so that God might fail to have a world, or in my view — fail to exist as creator. Divine *existential* independence and necessity contradict any such possibility. To say that worlds are possible is, for my or any high theism, to say that God could ground their possibility; to say that our world is actual is to say that God has grounded, also divinely prehended, and so, in the most complete sense, possessed it.

I think Judaism might do well to be cautious in accepting the medieval scheme so tainted with ontolotry, etiolotry (my words) and glorification of one-sided notions such as independence (in every possible sense) or cause (totally without any aspect of effect) or giving (without any kind of receiving), or permanence (without any kind of novelty). Deity is on both sides of such abstract polarities, as are the creatures. The difference that exalts God beyond any possible rival is in the *form* of independence, the *form* of dependence, the *form* of causation and of being caused. In the divine application these categories have their all-others-surpassing excellence. Independence, cause, and their contraries are not unequivocal value terms, any more than it is better to talk than to listen. No other kind of animal listens to other animals as variously as we do. Only God (analogically) listens to all.

Does the above unduly penetrate the divine mystery? I think not a whit more than it does to deny receptivity to God while exalting divine causative power. Try to imagine listening to all without being confused, or prehending a beginningless succession of "cosmic epochs" or worlds (of which ours is one), all forever after divinely prehended. Or to imagine a "knowing" not dependent upon and above language (as the other animals are below it). I think there is plenty of mystery.

In the long, often on the Christian side uncharitable (to put it mildly indeed), conflict between professed Christians and Jews, in my opinion Jews have in some important theological respects been more right than their opponents. For example, the Jews have been admirably cautious in indulging in dreams of Heaven and Hell. The fruits of this doctrine include Inquisitions, religious wars, crusades — a sad story. And I cannot overstate my gratitude for Rabbi Heschel's wonderfully apt pronouncement, "God is the *most* moved mover."

The divine fiat, "Let there be light" agrees with my doctrine. For, that there is light is indeed a divine act. No creature or set of creatures could decide the natural laws involved in the reality of light. God chooses this kind of world and has chosen many (infinitely many) kinds of world. The necessity to create *some* world is not a constraint upon any coherently conceivable deity. God could not choose to make no world because that is a foolish or nonsensical notion, a play with words. Why not leave such word-play to the Middle Ages with Dante, glorious poet though he was?

The Hebrew denial of a divine body verbally conflicts with my Platonic view of the cosmic Soul as the mind of which the universe is the body; but how clear is it that the makers of the denial did so while contemplating the thought of the *cosmos* as incarnating deity? "No graven images" — what graven image *of the cosmos* was even in anyone's mind at the time? Nothing is easier than to say 'incorporeal', but words are only as good as the minds that use them. As Hume remarked, and did well to do so, in nature the point of direct contact of mind, as we best know it, with body is in the nervous systems of animals. Surely God deals directly with each creature. Our minds deal directly with, and exert power in, our brains and nerves. What meaning can we give to mind that is in no analogous sense incarnate?

In my opinion Plato in the *Timaeus* reached a level of metaphysical insight that the Middle Ages did not attain. If God is not *literally* the soul of the cosmic body, then neither is God literally a magistrate, lord, father or mother, ruler, or maker in any humanly and easily accessible sense. Both (or all) analogies or none, in either case with judicious reservations, is my conclusion.

Concerning immortality, I cannot refrain from reiterating my enthusiasm for Theodore Walker's account of the African view of death, with its realism about that phenomenon, universal among animals, and its version of social immortality, a constituent of Whitehead's doctrine. What irony! The proud, nay conceited, Christians (and Muslims) who colonized or enslaved Africans to make them better, and in fact did give them some new possibilities — but at what a cost — were not unambiguously superior as human beings to those they conquered. The latter were closer to nature, to the sense of what it is to be an animal. They could live without the promise of infinitely prolonged careers of rewards and/or punishments. They could let God be the one with an endless career and not try to claim this divine attribute of indestructibility or career-infinity for themselves. In this respect I say they were, with the ancient Jews, on a very high level.

My metaphysical scheme is divine freedom, lesser forms of freedom, and otherwise nothing. What distinguishes neoclassical or, in the broad sense, process, philosophy is the "otherwise nothing" in the previous sentence. Peirce arrived at this before I was born and when Whitehead was less than twenty years old. There are no simply unfree single creatures, though various collectives of singulars may be called unfree, stones for example, or crystals, in contrast to atoms or molecules. If I do not rely on God to "arrange all things" it is because in process philosophy singular things are logically not, without qualification, arrangeable. To some extent they are self-arranging, or as Plato with a flash of genius said, they are self-moving.

Nothing "outside of or beyond the scope of God's will" is not unambiguously opposed to my belief. Outside, beyond, are vague terms. Besides, I hold with Fechner that "will" cannot be the entire content of any mental state, divine or otherwise. Will is the guide of impulse or feeling. Knowledge and will both presuppose perception and this involves sensing or feeling. If God is conceived by analogy with what we know of experience, mind, soul, or knowledge, there must, as Heschel says, be divine forms of *all* of these, not just of some of them. Otherwise "God" is an empty word, not a word of an exalted mystery. Schopenhauer tried to conceive reality as essentially mere will, without consciousness or superanimal purposiveness. Bradley tried to reduce it to mere feeling. "Human destiny is in God's hand" — yes indeed, understanding that we and all singular creatures have some freedom.

Why should God want to be independent of having some world or other? Subjects require and enjoy objects, and this is no deficiency in subjects; having no objects would be the same as not existing as subject. Nor will it help to say, "The divine subject is aware of itself." Awareness of that very awareness is language idling. Subjectivity is essentially social. I now as subject am aware of my past selves as subjects; I am aware of my just past bodily states which, according to the philosophers I've learned most from, beginning with Plato (interpreted through modern physics and psychology) and Leibniz, consist of radically subhuman forms of subjectivity.

I hope I do not seem unappreciative of Kaufman's honest effort to be fair to me and to his tradition, giving me a good springboard from which to make a few jumps, as they may seem to him. I trust he will not mind my recommending to him and those who think as he does the passages quoted from Heschel by McNamara. Is he sure that his way of modernizing the Judaic tradition is better than Heschel's? In that case, but scarcely otherwise, he must disagree rather radically with my way of saying what is best in religious traditions.

If I have any strong objection to Judaism it is on two accounts. Like Simone Weil I am horrified by the militarism of parts of the Old Testament, and the merciless treatment of enemies. I balance this against similar charges against traditional Christianity in the Inquisitions and religious wars. With some Jewish friends I am deeply troubled by the Israeli invasion of Lebanon and the present occurrences in the West Bank. My other trouble with

Judaism, which perhaps is unjustified, is the extent to which it seems to dwell mentally in the rather ancient past. But that is better than the almost complete disinterest in the past shown by many contemporaries. And I myself like to think of the Jews as they were before Greek ideas of immortality began to tarnish their vigorous this-worldliness. Aristotle and Socrates accepted mortality, and so did the author or authors of the Book of Job.

13. McNamara on Biblical Theology

I thank Martin McNamara for his vigorous summary of the Biblical tradition and its sources. Of the latter, the Egyptian is the only one I have any knowledge of, apart from the Greek element coming in near the end of the centuries he writes about. I take for granted the reliability of much of what he says concerning the stages of development of Hebrew thought about God and the diversity of opinions expressed in the old and new covenants and the *Apocrypha*. I have one complaint though: he virtually ignores *Job*. In my opinion the conventional interpretation of that sublime book is remarkably careless or lacking in insight. Even the sagacious poet Robert Frost does not seem very illuminating. The voice from the Whirlwind, which I take to symbolize the divine wisdom, does *not* say to Job: "You do not understand *why* I do what I do. It says, "You do not understand what it means to say that I *do* this or that. *You* have not created a world; you were not there when I created the Pleiades, you do not know how I make it possible for the wild animals to get their food, or so that the great whales can exist;" "you do not know" [I infer this from Job's ignorance of what it is to create] "that if something happens, I have done it or made it happen." After all, Job's sufferings in the fable were not decided by God, but by Satan. God allowed their infliction; but it is not even said that God knew what form they would take or just how Job would react.

Job's final response to the superhuman message does not show, as many seem to think, that God had frightened him into submission by a display or reminder of His (Her) power. God showed Job his *ignorance, not his mere physical weakness*, his *conceit* in thinking he could assign responsibility for his sufferings to God as creator and ruler of all, in spite of the fact that he did not know what 'create' or 'rule', in this in-principle-superhuman case, might mean. In this brief passage Jewish thought soared far above its earlier level and came closer to solving the religious problem of evil than medieval or classical theism ever did. If anything in ancient Greek thought came closer, it was in the late dialogues of Plato (and, of all people, in Epicurus): not in Aristotle, Plotinus, or the Stoics.

McNamara speaks of the mystery of creation and virtually admits that

305

bringing things to be merely be a simple command is a set of human words for which no human meaning is readily available. I submit, he is trying to have it both ways. God has "total mastery of creation," and we know this — though our description of this truth involves using words we cannot understand. Here he does what classical theists have always done. They are inconsistently modest and immodest. That God has "total mastery" is a human saying, not literally a divine saying. To take it as simply what God has said to us leads to dreadful consequences. For then allegedly there will be divine sayings of the Koran, or extreme Protestant and extreme Catholic fundamentalism, and much else. And what happens to the idea of freedom if divine decision settles everything? Then God is the ultimate murderer or torturer in the brutalities of history. We now know that no potter can exactly determine the motions or positions of the molecules or atoms constituting clay. There is nothing in current science to indicate that it makes sense to speak of precisely determining these.

I found the commentator's account of the emergence in Israel of belief in personal immortality helpful as history but quite unconvincing as showing the superiority of this belief in the form McNamara gives to it. In "perpetual union with God" and "God is not the God of the dead but of the living," I see no unambiguous incompatibility with Whitehead's doctrine (and mine) of objective immortality in God as "consequent" upon (that is, as everlastingly experiencing) the creatures in their momentary vividness, so that they "live forevermore" and are not mere corpses, or mere hosts of atoms scattered widely, first by creatures that live upon dead bodies and then by winds or waters that carry them about. As Spinoza said, once for all, the Bible is not a treatise in philosophy. Still less is it in any literal sense the word of God. It is a very human collection of writings by no doubt gifted and dedicated ancient members of our species interpreting their experiences.

Since God is by definition ubiquitous and essential to anything else, in experiencing anything we experience God, the only question being how far we are distinctly conscious of that aspect of our experience. I give the ancient Jews high marks in this respect, and regard their later contamination with Greek uses of Soul (as in the early Platonic dialogues) as regression. Remember that for God the remote past is as vividly given as the most recent past, so that all our experiences, and those of our bodily constituents, which for Whitehead are the actualities, are foreverafter cherished, once they have come to be. As Bergson said, becoming is creation "or nothing." Destruction is not of actualities but only termination of one or more of those series of (intimately connected) actualities we call careers of individuals, including persons. A person who dies prematurely remains for God just what he or she was, with all the value qualities he or she has ever possessed. What is "lost" is only that certain antecedently possible *further* actualizations will never be realized. Only real *opportunities* for actualization, not actualities, are lost.

As for supernatural justice after death I think this is a much too anthropomorphic idea. To think of God as judge, magistrate, and policeman in one is to pay undeserved tribute to our human efforts to influence behavior by rewards and punishments. I also think the idea is too ego-centric. If the ideal is to love the neighbor as the self, and if we are to help others because they are valuable or lovable to God, and help ourselves for the same reason, what does the question of desert have to do with this? Did I deserve the wonderful luck of having the parents I did? The cosmos cannot be a legal system. Emerson tried to persuade himself by clearly slip-shod arguments that everyone in this life gets what he (or she) deserves, but when his lovely little son died he admitted, even a year later, that this did not fit his theory! Perhaps he had not read the Book of Job, or he read it badly, or forgot it. (His religious education was shortened by illness.) Job's comforters, but *not* the voice from the Whirlwind, try to apply legal ideas cosmically. How good that this is so! Long before Dante there were nobler ideas of God than that genius entertained.

I wonder if McNamara ever met Rabbi Heschel. I did, and I have known some of his disciples. A truly great, wise, and good man. With, I hope, due respect, I cannot imagine that Berkovits compares with him. Or, for that matter, that most Christians do. The cited argument against Heschel seems to me a paradigm of special pleading. I am afraid that I feel the same about McNamara's argument that a *living* God must be impassive and *not* inactive. Of course God is not inactive. But to be passive in the sense of open to influence and able to change is not at all to be simply inactive. Passivity is the way one subject's activity takes account of the activity of others. What else is perception? It is the socially receptive side of activity, not its negation. So here is a definite fallacy in the service of an argument against a central form of twentieth century metaphysics. This *social* view of reality is the great distinction between the last twelve decades or so in the history of metaphysics and most of what went before (especially after Plato).

To be open to influence from free beings is the only conceivable way to be able to know these beings. To say that God is in dialogue with us but not open to influence by us is to talk nonsense or contradiction. And how is God to know our feelings? Not by mere concepts, for feelings are individual. For me to know how *you* feel while not feeling in the least myself could at most mean that I apply some word for feeling, or some special kind of feeling, but with no way to get beyond the word to an appropriate meaning.

I take the saying, "God is love," or the opening phrase of Wesley's hymn, "Love divine, all love excelling," to be the simplest characterization of God that is not hopelessly inadequate or misleading. And what is love? As the absolute minimum, it is "feeling *of* feeling," which is the primary form of Whitehead's "prehension." For Whitehead nature is "an ocean of feelings," to fully know it is to feel these feelings. Feel, not just conceive, or have beliefs about.

The nearest to a stark contradiction between Biblical and neoclassical theism is presented by the assertions in the former of eternal (not just everlasting) divine knowledge, and previously (or eternally, which is worse) established destination of concrete acatualities. With Kierkegaard I flatly reject, and regard as monstrous blunders, ideas of complete divine determination of concrete human decisions. With Lequier, Peirce, Bergson, Whitehead, and many others I see contradiction in the idea of timeless knowledge of concrete actualities. In any sense of the word, *timeless* truth (and timeless knowledge) there can be only of entities themselves timeless. And these are all highly abstract, like the ideas of pure mathematics or pure metaphysics. If any ancient writer said otherwise, so much the worse for his credibility today. And I see no such notion in Plato or Aristotle as that of timeless truth about concrete events. If the Stoics had it, that confirms my opinion of them. They were noble people who surpassed other Greeks in their freedom from Greek provincialism and male chauvinism, but in metaphysics they have the least to give us now. Here too I am echoing Peirce, as well as Whitehead and Bergson, James and Dewey.

One more quarrel with this author. He says we cannot know the "inner nature" of God. Suppose we know simply nothing of the inner nature of God, what then do we know? Is it the wholly external nature of God? And what is that? I should think, nothing at all. I ask also, Why say that God knows or loves, if the knowing or loving is not in the knower or lover? How can it be only an external nature? There are better ways to say what such language is intended to convey.

Do we know *adequately* the inner nature of God? Obviously not, for in that is knowing or cherishing of all there is. We have *some* knowledge (partly analogical and party literal) of what is in God, for in God is *all* truth. But according to the view I share with Whitehead, our entire cosmos for past billions of years, if physicists are right, is reality only as it has been in our "cosmic epoch," preceded by a beginningless series (known to God) of such epochs to which we may have no access, to be followed by countless other epochs, the details of which are unknown even to God, for there are no such details.

Recent philosophy has made a profound revolution that cannot be simply reversed. Whitehead's sublime formula "In the slow sunrise of a thousand years" symbolizes for me the profundity of a mind most of us cannot rival and are in grave danger of unwittingly cutting down to our size in criticizing. I do criticize him, but with care and with the help of some other giants, including Peirce, and some other great persons too little noticed, including Plato, particularly in his doctrine of the cosmos as divine body with a Soul transcending, by including, that is prehending, that body.

My issue with classical theists is not at all that of immanence *versus* transcendence. I affirm more transcendence than they do. My doctrine is labelled "dual transcendence." In whatever genuinely conceivable way (and I hold there are such ways) to be absolute is to be superior to all other beings (actual or conceivable), God is thus absolute (also immutable and impassable). In whatever ways (and such ways are conceivable) to be relative or changeable is to be superior to all others, God is in those ways relative and changing.

To transcend is to be superior to all possible rivals. It is not to be outside rather than inside the world, or vice versa; or absolute rather than relative, or vice versa. A merely finite God, wrote Peirce, is a "fetish." A merely infinite God, said to be like a person, is as close to stark nonsense as it is easy to come while appearing to talk sense. Finiteness is definiteness, it means this, rather than that, where both are conceivable. A mere negative like not-finite cannot describe what we ought to love with all our being. In sum God must be, in uniquely excellent ways, finite *and* infinite, as Brightman said before Whitehead, and as dozens of (mostly neglected) writers more or less clearly implied before Brightman.

Is "finite and infinite" a contradiction? Logic textbooks do not say that contrary properties cannot apply to the same subject if they are applied to different aspects or constituents of the subject; there is then no contradiction. If we are going to try to follow logical rules, and I do, let us be exact about the rules. If you say, "But God is simple and not complex," then the reply is clear: being simple in some aspect is entirely compatible with being complex as a whole. It is the complex that can include the simple, not vice versa. To take God as exclusively simple is to make deity an empty abstraction. Concreteness means complexity. To love all actualities is to be the most complex yet singular reality, not the simplest.

We are all human and fallible, and so are all sacred documents. Theology cannot dictate, for there are too many theologies; philosophy cannot dictate, for there are too many philosophies. The same holds for scientific views. But in some ways science is unique. I have heard an Episcopal preacher (in Savanna) actually say, "I consider science to be as much a revelation of God as the Bible." I would not put it that way, but I think it is irresponsible to ignore the basic changes in views of nature since the Biblical authors wrote their far from mutually coherent testimonies. And in deciding what to accept or not to accept, what rules are we to follow? Without philosophers, what happens, I think, is that no clear rules are followed. Even with philosophers there is trouble. We do what we can. We try to state rules. For nearly two thousand years classical theists oversimplified, by identifying God with one side of polar opposites; temporal-eternal, dependent-independent, passive-active, relative-absolute. They implied, but only half (or two-thirds) *consciously* and *responsibly* implied, that one side of these polarities is good, admirable, or worth praising. In reality these contrasts are not bad-good contrasts at all. There are good and bad ways of being any of these things. When we are *valuing* we should make clear that this is what we are doing. Infinity is one idea, deity quite another. The same with eternity or absoluteness. Worshipping these abstractions is subtle idolatry.

Obviously I have found McNamara's commentary on my kind of theism in relation to the Bible immensely stimulating, and I see this as putting me in debt to its author. He puts his cards on the table and this makes his contribution highly appropriate for this volume. For all I know, his textual scholarship is excellent, and where I disagree sharply with him he is in good company. By good, however, I do not mean the best, and certainly not the most representative of our time. Over three centuries ago the Socinian theologians saw that classical theism was incompatible with freedom and therefore, knowing well what they were opposing, rejected it and attributed change and partial passivity (but not inactivity) to God. Fechner in Germany, Lequier and others in France, Peirce in the U.S.A. went further, and others took up the task. The world was too busy or too conceited to much notice, or honestly consider, these efforts. Historians failed in this matter. Now at last the world must face the challenge. "The method of tenacity" (Peirce) has its limits.

I end with a bit of partial agreement. Yet indeed, God is analogous to a person and is the cosmic and supercosmic person; yes indeed, the divine wisdom is in nature, constituted by a set of natural laws, laws not deterministic and detail-determining, but statistical or somehow tolerant of freedom. The supreme freedom is the divine freedom; to say free is to say potential as well as actual, for to act freely is to have been able to act otherwise (which does not in the divine case mean less well). *Actus purus* is definitely, most exquisitely definitely, erroneous! As Popper says, great men make great mistakes. (Heidegger also said this and instantiated it. About the Nazis he could scarcely have been much more wrong.) Aquinas knew (in part) what he was denying and he was wrong. Socinus in disagreeing with him knew (still better) what he was denying and was right. The almost unwritten parts of history are not all trivial or lacking in relevance. Even Richard McKeon, little as he cared for Whitehead's system, once told me that he found Whitehead's historical comments illuminating. It was through Peirce that I learned where Aristotle's greatness was; yet Peirce also said one of the best things that can be claimed for Plato, that he "knew what philosophy is." This supports Whitehead's summary of Western philosophy: "A series of footnotes to Plato."

14. Pailin on Rigor, Reason, and Moderation

For decades now David Pailin has been trying to understand and reasonably evaluate my neoclassical theism or theory of dual transcendence. In his wish to understand I think he has achieved considerable success, and I have to hope that his judgments of value are *largely* reasonable for, as such things go in philosophy, they are mostly favorable. However, from Ockham to Wittgenstein and his admirers, the British tradition is so strongly anti-metaphysical that my rejection of thoroughgoing empiricism (in the sense of expecting *all* existential statements to be conceivably falsifiable as well as confirmable observationally) arouses his suspicions. I shall try to show some respects in which he has not entirely succeeded in understanding (and is not entirely reasonable in questioning) a few, to me important, points.

In his 5th and 6th paragraphs he characterizes as my ideal of metaphysical evidence the hope that all the options but one in answering a certain question will be found self-contradictory. I wonder if this is quite what my statements entail. If by *ideal* is meant, as God might see the matter, then I suppose that for God the wrong options would be no options, since God would see their absurdity as we see the absurdity of 2 and 3 making any sum other than 5. But I claim no close approximation to any such clarity as humanly attainable in metaphysics. That is just the distinction between the metaphysical and the mathematical, especially the finitely mathematical. What is for me almost beyond reasonable doubt is the possibility and importance of finitizing sets of mutually incompatible and collectively exhaustive sets of possible combinations of concepts that have been used in the history of metaphysical controversy. For example, God has been called *absolute*, in contrast to nondivine beings as *relative* or dependent (also *necessary*, in contrast to nondivine beings as *contingent*, and similarly with some other pairs of concepts). This implies for each conceptual pair four possible doctrines about God and four about the nondivine, giving 16 combinations in the mathematical sense. Historically a number of these sixteen have been definitely illustrated in the past. For example take 'N.c' meaning "God is wholly necessary and the nondivine wholly contingent." this fits practically all the scholastic theologians. 'N.cn' means, "God is wholly necessary and the nondivine is both necessary and contingent" (in diverse respects, to avoid contradiction). This is Aristotle's view. 'N.n' is clearly Spinozism as usually interpreted.

What the simple mathematics used here shows is that when controversy arose between any two of the 16 cases, a completely rational procedure would have been to consider all 16 combinations. Nothing like this was done! Here then is an historical discovery. Metaphysical controversy has not been conducted in accordance with the rules of appropriate procedure. Life is not so short that we must dismiss without consideration 14 cases in order to decide between the remaining two, or even dismiss 9 or 10 cases in order to decide among the remaining 7 or 6. Note that atheistic options are among the 16. Thus '0.cn' means "there is no divine being, whether necessary or contingent, only a nondivine reality or realities contingent in some respects and otherwise necessary." Also "acosmism" is included; thus, 'N.0' means "there is necessarily an eminent or divine being and otherwise nothing." Finally we have the double zero case 0.0, "neither concept applies to God or world."

If the above is granted, how do we decide among the options. Here mere formal logic will not suffice, for logical constants alone cannot define deity. Religious or irreligious intuition is bound to come in. This is why I am made uneasy by what Pailin says in his 5th paragraph about my recognizing no revelation or religious authority. I allow what the various theistic religions at their best have in common to define the term God (or divine, or deity). This is a non-provincial, non-sectarian appeal to religious experience. It involves more than such concepts as absolute or relative; it involves what I sometimes call psycho-analogy, application of terms like will, purpose, love, soul (also *body* as what a soul has, not just any physical thing). It also involves the use of value terms like *surpass, better than, worthy of worship or entire devotion.* The logic to which one appeals in the use of such terms, analogically applied to deity, may be called "informal logic." If there is no such thing, then there can be little rationality in religion. I think there is informal logicality and illogicality. But it is not so lucid and virtually infallible as the insight we all have that the sum of 3 and 4 is the same as the sum of 2 and 5, or that "all A is B, and some C is A" entails "some C is B." In informal logic we do the best we can.

Analogically God is said to have knowledge or love for the creatures, the nondivine beings. If it is also said that the existence of the latter is contingent, whether in some or in all respects, it then follows from any useful modal system that it is absurd to say that God is wholly or in all respects necessary. (To know infallibly that P* is true and contingent, is to have knowledge that one could not have had if P* were false, which by the assumption is regarded as possible.) Hence N.c or N.cn make the idea of divine knowledge contradictory. If one tries to deny this by saying that divine knowing is not like ours to the extent required for the contradiction to result, then the objection is, what really is left of the psychoanalogy? Is it merely verbal? If so, why play with words whose meaning is not available?

Are the historical metaphysical systems self-consistent? Not if one expects them to be clear enough for it to matter much whether we affirm or deny them. (We have new advantages that should enable us to do better.) I say the same about Kant's anti-metaphysical system. Did he really know what he meant by appearance or phenomenon in distinction from noumenon? I am far from alone in denying this. The goal is clarity without inconsistency, or consistency without hopeless unclarity. We do what we can. And in my opinion it is worth doing. I have arguments for the view that it is unreasonable to deny all progress or improvement in metaphysics. Kuhn does this in science, or comes perilously close to it. Popper is better. Kant denies progress in metaphysics. I think he was demonstrably ignorant of the history in question. In addition, Hume and Kant were not great logicians, in clarity comparable to that of mathematicians. Leibniz was exemplary in clarity but only avoided obvious inconsistency at certain points by evasions or transparently inadmissible verbal distinctions. We should do better. He had to try to reconcile dangerously combative religious groups. We have more freedom, better physics, biology, and psychology, and a more exact logic.

Pailin gives me a welcome opportunity to clear up one theological topic, that of the analogical use of psychological terms, such as knowing, loving, perceiving, willing, and the like. Does God "see" he asks, or "smell"? My answer is partly to express agreement with the great Rabbi Heschel, when he said that *all* the basic aspects of mind, soul, awareness, or experience must analogically apply to deity. It will not do to select will and omit feeling, or knowledge and omit perception. What knowledge might be without perception I am confident is not to be known. There is, however, at least one qualification. To see or smell in the normal sense is to be a fragment of the world made aware of the larger world to which the fragment belongs. God is no fragment. Nothing is larger than God. Since I accept Plato's doctrine of World Soul, having the cosmos as its body, my theistic analogy must set aside the way the distance receptors operate in us. God knows directly what we only see or hear as parts of a larger system of things. And we only do this by a more direct awareness of our bodily changes. This is true even when we see or smell our own bodies. This limitation cannot apply to deity. What God does do, however, is to be *directly* aware of or prehend *our* seeing and smelling *experiences* as the fragments they are of the inclusive whole forming the de facto contents of the divine bodily feelings.

How then do *we* directly feel the cellular processes in our bodies, especially in our nervous systems? I say, we (indistinctly, and more or less faintly) feel their several much more primitive feelings. Injure certain of our cells and we feel the sufferings of those cells; enable them to flourish and we feel their pleasures in this flourishing. This view is so simple in essence that I strongly suspect, to quote Goethe, that people will "refuse to believe that the truth can be so simple." Even Whitehead (who held this view, as I understand him) underemphasized it.

I see little power in Whitehead's system if we neglect his clearly stated doctrine that we know through prehending and that prehending of concrete actualities is always and everywhere "feeling *of* feeling," that is, qualitative experiencing (with a value aspect) *of other* qualitative experiencing. Two levels, at least, of qualitative feeling are involved, except where the first token of 'feeling' stands for a previous experience of the same individual (personally ordered society). God knows *our* olfactory experiences, and the qualitative experiences of the thing smelled and the molecules stimulating our sensory organs, and the singular constituents of the organs.

And this, for Whitehead, is all there is to know in the situation. In detail and specific respects there is vast complexity, in outline there is grandiose simplicity, illustrating what Whitehead called "the simplicity of genius." If the introduction of the concept of prehension was not genius don't ask me what genius in philosophy might be; for, on that condition, I do not know.

I trust I have made it evident that I admit the fallibility of my (in a technical sense) non-empirical argumentations about God. However, that for Anselm impassability as divine attribute was self-evident, while for me what is evident is rather that there must be both an impassable *and* a passable aspect of the divine reality, does not quite so strongly support skepticism as Pailin seems to suggest. For Anselm lacked many advantages that I enjoy in thinking about these topics. For just one, I have read him and many like him, and he has read neither me nor many like me (if any). Moreover, he adopted his position without making a serious beginning of exploring the theoretical options which, using concepts he did use, were involved in those concepts. In our "ape-like consciousness," to speak with Whitehead, it is not safe to accept some definite position — such as the attribution of independence or immunity to influence, in any and every conceivable sense, to deity — without exploring the different senses in which a being might be dependent or not dependent. No one that Anselm knew had done this. He had answered a question no one had conceptually examined calmly in logical terms. When my theological reflections began, much work had been done since the Middle Ages to clarify this problem.

As to the question, whether reality is or is not rational, "correspondingly to our rational thinking," and the possibility that how we, by our nature, *must* think may not agree with what reality is I have several remarks to make. First, there are various theoretical options as to the connotation of "rational." For Blanshard, Spinoza, or the Stoics it meant, to see everything as necessary. I reject this as a fine example of an irrational doctrine. I think, with Ernst Nagel and perhaps most logicians, that such extremes as everything is necessary (or everything is contingent) are counterintuitive and that no valid arguments have been given for them. Plato, Aristotle, and Epicurus argue against both. Logic requires necessity *and* contingency (or chance), also independence and dependence, of propositions, and so does empirical science. Without dependence, not only among propositions but among things propositions are about, we could not, by knowing some parts of the world be able to know anything about the rest of the world or about what is likely to happen the next moment; without independence we should have to know everything to know anything.

As to our simply having to think in certain ways although nature might not have to be or act in those ways, I remark that if we simply *have* to think in the ways in question we should not pretend to think otherwise sufficiently even to find sense in saying that we think reality might be otherwise. I see subtle ambiguities here, as in so many controversial topics. I share with Peirce the maxim, "Do not doubt in your philosophy what you believe in your heart."

There is another distinction. Metaphysical rationality is concerned only with hightly abstract matters. Every step from the extremely abstract or general toward the concrete and particular is contingent. The proposition that God knows all individuals tells nothing about what you or I, as unique individuals, are known to God as being. The divine wisdom remains a divine secret to a vast, if not in a definite sense infinite, extent.

Pailin, like John Hick, interprets the necessity of the divine existence to mean *only* that this existence is omnitolerant, everlasting, independent (and uncaused). Here Pailin is proclaiming, not arguing. I think differently, not only about the OA argument but about the whole question of necessity and contingency. Necessary as here used by me means, could not be or have been otherwise, no matter what. Unconditional necessity is in my view inherent in the high religions' idea of deity. The Hick-Pailin view is not only not my view, it is contradicted by a vast host of representatives of the great traditions. True enough, Hume and Kant are on Hick's side, along with Quine (see his *Quiddities*), so he has illustrious company. But I am not among them. Here we flatly disagree.

That the OA does not adequately prove the divine existence still obtains, and here I agree with Pailin; but for what I regard as the right reason, whereas he gives a wrong one. There is still, for me, the formidable positivist contention that the definition of deity fails to make clear and coherent sense. This means that perhaps deity, in the informal-logical sense, *could not* exist. The combination of clarity and coherence is hard to prove, as the now numerous famous paradoxes show. This is the Achilles heel of the OA, not Pailin's dogma that reality may be randomly pluralistic. If that dogma is even logically possible, then the idea of God is incoherent. As Findlay put it, "God must be Lord of possibility as well as actuality."

The meanings (other than my meaning) that Pailin ciites for necessity I accept because they are deducible from my meaning (could not have failed to be); moreover, I regard the converse as valid also, that the Hick-Pailin meanings make sense only if mine is added. What could-have-failed-to-be-but-is must have had some basis of its possibility and could not be uncaused. I am standing on Aristotelian ground here, that is, with the first, and still one of the best, giants in modal theory. Also, I think, Whitehead; his rejection of the OA is a way of stating the Achilles heel of that argument, which I grant.

That God's existence is "an inexplicable brute fact" or "simply what is the case" is precisely what I deny as making sense. The quoted passage gives not my view but a view I was attacking. God's concrete actuality is contingent, what is but might not have been the case; however, as I define existence, whether it be necessary or contingent, divine or not divine, it is in principle more or less abstract. Perhaps my paragraph was less clear than it should have been, but to me it does not say what Pailin takes it to say. The divine identifying traits or essences exist by being necessarily *somehow* instantiated, but *how, in what actual states*, instantiated is contingent. God's mere existence is an extreme abstraction; whereas God's actuality is the supreme concrete reality. It is contingent precisely because it is *not* uncaused, omnitolerant, or independent. It is, however, in a definite sense everlasting.

The statement "God's actuality is contingent" is open to the misunderstanding that God might have existed as only an empty abstraction lacking in concrete embodiment. This interpretation is ruled out by my definition of the divine existence as *necessarily somehow*, or in some state or states, *instantiated, concretized*. God's being somehow actualized is not contingent. That God enjoys concrete and (all others surpassing) life and consciousness is the same as that God exists. Apart from necessity and all-surpassing excellence that is how *we* exist, meaning that what makes us ourselves is somehow, in some states, instantiated. But our individual uniqueness is not capturable in a concept as the divine uniquenness is.

Pailin implies that theism is a proposition whose truth is necessary *if* it is true, but that it could have been contingently false. This gives me what someone has called "logical seasickness." What Hick and Pailin have done is to use a normally modal term nonmodally. It is, therefore, not surprising that it leads these authors to talk about the complete irrationality and inexplicability of the uncaused divine existence. The whole point of causality is the way it explains the possibility of contingent facts. The *how* or *in what* of the divine actuality must be caused, but not the being eternally somehow actualized.

Aristotle's "with eternal things to be possible and to be are the same" I interpret as supportive of the necessitarian aspect of my theism. 'Eternal' here need not mean immutable but only unborn and undying. In this sense deity could not be a mere *fact*. (I object to using this word so broadly that it covers, for instance, arithmetical truths. One can do this, but it tends to lead to fallacy, obscuring one of the deepest intellectual distinctions.)

That God exists whatever else happens to exist is my view; but note carefully that I hold that the existence of some world or other is not something that merely "happens" but rather is co-necessary with the existence of God in some state or states. God must have some world as the divine body. None of this is inexplicable, for it is explained by the idea of God itself, which is the supreme explanatory idea. As Peirce says, mind is self-intelligible, not matter. Burnet (an English scholar, please note) said that Plato's great discovery was not the immutable forms but the soul. Even in the divine case this is not immutable but a "moving [changing] image of eternity." And the World Soul must have a world body. Another English scholar, Cornford, is my authority in this.

That there can be no contradiction in denying the predicate "exists" of a subject because, if it does not exist, there is no *it* to have or lack the predicate is one of Kant's arguments. It misses the point that what does exist (if positivists are wrong here) is the idea of deity, the property divine. If there is no such idea, then the question of existence does not even arise. But if there is such an idea as definite and coherent, then either it is or is not conceivable that what it describes exists contingently (in the latter case it must also be conceivable that it contingently fails to exist). I say that neither of the two suppositions of contingency is coherent with the idea. What is coherent is that what it describes exists no matter what. A positivist can deny that the idea is coherent and definite, in which case theism has only the standing of an absurdity. Otherwise, so far as my understanding goes, God exists, not as a contingent fact but as a necessity, included as such in the content of any thinking that understands itself.

Necessity of existence is a predicate that inheres in all metaphysically general conceptions, including truth, beauty, actuality. The Anselmian principle entails, if positivism is wrong at this point, that it is not only the concept of deity that must exist, or be somehow concretely actualized; *all comparably general ideas must be so*. If "God exists" could not have been false, neither could the vaguer "something exists." Deity is, in my theory, the concept of an *individual with strictly universal functions*. Its universality defines its individuality. (Hegel should have meant this by his concrete universal, but probably did not.) The point here is the Buddhist-Whiteheadian point that individuality is not the final particularity. Here as at many points, Peirce was a Whiteheadian without Whitehead. He said a human person is an idea. I recall Whitehead talking about "the Demos idea," referring to his friend (and my tutor once) Raphael Demos. Personal identity is concrete and definite only retrospectively. Since God does not die, the divine concreteness is not a fixed sum of actuality and value but an ever growing one. Only dead individuals are completely particular. Their further potentiality (which, as Peirce insisted, is in principle general not particular) is no longer actualizable.

Grant Quine or Santayana their view of the future as no less particular than the past and all truths about what happens as timelessly there "from the standpoint of eternity," the entire intellectual revolution some of us have been trying to bring about collapses. Quine has an argument here and I am ill-equipped to combat it. I can, however, put the question, "Is there no danger of our deceiving ourselves when we suppose we can see things in principle as classical theism thought God saw them?" Perhaps Quine is trying to transcend our human fragmentary status, and perhaps this cannot be done except when dealing with purely mathematical or purely metaphysical or logical truths, one of which, according to Quine (by implication) is that no individual whatsoever can exist except contingently. Does this mean that for all we know there might have been nothing at all? I do not know what Pailin (or Quine) think about this. I say, 'the being of total nonbeing' is nonsense or mere contradiction.

Anselm knew what he was doing in denying that God can be conceived (not just verbally stated) not to exist. Dodos do not *now* exist means that every place in the present cosmos suitable for Dodos is occupied by something that could not be there if a Dodo were there. Nonexistence as knowable is exclusion by what does exist. this will not work with God. If the evils in the world could show God not to be there, then theism is indeed in bad shape. But the classical argument from evil assumes, as ideal of divine power, ability unilaterally to determine what concretely happens. Grant universal creativity as the essence of life and activity, and what is left of the argument? Why should there not be conflict and suffering, yes and wickedness if there is life on a high level? And if evils cannot show the absence of God, what could? I hold with Carnap that the theistic question is essentially one of meaning, not of contingent fact. We agreed that a *merely* finite or contingent deity is made unplausible by science, and I say it is not religiously helpful anyway.

I believe it was Sylvester Schilling who made a serious attempt to show how theism (in which he believes) could conceivably be falsified by observation of evils. He tried to describe a world in which nothing went well and animals and people were largely frustrated in their efforts. It was a thoroughly nasty cosmos that he described. I have lost the reference, and the essay in which I commented on this attempt to apply empirical tests to the belief in God. My contention was and is that the world he purported to describe as conceivable was one in which nothing like observation to test a theory could arise, and which there is no good reason to suppose could exist. Animals cannot live without achieving some satisfaction in doing so. The energy that drives the world is, as Whitehead says, emotion, and merely negative emotion is in principle life-destroying not life maintaining. The enjoyment of eating reinforces eating, disenjoyment in eating tends to discourage eating, and this is not an arbitrary law of our world, but a tautology. Worlds are made possible by a form of order that admits of symbiosis, mutual compatibility of life-forms, which means general happiness. This is what Plato's doctrine that the Good is the basic principle (as light from the sun is of life on this planet) comes to in concrete terms.

If Schilling's argument were valid, then the case for theism would not be very good, to put it mildly. For Jews in Hitler-controlled Europe, our world had quite a little in common with Schiller's supposed one. Then too the Kalahari desert in Africa, in a bad drought year, is like it for the animals there, the fish deprived of water and the vegetable-eating animals deprived of grass, foliage, or fruits. All things considered this is not a promising line for theists to follow, except as supplementary to a metaphysical grounding of theism, properly formulated according to the best that is now known in logic and metaphysics (especially of the last dozen decades or so).

Post-Middle-Age science and philosophy have been struggling to escape from certain one-sided assumptions of metaphysical, not genuinely empirical scope; particularly (1) that of strictly sufficient or determining reasons or causes, unpermissive of creativity or freedom in the strong sense; (2) the idea of matter as, except in cosmically rare, highly exceptional forms, entirely insentient, vacuous of feeling or intrinsic value. By the time of Peirce and Maxwell, strict determinism had already been dismissed by several high authorities as a needless, and perhaps no longer harmless, metaphysical extravagance; so, and much more widely, had the classical concept of *wholly dead and insentient* matter been rejected by a number of scientists and philosophers. With relativity physics and quantum physics a third one-sided view — likewise not genuinely empirical — that of radical pluralism, the doctrine of externally related simples, logically independent of one another and able to influence each other only by collision, the push-pull mode of transaction, also began to exhibit its irrelevance or falsity. Hume's "what is distinguishable is separable" is demonstrably an ambiguous or untrue statement as it stands, since the first half of a certain hour is distinguishable from the entire hour but the latter cannot be without the former. The formula makes no quantum theoretical sense, or relativistic sense either, so far as I can see. If these three changes from traditional materialism and mechanism are adequately digested, the case for a theistic metaphysics is much easier to make.

A fourth important change is that we no longer trust verbal smoothness as guarantee of logical possibility, and we are more careful in dealing with extremely wide gaps in scale or degree between examples for the meanings of words given by everyday common-sense objects, such as other macroscopic animals, sticks or stones, trees and the like as somehow intermediate between the animal and the inanimate, compared with the microscopic and ultra-microscopic entities below us at one extreme, and the megaloscopic, cosmic, and divine above us at the other extreme. For example, our sense of the "power" we have over ourselves, other animals, plants and seemingly insentient materials extends easily enough to micro-animals, (even micro-plants), but not so easily to molecules, atoms, particles; still less does it transfer easily to cosmic or supercosmic power.

Theological analogy was the central theme of classical theism. Mortimer Adler tried to defend the Thomistic view of analogy and gave up. A large book was left unpublished, if I recollect correctly. Whitehead took up the problem and adopted from the Greeks the Platonic-Aristotelian analogy between the way a human being influences others, not by physical rewards or punishments, or by pushing, pulling, or carrying, but by the persuasive force of personal knowledge, intellectual or artistic insight, or charm. The Greeks said that we admire, love, or wish to be like God; the divine power is ability to persuade, charm, induce admiration or fondness. So Whitehead says, "God's power is the worship he inspires." Alas, Plato said one more thing which Whitehead refused to say, that God's power is like that which we have over our own bodies. Whitehead was upset by historical usages to which Plato's psycho-somatic analogy was put in the remote past. I consider this a weak argument, one of the worst in Whitehead. I also think he somewhat misread Plato. Several theologians of recent times have seen Plato's point, including a prominent German and a prominent American. I agree with them.

Even Hume can be cited in favor of this strategy. The mind-body relation, one of his dialogue disputants points out, is our human example of a direct relation between mental purpose and physical result. We must first change our bodies to change things outside our bodies. Our mere feelings or thoughts do not suffice for outside changes; neural, muscular or other inner changes must also come in. Whitehead's own theory of prehension as the bridge over which all concrete causal efficacy travels, supports Plato better than any other causal theory there has been. "Feeling of feeling," involving at least two sentient subjects, implies a sympathetic connection whereby one subject contributes to the emotional life of another subject. There is a one-way transmission of energy and direction between two or more active and at least in some slight degree free actualities.

Since we prehend God and God prehends us, we (normally unconsciously) feel something of the emotional life of God and God feels with ideal consciousness our emotional lives. Thus there is persuasion both ways. But there is also radical asymmetry, for we merely enrich the divine life, which was there before we were even definite potentialities and which could have maintained its continuity had our parents, as might easily have happened, not had children with our particular gene mixtures and so not had us — or even any children. Deity is a self-individualizing concept, there is no such concept for you or me. Even "world" is not an individual, just as your or my body is not. You are not well described as 'your body and its contents.' You have (prehend) it, it does not have you. Each of your brain cells has (prehends) you, but that is not the same thing at all. In dreamless sleep your body is there, but where are you as a conscious or even sentient person? (There is a Buddhist saying I could quote here.) What makes your body a single active agent in the full sense in which a tree is no such agent is your experiences. Otherwise it is like a tree or a termite colony. How well did Aristotle say it, "A tree is like a sleeping [and not dreaming] man who never wakes up."

Being without our knowledge of cells, both in trees and in animals, and of the cells composing the nervous system, Aristotle could not have done nearly as much with this animal-vegetable distinction as we are in a position to do. I have yet to be persuaded that most teachers of philosophy are making much use of this new opportunity. It is not a detail. My essay about *The Compound Individual* (1936) tried to spell out what is involved. Without far better grasp of microbiology than I have I am not in a position to go much beyond that essay. But it is clear to me that the Greeks were hopelessly handicapped in dealing with the mind-body or the mind-matter problems. Aristotle was in some ways farther from modern science than Plato. And Epicurus was less handicapped than either of them in some respects. But they were *all* largely in the dark on these topics.

Obviously my long-time friend has done me, and I hope the reader, a favor by his candid commentary.

CONCLUDING REMARKS

I wish to conclude my replies with appreciation of Dr. Sia's selection of contributors who, in my judgment, have fully justified his confidence in them. The idea for the book, which we owe to him, is remarkable for the wide range of significant perspectives from which my kind of philosophy is regarded. The complexity of the religious problems posed by the human condition is, I think, splendidly illustrated by this range. (Unfortunately, the intended representative of Islam and one other invited contributor did not furnish essays in the allotted time.) Sia is one of those who came to understand my thought before he ever saw or heard me. As I have always liked writing even more than teaching classes, I feel complimented and gratified by these cases where it is the writing that did the job of communication. Eventually Sia and I did meet and he did hear me lecture, but he was already an interpreter and skillful defender of my views. I now think that his previous book, *God in Process Thought*, is probably the best summary of my view. The book is a superb and for some purposes conveniently brief account of the issues between my view and traditional ones and shows that Sia is not unaware of some of the recent objections to process thought. Several other reviewers, especially John Cobb, support me in this evaluation.

In this age of television it is important to realize the immense value of the silent written word. I never saw or heard (except in a vivid dream) C. S. Peirce; however, that I have been (perhaps) more influenced by Whitehead was not so much because I did, two years after my doctoral dissertation was written and my degree obtained, begin to see and hear and talk to Whitehead, as it was because Whitehead was born a generation later and lived a longer active life. He had the stimulus of comparing his own thought with that of F. H. Bradley, G. E. Moore, Bergson, S. Alexander, Wm. James, Santayana, Dewey, Roy Sellers, and responded to much of the climate of opinion in which I grew up. He had as colleagues my chief Harvard teachers. He worked for ten years with Bertrand Russell; I knew Russell somewhat well and once taught a course on his book on knowledge. Compared with him, Peirce, or Whitehead, I am (to adapt a phrase of Whitehead's) only "a baby in mathematics."

I never saw or heard Plato or Aristotle, yet they are vividly real for me, especially Plato, and this in spite of the fact that he distrusted the written word. Or did he? His dialogues were written, even though several people "speak" in them and they usually reach only tentative conclusions. His seventh letter questions the possibility of capturing philosophical truth in words — almost a deconstructionist scepticism! Yet for me Plato often did this allegedly impossible thing, or came reasonably close to it. So did the contributors to this volume. We are all heirs of many post-Aristotelian writers. That we are so stupid, or language so treacherous or impotent, that these chronological advantages bring us no closer to the truth about reality seems less than the truth about us or about language. One of Heidegger's last words was also one of his best — "gratitude". My thanks to everybody!

Notes on Contributors

BASU, Arabinda. Professor of Philosophy, Sri Aurobindo International Centre of Education, Pondicherry, India. He was formerly Sri Aurobindo Professor of Philosophy, Banaras Hindu University, India, and Shalding Lecturer in Indian Philosophy and Religion, University of Durham, England. He has held visiting Professorships in various universities in the USA, Israel and India. He is the author of a number of books and articles on Indian thought, associate editor of *Dharma*, and a member of the Advisory Board of *Process Studies*.

BRACKEN, Joseph A., S.J. Professor of Theology at Xavier University, Cincinnati, Ohio, USA. He studied for his doctorate at the University of Freiburg, West Germany under Prof. Dr. Eugen Fink. Among his publications are: *What are They Saying about the Trinity?* (N. Y.: Paulist Press, 1979) and *The Triune Symbol: Persons, Process and Community* (Lanham, MD: The University of America Press, 1985). Currently, he is preparing for publication a book-length comparative study of the cosmologies of Pierre Teilhard de Chardin and A. N. Whitehead, tentatively titled: "Spirit and Society: Toward a New Philosophical Cosmology."

CLARKE, Norris W. S. J. Professor Emeritus of Philosophy at Fordham University, New York, USA, where he spent most of his teaching career (1955—1985). He took his Ph. D. at the Catholic University of Louvain. Since his retirement he has been Visiting Professor at Santa Clara University, Villanova University, and Xavier University. He was also Co-Founder and Editor of the *International Philosophical Quarterly* (1961—1985). He has been President of the Metaphysical Society of America and the American Catholic Philosophical Association, and is the author of *The Philosophical Approach to God: a Neothomist Perspective*, as well as of some fifty articles and chapters in books on St. Thomas, metaphysics, philosophy of God, and the person. He is known also for his dialogues with process philosophy.

CLOOTS, André. Lectures at the Catholic University of Leuven (Campus

Kortrijk), Belgium, on metaphysics, contemporary philosophy, and philosophy of science. He received his Ph. D. in philosophy from the Catholic University of Leuven with a dissertation on the problem of the ultimate in process philosophy. In 1974-75 he was at the Center for Process Studies, Claremont, as a CRB-Fellow. He has published articles on process thought in different journals.

DAVANEY, Sheila Greeve. Associate Professor of Theology at the Iliff School of Theology, Denver, Colorado, USA. Her master's and doctoral degrees are from Harvard University where she was also a Research/Resource Associate in Women's Studies. She is the author of *Divine Power* (Fortress Press, 1986) and the editor of *Feminism and Process Thought* (Edwin Mellen Press, 1981). Her current research is focused on the relation between feminist theology and social theories of knowledge, in particular the relation between power and knowledge.

ENDO, Hiroshi. Professor of Philosophy at Waseda University, Tokyo, Japan. He has been the Director of the Japan Society for Process Studies since 1980. His publications are mostly in Japanese, among which is *Sonsai-no-ronri* (*Logic of Being*) (Waseda University Press, 1974). He has also published in English in *Bulletin of the Japan Society of British Philosophy* and in other journals.

GUTOWSKI, Piotr. Assistant to the Chair of the History of Modern Philosophy, Katolicki Uniwersytet Lubelski, Lublin, Poland. He studied for his master's degree in philosophy at Katolicki Uniwersytet Lubelski and wrote on the epistemological and ontological foundations of Thomas Reid's philosophy of common sense. He is specialising in the history of contemporary American philosophy in general and process philosophy in particular. He is preparing his doctoral dissertation on Charles Hartshorne's concept of metaphysics.

ISHIHARA, John Shunji. Assistant Professor at Chikuahi Jogakuen College, Fukuoka, Kyushu, Japan, and a Buddhist priest (Jodo Shinshu Honganji-han). He studied in Japan and the USA. His doctorate is from Claremont Graduate School. He taught previously at California State University, Long Beach, and the University of Calgary. He has published in *The Pacific Journal* and in *Japanese Religions.*

KAUFMAN, William E. Rabbi of Temple Beth El in Fall River, Massachusetts, USA, and Visiting Lecturer in Philosophy at Rhode Island College. He was ordained as Rabbi at the Jewish Theological Seminary of America and received his doctorate in philosophy from Boston University. He is the author of two books: *Contemporary Jewish Philosophies* and *Journeys: An Introductory Guide to Jewish Mysticism* as well as numerous articles on

Jewish philosophy, mysticism and theology. He has taught at Clark University, the University of Rhode Island, Our Lady of the Lake University and Southeastern Massachusetts University.

McNAMARA, Martin, MSC. Professor of Scripture at Milltown Institute of Theology and Philosophy, Dublin, Ireland. He took up Biblical Studies in Rome (Pontifical Biblical Institute) and Jerusalem (Ecole Biblique) and holds a doctorate in Scripture on Aramaic translations (Targums) and New Testament. He obtained a Ph.D. from the National University of Ireland with a dissertation on early Hiberno-Latin Psalm commentary. His chief publications are: *Palestinian Targum to the Pentateuch and the NT* (1966); *Targum and Testament* (1972); *Palestinian Judaism and the NT* (1983); *Intertestamental Literature* (1983); *The Apocrypha and the Irish Church* (1976); *The Psalms in the Early Irish Church 600—1200* (1973); *Codex Palatinus Latinus 68* (critical ed., 1987).

MORRIS, Randall. Instructor in Modern Theology at Texas Christian University, Fort Worth, Texas, USA. He received his B. A. and D. Phil. degrees from the University of Oxford (Regents Park College and The Queen's College). His doctoral dissertation was on the social and political thought of Whitehead and Hartshorne. He has published in *Process Studies*.

PAILIN, David A. Senior Lecturer and Head of the Dept. of Philosophy of Religion at Manchester University, England. He was educated in England and the USA. Ordained in the Methodist Church in 1962, he served as the Methodist minister in Romiley, Cheshire (1961—1966). He is the author of three books: *The Way to Faith: An Examination of Newman's Grammar of Assent; Attitudes to Other Religions: Comparative Religion in 17th and 18th Century Britain*; and *Groundwork of Philosophy of Religion*. A study of process theology entitled *God and the Processes of Reality* is due to be published in 1989.

PHAN, Peter C. Professor of Systematic Theology at the Catholic University of America, Washington, D.C., USA. A native of Vietnam, he holds an STD from the Salesian Pontifical University, Rome, and a Ph. D. from the University of London, England. He was formerly Professor of Theology at the University of Dallas. His published works include: *Social Thought: The Message of the Fathers of the Church; Culture and Eschatology: The Iconographical Vision of Paul Evdokimov; Eternity in Time: a Study of Karl Rahner's Eschatology; Divine Grace and the Human Condition*. He is presently the general editor of an eight-volume series on systematic theology to be published by Michael Glazier, Inc., to which he contributes the volume on theological method.

SIA, Santiago. Senior Lecturer in Philosophy and Theology, Newman College,

University of Birmingham, England. After undergraduate and graduate studies in the Philippines, where he was born, he studied for his doctorate at Trinity College, University of Dublin, Ireland. He has taught at colleges and universities in the Philippines, Ireland and the USA. He is the author of *God in Process Thought: a Study in Charles Hartshorne's Concept of God* (Martinus Nijhoff, 1985), editor of *Process Theology and the Christian Doctrine of God* (St. Bede's Publications, 1986) and of articles in philosophy of religion, ethics and modern thought. He has recently joined the dept. of philosophy of Loyola Marymount University, Los Angeles, USA.

VAN DER VEKEN, Jan. Professor of Metaphysics at the Higher Institute of Philosophy of the Katholieke Universiteit te Leuven, Belgium and Director of the Center for Metaphysics and Philosophy of God in Leuven, which houses the largest collection of documents on process thought in Europe. He is the president of the European Society for Process Thought and the author of *Proces-denken: Een orientatie* and of several articles on process thought and phenomenology.

WALKER, Theodore Jr. Assistant Professor of Ethics and Society at Perkins School of Theology, Southern Methodist University, Dallas, Texas, USA. His appointment at Perkins was preceded by one year of service to Bethune-Cookman College in Daytona Beach, Florida, and three years of service to Hood Theological Seminary in Salisbury, North Carolina. He holds graduate degrees (Ph.D. and M.A.) from University of Notre Dame. He is the son of an African-American preacher and retired church pastor, Rev. Theodore Walker, Sr. of Greensboro, North Carolina, and is a member of Shiloh Baptist Church.

Index of Names*

Abraham 186, 209, 211, 216, 227
Adapa 215
Adler, Motimer 253, 254, 255, 318
Ahaz 213
Alexander, S. 321
Allen, George 162, 236
Altizer, Thomas J. 59, 73
Ambrose, Bierce 246
Amida 181
Anath 215
Anselm 130, 133, 149, 222, 223, 224, 236,
    237, 257, 313, 317
Aqhat 215
Aquinas, Thomas 102, 103, 104, 105, 107,
    108, 109, 111, 112, 113, 114, 115, 117,
    118, 119, 120, 122, 206, 237, 252, 269,
    270, 273, 274, 275, 276, 295, 309
Araya, Victorio 33, 36, 38, 39
Aristotle 28, 82, 102, 115, 125, 164, 210,
    229, 233, 252, 257, 259, 260, 267, 272,
    273, 277, 282, 288, 304, 307, 309, 311,
    313, 314, 315, 318, 319, 321
Armah, Ayi Kwei 19, 22
Assmann, Hugo 36
Astarte 200
Augustine 112, 270, 273
Aurobindo 83, 84, 85
Austin, J. L. 249, 261
Axel, Larry E. 101

Baal 200, 218
Banez 107
Barcan 149
Barbour, I. G. 160, 162
Barth, Karl 35, 74, 122, 273
Basu, Arabinda ix, xiii, 77, 263, 264, 265

Beethoven, Ludwig 246, 247
Becker 149
Bell 122, 276
Belo, Fernando 37
Berdyaev 266, 273, 297
Bergson, Henri 126, 145, 166, 219, 243,
    250, 263, 273, 284, 289, 296, 297, 307,
    321
Berkeley 138
Berkovite, Eliezer 198, 205, 206, 217, 306
Berryman, Phillip 35
Bertocci, P. 152
Blake, William 296
Blanshard 213
Boff, Clodovis and Leonardo 29, 35, 37
Bohm, David 126
Bonventure 277
Bosan, Guet 45, 259
Bracken, Joseph x, xiii, 89, 266, 267, 272
Bradley, F.H. 143, 301, 302
Brightman 308
Brown, Delwin 23, 36
Brown, William W. 8, 9, 20
Buddha 150
Bultmann 291
Burnet 315

Carlyle 282
Campanella 277
Camus 296
Capra, Fritjof 126
Cardanus 277
Cargas, Harry J. 75, 198, 217
Carnap 317
Carroll, Lewis 270
Carter, Jimmy 247

* I am grateful to my research assistant, Bard Widmer, who prepared the index and to Loyola
Marymount University for research funds.

328

331

Sia, Santiago ix, xi, xiii, 26, 35, 37, 38, 39,
44, 151, 161, 185, 190, 191, 194, 195,
198, 217, 236, 321
Simeon 186
Simons, Henry 252
Sirach 200
Smith, Arche 17
Smith, Gerard 122
Smith, John E. xi, 162
Smith, Mrs. 241
Smith, N. K. 236
Snow, C. P. 247
Sobrino, Jon 24, 25, 27, 28, 30, 31, 33, 35,
38, 39
Socinus 297, 309
Socrates 259
Solomon 201
Solovyov 166
Spinoza 133, 273, 275, 282, 292, 305, 311,
313
Stanton, Elizabeth C. 57
Stcherbatsky, T. 170, 172, 174, 175, 176,
177, 184
Stengers, Isabelle 126
Strasser, S. 151
Suso, Heinrich 134
Suzuki, D. T. 182, 264
Szilard 245
Szubka, T. 160, 161

Tarsky 261
Taylor, Mark C. 59, 73, 74
Teller, Edward 245, 246
Thandeka 17
Thomas, Charles 74
Thurman, Howard 20, 22, 241, 242
Tillich, Paul 206, 281
Toulmin, Stephen 126
Tonybee, Arnold 45
Tscherbatski 294

Trethowan, Illtyd 102
Ture, Kawme (Stokely Carmichael) 20, 22
Twain, Mark 246
Tymieniecka 151

Underhill, Evelyn 187, 188, 194, 195

Van Der Veken, Jan x, xiii, 125, 136, 160,
235, 280
Varick, John 2
Vanter, Bruce 218
Viard, Andre A. 218
Viney, D. W. 152
Von Balthasar, H. U. 217
Von Rad, Gerhard 218
Von Wright 290

Walker, Theodore ix, xiii, 1, 241, 242, 301
Walls, William J. 21
Waloszczyk, K. 160
Warner, Lucille 5, 21
Weil, Simone 302
Weis, P. 151, 254
Wells, H. G. 287
Wesley 306
West, Cornel 60
Westphal, Merold 122
Wharton, Edith 261
Wildiers, N. M. 160
Winston 74
Wittgenstein, L. 145, 151, 222, 273, 296,
297, 310
Wolfson, Harry A. 185, 194
Wordsworth 286, 287

Young, Henry 17

Zaner, Richard 286
Zycinski, J. 160

STUDIES IN PHILOSOPHY AND RELIGION

1. FREUND, E-R. *Franz Rosenzweig's Philosophy of Existence. An Analysis of The Star of Redemption.* 1979. ISBN 90-247-2901-5.
   viii + 189 pp., cloth, Dfl. 96,00/US$ 48.00/EP 26.50.

2. OLSON, A. M. *Transcendence and Hermeneutics. An Interpretation of the Philosophy of Karl Jaspers.* 1979. ISBN 90-247-2092-3.
   xxiv + 198 pp., cloth, Dfl. 101,00/US$ 50.50/EP 27.75.

3. VERDU, A. *The Philosophy of Buddhism. A 'Totalistic' Synthesis.* 1981. ISBN 90-247-2224-1.
   xii + 207 pp., cloth, Dfl. 109,00/US$ 54.50/EP 29.95.

4. OLIVER, H. H. *A Relational Metaphysics.* 1981. ISBN 90-247-2457-0.
   xiv + 228 pp., cloth, Dfl. 109,00/US$ 54.00/EP 29.95.

5. ARAPURA, J. G. *Gnosis and the Question of Thought in Vedanta. Dialogue with the Foundations.* 1988. ISBN 90-247-3061-9.
   vi + 211 pp., cloth, Dfl. 165,00/US$ 82.50/EP 45.75.

6. HOROSZ, W. and CLEMENTS, T. (eds.). *Religion and Human Purpose. A Cross Disciplinary Approach.* 1987. ISBN 90-247-3000-7.
   x + 309 pp., cloth, Dfl. 140,00/US$ 70.00/EP 46.50.

7. SIA, S. *God in Process Thought. With a Postscript by Charles Hartshorne.* 1985. ISBN 90-247-3103-8.
   x + 153 pp., cloth, Dfl. 105,00/US$ 52.50/EP 28.95.

8. KOBLER, J. F. *Vatican II and Phenomenology.* 1985. ISBN 90-247-3193-3.
   xvi + 238 pp., cloth, Dfl. 116,00/US$ 55.00/EP 30.25.

9. GODFREY, J. J. *A Philosophy of Human Hope.* 1987. ISBN 90-247-3353-7.
   xiv + 272 pp., cloth, Dfl. 110,00/US$ 55.00/EP 31.25.

10. PERRETT, R. W.: *Death and Immortality.* 1987. ISBN 90-247-3440-1.
    x + 220 pp., cloth, Dfl. 85,00/US$ 42.50/EP 30.25.

11. GALL, R. S. *Beyond Theism and Atheism: Heidegger's Significance for Religious Thinking.* 1987. ISBN 90-247-3623-4.
    xii + 174 pp., cloth, Dfl. 105,00/US$ 49.50/EP 32.00.

12. SIA, S. (ed.). *Charles Hartshorne's Concept of God.* 1989. ISBN 0-7923-0290-7.